AF291523

# WINE

# AN ILLUSTRATED GUIDE TO
# WINE

A GRAND TOUR OF THE VINEYARDS, FROM BORDEAUX TO THE BAROSSA
VALLEY, THE BEST GRAPE VARIETIES AND THE PRACTICALITIES OF BUYING,
KEEPING, SERVING AND DRINKING WINE, WITH 450 PHOTOGRAPHS

## STUART WALTON

LORENZ BOOKS

# CONTENTS

# INTRODUCTION

*Van Gogh's depiction of grape-harvesting at Arles in the 1880s (above) would still be recognizable today in parts of southern France.*

THE WORLD OF WINE, like many other categories of human experience, is changing fast. In the last ten to twenty years in particular, it has developed, grown, and innovated in ways that would have been inconceivable to the young man who wrote the first edition of this book in 1996. It isn't just that wine is being made in regions and countries that simply didn't appear in a general wine guide in the 20th century. It's also that styles of wine are now being produced to shock the purists among us, some of it barely recognizable as the fermented juice of the grape, and before we plunge in to this exciting, often challenging, occasionally infuriating world, it's worth stepping back and taking a deep breath, by means of a general overview of those convulsive changes.

## A CHANGING COMMODITY

First of all, the way wine is viewed as an item of daily or weekly shopping, the contexts in which it is drunk, have changed considerably over the 30 years since this book first appeared. When I got into wine by setting up a tasting group with an old schoolmate at home in northern England, it was still relatively unusual for people to drink wine at home. Most homes had a drinks cupboard, and there was very often beer in the fridge, but wine was still seen as something of a

niche category. It was a growing niche category, but the ordinary consumer still typically confessed to being baffled, even a little intimidated, by it as a commodity. It seemed to require a lot of specialist knowledge, and there was a feeling that, unless you spent a small fortune on it, you were probably drinking the most basic slosh.

Today, wine is everywhere. Not only do pubs and bars now have little wine lists, or at least a range of options, but wine bars and eateries that specialize in wine compete to offer interesting and surprising examples that you might not have come across before. People are drinking more experimentally, more adventurously. They want to know the back-story of a wine, as much as what it promises to taste like. Characters in TV drama drink wine from huge designer glasses when they get in from work, when they are tapping away on their laptops, when they sink into a bubble bath. It has become a perceived aspect of everyday life.

What initially led this cultural revolution in wine was the sometimes astonishing range available in supermarkets. In the UK at least, the supermarkets effectively did away with the high-street off-licence chains, but they did help generate a shift towards specialist wine merchants, bottle-shops and the wholesale trade that had always been a big part of wine retail in the United States, Australia and New Zealand. Then, too, wine by the glass has played a big part in expanding people's horizons in bars and restaurants. The profit take is considerably higher for the business, but customers like being offered a choice of glass sizes, and being able to ring the changes from a list as they make their way through dinner, rather than being stuck with the one note of a whole bottle.

## CHANGING TASTES

A generation ago, what chiefly worried me was the creeping standardization that seemed to be setting in worldwide. Everybody was making sweetly oaky Chardonnay, Cabernet Sauvignon that tasted like cheeky blackcurrant Gatorade, and – a little later – juicy-fruited, knock-it-back Sauvignon Blanc. It was getting harder to tell wines apart. If you were tasting it without sight of the bottle, it became increasingly difficult to say where a simple unoaked Chardonnay came from: Southern Burgundy? Chile? Northern Italy? Canada? In other words, we were losing the sense of place that had always been such an important factor in making wine the inspiring commodity it was.

One of the best developments to happen since then has been the dynamic diversification that has taken place on the global wine scene. There are wine-producing countries in this book now that weren't mentioned at all in the 1990s, all of them turning out wines that are worthy of investigation by the open-minded consumer. My particular tips? Greece at last has a modern wine industry to be proud of. Look for Uruguay when you are lingering near the South America section of the wine shop. There are great wines being made all over central and southern Europe, from Austria's Grüner Veltliners to the wild and wonderful spice-splashed reds of Croatia.

And it's not just new countries that are coming on stream. There are also new grape varieties coming to public notice. I've rounded up a few of those at the end of my Grapes section, but the notion that people have an idea of what to expect now from a wine labelled Albariño or Malbec is another small miracle that would have been unthinkable back in the day. You might not necessarily remember the Croatian Plavac Mali or the Turkish Buzbağ next time you venture into the wine bar, but the fact that they had them at all is worth celebrating.

I wish I could say it's all good. But if you sensed a 'but' coming, here it is. The biggest enemy now of quality wine production will be climate change. In certain areas, previously considered too marginal to grow grapes or make successful balanced wines, new opportunities have arisen. England's palette of feasible grape varieties has expanded encouragingly, and if you had been waiting for Danish wine to start making an appearance on wine lists, your patience will shortly be rewarded. Down in Spain and central Italy, though, it's a different picture. Heat-stressed vineyards (not to mention vineyard workers) may one day make these areas too torrid for wine cultivation, and viticulture that has been a family concern through countless generations will have to be abandoned, which will mean we could well lose some classic wine styles.

In the meantime, before the climate apocalypse sets in, the effect of hotter vintages is more alcohol in the wines. This is not a blessing. Apart from the fact that it is insidiously increasing the intake of regular drinkers, it has also resulted in wines that lack balance. Try finding a southern Rhône or Languedoc red now that has less than 14–14.5 per cent alcohol.

*The vintage has traditionally been one of the ceremonial high points of the year in Europe's wine-growing regions, as this illustration from the medieval Book of Hours, c.1520 (above) vividly demonstrates.*

You may not notice this if you are drinking it at the barbecue, or partnering it with something rich and spicy, a robust red meat or a dish full of mushrooms or lentils, but on its own, it burns the throat before delivering a whopping great thud to the head. Unless it's a wine I really want, from a favoured producer I trust to have compensated for its alcohol, I won't buy anything higher than 13.5 per cent, and even that can be heavy going on a hot summer's evening, or before you have had anything to eat.

## CHANGING RECIPES

While that revolution in retail and restaurant trades has been going on, there has been another creative upheaval in the way wine is made. More than ever, the words on the label that tell you what grape(s) are in it, where it was grown, what was done with it in the winery, and what you might drink it with, have become meaningful indicators of what you will find when you unscrew the top. Yes, that's right. Screw-capped wine has largely replaced the old natural cork. Cork was a wonderful resource for sealing wine, and helping it to age in your underground cellars through the decades. But it did occasionally bring with it problems of cork taint (caused when the chemical it was treated with became unstable and contaminated the aroma and flavour of the wine – think old dishcloth), particularly irritating when it was the one bottle you had bought for the evening.

The biggest transformation in traditional practice has taken place in the vineyard itself. Where vines are grown, how they are trained, what interventions are carried out to expose the ripening berries to more sun or protect them from the glare, when they are picked and what judgments come into play to decide that, have all resulted in wines that are much more carefully made, even at the modest end of the commercial scale.

Different approaches to viticulture have provided interesting talking points for the wine scene's chattering classes. Organic vineyard management speaks for itself. Biodynamic viticulture is something else entirely. It derives from the holistic philosophies of the Austrian occultist Rudolf Steiner, and involves treating the earth as a whole living organism in itself. Not just treatments during the growing season, but the organic compounds that are added to the soil after harvest play their part, while the viticultural agenda, all the way through to harvesting, occurs according to the phases of the moon and other astrological calculations. A significant number of prominent quality wine estates have now converted to biodynamic agriculture. It was quite the norm in the wine press 20 years ago to say that, while you personally had no truck with the blather of astrology, and such arcane rituals as fertilizing the soil with manure-filled cow-horns, the wines themselves were undoubtedly superb. Whether they would have been equally as superb if produced from simple organic farming was another question, but biodynamic growers proved quite as prickly as people who plan their lives according to horoscopes if you suggested as much.

What has succeeded the biodynamic wave is the natural wine movement. This is predicated on the seductively simple idea that the less you do to wine, the better. There are few or no treatments in the vineyard, so no pesticides or herbicides, and when the juice gets to the winery, you resist treating it with sulphur dioxide, a preservative and antioxidant, and you do little or no clarifying or filtering of the wine before bottling. Natural reds may not taste all that different to the industrialized reds we all grew up with, but the white wines are something else. For one thing, they aren't white but yellowy, or even positively browned. The official term is 'orange wine', which is now a category in itself for wines that would, at one time, have been thought straightforwardly faulty, oxidized to a state that tastes more like cider than something from a recognizable grape variety. A period of extended skin contact brings out a waxy, slightly abrasive texture, producing what is essentially a white wine with tannin. I personally can't stand these wines, but I'll keep my opinion to myself in what follows.

And what are you going to ferment your wine in? A stainless steel tank? A brand-new oak barrel? How last-century. Oval fermenters that look like

*Serving wine from a traditional Georgian* qvevri *(below) involves ladling it out with a long-handled gourd called an* orshimo.

giant eggs, made from concrete, ceramics, even permeable plastics, theoretically ensure more even distribution of the carbon dioxide generated during fermentation. In Georgia (the Caucasian country, not the American state), they ferment in stone vessels called *qvevri*. They wouldn't have looked unusual to a Roman cellarmaster in the time of the Caesars, being effectively modern-day amphorae. The Georgians seal them and then bury them in the ground (I promise I'm not making this up) and leave nature to take its course. They don't even separate the grapes from their skins or stalks or pips. It's how wine was made two thousand years ago. I actually like these wines. To me, they are more rewarding than those orange and skin-contact oddities.

I mentioned carbon dioxide, one of the by-products (along with ethyl alcohol) of fermentation. A wine that still had fizz in it when it was bottled was also once deemed faulty. Partially fermented wines, though, have now become a novelty. There is a sparkling wine category called pét-nat, which is short for the French term *pétillant naturel* (naturally bubbly), meaning that there is a natural degree of intentional spritz in the wine, giving it a livelier, fresher feel in the mouth. This is nothing to do with the traditional method of producing sparkling wine such as champagne, where the wine undergoes a whole second fermentation in the bottle. In the case of pét-nat, the first fermentation is interrupted, and then the wine completes it after it is bottled. This was once known as the *méthode ancestrale* in France, and is now all the rage. Like the low-intervention wines, it caters to a taste for reducing technological interference as much as possible, so that we can imagine we have returned, in the mid-21st century, to much simpler ways of doing things, as though the industrial revolution had never happened.

## Changing Habits

In fact, the developments of the most recent era are effectively pulling in opposing directions. On the one hand, we are being asked to get used to drinking wine made by Victorian, or even Greco-Roman, methods, to get back to nature and put up with funny smells and peculiar tastes. On the other, though, all that vineyard science and the full battery of treatments that may be applied to wine in the winery, even when growing conditions have been particularly challenging this year, have meant that vintage variation is, for many wines, becoming a thing

of the past. When I updated the vintage guides in this edition for the great European classic wines (Bordeaux, Burgundy, Piedmont, Tuscany, Germany's Rhine and Mosel valleys), I was struck by how little the rollercoaster effect there once was, from mediocre years to outstanding ones, via the odd absolute stinker, now applies. It was hardly necessary at all to give evaluations for dry white Bordeaux (though I have done) as most of its vintages are now fine. I can't tell you how much that wasn't true 30 years ago.

And why did it used to matter what the vintages were like? Because you might want to buy the best by the case, and squirrel them away – or lay them down, as the wine trade puts it – while they evolved and changed and blossomed in the bottle. Almost nobody has the resources, or indeed the patience to do this, other than those at the top end of the income scale. I often talk in the pages that follow about wines being age-worthy, built to last, etc. These assessments are as accurate as they ever were, but the fact that so very few people will ever find out what 30-year-old burgundy tastes like is, to put it mildly, a pity.

Sermon over. Now, let's jump right in.

Stuart Walton

*Cabernet Sauvignon grapes (above) ripening at a vineyard in Bordeaux. Vintage variation is much less of an issue now than it was a generation ago.*

# PRINCIPLES OF TASTING

*All that sniffing, swirling and spitting that the professional winetasters engage in is more than just a way of showing off; it really can immeasurably enhance the appreciation of any wine.*

WATCHING A PROFESSIONAL winetaster at work, you could be forgiven for wondering whether they really like wine at all. The ritual of peering into the glass, swirling it around and then sniffing suspiciously at it, before taking a mouthful only to spit it out again, doesn't look much like the behaviour of someone who loves the stuff. It is, however, a sequence of perfectly logical steps that, quite apart from helping you evaluate a wine's quality, can also immeasurably enhance the enjoyment of good wine. Here's how.

Don't pour a full glass for tasting, because you're going to need room for swirling. About a third full is the optimum amount.

Firstly, have a good look at the wine by holding it up to the daylight or other light source. Is it nice and clear? Does it contain sediment or any other solid matter? In the case of red wines, tilt the glass away from you against a white surface, and look at the colour of the liquid at the far edge. Older wines start to fade at the rim, the deep purplish-red taking on lighter crimson tones, and later an autumnal brownish hue with dignified old age.

Now swirl the glass gently. The point of this is to activate the aromatic compounds in the wine, so that when you stick your nose in, you can fully appreciate the bouquet. The aim is to get a fairly vigorous wave circulating in the glass. Some people swirl the glass while it's still resting on a surface, before bringing it to their nose, but make sure the surface isn't likely to damage any good glassware.

When sniffing, tilt the glass towards your face and get your nose slightly inside it, keeping it within the lower half of the opening of the glass. The head should be bent forward a little. Inhale gently (as if you were sniffing a flower, not filling your lungs on a blustery clifftop) and for a good two or three seconds. Nosing a wine can reveal a lot about its origins and the way it was made, but don't overdo it. The sense of smell is quickly neutralized. Two or three sniffs should tell you as much as you need to know.

Now for the tricky part. The reason that wine experts pull those ridiculous faces when they take a mouthful is that they are trying to spread the wine all around the different taste-sensitive parts of the tongue. At its very tip, the receptors for sweetness are most densely concentrated. Just a little back from those, saltiness is registered. Acidity or sourness is tasted on the edges of the tongue, while bitterness is sensed at the very back. So roll the wine around your mouth as thoroughly as you can.

It helps to maximize the flavour of a wine if you take in air while it's in your mouth. Using gentle suction with the lips pursed, draw in

*When pouring a tasting sample, be sure to leave enough room in the glass for giving it a good swirl (below).*

some breath. Allow only the tiniest opening (less than the width of a pencil), and suck in immediately. Close your lips again, and breathe downwards through your nose. In this way, the flavour of the wine is transmitted past the taste receptors in your nasal cavity, as well as via your tongue, intensifying the whole sensation.

In polite company, swallow it. If you are tasting a number of wines at a time of day when you wouldn't normally be drinking, say at a market or fair, spit it out into whatever receptacle is provided (the ground will do). Spit confidently, with the tongue behind the ejected liquid, and spit downwards.

There are five principal elements to look for in the taste of a wine. Learn to concentrate on each one individually, and you will start to assemble a set of analytical tools that will stand you in good stead for evaluating any wine.

**Dryness/Sweetness** From a bone-dry Sancerre at one end of the spectrum to the most unctuous Liqueur Muscats at the other, the amount of natural sugar a wine contains is its most easily noted attribute.

**Acidity** There are many different types of acid in wine, the most important of which is tartaric, which is present in unfermented grape juice. How sharp does it feel on the edges of the tongue? Good acidity is necessary to contribute a feeling of freshness to a young wine, and to help the best wines to age. Don't confuse dryness with acidity. A very dry wine like fino sherry can actually be quite low in acid, while the sweetest Sauternes will contain sufficient acidity to offset its sugar.

**Tannin** Tannin is present in the stalks, seeds and skins of grapes. Since the colour in red wine comes from the skins (the juice being colourless), some tannin is extracted along with it. In the mouth, it's what gives young red wines that furry, sandy or abrasive feel, but it disappears with age.

**Oak** Many wines are matured (and sometimes even fermented too) in oak barrels. An aroma or taste of vanilla, nutmeg or cinnamon is an indicator of oak in white wines, and an overall feeling of creamy smoothness in richer reds. A pronounced smokiness like slightly burned toast indicates that the barrels were heavily charred (or 'toasted') on the insides.

**Fruit** We're all familiar with wine writers' flights of fancy ('I'm getting raspberries, passion-fruit, melon…'), but there are sound biochemical reasons for the resemblance of wines to the flavours of fruits, vegetables, herbs and spices. We'll come across these in the Grape Varieties section, but let your imagination off the leash when tasting. Bright fruit flavours are among the great charms of wine.

**Faults** Not everything in the garden is lovely, and sometimes wines can display problems. Cork taint, leading to corked wine, bestows a nasty, stale aroma of old dishcloth or bread mould, but is much less widespread now that screwcaps have begun to replace real cork. Older wines can sometimes show oxidation, which deepens the colour of white wines alarmingly, and makes all wines taste flat and dead. Take back any wine that shows either of these faults. Sometimes tartrate crystals can be present in an imperfectly stabilized wine, but these don't affect its drinking quality.

*Wait for the mousse to subside in a sparkling wine before tasting it (above).*
*The different shades of colour in wine can convey a lot of information to the taster (below).*

*A gentle swirling action of the hand is sufficient to produce quite a vigorous wave in the glass (above).*

*Sniff lightly and long, with the nose slightly below the rim of the glass (above).*

*Take a good mouthful of the wine, in order to coat all surfaces of the mouth with it (above).*

# STORING AND SERVING

*Where is the best place to keep wine for maturation? Should it be allowed to breathe before being served? What does decanting an old wine involve? None of these questions is as technical as it seems.*

NONE OF THE TECHNICALITIES involved in the storage and serving of wine needs to be too complicated. The following guidelines are aimed at keeping things simple.

**Creating a cellar** Starting a wine collection requires a certain amount of ingenuity now that most of us live in flats or houses without cellars. If you have bought a large parcel of wine that you don't want to touch for years, you can pay a nominal fee to a wine merchant to cellar it for you, but the chances are that you may only have a couple of dozen bottles at any one time. Where to keep it?

The two main points to bear in mind are that bottles should be stored horizontally and away from sources of heat. You can pile them on top of each other if they are all the same shape, but it's safer and more convenient to invest in a simple wooden or plastic wine rack. Keeping the bottles on their sides means the wine is in constant contact with the corks, preventing them from drying out and imparting off-flavours to the wine.

Don't put your bottles in the cupboard next to the storage heater or near the cooker because heat is a menace to wine. Equally, don't leave it in the garden shed in sub-zero temperatures.

*A simple wine rack is much the best way of storing bottles (right). This one allows enough space to see the labels too, so that they don't have to be pulled out to identify them.*

Choose a cool cupboard that's not too high up (remember that heat rises) and where it can rest in peace in the dark.

**Serving temperatures** The conventional wisdom that white wine should be served chilled and red wine at room temperature is essentially correct, but it isn't the whole story.

Don't over-chill white wine or its flavours will be muted. Light, acidic whites, sparkling wines and very sweet wines (and rosés too for that matter) should be served at no higher than about 10°C (50°F) but the best Chardonnays, dry Semillons and Alsace wines can afford to be a little less cool than that.

Reds, on the other hand, generally benefit from being slightly cooler than the ambient temperature in a well-heated home. Never warm the bottle by a radiator as that will make the wine taste muddy. Some lighter, fruity reds such as young Beaujolais, Dolcetto or the lighter

Loire or New Zealand reds are best served lightly chilled – about an hour in the refrigerator.

**Breathing** Should red wine be allowed to breathe? In the case of matured reds that are intended to be drunk on release, like Rioja Reservas or the softer, barrel-aged Cabernet Sauvignons of Australia, the answer is that there is probably no point. Young reds with some tannin, or immature hard acidity, do round out with a bit of air contact, though. Either pour the wine into a decanter or jug (pitcher) half an hour or so before serving or, if you haven't anything suitable for the table, pour it into another container and then funnel it back into the bottle. Simply drawing the cork won't in itself make any difference because only the wine in the neck is in contact with the air. And remember the wine will develop in any case in the glass as you keep swirling and slowly sipping it.

*Here is an ingeniously designed wine rack that ensures that the undersides of the corks are kept constantly in contact with the wine, thus preventing them from drying out.*

**Corkscrews** With the increasing use of the Stelvin closure (aka the screwcap) for all quality levels of wine – pioneered in the southern hemisphere, but now widely in use in Europe too – you can leave the corkscrew in the drawer. The great advantage is that any leftover wine can be easily resealed, and of course there is no risk of cork taint.

For corks, the spin-handled corkscrew is the easiest to use, because it involves one continuous motion, and very little effort. The type with side-levers is less good, because it often needs two or three attempts with longer corks, and can break a fragile cork in two, especially if it's the type with a solid shaft as opposed to a hollow spiral. The simplest model, the Wine Waiter's Friend, is good for those who like displaying their brute strength, but an obstinate cork can reduce you to a study in red-faced futility.

*The Spin-handled Screwpull (above) was the corkscrew that revolutionized the business of bottle opening. Not only does it require very little in the way of brute force, but it virtually never breaks a cork in two. That is because the screw itself (or thread) is so long.*

*The most basic type of corkscrew (above left) involves simply tugging. The levered model (above right) can sometimes break a long or old cork. A bottle with a screwcap (right) avoids the need for any sort of special implement at all. There are now three kinds of bottle closure (far right): natural cork, synthetic cork and the Stelvin or screwcap.*

Avoid if you can any wines sealed with synthetic cork. When they get stuck, they stay stuck. They are the only closure that won't go back in the bottle, and they can break a plastic corkscrew. Briefly seen as the alternative to real cork some years ago, they have now thankfully begun to be widely superseded as a technology by more efficient screwcaps.

**Opening fizz** Many people are still intimidated about opening sparkling wines. Remember that the longer a bottle of fizz has been able to rest before opening, the less lively it will be. If it has been very badly shaken up, it may need a week or more to settle. Also, the colder it is, the less likely it will be to go off like a firecracker.

Once the foil has been removed and the wire cage untwisted and taken off too, grasp the cork firmly and take hold of the lower half of the bottle. The advice generally given is to turn the bottle rather than the cork, but in practice most people probably do both (twisting in opposite directions, of course). Work very gently and, when you feel or see the cork beginning to rise, control it every millimetre of the way with your thumb over the top. It should be possible then to ease it out without it popping. If the wine does spurt, put a finger in the neck, but don't completely stopper it again.

When pouring, fill each glass to just under half-full, and then go round again to top them up once the initial fizz has subsided. Pour fairly slowly so that the wine doesn't foam over the sides. Pouring into tilted glasses does preserve more of the fizz, though some see it as vulgarly reminiscent of pouring lager.

**Decanting** Decanting can help to make a tough young wine a bit more supple, but it is only absolutely necessary if the wine being served is heavily sedimented. In that case, stand the bottle upright for the best part of the day you intend to serve it (from the night before is even better) so that the deposits settle to the bottom. After uncorking, pour the wine in a slow but continuous stream into the decanter, looking into the neck of the bottle. When the sediment starts working its way into the neck as you reach the end, stop pouring. The amount of wine you are left with should be negligible enough to throw away, but if there's more than half a glass, then strain the remainder through a clean muslin cloth. Do *not* use coffee filter-papers or tissue as they will alter the flavour of the wine. Decanting is particularly essential for old bottles of vintage port.

*When opening sparkling wines, it is important to restrain the release of the cork (left). Control it every millimetre of the way once it begins to push out.*

*The quicker you pour, the more vigorous will be the foaming of the wine in the glass (left). Pour carefully to avoid any wastage through overflowing.*

*The Champagne Saver is a good way of preserving the fizz in any unfinished bottles of sparkling wine (left). Some swear, quite unscientifically, by inserting a spoon-handle in the neck.*

# GLASSES

*Wine doesn't have to be served in the most expensive glassware to show it to advantage, but there are a few basic principles to bear in mind when choosing glasses that will help you get the best from your bottle.*

*Glasses these days come in all shapes and sizes (below). From left to right in the foreground are: a good red or white wine glass; a technically correct champagne flute; the famous 'Paris goblet' much beloved of wine-bars, not a bad shape but too small; an elegant-looking but inefficient sparkling wine glass with flared opening, causing greater dispersal of bubbles; a sherry* copita, *also useful for other fortified wines.*

ALTHOUGH I CAN scarcely remember any champagne that tasted better than the stuff we poured into polystyrene cups huddled in my student quarters after the examination results went up, the truth is that, certainly when you're in the mood to concentrate, it does make a difference what you drink wine from. Not only the appearance but the scent and even the taste of wine can be substantially enhanced by using appropriate glasses.

They don't have to be prohibitively costly, although – as with everything else – the best doesn't come cheap. The celebrated Austrian glassmaker Georg Riedel has taken the science of wine glasses to its ultimate degree, working out what design features will emphasize the specific aromatic and flavour compounds in dozens of different types of wine. Some of them are very peculiar shapes and they're expensive, but they undeniably do the trick.

There are some broad guidelines we can all follow, however, when choosing glasses. Firstly, always choose a plain glass to set off your best wines. Coloured ones, or even those with just the stems and bases tinted, can distort the appearance of white wines particularly. And, although cut crystal can look very beautiful, it has now fallen from fashion. I tend to avoid it for wines because it doesn't make for the clearest view of the liquid in the glass.

Look for a deep, wide bowl that tapers significantly towards the mouth. With such glasses, the aromas of the wine can be released more generously, both because the deeper bowl allows for more vigorous swirling, and because the narrower opening channels the scents of the

wine to your nostrils more efficiently. Also, the thinner the glass it's made from, the less it will interfere with tasting.

Traditionally, red wine is served in bigger glasses than white. If you are serving both colours at a grand gastronomic evening, it helps to allot different wines their individual glasses, but the assumption is that reds, especially mature wines, need more space in which to breathe. More development of the wine will take place in the glass than in any decanter or jug you may have poured it into. If you are only buying one size, though, think big. A wine glass can never be too large.

Sparkling wines should be served in flutes, tall thin glasses with straight sides, so that the mousse or fizz is preserved. The champagne saucers familiar from old movies (and originally modelled, as legend has it, on the breast of Marie Antoinette) are less efficient because the larger surface area of the wine causes faster dispersal of the bubbles. That said, they have defiantly come back into fashion in some quarters, and I have to own up to a guilty fondness for their elegance myself.

Fortified wines should be served in smaller, narrower versions of the ordinary wine glass, in recognition of their higher alcoholic strength. The *copita*, traditional glass of the sherry region, is a particularly handsome receptacle, and will do quite well for the other fortifieds too. Don't use your tiniest liqueur glasses: apart from looking spectacularly mean, they allow no room for enjoying the wine's aromas.

*These three glasses (left) are all perfectly shaped for tasting. The one on the right is the official international tasting-glass.*

# DRINKING WINE WITH FOOD

*Matching the right wine to its appropriate dish may seem like a gastronomic assault course but there are broad principles that can be easily learned. And very few mistakes are complete failures.*

AT ONE TIME, the rules on choosing wines to accompany food seemed hearteningly simple. It was just a matter of remembering: white wine with fish and poultry, red wine with red meats and cheese, with sherry to start and port to finish. Recent thinking has hugely complicated that basic picture, although its essential principles remain sound.

What is clear is that this is one of those areas in which there are no fixed rules. Even though a particular dish may be a firm favourite, why drink the same wine with it every time? Whenever I go to tastings of wine with food, there are always at least a couple of matches that are completely surprising successes.

The following are rough guidelines that are intended to send you off in some new directions. On the whole, you can afford to be bold: very few combinations actually clash.

## APERITIFS

The two classic (and best) appetite-whetters are sparkling wine and dry sherry. Choose a light, non-vintage champagne (blanc de blancs has the requisite delicacy), or one of the lighter California or New Zealand sparklers. If you are serving highly seasoned canapés, olives or nuts before the meal, dry sherry is better. Always serve a freshly opened bottle of good fino or manzanilla. Kir has become quite trendy again: add a dash of cassis (blackcurrant liqueur) to a glass of crisp dry white – classically Bourgogne Aligoté – or to bone-dry fizz for a Kir Royale.

## FIRST COURSES

**Soups** In general, liquidized soups are happier without wine, although thickly textured versions containing cream or truffle oil work with richer styles of fizz, such as blanc de noirs

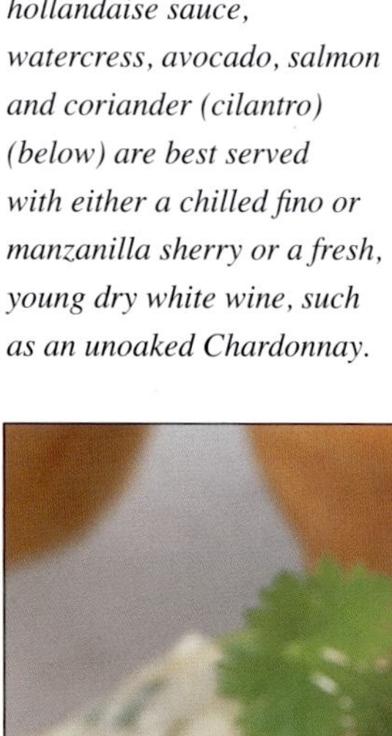

*Pre-dinner nibbles with strong flavours such as prawns (shrimp), tomato, hollandaise sauce, watercress, avocado, salmon and coriander (cilantro) (below) are best served with either a chilled fino or manzanilla sherry or a fresh, young dry white wine, such as an unoaked Chardonnay.*

*Chicken and pistachio pâté with crusty bread (above) is best with a white wine that has some aromatic personality, perhaps a Torrontes.*

*Salt-cured salmon (above) needs a white wine with plenty of weight, such as an Alsace Gewurztraminer or a Pinot Gris.*

champagne. A small glass of one of the nuttier-tasting fortified wines such as amontillado sherry or Sercial madeira is a good friend to a meaty consommé. Bulky chowders and minestrones may benefit from a medium-textured red – perhaps a Montepulciano d'Abruzzo – to kick off a winter dinner.

**Fish pâtés** Light dry whites without overt fruit are best: Chablis, Alsace Pinot Blanc, Muscadet *sur lie*, Spanish Viura, South African Chenin Blanc, shading to something a little richer, such as Spain's Rias Baixas, with the oilier fish like smoked mackerel.

**Chicken, duck or pork liver pâtés** Go for a big, pungently flavoured white – Alsace Gewurztraminer, dry Bordeaux from Pessac-Léognan, Hunter Valley Semillon. The traditional partner for foie gras is Sauternes (which I find much too sickly a combination).

**Smoked salmon** Needs a hefty white such as Gewurztraminer or Pinot Gris from Alsace, or an oak-fermented Chardonnay from the Côte de Beaune or California. Beware: champagne will wither under the onslaught of salt, smoke and fat, however traditional it seems.

**Melon** The sweeter-fleshed aromatic varieties require a wine with its own gentle sweetness. Try late-picked Muscat or Riesling from Washington or California, or even young Canadian Ice Wine.

**Prawns, shrimp, langoustines, etc** Almost any crisp dry white will work – Sauvignon Blanc is a good grape to choose – but avoid heavily oaked wines. Go for high acidity if you are serving mayonnaise or garlic butter.

**Deep-fried mushrooms** Best with a midweight simple red such as Côtes du Rhône, Valdepeñas or Valpolicella.

**Asparagus** Richer styles of Sauvignon, such as those from New Zealand, are perfect.

**Pasta dishes and risottos** These really are best with Italian wines. Choose a concentrated white such as Vernaccia, Arneis, Falanghina or good Soave for cream sauces, or dishes involving seafood. Light- to medium-bodied reds from Italian grapes (Barbera, Montepulciano) work best with tomato-based sauces. A wild mushroom risotto with Parmesan is great with one of the richer styles of Chianti.

### FISH AND SHELLFISH

**Oysters** Classic partners are champagne, Muscadet or Chablis. Most unoaked Sauvignon also makes a suitably bracing match.

**Scallops** Simply poached or seared, this most delicate of shellfish needs a soft light white – Côte Chalonnaise burgundy, medium-dry German or New Zealand Riesling, Italian Pinot Grigio – becoming correspondingly richer, the creamier the sauce.

*Lobster Thermidor (above) is best with a rich, ideally oak-aged white. Best white burgundy or hot-climate Chardonnay are ideal.*

*Rabbit dishes (right) will take either red or white wines, depending on the treatment. A rich white would be good with mustard sauce, while Pinot Noir would work well alongside rabbit with red wine and prunes.*

**Salmon** Goes well with elegant, midweight whites with some acidity, such as *premier cru* Chablis, Chilean Chardonnay, dry Rieslings from Alsace or Germany. Equally, it is capable of taking a lightish red such as Côte de Beaune Pinot Noir.

**Tuna** Go for a fairly assertive red in preference to white: well-built Pinot Noir (California or New Zealand), mature Loire red (Chinon or Bourgueil), Chilean Merlot.

**Sushi and sashimi** What else but sake?

## MEAT AND POULTRY

**Chicken** If roasted, go for a soft-edged quality red, such as mature burgundy, Rioja Crianza or California Merlot. Lighter treatments such as poaching may need one of the richer whites, depending on any sauce.

**Turkey** The Christmas or Thanksgiving turkey deserves a show-stopping red with a little more power than you would serve with roast chicken: St-Emilion claret, Châteauneuf-du-Pape, California Cabernet.

**Rabbit** As for roast chicken.

**Pork** Roast pork or grilled chops are happiest with fairly full reds with a touch of spice: southern Rhône blends, Australian Shiraz, Chianti Classico.

**Lamb** The two best mates are Cabernet Sauvignon (Médoc, Napa, Chile, etc) and Rioja Reserva.

**Lobster** Cold in a salad, it needs a pungent white with some acidity, such as Pouilly-Fumé, dry Vouvray, Chablis *premier cru*, South African Chenin Blanc, Australian Riesling. Served hot as a main course (e.g. Thermidor), it requires an opulent and heavier wine – Meursault, California or South Australian Chardonnay, Alsace Pinot Gris.

**Light-textured white fish** Sole, lemon sole, plaice and the like go well with any light, unoaked or very lightly oaked white from almost anywhere.

**Firm-fleshed fish** Fish like sea bass, brill, turbot, tilapia or cod need full-bodied whites to match their texture. *Cru classé* white Bordeaux, Australian Semillon, and most of the richer Chardonnays of the southern hemisphere will fit the bill.

**Monkfish** Either a weighty white such as Hermitage or top burgundy, or – if cooked in red wine or wrapped in ham – something quite beefy such as Moulin-à-Vent or Rioja Crianza.

**Beef** Rump or sirloin can cope with the burliest reds from anywhere: Hermitage, the sturdiest Zinfandels, Barolo, Coonawarra Shiraz. A little lighter for fillet: South African Merlot, Bordeaux. Peppered steaks, mustard sauces and horseradish all demand a wine with bite, perhaps Crozes-Hermitage.

**Duck** A midweight red with youthful acidity to cut the fat is best: Chianti Classico, Zinfandel, New Zealand Pinot.

**Game birds** Best with fully mature Pinot Noir.

**Venison** Highly concentrated reds with some bottle-age are good. Cabernet, Shiraz or Zinfandel from hotter climates work well.

**Offal** Liver and kidneys are good with vigorous young reds such as Chinon, Barbera or *cru* Beaujolais. Sweetbreads are better with a high-powered white such as a mature Alsace.

**Indian** Fruity whites with a cutting-edge of acidity (Chenin, Riesling) are best with highly spiced dishes, but go red (Cabernet, Merlot) for lamb dishes like rogan josh.

**Thai** The chilli heat and abundance of lime and ginger make Sauvignon Blanc the surefire choice, whether from Sancerre, South Africa or New Zealand.

**Chinese** Perfumed whites such as Gewurztraminer, Viognier, Argentinian Torrontés and most Riesling are good cover-all wines for the huge diversity of Chinese food.

## DESSERTS

Fresh fruit salads are best served on their own, on account of their natural acidity. Similarly, frozen desserts like ice-creams and sorbets tend to numb the palate's sensitivity to wine. Anything based on eggs and cream, such as mousses, crème brûlée and pannacotta, deserves a noble-rotted wine such as Sauternes, Coteaux du Layon, or equivalent wines from outside Europe. Chocolate, often thought to present problems, doesn't do much damage to botrytized wines, but think maximum richness and high alcohol. Fruit tarts are better with a late-picked rather than fully rotted wine, such as Auslese German or Austrian Riesling, Alsace Vendange Tardive, or late-harvest South African Muscat. Meringues and creamy gâteaux are good with the sweeter styles of sparkling wine, while Asti or Moscato d'Asti make refreshing counter-balances to Christmas pudding. Sweet oloroso sherry, Bual or Malmsey madeira and Australian Liqueur Muscat are all superb with rich, dark fruitcake or anything nutty such as pecan pie.

*The classic partner for boeuf bourguinonne (left) is a soft, mature burgundy – the region from which the dish originated.*

*Mince pies with orange whisky butter (below) could be paired either with sparkling Italian Asti, or with a marmaladey Australian Liqueur Muscat.*

# LABELLING

Champagne labels are rarely complicated. The house name will always dominate, since it is a form of brand, in this case Billecart-Salmon at Mareuil-sur-Ay. Below is the style, Brut being virtually the driest, and this one is pink. Champagne is the only AOP wine that doesn't require the words *appellation contrôlée* to appear. Along the bottom, the reference number of this house denotes that it is an NM (*négociant-manipulant*), a producer that buys in grapes and makes its own wine.

The most prominent detail on a Bordeaux label is the property at which the wine was made. A classed growth always announces itself with the formula "*cru classé* en 1855". Lower down, the sub-region from which the wine hails is stated, in this case St-Julien, which also forms the name of the appellation.

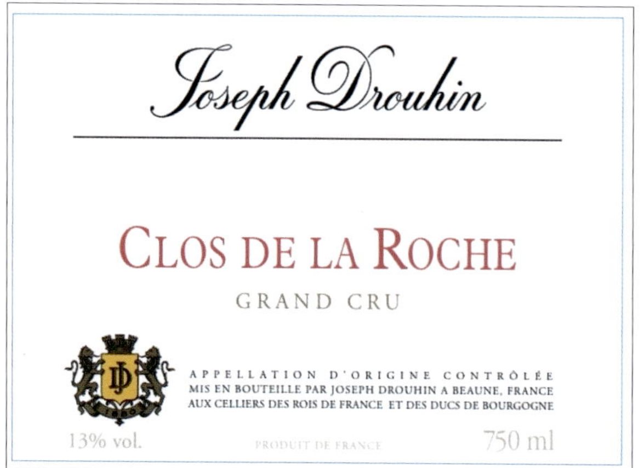

Burgundy labelling can be a minefield. The merchant's name (Drouhin) is followed by the appellation. This label tells you this is a *grand cru* wine, but doesn't have to state which village it belongs to (Morey-St-Denis, in fact). Note that *mis en bouteille* is not followed by *au domaine*, because it has not been bottled on an individual estate, but by a négociant based elsewhere.

Reading down this Italian label, we have the name of the vineyard (Vigna del Sorbo), then the producer (Fontodi) and then the appellation or denominazione (Chianti Classico). Then comes the quality level – Italy's highest, DOCG. Riserva denotes a wine aged for at least three years before release. Below is the information that the wine was bottled at the estate by its producer.

The practised eye begins to discern similarities among the labels of different European countries. On this Spanish label, we see the name of the producer (La Rioja Alta SA), then the appellation or denominación (Rioja), and the standard formula that announces its quality level – DOCa, Spain's highest. Under the vintage comes the wine name. Gran Reserva denotes a wine that has been kept for five years before release, of which at least two must be spent in oak, 904 being a kind of brand name for this producer's top wines. *Embotellado en la propiedad* means 'bottled on the estate'.

German labels can look even more fiendishly complicated than the French. Underneath the proprietor's name here (Dr Pauly-Bergweiler), we have what amounts to the designated appellation. This one comes specifically from the Alte Badstube am Doctorberg vineyard in the village of Bernkastel on the Mosel, which happens to be solely owned by this producer, and is so called because it adjoins the famous Bernkasteler Doctor vineyard. This is roughly comparable within the classification structure – and also in size – to a tiny *grand cru* within one of the village appellations of Burgundy (say, the Romanée-Conti vineyard of Vosne-Romanée). Next to the vintage date, we are told the grape variety is Riesling, and the style of this wine is Spätlese (late-picked). In the absence of any other qualifier, we can therefore take it to be very delicately sweet in style. A dry version would be labelled Spätlese Trocken.

In the sometimes complex world of bottle labelling, what could be simpler than the information on this varietal wine from an acclaimed South Australia producer? The proprietor has given his own name to the estate, which appears prominently at the top (Tim Adams), with the vintage (2009), grape variety (Semillon) and region (Clare Valley) following on below it. In essence, this is pretty much what that German label is also telling you, but notice how much more straightforward the Australian label looks.

This label simply tells us the name of the estate (Thelema), the vintage year (2007), the grape variety (Merlot) and the region of the country in which it was grown and produced (Stellenbosch). Even though there is a regional denomination system in South Africa, the label itself still manages to be crystal-clear.

# GRAPE VARIETIES

*Soil is furrowed the ancient way to catch winter rain (above), in the sweltering south of Spain.*

S uch is the mystique and reverence attached to the appreciation of wine that it is easy to forget just what a simple product it is.

Visiting a modern winery today, with its acres of carefully trained vines, the giant tanks of shining stainless steel, the automated bottling line, and perhaps the rows of oak barrels resting on top of one another in deep cavernous cellars, you might think this was the end product of centuries of human ingenuity.

To the extent that the techniques for making good wine have been steadily refined through succeeding generations, indeed it is. Unlike beer, though, which had to await the discovery of malting grains before it could be produced, the rudiments of wine have always been there, for it is nothing other than spoiled grape juice.

Any substance that is high in natural sugars – whether it be the sticky sap of palm trees, or honey, or the juice of ripened fruit – will sooner or later start to ferment if it comes into contact with yeast. Wild yeasts, transported on the bodies of insects and falling on to the fruit that they hover around, feed on the fruit sugar and initiate fermentation, creating two principal by-products in the process.

One is carbon dioxide gas, which is why anything that has accidentally started fermenting tastes slightly fizzy, and the other is alcohol. And we know what that does to us.

Long before the earliest human societies had begun to live settled rather than nomadic existences, and begun to cultivate the land, a basic type of alcoholic drink could be derived from the controlled fermentation of fresh fruit or honey. This was the prototype of wine.

One particular species of wild vine, which originated in the area around the Black Sea that today takes in Georgia, Armenia and eastern Turkey, proved especially well suited to quick fermentation, owing to the naturally sweet berries it produced. It is in fact the only vine species native to Europe and the Near East and, because it came to play such a pre-eminent role in the development of winemaking all over the world, it was later given the botanical classification *Vitis vinifera* – 'the wine-bearing grape'.

Within that one species, however, there are as many as 10,000 different sub-types, known as varieties. Some of these developed by natural mutation; many have been created by deliberate cross-fertilization. Only a small percentage of those 10,000 are important in the commercial production of wine today (the French wine authorities recognize around 200), and many of those are fairly obscure and consequently hardly ever used. A mere handful, overwhelmingly French in origin, now constitutes the international language of wine, and it is these that this section deals with.

*A breathtaking springtime scene (right), with flowering mustard seed growing in the vineyards of Sonoma, California, the state that has become a major player on the world wine scene.*

Not all of the varieties we'll look at are grown throughout the world, and one of them – Gamay – is mostly concentrated in its own little corner of France (Beaujolais). But these are the varieties whose flavours it is most useful to become familiar with. They are responsible between them for producing all the most famous French wine styles, from champagne in the north to the richly heady reds of the sweltering south, and they therefore provided the original models when serious winemaking first began to be pioneered beyond the shores of Europe.

All the European countries have indigenous grapes of their own, some of which have made it on to the international wine scene. There are plantings of some of the best Spanish, Italian and Portuguese grapes in North and South America, and in the enterprising wine cultures of Australia and New Zealand. We begin in this section, though, with the mostly French grapes, because those have been the earliest and most widely travelled ones.

All sorts of factors influence the taste of wine. The climate in which the grapes are grown; the type of soil in the vineyards; the way the vines are trained and managed during the growing season; the temperature at which the juice is fermented; what it ferments in (stainless steel or wood); how much contact red

wines have with the grape-skins; the duration and type of any cask-ageing. But nothing affects the style more importantly than the grape or grapes the wine is made from.

If you want to drink a delicately crisp, simple white, it doesn't make sense to go for Gewürztraminer. Similarly, if you're after a featherlight, fruity red for a summer's day, you may get more than you bargained for from Cabernet Sauvignon. The most widely met grape varieties have innate common characteristics.

As we are introduced to each of these VIPs of the wine world, we shall also take a look at the different regions in which they feature, both at home and abroad, and explore the typical styles and flavours to be found in each of them.

Following extensive introductions to 12 of the most familiar grapes, largely French in origin, along with Riesling and Gewürztraminer, we'll take a look at a handful of varieties that have achieved brand recognition in more recent times – grapes like Malbec, which has emerged from the shadow of Bordeaux to become a star in its own right in South America.

*The impressive vaulted cellars of Ch. de Meursault, in Burgundy's Côte de Beaune (above), filled with wine ageing in oak barrels.*

# CHARDONNAY

*From its homeland in Burgundy, Chardonnay has travelled the world to become the most fashionable and sought-after of white varieties. This chameleon of grapes bows to the whim of the winemaker, offering a diversity of styles to appeal to all palates.*

AS SOMEBODY once (nearly) said, if Chardonnay didn't exist, it would be necessary to invent it. No other grape, white or red, has even now achieved quite the degree of international recognition that Chardonnay has. In many consumers' minds, it stands as a synonym for dry white wine in general, and the reason is not hard to find. It is grown is some proportion in virtually every wine-producing country on the planet.

Its adaptablity in the vineyard and its almost limitless mutability in the winery are what made Chardonnay the first big success story among grape varieties. Compared with most other major grapes, it is relatively easy to grow. It can take a wide spectrum of climatic conditions in its stride, from the pinched summers of northern France to the broiling sun-traps of South Australia, and it isn't especially fussy about the kinds of soils it grows in. It ripens well, and it yields plentifully in most vintages. While it's true that great wines are for the most part produced from low-yielding vines, the truth is that the vast bulk of worldwide Chardonnay is destined for straightforward, everyday wines that are intended to be drunk young.

Just as Chardonnay has been everybody's flexible friend in the vineyard, so it proves similarly malleable in the winery. It isn't in itself an especially characterful variety (although there are certain sub-types of it that do have some intriguingly musky perfume), hence its suitability for everyday drinking. On the other hand, it is precisely that innate neutrality that fits it so well – perhaps more obviously than any other white variety – for responding to oak treatments.

Given even a short period of maturation in oak barrels, whether new or used once or twice already, it begins to take on some of those buttery or vanilla scents we classically associate with premium Chardonnay. Ferment it in barrel to begin with, with a further period of ageing in the cask, and those buttery notes are backed up by savoury, toasty aromas. If the insides of the barrels have been given a thorough charring, we may end up with something that is, in effect, smoked wine.

Various economic shortcuts to impart the taste of oak to a wine can be used by producers keen to avoid the outlay of putting their Chardonnays through an expensive finishing-school. A 'chipped' Chardonnay has had a bag of oak chippings (something like a giant teabag) macerated in the wine. One that has been 'staved' has been held in specially designed steel vats that incorporate vertical strips of oak on their inner surfaces. All of which is far cheaper than investing in a consignment of new barrels every year.

*Chardonnay matures in the warm vineyards of California (right). A vigorous vine, relatively unfussed by climate or soil, this golden grape is neutral in character and has a natural affinity with oak. It is as suited to classic white burgundies as to Australian sparkling wines.*

With the asset of huge popularity comes the liability of changing fashion. In the years since the 1990s, Chardonnay has undergone something of a rocky period in consumers' affections. The international palate eventually grew fatigued with wines that tasted as though the oak had been laid on with a trowel. Australia's Chardonnays (a little unfairly) were suddenly seen as the prime culprits, leading to the wholesale abandonment there of oak-ageing at the simpler end of the spectrum. Suddenly, labels proudly proclaimed their Chardonnays to be 'unoaked', as though they were being declared free of some adulterating substance.

While that welcome development certainly led to a generation of more finely balanced wines, it also contained within it a paradoxical drawback. As we learned above, Chardonnay is an extremely simple wine when it doesn't have anything beyond basic vinification done to it. And the sudden worldwide preponderance of what were essentially rather prosaic, lightly lemony dry whites of no great personality is what led to Chardonnay fatigue, best expressed by the emergence of a movement among dissenting drinkers in the United States known as ABC – Anything But Chardonnay.

The search was on for a white grape that could replicate some of the reliability of Chardonnay, while providing drinkers with something a little more idiosyncratic, a little more varied from one wine to the next, than Chardonnay is capable of. Viognier (see page 86) was where a lot of the smart money went, although the answer has turned out for the time being to lie more readily to hand in the shape of another already established variety, Sauvignon Blanc (see page 52).

As well as making one of the most famous styles of white table wine, Chardonnay is also indispensable to the production of quality sparkling wines the world over. It forms one of the triumvirate of grapes used in champagne, and nearly all producers of classic sparklers elsewhere have plantings of Chardonnay. Once again, it is the grape's inherent neutrality that bestows elegance and finesse on the best fizz.

# Burgundy

If Chardonnay represents the monarch among white wine grapes, then the Burgundy region in eastern France is its official residence. From the isolated enclave of Chablis in the *département* of the Yonne down to the wide swathes of vineyard known as the Mâconnais to the west of the river Saône, Chardonnay is the overwhelmingly predominant white grape variety.

The entire gamut of styles is produced. There are easy-drinking, everyday whites of honest simplicity, as well as powerfully complex wines intended to be aged in the bottle. There are wines that rely on youthful acidity and freshness alone for their appeal, while others mobilize the fat buttery opulence imparted by oak.

Cooperatives and négociants (merchants who buy in grapes from growers under contract and bottle the resulting blend under their own name) tend to be the sources for much of the commercial white burgundy seen in high-street drinks outlets, while the many individual producers who operate entirely self-sufficiently are responsible for some of the world's most extravagantly rich – and extravagantly expensive – dry white wine.

Chablis in some ways deserves to be considered as a region in itself, because it is not geographically part of Burgundy proper, lying as it does slightly nearer to the most southerly part of the Champagne vineyards than to the northernmost tip of the Côte d'Or. Its climate is cool and fairly wet, its winters often severe, and late frosts in spring are a regular occurrence. Those conditions mean Chardonnay ripens quite late, tending to produce a high-acid wine, often described as steely.

At their best, these are squeaky-clean, bone-dry wines that can be crisp to the point of brittleness in their youth. As they age, they lose some of that sharp edge and become mellower. That said, there is a general tendency to make softer wine these days, which runs the risk that they lack bite when young, and don't mature with quite the same complexity as the traditional style.

The great majority of the wines are made without oak, Chablis being the original reference for the world's unwooded Chardonnays. Some producers, however, do use a certain amount of oak on their best *cuvées*, particularly those with land in one or more of the seven *grand cru* vineyards that sit at the top of the quality tree. Even without oak, Chablis from a good producer in a fine vintage (such as 2007 or 2009) can develop its own inherent richness, often tantalizingly hinting at some phantom oak presence, with a few years in the bottle.

Southeast of Chablis, white wines from the Côte d'Or – and in particular the Côte de Beaune, its southern stretch – represent the pinnacle of Burgundian Chardonnay. It is here, in the exalted appellations of Corton-Charlemagne, Puligny-Montrachet, Meursault and others, that oaked Chardonnay really began.

The top wines, often produced in tiny quantities selling at dizzyingly elevated prices, are sumptuously rich and concentrated, often deep golden in colour from months of ageing in oak barrels, and generally high in alcohol (13–13.5 per cent is the norm). Many possess an intriguingly vegetal flavour, like green beans, leeks or even cabbage, that can be something of a shock to

*The rich, golden colours of a Burgundian autumn (below) spread through the sloping* grand cru *vineyards of Vaudésir (nearest) and Grenouilles, in Chablis.*

those used to fruitier-tasting Chardonnays. The Burgundians argue that this is their famous *goût de terroir* – the unique taste of the limestone soils in which the vines are grown.

It is still fair to say that many winemakers aiming to produce premium-quality oaked Chardonnay began by looking to the top wines of the Côte d'Or for their original inspiration, however much they may since have diverged from that earliest model.

The Côte d'Or is connected to the Mâconnais by a strip of land called the Côte Chalonnaise, so called because it lies just to the west of the town of Chalon-sur-Saône. Its Chardonnays, from appellations such as Montagny, Rully and Mercurey, are considerably lighter in style than those from further north, but can possess their own lean elegance. They tend to have correspondingly less oak (if any) than the Côte d'Or wines, but as so often, certain individual producers can provide the exception to the rule.

In the south of Burgundy, the Mâconnais is the largest of the sub-regions. Here is where most of the everyday quaffing wine is made, much of it of rather humdrum quality, often vinified without oak. The best appellation, Pouilly-Fuissé, can have something of the depth and ageability of lesser Côte de Beaune wines, while St-Véran is often as good as anything from the Chalonnaise.

Certain villages within the overall appellation of Mâcon Blanc-Villages are considered to produce wines of sufficiently distinct quality for their names to be added to the label (hence Mâcon-Lugny, Mâcon-Verzé, and so forth).

In recent years, some quality producers have taken to selling wine under the simplest appellation of all, Bourgogne Chardonnay, the result sufficiently full and rich (and perhaps oaky) as to belie the apparently humble designation – and also to allow them to compete on the shelves with Chardonnays from elsewhere.

The rare white wine of Beaujolais, Burgundy's southernmost sector, is Chardonnay too, a chalky-dry, usually unoaked style a little like a less graceful Chablis.

Burgundy's sparkling wine, Crémant de Bourgogne, made by the same method as champagne, relies principally on Chardonnay. The grapes can theoretically come from anywhere in the region, and the bottle maturation varies between producers, so styles run the range from overly delicate to something approximating the complex, yeasty fullness of champagne itself.

*Hand-picked Chardonnay grapes are loaded on to a trailer at Fuissé (above) in the Mâconnais, the largest sub-region of Burgundy.*

# United States

*Wineries in New York State, especially those on Long Island (above), are increasingly producing elegant, complex Chardonnays.*

Undoubtedly, the most dynamic Chardonnay developments outside Europe have taken place in the United States. Indeed, by the end of the 1980s, the state of California alone had more extensive plantings of the grape than the whole of France, where its growth has not exactly been stagnant. No group of winemakers beyond the ancestral heartland of Burgundy has taken greater pains with the variety than the Californians, and the transformations that the wines have undergone in the last two decades have been a fascinating barometer of changing Chardonnay trends.

In the 1970s and 80s, the fashion was for a massively overblown style of rich golden wine, with dollops of sweet new oak all over it, not dissimilar to what was then the southern hemisphere mode. When the backlash came, it sent the pendulum hurtling in the other direction, so that it suddenly seemed as if everybody was competing to produce West Coast Chablis, so lean and green and biting were many of the wines.

By the late 1980s, the picture was beginning to even out, and there is now a much greater diversity of styles, each representing a more relaxed expression of its microclimate and the intentions of the individual winemaker.

The very best Stateside Chardonnays – such as those from the cooler areas of California like Carneros and Sonoma Valley, from Oregon and New York State – can sometimes achieve an almost eerie similarity to certain top burgundies, partly because of the comparable levels of acidity, and partly because of the sensitive use of new French oak.

A lot of work has been done in researching types of oak, and the different levels of flame treatment the cooper can give the barrels, to find out what best suits American Chardonnay. Some producers, veterans of field trips to Burgundy, put their faith in the flavours of French oak, but others have looked again at native American woods and have disproved the theory that you can't make a subtle Chardonnay in US oak.

Another French habit that has taken root among many of the premium producers is avoidance of the filtration procedure, in which microscopic solid residues of the fermentation are cleaned out of the wine. While filtering a wine certainly results in a crystal-clear, stable

*Madonna Vineyards in the cool Carneros region of northern California (right), a region that produces some of the state's finest Chardonnays, eerily similar in style to certain top burgundies.*

product, many feel that it also strips it of some of its flavour complexity and richness of texture. The anti-filtration brigade has often proudly inscribed the word 'Unfiltered' on the labels.

It is no more possible to generalize about a typical California style of Chardonnay than it is to talk about a French style. The state contains a multitude of different microclimates, reflected in the various AVAs (American Viticultural Areas, the equivalent of appellations): Calistoga, at the northern end of Napa Valley, is one of the hotter areas, as are the inland districts of San Joaquin, while Santa Ynez, to the south, is relatively cool.

Most of California's coastal regions are affected each day by Pacific fog drifts, which can take until mid-morning to clear. Those, and cool night-time conditions, help to ensure that the ripening grapes don't become heat-stressed, so that acidity levels at harvest-time are not too low.

Good California Chardonnays have the same sort of weight in the mouth as wines like Puligny-Montrachet, with a carefully defined balance of oak and fruit. Acidity is usually fresh, though with perhaps not quite the same tang as young burgundy. Owing to the specific clonal types of the grape favoured, the fruit flavours are altogether more overt, California wines often having a riper citrus character

(mandarin orange), even a tropical element like fresh pineapple. By and large, despite what some producers intend, they are not particularly susceptible to improvement in the bottle, other than an allowance for the softening of youthful acids. Most will never be better than they are at one or two years old, and may already be beginning to taste a little tired at not much more than three. Drink young and fresh.

In the Pacific Northwest, Oregon Chardonnay tends to be crisper and slightly more austere on the palate than the wines of California, and the characteristic style is leaner, and less ostentatious as to fruit. Washington State has some fine Chardonnays, their erstwhile tendency to flabbiness having been overcome by some attractively balanced wines, though again with somewhat less fruit than California examples. Idaho has a more extreme climate, and tends to produce wines with high acidity, though they can be rounded out with gentle oak treatment.

Back east, New York State has a much cooler climate than the West Coast, and the Chardonnays it produces are in a correspondingly more bracing style, but the best wineries – notably on Long Island – are capitalizing on that to turn out some elegant and complex wines with ageing potential.

Chardonnay is also gaining in importance in Texas, where it makes a broad, immediately approachable style with plenty of ripe fruit.

*Chardonnay ageing in new oak barrels (above). A lot of research has been carried out in the US to find out which oak best suits American Chardonnay, leading to a trend among certain producers away from French oak to native American oak.*

# Australia

Such was the soaring popularity of Australia's Chardonnays on external markets by the late 20th century that, at one stage, it began to look as if the country might not be able to produce enough to cope with the worldwide demand for them. One consequence is that there is now more Chardonnay planted across the country's vineyards than any other grape variety, white or red.

With the advent in the 1990s of the so-called flying winemakers – travelling wine consultants who flit between the hemispheres working as many vintages as they can fit into their schedules – the success of Australian wine had received the global endorsement that it was due.

Although it often involved a great swallowing of cultural pride on the part of the natives, the Australian itinerant winemakers were instrumental in revolutionizing winemaking practices in the viticultural backwaters of southern Europe. It was their skill with Chardonnay that, more than anything, served to create the demand for their services.

*Carpets of purple flowers surround Mountadam Estate (below) on the High Eden Ridge, in South Australia. Eden Valley, part of the Barossa Range, shares the soils and climate of the Barossa Valley, source of richly concentrated Chardonnays.*

Australia taught the wine world that Chardonnay could be as unashamedly big and ripe and rich as you wanted it to be. Since the climate in most of the vineyard regions, the majority of which lie in the southeast of the country, is uniformly hot and dry, the fruit grown there regularly attains sky-high levels of natural sugar. Winemakers thus generally have to sharpen their wines up by controlled additions of tartaric acid to prevent them from tasting too sweet.

Nonetheless, the benchmark style of Aussie Chardonnay for years was a sunshine-yellow, extraordinarily luscious wine that, married with the vanilla and butterscotch flavours of new oak, was quite a way off being fully dry. High sugar means high alcohol (up to 14.5 per cent in some wines) so that, at the end of a generous glass, you certainly knew you'd had a drink.

As British and American wine consumers discovered an almost insatiable thirst for Australian Chardonnay, it became the habit in some critical quarters (myself included) to start calling into question whether these wines possessed true balance.

In latter years, trends in Chardonnay have begun to diversify in Australia, just as they have in California. There is a desire on the part of many winemakers, notably in the state of Western Australia, in South Australia's Coonawarra region, and in the Yarra Valley in Victoria, to make a subtler, more ageworthy (dare one say, more European?) style of Chardonnay, with better complexity.

At the top end of the quality ladder, there are some world-class wines. The problem, as so often, arises lower down the scale, where the unoaked Chardonnays in particular often seem to fighting to attain an elusive balance. Acidification is not always as finely judged as it might be, and where it isn't, a feeling of conflict with the obviously ripe fruit can be the result. Residual sugar levels are still often uncomfortably high, leading to wines that taste cloying after a glass, and are not best suited for accompanying food.

Much of Australia's wine is made from grapes sourced from different areas, blended to get the best balance of attributes in the final wine, so regional characteristics are proportionately less significant. However, an

increasing number do bottle wines that are the produce of particular vineyard areas (the system of Geographical Indications, or GIs, is loosely and much less restrictively based on the European appellation approach), vinified separately so as to give a true expression of what the French would call their *terroir*.

In the state of South Australia, the Barossa Valley GI is one of the most important regions, producing broad-beamed, richly concentrated Chardonnays that make a dramatic impact on the palate. The McLaren Vale and Padthaway GIs are responsible for wines with perhaps a touch more finesse. Clare Valley is distinctly cooler, and its wines are correspondingly lighter and less upfront in style.

Chardonnays from the Goulburn Valley GI, Victoria, often possess hauntingly tropical fruit characters, while the cooler-climate Yarra Valley wines can resemble those of the less torrid parts of California. In Western Australia, the Margaret River GI is producing some unabashedly Burgundian wines that sometimes have that pungent whiff of green vegetable found on the Côte d'Or. For me, these are some of the most refined and attractive wines Australia has yet produced.

On the island of Tasmania, which constitutes its own GI, Chardonnay can be more austerely European still in its orientation, owing to the cool and fairly wet climate. Levels of grape acidity comparable to Chablis are not unheard of.

*Stormy skies at first light (above) over the high ridges of the Barossa Range, South Australia.*

# New Zealand

*(Above) Brancott Estate, Marlborough, South Island. New Zealand Chardonnay is light, with juicily ripe fruit.*

Chardonnay is New Zealand's second most widely planted white grape, behind Sauvignon Blanc. Grown in what is a considerably cooler and damper climate than Australia, the wines it produces tend, on the whole, to be noticeably lighter and more acidic.

That doesn't mean to say that Chardonnay lacks anything in terms of character because, in common with the even more fashionable Sauvignon, it nearly always possesses a positively unearthly degree of juicily ripe fruit. It is quite the norm to find pineapple and mango, grapefruit and apple, chasing each other around the glass, almost as though the grower had set out to confound the notion that Chardonnay isn't an aromatic variety.

About the richest styles come from the Gisborne and Poverty Bay regions on the eastern tip of the North Island, and these are the ones that respond best to oak-ageing. A little to the south, the wines of Hawke's Bay have more of a tang to them, and require a correspondingly more delicate touch with the wood.

Hopping over to the South Island, the climate becomes distinctly cooler still, and the typical Chardonnay style is snappier and more citric in Marlborough, and then quite taut and austere from Waipara and Central Otago.

# South Africa

*The lush green vineyards of Stellenbosch wineries Warwick Estate (above), and Thelema Vineyards (right), producers of rounded, golden Chardonnays. Coastal Stellenbosch is home to many of South Africa's finest producers.*

When South Africa began to play a full part on the international wine scene in the early 1990s, many consumers were surprised to discover that Chardonnay was not the major force that it is elsewhere in the southern hemisphere. It played second fiddle to the much more widely planted Chenin Blanc. It still accounts for only a small percentage of vineyard land planted with white grapes, and what there is has been losing ground to Sauvignon Blanc.

Although South Africa remained largely isolated from world trade while the wine boom of the 1970s and 1980s was gathering momentum, it did profit in one respect. It was able to observe the trend for the heavily oaked, blockbuster style of Chardonnay (then inextricably associated with so-called New World winemaking) as it fell from favour among forward-looking winemakers, and simply sit it out.

How today's Chardonnays taste depends crucially on how far the vineyards lie from the southern coast. Those from further inland are grown in hotter conditions. So the Breede River Valley – over 96km (60 miles) from the cooling maritime influence of the Indian Ocean – is home to some of the Cape's biggest, burliest Chardonnays, while those from coastal Walker Bay are subtler, with the emphasis on fruit and more sharply defined acidity.

# Other Regions

## SOUTH AMERICA

Chile's Chardonnays, as with its Cabernet Sauvignon wines, are made in two broad style categories. Some are made in a recognizably French vein, with pronounced acidity, light appley fruit and restrained oak maturation. Others go the whole hog, with full-blown charred oak flavours and a high-extract, alcoholic feel. It depends on the producer as much as the region. Argentina's wines, made largely in Mendoza in the foothills of the Andes, occupy a midway point between those two styles, with impressive balance and class.

## EUROPE

Increasing concentrations of Chardonnay are cropping up across Italy now, from Aosta in the northwest all the way down to Puglia and Sicily, so that the variety is now the fourth most widely planted white grape. Although some rugged individualists are aiming for top-flight, barrel-fermented wines (and charging energetically for them), the basic style – best typified by the wines of the Alto Adige DOC on the Austrian border – are delicate, very lightly creamy wines made without recourse to wood.

Northern Spain is getting in on the act too, with plantings of Chardonnay vines in Penedés, Lérida, Somontano and Navarra, where it is often blended with local varieties such as Macabeo and Viura to make clean-cut, nutty, dry modern whites. It has achieved some significance in the production of the sparkling

*Chardonnay is taking root in northern Italy, especially in Piedmont (above), in the foothills of the Alps, where it produces delicate, lightly creamy wines.*

wine, cava, although many quality-conscious producers feel they can do without the reflected glory a non-Spanish variety appears to confer on the wines.

Chardonnay is of some modest importance in central Europe, particularly in Hungary, where the flying winemakers have been regular visitors. The wines tend to be made in the straightforward neutral style, clean and sharp for everyday drinking. When they do have some oak on them, it is only to add a gentler, rounder feel to them.

Further east, Bulgaria has been making Chardonnays since its heavily state-subsidized entry into western markets in the 1980s. A little on the clumsy side, they often didn't taste especially fresh, although the odd wine from Khan Krum in the east of the country could display a sort of sour-cream palatability.

There are also limited plantings in Slovenia and Romania but, among the other big western players, only Germany and Portugal managed largely to bypass the Chardonnay craze of the late 20th century.

*Harvesting Chardonnay grapes (left) in Blatetz, Bulgaria. The quality of Chardonnay, one of many wines produced for the export market, varies, some of the best coming from Khan Krum.*

# CABERNET SAUVIGNON

*Its pedigree is firmly founded in the gravelly soils of the Médoc, in the heart of Bordeaux. The king of red grapes, Cabernet Sauvignon has conquered vineyards across the world without losing the classic character that brought it such renown.*

THE RED HALF of that hugely successful partnership that came to dominate international winemaking in the most recent generation is Cabernet Sauvignon. Alongside Chardonnay, it strode imperiously through the world's vineyards in the 1980s, often insisting that native varieties get out of its way wherever serious red wine was to be made. Although the example set before Cabernet growers – the classed-growth clarets of the Médoc in Bordeaux – is an illustrious one, it wasn't immediately easy to see why Cabernet came to be perceived as the pre-eminent red counterpart to the crowd-pleasing Chardonnay.

Its adaptablity to a variety of soils and climates is quite as impressive as that of Chardonnay, but its crop yield is more grudging, meaning that, even in the warmest climates, it has a heavy responsibility to earn its keep. Producers in regions with high climatic variation can often find that their higher-volume wines are basically subsidising the Cabernet.

As against that, Cabernet Sauvignon has suffered far less from the contempt induced by over-familiarity that has been Chardonnay's fate, for all that, among educated American consumers, ABC implicitly represents Anything but Cabernet as much as it stands for Anything but Chardonnay. There are three principal reasons for this.

Firstly, Cabernet comes in a much broader and more nuanced range of styles than Chardonnay. It isn't simply a question of deciding whether you want to make an unoaked, lightly oaked or very oaky wine. There are much finer gradations of style, and the grape is much less led by the nose when treated with oak than Chardonnay is.

Secondly, being a red wine, it is more often than not capable of developing with age. Just as the basic styles can be vastly different, so too the reactions of the wine to bottle maturation are excitingly divergent.

And thirdly, while it certainly conquered the known wine world quite as extensively as Chardonnay did, it somehow never became quite as axiomatically synonymous with red wine as Chardonnay did with white. Nobody ordering in a wine bar was ever heard asking for 'a glass of Cabernet' in the way that the fabled 'glass of Chardonnay' became the *lingua franca* of everyday white wine.

When on song, Cabernet Sauvignon wines deliver a heady rush of pure blackcurrant fruit, bolstered by density of texture and substantial ageing capacity, the sum of which seems to many wine-lovers the essence of all that is noble in a red wine. The greatest productions of the Médoc – Châteaux Lafite, Latour, Margaux, Mouton-Rothschild – are among the most famous names in wine, and if some of the class of those wines could be seen, however distantly, in a Cabernet Sauvignon from Chile, California or Australia, then the winemaker behind it might stand a fair chance of making the big time. (And so they have.)

Cabernet responds supremely well to oak-ageing, when the vanillin in new wood helps to soothe some of the natural acerbity of the young wine. That acerbity is basically tannin, that substance in youthful red wine that furs up the drinker's mouth, and which can obscure the fruit flavours. Cabernet is a thick-skinned variety, so its vinification results in naturally high tannin. Furthermore, its berries are relatively small compared to other red varieties, meaning that the proportion of tannin-bearing pip to flesh is higher.

What this means is that Cabernet producers need to make some finely detailed decisions in the winery about how to treat their wine. If you're selling to an audience that will kill for your next vintage, and expect to cellar the wine for upwards of a decade, you can spread your wings. If, on the other hand, your market positioning is about quick turnover from the winery to the retail industry, a great unwieldy slew of indigestible tannin is going to be box-office poison. And how much youthful fruit is too much for today's palates?

*The small, dusty-blue Cabernet Sauvignon grape (right) produces wines of good tannin, body and aroma. It adapts easily to differing soils and climates, and in its finest form, with warm, late summer sun to ripen it fully, Cabernet creates complex, deeply coloured reds, packed with juicy blackcurrant fruit.*

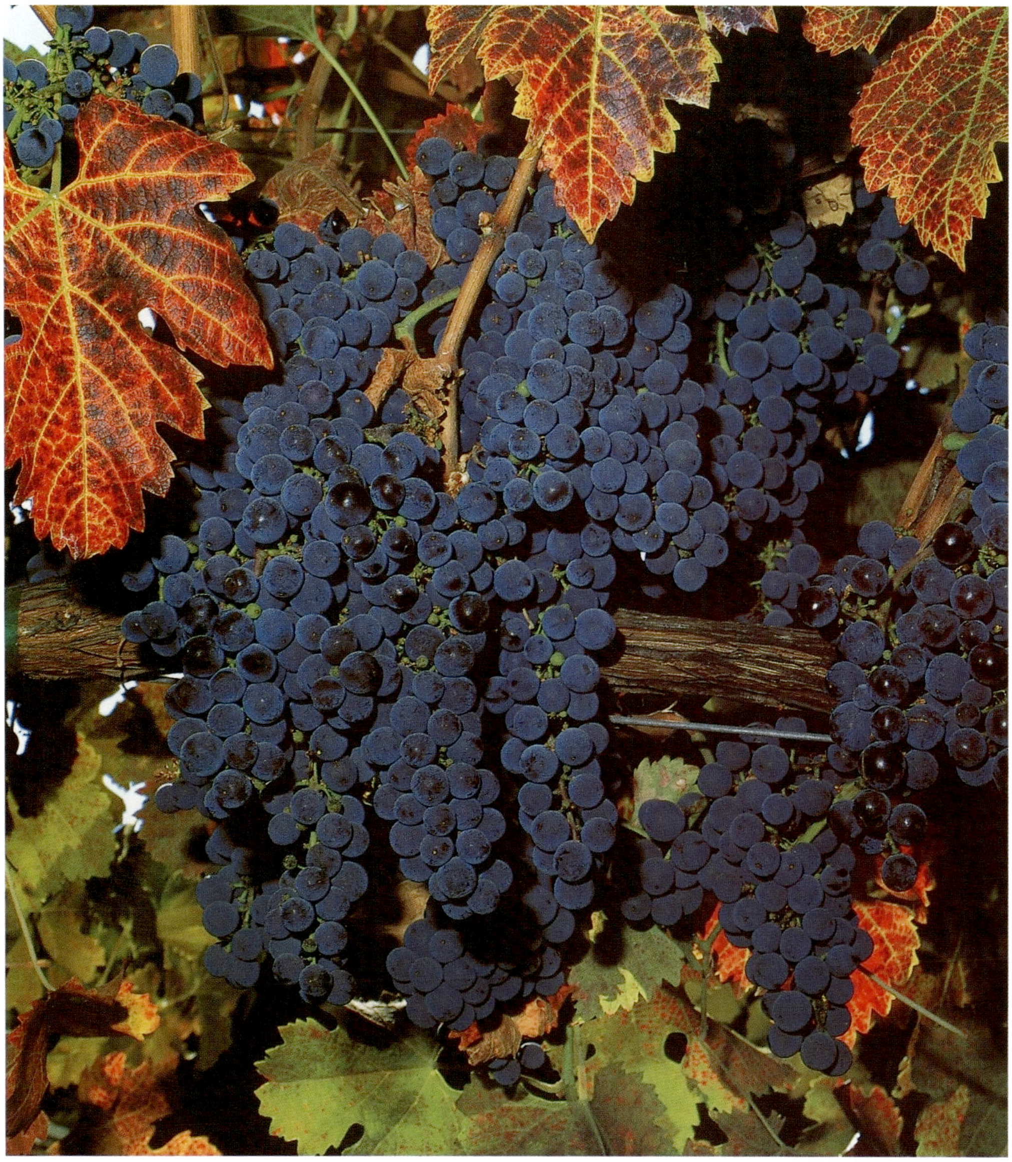

It's partly those considerations that have led to the realization that Cabernet Sauvignon is often much better-behaved in company. The original Bordeaux model is about blending in any case, and even a modest admixture of one or two other grapes can negotiate the toughness and brutality out of young Cabernet. Enter Merlot, Cabernet Franc and others in Bordeaux. Hello Shiraz in Australia.

Whatever the blend, the holy grail is a wine capable of acquiring complexity through long cellaring. Cabernets and Cabernet-based blends evolve in fascinatingly various ways as they age, depending on the quality of the primary fruit, the type of wood used for maturation, duration in the cask, and the length of time the wine spends in the bottle before you open it. Even in quite advanced old age, the telltale mineral purity of Cabernet Sauvignon still shines invitingly through.

Lighter styles of Cabernet are made in regions such as northern Italy and New Zealand, and many of these rub along quite well without oak. Indeed, when the wine is fully ripe and made from low-yielding vines, it can often be quite difficult to tell whether it has any oak on it or not. It can also, in common with others of the more assertive red varieties, make an attractive, full-flavoured rosé.

It is this potential for gathering complexity, though, that explains the high prices consistently paid for top Cabernets around the world. And that in turn is why so many winemakers take such enormous pains with it, when they may well be able to turn a faster buck growing something more mundane.

### FRENCH ORIGINS

Bordeaux, specifically the left bank of the river Gironde, from the north of the Médoc down to the Graves. (On the right bank, it tends to play second fiddle to Merlot.)

### WHERE ELSE IS IT GROWN?

Just about everywhere, although it has not made significant inroads into the cooler climates of northern Europe.

### TASTING NOTES

In warm climates, almost any of the purple-skinned fruits – classically blackcurrants (perhaps most startlingly so in the best wines of Chile), but also black plums, brambles, damsons, etc. Often has a distinct note of fresh mint or even eucalyptus, especially in parts of Australia and Chile. Cooler climates can create a whiff of bitterness in it, often uncannily like chopped green pepper. Oak treatments generally emphasize a mineral austerity in the wine, likened in Bordeaux to the smell of cigar-boxes, cedarwood or – most recognizably – pencil shavings. With several years' bottle-age, it can take on aromas such as well-hung game, plum tomatoes, warm leather, dark chocolate, even soft Indian spices like cardamom, while the primary fruit begins to taste more like preserved fruit.

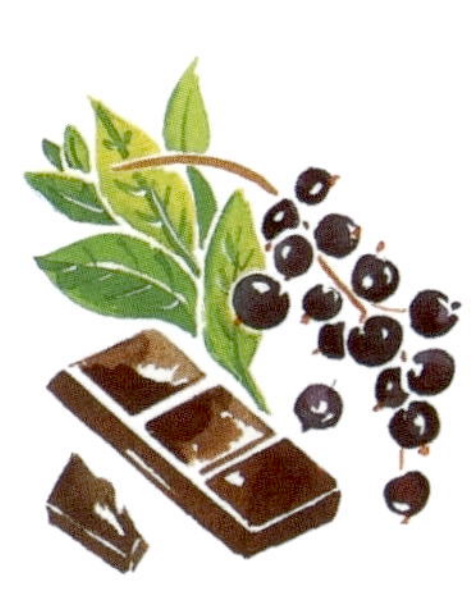

# Bordeaux

*A landmark in the Pauillac vineyards of first growth Château Latour (above), one of the five great premier cru châteaux of the Médoc.*

*The chai at Château Mouton-Rothschild, Pauillac (below). The four famous communes of the Médoc – St-Estèphe, St-Julien, Margaux and Pauillac – are where the reputation of red Bordeaux is founded.*

Although Cabernet Sauvignon occupies far less vineyard land in Bordeaux than its traditional blending partner Merlot, it is nonetheless widely considered the pre-eminent grape variety in the region. This is because it plays a major part in the wines on which the reputation of Bordeaux is primarily founded – the *crus classés*, or classed growths, of the Médoc and Graves. When the region's classification system was drawn up in 1855, it was not that the judges ignored the Merlot-based wines of Pomerol and St-Emilion on the right bank; they simply didn't think they were in the same class.

That classification (outlined in detail in the chapter on Bordeaux) is now considered seriously outdated by many commentators, but the general perception that the majority of Bordeaux's most illustrious wines derive the greater part of their authority from the presence of Cabernet Sauvignon has never really changed, Pomerol notwithstanding.

Cabernet equips the young wine with those austere tannins that give it the structure it needs to age well, its pigment-rich skins endowing the wine with full-blooded depth of colour too. When claret-lovers refer to their favourite wine as having a profoundly serious quality that appeals as much to the intellect as it does to the senses, it is essentially Cabernet Sauvignon they have to thank for it.

If Cabernet enjoys such an exalted status, you may ask why more châteaux don't simply produce an unblended Cabernet wine, instead of making it share the bottle with Merlot and other varieties. The answer is partly that the grape works better in a team. Solo Cabernet, as some winemakers in California have found, is not necessarily an unalloyed blessing. In hot years, it can be just too much of a good thing, the resulting wines having colossal density and concentration, but not really seeming as though they are going to be ready to drink this side of the next appearance of Halley's comet.

The other reason for blending in Bordeaux is that, even though its southerly position makes this one of the warmest of France's classic regions, the summers are still highly variable. In problem vintages (such as the region endured through most of the 1970s, in 1980, 1984, during much of the early 1990s, and in 2002), Cabernet Sauvignon is the grape that suffers most. If the late summer is cool – and, what's worse, wet – it simply doesn't ripen properly, resulting in those vegetal, green-pepper tastes that make for harsh, depressing wine.

Since Merlot has much better tolerance for less-than-perfect vintage conditions, it makes sense for the growers to have the option of blending in some of the lighter Merlot to soften an overly astringent or green-tasting

Cabernet. In the great vintages, however, such as 2000, 2005 and 2009, the richness and power of Cabernet are worth celebrating, and the Merlot will only play a discreet supporting role, just smoothing the edges a little, so that the full glory of ripe Cabernet can be shown to maximum advantage.

Most of the wines that occupy the five ranks of the 1855 hierarchy come from four vineyard areas to the west of the river Gironde: St-Estèphe, Pauillac, St-Julien and Margaux. From top to bottom, collectively, they extend over not much more than 40km (25 miles), but there are subtle differences in the styles of Cabernet-based wine they produce.

St-Estèphe generally makes the fiercest wine, with typically tough tannins that take years to fall away, and a very austere aroma that is often compared to fresh tobacco. Pauillac – the commune that boasts three of the five first growths in Lafite, Latour and Mouton-Rothschild – is a little less severe, even when young. Its wines have more emphatic blackcurrant fruit than those of St-Estèphe, and a seemingly more complicated pot-pourri of spice and wood notes as they age.

St-Julien, which adjoins Pauillac, exhibits many of the characteristics of its neighbour, although its wines somehow display a softer fruit – more like dark plums and blackberries than blackcurrants – as they begin to mature. The best wines of Margaux are noted for their extravagant perfume, although in general the

underlying wine is lighter than anything from further north, the exception being first-growth Château Margaux itself.

South of the city of Bordeaux, the large area of the Graves makes wines that vary in character. These range from relative featherweights that constitute some of the region's lightest reds, to those that have a mineral earthiness to them, thought to derive from the gravelly soils that give this part of Bordeaux its name. Elsewhere, the quality becomes gradually more prosaic until, at the lowest level of AOP Bordeaux, the bulk of the produce is hard red jug-wine of no obvious appeal.

In Bordeaux, it is the name of the property rather than the producer that goes on the label. Much time and attention is devoted to studying the relative form and fitness of the most famous estates as each new vintage appears on the market. Those planning to buy even a single bottle of top-flight Bordeaux would do well to consider the present reputation of a château as well as the quality of the vintage.

*Cabernet Sauvignon vines (above) planted in the poor, gravelly soils of St-Estèphe, in the Médoc, on the right bank of the Gironde river.*

# United States

Cabernet Sauvignon was introduced to California in the 19th century in the form of cuttings from Bordeaux. The readiness with which it took to the fertile soils in which it was planted is evidenced by the fact that it already had something of a reputation among the American wine cognoscenti before that century was out. The best was held to come from the Napa Valley, north of San Francisco, where the late hot summers resulted in strapping great wines of swarthy hue, thickly textured, and capable of delivering a hefty alcoholic blow to the unsuspecting drinker.

Some might facetiously say that not much has changed. Certainly, in many consumers' minds, the benchmark style of California Cabernet has been fiercely tannic, often virtually black wines that potentially took a decade or two to unravel into a state of anything like drinkability. It would be grossly simplistic to characterize all California Cabernets in that way today, but it was undeniably the predominant style of the wine in the 1970s and 1980s, and there are certainly some wineries that still nail their colours to that particular mast.

Moreover, it is not as though there aren't perfectly good antecedents for it. Most classed-growth Bordeaux in the hot years like 2003 and 2005 would answer that description – or something very like it – when first released. The wines are not intended to be drunk straight away in any case. Château Latour is after all still black as sin and guarded by snarling tannins at ten years old. It's almost as though a dose of old-world condescension were at work here: it's fine for the Bordelais, but really doesn't suit you.

The problem lay in the fact that not many consumers are attuned to drinking wine that tastes so forbidding, even if they can readily afford the prices commanded by it. Producers realized a middle way had to be found between budding West Coast Latours and insipid commercial jug-wine.

What happened from the 1970s on was a huge upsurge in experimental plantings of Cabernet Sauvignon across the state of California, as growers set out to find the optimum microclimates for the variety. Experiments, by their nature, can produce failures, and where the

*The tower in the vineyard at Silver Oak Cellars, Napa Valley (below).*

*Picking Cabernet Sauvignon grapes in vineyards south of Prosser, Washington State (left). Despite the fairly cool climate, some fine Cabernets have been made in the Pacific Northwest.*

*A vineyard worker harvesting Cabernet Sauvignon grapes in Calistoga, California (above).*

grape was grown in cooler areas, the outcome was wines that had more than a touch of the familiar green bell pepper/asparagus vegetal quality that Cabernet is prone to when it lacks sufficient ripening time. Oak maturation was sometimes excessive too, giving wines with an exaggeratedly woody taste.

Without a doubt, however, California – the Napa Valley in particular – has also turned out some wonderfully sleek, opulently fruit-filled Cabernets of world-class status, many of them blended with others of the Bordeaux varieties (these blends sometimes given the label Meritage).

In the Pacific Northwest, the climate is generally a little too cool for producing great Cabernets, although Washington State has come up with some fine examples. The tendency is to compensate for less than generous fruit flavours by applying fairly heavy oak maturation, which runs the risk of creating top-heavy wines. Oregon indeed is a much safer bet for cool-ripening Pinot Noir than sun-seeking Cabernet.

Texas, on the other hand, is proving to be highly Cabernet-friendly, and the grape is now the most widely planted red variety there, having expanded rapidly over the last 20 years. The state style is one of big, rich, upfront fruit, some savoury herb characters and good weight, but with tannins kept in check. In time, this could emerge as the best American Cabernet territory outside the Napa Valley. Virginia too is producing some distinguished Cabernets.

# Australia

Australia's approach to Cabernet Sauvignon, its second most planted red grape after Shiraz, has been much less conflicted than than of California. The aim among its growers is all about emphasizing the kind of ripe juicy drinkability that wins friends even among those who don't consider themselves fans of rich red wine. In the ultra-reliable climates enjoyed by most of Australia's wine-growing regions, Cabernet more often than not attains levels of ripeness Bordeaux's producers would give their eye-teeth for.

Oak barrel ageing is used enthusiastically by the great majority of Cabernet growers. When your wine is as rich and dense and blackcurranty as much Australian Cabernet is, you can afford to be generous with the oak treatment. At the same time, however, the classic style aims to maximize fruit characters without extracting too much tannin from the grapeskins. Thus, although it is an intensely concentrated wine, it doesn't necessarily scour your mouth with harsh astringency when it's young.

The chances are that, even if you are unfamiliar with the producer, a Cabernet from practically anywhere in Australia will deliver plump, soft, cassis-scented wine with an enagaging creamy texture and no hard edges. That is not to say that there aren't wineries intent on producing more austere Cabernets in a style built to age, but even these tend to come round far sooner than most California Cabernets, or Cabernet-based clarets, made in the same idiom. Even tasted in their infancy, the tannins on Australian wines such as these are nowhere near as severe as the colour may lead you to expect.

Blending is widely practised for Cabernet here too, with Shiraz having been its best bottle-friend since the 1960s, a recipe that Australia taught the world.

Australia's Cabernet pioneer was one John Riddoch (honoured in the name of one of the country's best classic Cabernets), who first planted the variety in the last decade of the 19th century in a part of South Australia called Coonawarra. Coonawarra's chief distinguishing characteristic is a narrow strip of red soil the colour of paprika, known as *terra rossa*. And it is here that Cabernet Sauvignon still produces its most gorgeously distinctive performances in Australia, and some of the world's best.

*Endless rows of Cabernet Sauvignon vines under an endless Australian sky (below), in Clare Valley, South Australia. The hotter, drier climate encourages rich, dense Cabernets.*

Coonawarra wines often have a chocolatey richness to them, tinged with hints of mocha coffee beans. Some, noting the relatively cooler climate the region enjoys, have compared it to a southern-hemisphere Bordeaux, but Coonawarra stands in no need of such vicarious honour. Its wines are nothing like claret; they have their own uniquely spicy style.

South Australia is the most important state overall for Cabernet wines. In the heat of the Barossa Valley GI, they tend to be richly coloured and thickly textured, with an intensity like preserved fruits. From McLaren Vale, the wines are often more delicately proportioned, with slightly higher acid levels. In the Eden Valley, Cabernets of almost European profile are being produced, with aromatic spice notes in them, and often a dash of mint.

Coonawarra takes that spice component a little further, and there is sometimes a fugitive hint of something exotically pungent, like Worcester sauce. Riverland is a much less distinguished bulk-producing region, where the wines are made in an easy-drinking, uncomplicated style.

Victoria makes Cabernet in the leaner, mintier manner. The vineyards are mainly located in the centre of the state, especially in the fashionable region of Bendigo. Despite its notably cool climate, Yarra Valley has been responsible for some of Australia's most extraordinarily intense Cabernets, with astonishing depth.

Cabernets from the Margaret River GI in Western Australia tend to the hauntingly scented end of the spectrum, with particularly defined acidity and consequently good ageing potential.

Tasmania's cool, damp climate is better suited to other varieties, but there have been successes with lighter, more sharply angled Cabernets than are found on the mainland.

*The famous* terra rossa *soil of Coonawarra, South Australia (above). Vineyard land here is highly prized for the quality of grapes it yields.*

# Other Regions

### SOUTH AFRICA

Cabernet Sauvignon became, in the early 1990s, the most widely planted red grape variety in South Africa. Early efforts were often discouraging, partly as a result of Cabernet being grown in sites that were either too cool or too hot for it, and partly because the specific variant of the grape widely grown in Cape vineyards wasn't of the best quality. The results were often wines that lacked convincing fruit definition.

All that has changed in recent years, with new clones of the grape yielding riper, richer fruit flavours, and growers allowing them full ripening time on the vine. Coastal Stellenbosch, Franschhoek, and inland Paarl have turned out to be the most promising regions, with many convincingly classy, ageworthy wines emerging. Wines made according to the Bordeaux recipe, using Cabernet Franc and Merlot to soften some

of Cabernet Sauvignon's severity, have been the best, but blends with Shiraz can be juicily appealing too in their way.

### CHILE

During the course of the 1980s, Chile was the southern-hemisphere epicentre for European wine consultants, and no variety was more consulted on than Cabernet Sauvignon. When no less an eminence than Gilbert Rokvam of Château Lafite arrived at the Los Vascos winery in Colchagua, it seemed pretty clear that Chile had made its entrance on the world wine map with due fanfare, at least as far as Cabernet was concerned. Early results were amazing.

What has happened since is that Chilean Cabernet has diverged into two broadly identifiable styles. One is what Europeans tend to think of as the benchmark New World idiom, ripely blackcurranty Cabernet of sumptuous, velvety texture, with low tannins and plenty of oak. There are numerous examples of this style and, while they all benefit from a couple of years' ageing, they can be enjoyed relatively young, at barely more than a year old.

The other style is much more austere, cedary wine of high acidity and more pronounced tannins, vinified in a way that is intended to help it to age in the bottle, and owing much to the taste of classic Médoc claret. Wines from the Maipo, Rapel and Casablanca regions have registered some stunning successes in this style.

At its best, Chilean Cabernet Sauvignon can display scents of the most intensely pure essence of blackcurrant to be found in any Cabernet produced anywhere. They may taste a little one-dimensional at first, but they broaden and deepen with age into something altogether thrilling. The wines made in the French style are the longest-lived, with older vintages taking on the savoury complexity of fine mature Médoc.

### ARGENTINA

On the other side of the Andes, the Mendoza province of Argentina is now showing its own potential as a major runner in the Cabernet stakes. Strangely enough, the grape has had to play understudy in the vineyards to Malbec, one of the bit-part players in red Bordeaux (blending the two is widely practised), but plantings are steadily on the increase.

*The towering Drakensteinberg mountains form a stunning backdrop to the higher and cooler district of Franschhoek in coastal Stellenbosch, South Africa (below), source of classy Cabernets capable of ageing.*

Initially, varietal Cabernets were rather sternly tannic, and dominated by wood flavours rather than fruit, on account of their having been aged too long in old oak casks. Outside investment was slower to arrive in Argentina than it was in Chile, and so the wines, Cabernet in particular, took a little longer to settle into their best style.

Cabernet is now being made in a generally French-oriented manner, from plantings in high-altitude vineyards to mitigate some of the formidable heat of the growing season. Expect rich plum and cassis fruit, backed by savoury herb flavours and a judicious amount of tannin.

High-altitude sites in Argentina's second biggest region, San Juan, look equally promising for Cabernet.

## NEW ZEALAND

Most of New Zealand's vineyard land has proved to be too cool and damp for Cabernet, which is notoriously bad-tempered if it doesn't get enough sun. Some varietal Cabernet has that telltale green pepper flavour, with high acidity, though low tannin. Painstaking site selection has, however, produced some encouraging successes on the North Island, particularly in the Hawke's Bay area, and from Waiheke Island near Auckland.

As elsewhere, blending is the key, and the Cabernet-Merlot partnership has emerged as a surefire winner for many growers. There are now some very attractive wines of real complexity and depth, in a midweight style not a million miles from the softer wines of Bordeaux, though quicker to mature.

*Harvesting Cabernet Sauvignon at Los Vascos (above) in the hot Colchagua Valley, Rapel, Chile. Los Vascos produces Cabernets moulded in the classic Médoc style.*

*Old Cabernet Sauvignon vines owned by the grand 19th-century bodega, Cousiño Macul (left), in Maipo, Chile. The vines date back to the 1930s.*

*Pickers on the Marqués de Griñón's estate near Toledo, in the hot centre of Spain (above). The estate has drawn attention for its structured, long-ageing Cabernets.*

*The Torres Mas la Plana vineyard in Penedés, planted solely with Cabernet vines (below). Torres and Jean León set a precedent for Cabernet in Spain in the '60s.*

## FRANCE

Just outside Bordeaux, in appellations such as Bergerac and Buzet, the permitted grape varieties are the same as in Bordeaux itself, and from certain producers, the wines can rival everyday claret. Cabernet Sauvignon has made major inroads into the Languedoc-Roussillon, in France's warm southern zone, where it most often appears as varietal Vin de Pays d'Oc. A small amount is also grown in the Loire as blending material with Gamay, or as a minor component in sparkling rosés.

## SPAIN AND PORTUGAL

Cabernet Sauvignon established a bridgehead on the Iberian peninsula when it was planted in Penedés by the Torres family and Jean León in the 1960s. Varietal Cabernets from that region, from Castile and the Montes de Toledo are often made in the opaquely concentrated, monumental style for long keeping.

Many producers, in regions such as Ribera del Duero and Costers del Segre, have developed blends of Cabernet Sauvignon with Spain's indigenous superstar grape Tempranillo, often with exciting results.

The same inclination towards blended wines has tended to be followed by those Portuguese growers who have planted Cabernet, although there are some accomplished varietal wines produced on the Setúbal peninsula south of

Lisbon. Otherwise, the grape has become an important blending ingredient for many growers in the Douro and Alentejo regions.

## ITALY

Italy's growers have always been a little cavalier, particularly in the northern regions, in distinguishing Cabernet Sauvignon from its Bordeaux sibling Cabernet Franc. Thus a Trentino wine labelled Cabernet may be one or the other, or both. Yet the two grapes are in reality quite distinct, and produce different styles of wine.

Less confusion arises in Tuscany, where Cabernet Sauvignon is allowed to make up a minor part of the blend in Chianti, and in lesser-known reds such as Carmignano. A revolution in Italian wine was effected in the 1970s by a group of Tuscan innovators, led by the highly respected family house of Antinori. They began working outside the Italian DOC regulations to produce towering reds that made free use of Cabernet Sauvignon, either blended with the Chianti grape Sangiovese, or the other Bordeaux varieties. Eventually, these wines were brought into either the Bolgheri DOC or the wider regional IGT designation for Tuscany.

Cabernet has also gained a foothold in Piedmont in the northwest, where it is often bottled either wholly or almost unblended in the Langhe DOC.

## CENTRAL AND EASTERN EUROPE

The cheap red wine boom in the 1970s and 1980s was sustained almost single-handedly by the state-subsidized exports of Bulgaria. For a supposedly marginal winemaking climate, Bulgarian Cabernets generally offered the sorts of easily lovable, softly plummy fruit flavours that producers of less expensive Bordeaux could only dream about. The wines were smoothed with plenty of oak, and were often released as Reserve bottlings after several years' ageing in the state cellars.

At their best, these wines managed to combine enough depth of character to grace a serious dinner table with the kind of instant drinkability that made them surefire party wines. Sadly, the breakup of the old communist state monopoly immediately resulted in wild inconsistencies in quality but, with gathering private investment, Bulgaria is gradually coming back into contention.

Hungary, Moldova and Romania are all capable of producing good Cabernet at a price the wine-drinker wants to pay. Hungary's Villany and Romania's Dealul Mare are among the most propitious regions.

Other Cabernet-based one-offs include the legendary Château Musar of Lebanon, a blend of Cabernet with Cinsault and Carignan made in the Bekaa Valley by the late Serge Hochar. Where other growers worry about problems like spring frost, the Bekaa has been more prone to war, invasion and rocket attacks. That the fruit of Musar's labours is a magnificently long-lived and powerful wine is a due tribute to human indomitability.

Greek Cabernet Sauvignon may one day be a force to be reckoned with, if varietal and blended bottlings from areas such as the Atalanti Valley in central Greece, and the Thracian peninsula in the far northeast, are anything to go by.

*Bulgaria's vineyards, like these overlooking the village of Ustina, near Plovdiv (above), were the source of much commercially successful Cabernet in the 1980s.*

# SAUVIGNON BLANC

*The grape of the famous Loire whites, Sancerre and Pouilly-Fumé, Sauvignon also brought New Zealand to the attention of the wine world, with a fruit cocktail of a wine that proved the versatility of this variety.*

THE PREDOMINANT shift in consumer tastes in white wine in the last decade or so has been the transfer of allegiance from Chardonnay to Sauvignon Blanc. In many ways, it's easy to see why. The two grapes' characteristics are diametrically opposed. Whereas Chardonnay was typically seen as a golden, fat-textured, buttery white wine that owed much of its identity to the influence of wood, Sauvignon is a pale, relatively light and acidic wine nearly always vinified without oak and endowed with a piercingly distinct perfume. In other words, when Chardonnay fatigue began to set in, here was the antidote.

A well-made Sauvignon performs its role as light refreshment almost too well. The simplicity of this style has led some in the wine commentariat to treat the grape with mild contempt. This undoubtedly does it a great injustice; it is in fact capable of impressive complexity. Sauvignon is responsible for two of France's most celebrated dry white wines – Sancerre and Pouilly-Fumé, stylistically inimitable stars of the Loire. And when the vine's yields are controlled, it can display a wealth of uninihibited ripe fruit, as shown by the roaring success of New Zealand Sauvignon.

In addition to its upfront fruit, Sauvignon grown on certain flinty soils of the upper Loire valley in the centre of France can take on an inexplicable, but oddly powerful, smoky quality that deceives many into thinking it must have had some oak treatment. At its most pungent, it can resemble the savoury fume of woodsmoke; in a gentler vein, it may remind you of the wisps of steam from an espresso machine. This attribute is celebrated in the suffix of the name of Pouilly-Fumé, and it came to be much imitated in the California of the 1970s and 1980s, after Napa Valley winemaker Robert Mondavi renamed his Sauvignon wine Fumé Blanc. Sometimes the elusive smokiness was there; quite often one searched in vain.

Styles in Sauvignon have been subject to wide international vicissitudes in the last 20 years. Some Fumé Blanc was given time in oak, as a way of imitating the flint-derived smokiness of the upper Loire wines. Many California growers, though, have resorted to bottling the wine with relatively high residual sugar, as a way of mitigating its acidity and masking its herbaceous pungency. But if they

*The green Sauvignon Blanc grape (right), here in Pessac-Léognan where it is destined for blending with Sémillon for the dry white Bordeaux. A prolific vine, but when yields are controlled it is capable of massive fruit character.*

feel it needs such cosmetic disguising, why grow it at all? Even now, Sauvignon is often California's weakest shot.

In Bordeaux, where it was traditionally blended with Sémillon (see page 64) for both dry and sweet whites, it has begun to take centre-stage as a solo performer in the dry wines. Plantings have increased to reflect the worldwide modishness of the grape, and there are some intriguing flavours being coaxed out of it, pineapple as well as gooseberry.

More than any other region outside France, though, it is New Zealand that helped to establish the international status of Sauvignon. It may very well be that, across the board, New Zealand's winemakers now have a better understanding of the grape than the French. Wines from Marlborough in particular offer more ecstatically happy fruit flavour per mouthful than practically any other dry whites in the world. For every trend, however, there's a backlash, and in the last few years, I've begun to detect a slight fatigue among consumers with the thorough-going juicy-fruit style of Marlborough Sauvignon.

In general, Sauvignon is lost without a healthy measure of good crisp acidity, which is why, in very hot areas, it can result in a rather flabby and fruitless wine. It's important to remember that Sauvignon is not meant to be a neutral-tasting glass of nothing-in-particular. We've got Pinot Grigio for that.

## FRENCH ORIGINS

Bordeaux, where it is nearly always blended with Sémillon (and perhaps a drop of Muscadelle). The upper Loire valley is where France's top varietal Sauvignons are based, and less exalted wines are made further west along the Loire in Touraine.

## WHERE ELSE IS IT GROWN?

Fairly widespread, but particularly important in New Zealand, Chile and South Africa, less so in the United States and Australia. Increasing plantings in the warmer Languedoc and northern Spain have proved surprisingly successful.

## TASTING NOTES

Practically the whole gamut of fruit flavours, ranging from sour green fruits like gooseberry and tart apple or pear to astonishingly exotic notes such as Charentais melon, passion fruit and mango. It very often has a precise nose of blackcurrants.

Vegetable flavours can loom large too. Green peas, asparagus and sweet red (bell) peppers often crop up in New Zealand examples. Then there is a curiously pungent animal quality in many cool-climate, especially Loire, versions that is often compared to cat's pee, or even to male sweat. If you're lucky, that fugitive wisp of faintly acrid smoke is there as well.

# France

*Early-morning mist (above) over Sauvignon vines in the Loire's famous Pouilly-Fumé appellation.*

### LOIRE

In the vineyards around the upper reaches of the river Loire, in the centre of France, unblended Sauvignon Blanc reigns supreme. It wasn't that long ago that these crisp, scented dry white wines, designed to be drunk within a couple of years of harvest, were not especially highly regarded even within France itself. As fashion has shifted away from richer and oakier styles of white, Loire Sauvignon – Sancerre in particular – has found itself catapulted to the height of popularity.

Pouilly-Fumé and Sancerre are the two most famous appellations for Sauvignon. They are situated on opposite sides of the river, on the east and west banks respectively. It is a very accomplished taster indeed who can spot one from the other when, at their best, they both capture the combination of refreshing green fruit flavours, snappy acids and distant smoky aromas that typify the grape in these parts.

The fashionability of the wines has elevated their prices, which – at the generic supermarket own-brand end of the quality spectrum – have become all but unpalatable, given the fact that there is nothing particularly expensive about their production. As well as that, there is the uncomfortable fact that, in Pouilly-Fumé particularly, there are too many indifferent producers making unfocused wines from the product of overcropping vines.

To the west of Sancerre are three less well-known Sauvignon appellations. They offer most of the flavour of the wines of their more exalted neighbours at generally kinder prices. The best, and closest to Sancerre, is Menetou-Salon. Further west, across the river Cher, Quincy and Reuilly produce brisk, assertive Sauvignons in a clean but slightly less concentrated style than the others.

In the heartland of the Loire region, the Touraine district – more famous for its Chenin Blanc wines – also has a lot of Sauvignon. A fair amount of it gets used as blending fodder, but some varietal wines are bottled under the label Touraine Sauvignon. In good years, they too can offer a glass of cheerfully fruity white, increasingly showing something of the intensity of the wines of the upper Loire.

*The village of Sancerre (right) that gives the appellation its name stands on a hilltop close to the river Loire, overlooking the vineyards.*

## BORDEAUX

The dry white wines of Bordeaux were taken by the scruff of the neck and marched into the modern world during the 1980s. Too often stale and dispiriting creations based on over-produced Sémillon prior to that, they have benefited hugely from the trend towards cooler fermentations in temperature-controlled stainless steel.

As Sauvignon wines from further north gained in modishness and therefore retail value, it dawned on the Bordelais that perhaps they could play a part in the Sauvignon craze by vinifying more of what was after all one of their own main grapes. The percentage of Sauvignon in many of the blends has accordingly sharply increased, bringing in its train a greater freshness and zip to the wines.

Top of the quality tree is the region of Pessac-Léognan at the northern end of the Graves, where a healthy scattering of wines from properties such as Domaine de Chevalier, and Châteaux Haut-Brion and Laville-Haut-Brion, have always shown true class. Some producers, such as Couhins-Lurton, use only Sauvignon in their whites. The smart operators have also employed barrel-ageing (and even fermentation in oak too) in order to achieve a rich, tropical-fruit style that is far more opulent than the unoaked Sauvignons of the Loire.

The large production of the Entre-Deux-Mers region is generally more humble stuff, although the best of even these are beginning to shine, and there are producers turning out oaked, unblended Sauvignon to rival the best of Pessac-Léognan. Sauvignon also plays a supporting role in the great sweet wines of Bordeaux, to lend a flash of balancing acid to the noble-rotted Sémillon.

## ELSEWHERE

The Bergerac appellation on the river Dordogne has the same grape varieties as Bordeaux, and can turn out some light, refreshing Sauvignon-based blends, as can the Côtes de Duras to the south. White wines labelled Vin de Pays des Côtes de Gascogne, from further down in southwest France, may be made from any of a number of grapes, and there is a smattering of varietal Sauvignon among them.

Although it may seem inauspiciously hot, the increased plantings of Sauvignon in the Languedoc are yielding some attractively crisp, fruity Vins de Pays d'Oc that owe their super-

fresh quality to cold fermentation in stainless steel. Choice of the right harvest-time is all. That, and controlling the vigour of the vines so they don't over-produce.

Finally, there is a lone outpost of Sauvignon in the far north of what is technically the Burgundy region, near Chablis. Sauvignon de St-Bris is an historical oddity, best described as tasting like Sauvignon made in the style of Chardonnay, with the recognizable green fruit but with smoother contours than are found in the Loire versions. (Some Chablis growers also possess vineyard land here.) The wines were promoted to the full AOP (*appellation d'origine protégée*) designation in 2003.

*In the Sauternes region, as here at Château Suduiraut (below), Sauvignon Blanc brings a streak of fresh acidity to balance the sweetness of noble-rotted Sémillon.*

# New Zealand

*The Cloudy Bay winery in New Zealand's Marlborough district (below), one of the country's greatest success stories with the Sauvignon grape.*

Sauvignon Blanc devotees weaned on the exhilarating flavours of New Zealand's finest efforts won't be surprised to learn that it is now the country's most extensively planted white variety, recently overtaking Chardonnay in acres of vineyard. The grape shot to prominence here in the 1980s on the back of the wine made by the bulk-producing Montana winery in Marlborough on the South Island. The commercial success of its Sauvignon – never less than a harvest festival of pure raw-fruit ripeness – was founded on its sheer exuberance of flavour, and shored up for many years by the fact that its export price hardly moved. And that despite the fact that few wines have further to travel to the international marketplace than those of southern New Zealand.

Having sparked a trend, Montana's example was quickly followed by a host of other wineries. That surge of abundant fruit is present in nearly all the wines of the Marlborough region, although occasionally the acidity can be out of focus, or – as in the troubled vintages of 2003 and 2008 – just a little too aggressive. There has been a distinct tendency among some producers to aim for more Loire-like levels of acidity, which has resulted in wines that have some of the flintiness of their French counterparts, and correspondingly less obvious fruit. Blending with Semillon can achieve a textural depth and lushness in certain wines.

Adjacent to Marlborough, the South Island region of Nelson makes some sharply defined, cool-climate Sauvignons in the nettly, herbaceous style.

The slightly softer style of Sauvignon really comes into its own in the North Island region of Hawke's Bay. The fruit here seems less green and more peachy, and there is a concomitantly greater readiness to use a little oak in the vinification, though by no means universally. These can be very attractive wines.

# Other Regions

## SOUTH AFRICA

As elsewhere, it's the cooler areas that do best with Sauvignon Blanc in South Africa, and there are now some brilliantly aromatic, concentrated wines being produced. Most of the premium examples are made in the acerbically dry, smoky style of the Loire, with some even recalling the flintiness of good Pouilly-Fumé. The fruit characters of the wines tend to the green, sappy end of the scale, but there is the odd one with something like the fruit-basket juiciness of the textbook New Zealand style. Walker Bay, Elgin, Durbanville and the cooler parts of Stellenbosch have been the best regions for Sauvignon.

## SOUTH AMERICA

There was a large, and for some time intractable, problem with Sauvignon Blanc in Chile, which was that a lot of it wasn't. Quite a few growers had a grape called Sauvignonasse, thinking it was the Loire variety, whereas it was in fact the dull, neutral-tasting relative of a grape native to northeast Italy. Chilean Sauvignon, however, can now be bought with confidence, with most wines representing a gentler version of the crisp Loire style. Wines from the cooler Casablanca region are a good bet.

Astonishingly well-defined Sauvignons with tropical fruit, sharply etched acids and a touch of smoke are being made in Argentina's high-volume Mendoza province.

## AUSTRALIA

The hotter the wine region, the less likely it is to be capable of producing the appetizing fruit and natural crispness that Sauvignon wines need. Many of Australia's efforts have traditionally been hampered by a lack of sharp definition. Not unexpectedly, the cooler Margaret River GI in Western Australia has proved the most propitious, with some refreshing, sappy wines.

## UNITED STATES

The Mondavi winery's attempt to elevate the status of California Sauvignon by renaming it Fumé Blanc didn't manage to persuade many other growers to take the variety to their hearts. If they have Sauvignon at all, they often try to disguise what they see as a troubling pungency in the flavour of the grape by ageing in oak, or

else leaving a distracting quantity of residual sugar in the wine. Washington State is very often a better source of fruit-driven, tangy Sauvignon for drinking young.

*The Cullens winery in the Margaret River area of Western Australia (above) has consistently produced one of the country's more sharply defined Sauvignons.*

*Chile's cooler Casablanca Valley (left) is proving a good spot to grow characterful, fruity Sauvignon Blanc.*

# PINOT NOIR

*Difficult to grow, difficult to vinify, but still producers across the globe are attracted to this temperamental grape variety, tempted to try matching the classic style of Burgundy's greatest red wines.*

OF ALL THE French grape varieties that have migrated around the viticultural world, this is the one that excites the greatest passions. More tears are shed, greater energy expended, more hand-wringing despair engendered over it than over any other variety. It is not, by and large, an endeavour for those who relish a quiet life.

Pinot Noir is the only grape permitted in the great majority of red burgundies (the only exceptions being at or near the bottom end of the quality ladder). At the summit sit the *grand cru* wines of the region's most illustrious estates, wines of positively exotic complexity that offer a once-in-a-lifetime experience of dazzling opulence at a once-in-a-lifetime price. All the red-wine appellations of the Côte d'Or, however, are capable of producing great Pinot at one time or another – they don't call it the Slope of Gold for nothing.

So why all the heartbreak?

First off, it emphatically doesn't like being heat-stressed. Burgundy is cool and wet, prone to spring frosts and hail, to an extent that, even here in its ancestral home, it is profoundly vintage-dependent. It has been estimated that, on average, two years out of every three are inadequate for producing great wine (although climate change may gradually be lending its producers a helping hand for the time being).

In off-vintages, the result is a thin, bitter wine with no fruit to speak of, and a streak of hard, spiteful acid that acts as a powerful repellent in its youth. Pinots produced in these conditions are among the feeblest red wines in the fine wine sector, and the labour of love that has to be lavished on them accounts for that part of the sky-high asking prices that isn't accounted for by the region's reputation.

Early experiments with Pinot outside Europe too often fell into this trap. Plantings in the cooler areas of the United States and in New Zealand often combined scything acidity with chaotically high alcohol, while Australian

efforts grown in sweltering conditions were muddy, unfocused and clumsily smothered with extraneous oak.

So should we just draw a veil over Pinot Noir and move on to the next grape? Ah, no.

Grow it in the right climate, preferably in soils with some limestone in them (as in Burgundy), and protect it against the rash of diseases that its flesh is heir to, including rot if there is any rain at harvest-time, and the potential payoff is wine of uniquely haunting beauty, and extraordinary longevity.

*Ripe, healthy bunches of Pinot Noir grapes (right). A thin-skinned grape that is highly sensitive to climate and soil, and notoriously difficult to nurture, Pinot Noir can make ripely fruity reds of great class. It is also invaluable in the production of sparkling wine.*

It is a thin-skinned variety – physically as well as temperamentally – which means that it generally produces lighter, less forbiddingly tannic wines than Cabernet Sauvignon does. They are correspondingly approachable earlier in their development, although their naturally high acidity does need time to settle. Keep the most concentrated ones for a few years more, and their maturation is astonishing for such a comparatively light wine. An intense gaminess comes over them, something between well-hung meat and black truffle, and their initial red fruit deepens into the savoury scents of herbs and grilling meat.

Increasingly, since the 1990s, growers outside France have got the hang of Pinot Noir. In California (particularly Carneros) and Oregon, and in selected sites across New Zealand, fantastic results are being achieved. The wines often possess brighter, more resonant red fruit in their first flush than burgundy does (think raspberries and red cherries), but the savouriness is there too, and the acid profiles are such that they age majestically. They aren't necessarily much more affordable than mid-range burgundy, but you are appreciably getting your money's worth.

Additionally, Pinot Noir plays an important role in the production of champagne and other sparkling wines, where it adds depth and potential longevity to the Chardonnay, as well as colour to the rosés. Red Pinot wine adds scented charm to much pink champagne. It has enjoyed a highly successful entrée on to the Spanish cava scene, for example, where its delicacy compared to the traditional Spanish red grapes has made for some more graceful pink sparklers than was usually the norm.

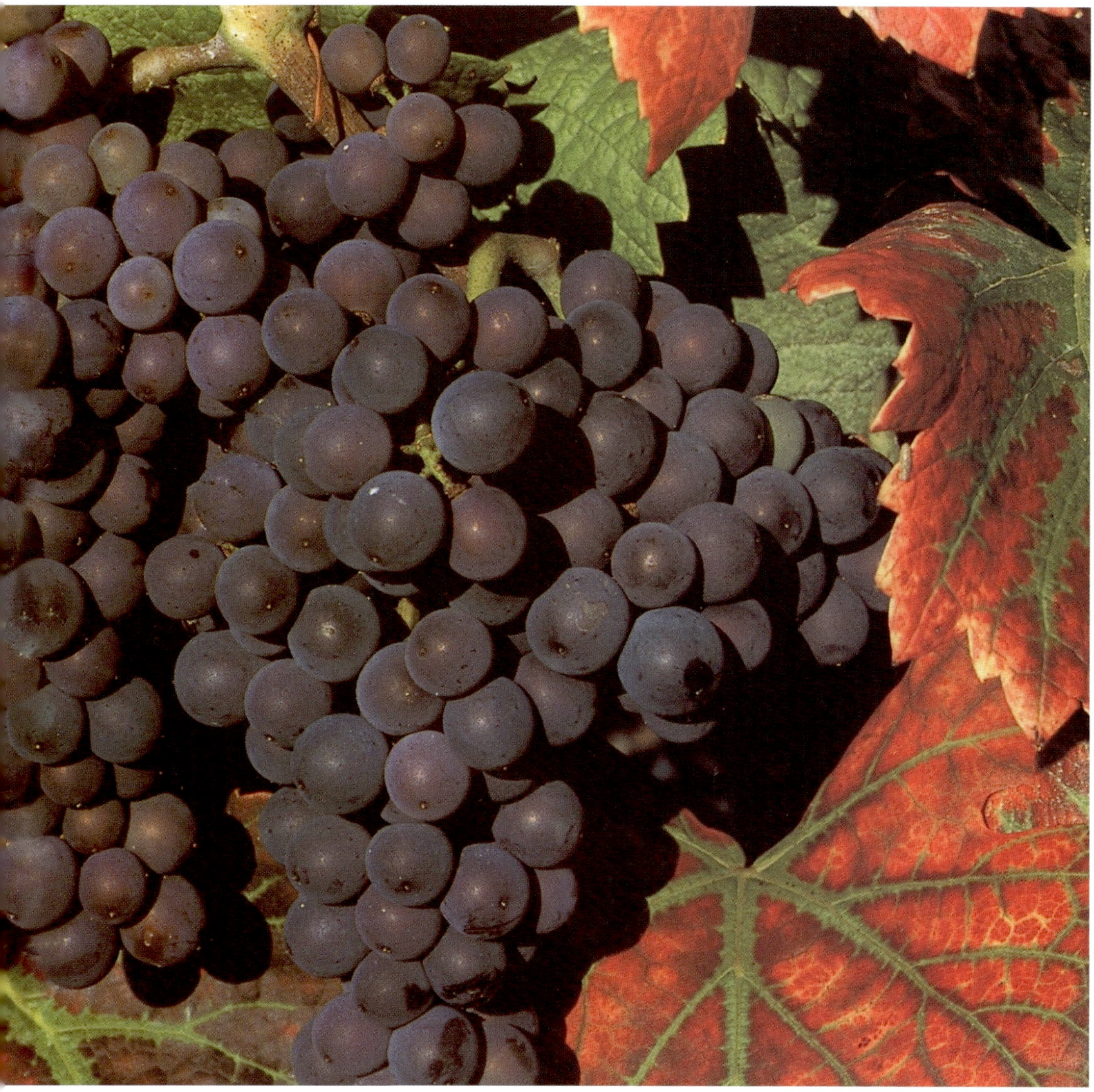

### French Origins

Burgundy and Champagne. Also used in some of the light reds and rosés of the Loire, and the red wine of Alsace.

### Where Else is it Grown?

California, Oregon, Australia, New Zealand, Chile and South Africa. Quite important in central Europe – southern Germany, Switzerland, and points east – but still fairly rare along the Mediterranean. Anybody making sparkling wine by the traditional champagne method is likely to use some Pinot.

### Tasting Notes

In youth, it can possess light aromas of red fruits, typically raspberry, strawberry, redcurrant, cherry. In parts of California and Australia, it also has a faint note of coffee bean or mocha. Nearly always has an element of meatiness – beef stock in young wines, shading to well-hung game as it ages, overlaid in the very best with the other-worldly pungency of black truffle. Classically (or notoriously, depending on your tastes) mature wines can also display a distinctly rank smell, politely described as 'barnyardy', but really referring to what you might accidentally put your foot in as you walk through the barnyard.

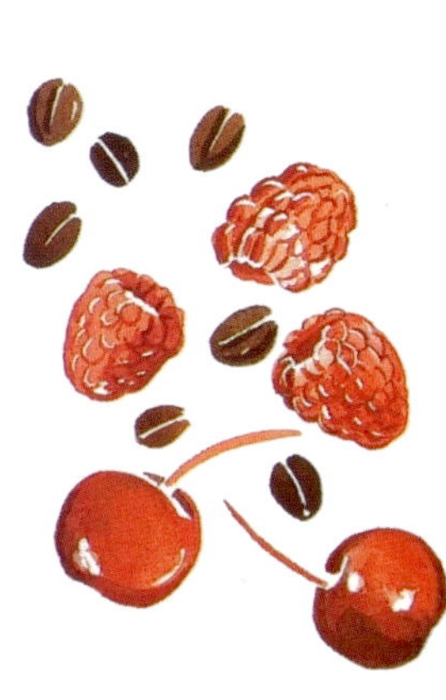

# France

*Levelling Pinot Noir grapes in the traditional wooden press at Champagne Bollinger (above).*

*Harvested Pinot Noir grapes resting in traditional wicker baskets (below) at Louis Latour, in Aloxe-Corton on the Côte d'Or, the home of most of Burgundy's famous names.*

Betting on vintage conditions in Burgundy as harvest-time approaches makes for slightly more peace of mind than playing Russian roulette – but only just. In most years, the region's white grape variety, Chardonnay, fares reasonably well: only torrential rain during the picking can really ruin it at the eleventh hour. Pinot Noir, the only runner in the red wine stakes, is a horse of another colour altogether.

At least until the late 1990s, it was possible to say that, more often than not, Pinot Noir yielded disappointing results. Precisely because out-and-out successes were so hard-won, great red burgundy came to be valued by many as the most precious of all France's classic wines, consort to Bordeaux's monarch perhaps, but held in special esteem just because of its relative scarcity. (As well as being less reliable from one vintage to the next, the produce of the Burgundy region is a tiny fraction of that of Bordeaux.)

The Pinot grape reaches the apex of its potential on the Côte d'Or, the narrow escarpment running southwest of the city of Dijon, and home to most of Burgundy's famous names. Its narrower northern strip, the Côte de Nuits, which includes such appellations as Gevrey-Chambertin, Nuits-St-Georges and Morey-St-Denis, tends to produce the weightiest style of Burgundian Pinot, with all sorts of meaty notes ranging from the singed skin of roasting poultry to gravy bubbling in the dish. Further south, the Côte de Beaune, which takes in Aloxe-Corton, Pommard and Volnay among others, specializes in a lighter, gentler Pinot, scented with soft summer fruits and sometimes flowers as well.

The further south of the Côte d'Or you travel, into the Côte Chalonnaise and then the workhorse region of the Mâconnais, the more ordinary the Pinot Noir wines become. At the bottom of the scale, wine labelled Bourgogne Rouge may be a blend of grapes from different sources in the region. It once covered a multitude of sins, but is now increasingly a useful varietal designation for some simple but conscientiously crafted wines.

If the growing season has been relatively chilly or, worse, plagued with intermittent rainfall (as in 2008), the resulting wines can be extremely light, both in colour as well as texture. When a red wine is full of hard acids and bitterly unripe fruit, and feels no richer on the palate than a heavyish rosé, then it's hard to get consumers to see why they should pay the inflated prices.

On the other hand, if burgundy is noted for one thing, it is a resistance to generalizations. Some producers can manage to make densely concentrated wines in even the less auspicious vintages, even while their near neighbours may be wringing their hands. It pays to know who the high fliers are.

Because Pinot often lacks adequate natural sugar to ferment into a full-bodied red that will stay the distance, producers may be permitted to add ordinary cane sugar to the freshly pressed juice. The process is known as chaptalization after its inventor, Jean-Antoine Chaptal. By giving the yeast more sugar to work on, the potential alcohol content of the finished product is raised in the direction of the regional average of 13 per cent. Sometimes, especially when young, it can give off a telltale whiff of burnt sugar, a probable indicator that the winemaker has resorted to fairly heavy chaptalization.

In the best vintages, however, such as 2002, 2005 and 2009, when the Pinot Noir has attained full ripeness, it turns out richly perfumed, exquisitely elegant wines that go at least some way to explaining the heart-stopping prices they sell for. These are the wines that are most worth stashing away for a rainy day.

*Autumnal Pinot Noir vines (left) running down towards the town of Aÿ, in Champagne. The inclusion of Pinot in champagne lends it a nuttier, darker hue, and gives the wine depth and good ageing potential.*

*The beginnings of a red burgundy – Pinot Noir gently fermenting in an open wooden vat (above).*

Although it is a red grape, Pinot is hugely important in the making of champagne. The colourless juice is vinified without its skins so that the resulting wine remains white, although if you compare a blended champagne with one that has been made entirely from Chardonnay, you will notice a deeper, nuttier hue in the one that contains Pinot Noir.

Champagne producers consider that Pinot gives their wines depth and the ability to age well. Some champagne, labelled Blanc de Noirs, is made entirely from Pinot Noir and/or the region's other red grape, Pinot Meunier, but is still a white wine. A small amount of still red wine, vaguely Burgundian in style though even more crisply acidic, is made, and may be added to white wine to make rosé champagne. Tiny quantities of pink champagne are made by the painstaking method of infusing the red grape skins briefly in the white juice to tint it to the desired shade.

In the eastern Loire, Pinot Noir is used to make the red (and rosé) versions of Sancerre and Menetou-Salon. These are much lighter in style than burgundy, often with a slightly vegetal hint. They aren't intended for ageing but, served lightly chilled, can make good summer drinking.

Pinot Noir also makes the only red wine of Alsace, again in a typically featherlight and not overly fruity style. Increasingly, though, a handful of producers are starting to take it more seriously, and making wines with the muscle to take some well-judged oak-ageing in their stride.

# United States

### CALIFORNIA

California has undoubtedly been the most successful region across the board for Pinot Noir outside Burgundy itself. Although they are extremely unlikely to admit it, Burgundy's growers could profitably learn a fair bit from the approach of the more conscientious producers of Pinot Noir in America.

The most successful area to date has been the Carneros AVA, a cool district straddling Napa and Sonoma Counties and benefiting from the coastal fogs that waft in from San Francisco Bay. The afternoons and early evenings in Carneros are sufficiently warm to endow the developing grapes with the exciting flavours of ripe red fruits that are characteristic of the best Pinot wines. At the same time, the cooling influence of those thick mists, which often hang around until mid-morning, ensures adequate levels of fresh acidity, so the wines are impeccably balanced and capable of ageing.

Its ripe fruit intensity means that California Pinot is generally ready for drinking earlier than traditional burgundy, although it does benefit from keeping for a couple of years after release just to allow the nervy edge on those acids to calm down. If the top wines have any noticeable problem, it is that alcohol levels are frequently uncomfortably high. That can result in wines that are very attractive until you swallow them, whereupon they leave a definite smoulder at the back of the throat. There are more balanced wines around now, though, than there were, say, 20 years ago, and the truth is that a lot of them do have the stuffing to carry a weighty alcohol load. Get to know your producers.

In addition to Carneros, parts of Santa Barbara County south of the Bay have proved successful for Pinot Noir, as has the mountainous inland AVA of San Benito, and the AVAs of Russian River Valley and the Santa Cruz Mountains to the north and south of San Francisco respectively.

### OREGON

Because of its cooler, damper climate, this Pacific Northwestern state was seen as ideal Pinot territory when the search for appropriate vineyard sites began to gather momentum. Climatically, it is indubitably much closer to Burgundy than most of California, and there are indeed now some stunning wines. The trailblazer was David Lett of Eyrie Vineyards, who first planted Pinot in the 1960s.

It wasn't all plain sailing for many growers. High yields, lack of true physiological ripeness in the grapes and uncertain site selection hampered many early efforts, but Oregon's has been a true tale of dedication to a cause. A succession of good to great vintages since the late 1990s has helped, and some wineries are now showing just what thrilling Pinots the state is capable of making.

Oregon's *premier cru* region is the Willamette Valley AVA, which lies to the west of the Cascade Mountains. A series of smaller AVAs has been demarcated within the overall valley region, with the Dundee Hills and McMinnville looking especially enthralling. The style is generally lighter than in most of California, less meaty but with more accentuated strawberry fruit, and generally approachable sooner.

*Terracing a new Pinot Noir vineyard in Oregon (below). The grape of Burgundy is making itself at home in the Pacific Northwest.*

# Other Regions

## NEW ZEALAND

The coolest wine climate in the southern hemisphere has proved perfectly hospitable for Pinot Noir, which is now its most widely planted red grape. Although initial efforts often lacked for enough flesh to cover their bare bones, there are now dozens of world-class producers of top-flight Pinot, and prices have climbed accordingly. The very best display that elusive savoury intensity that adds complexity to the ripe raspberry fruit.

So far, the most exciting wines have come from the Wairarapa region, around the town of Martinborough in the south of the North Island. Most of the cooler South Island is turning out quality Pinot Noir too, from Marlborough and Nelson at the northern end, down through Canterbury and – perhaps most electrifyingly of all – Central Otago. If there is a flaw, it is that some wines are made in a more highly extracted, densely coloured, even tannic style than they need to be (some lighter Beaune-like showings would be nice to see), but these are without question among the world's most attractive versions of this most demanding grape.

## AUSTRALIA

As with other cool-climate grapes, it is crucial to find the right site for Pinot Noir in Australia, in order to avoid the gloppy or jammy characters

that can so easily spoil it. The Yarra Valley GI in Victoria fits the bill because of its altitude. Western Australia's Margaret River GI has made great strides, while on Tasmania, the cool conditions are responsible for some of the most Burgundian Pinot Noir produced outside France.

## SOUTH AFRICA

As in Australia, much of the country is simply too hot to achieve great elegance in wines made from Pinot Noir, and the grape is not that important in South Africa, except for fine sparkling wines. The best varietal red Pinots have so far come from the coastal Walker Bay region.

## SOUTH AMERICA

Chile now has some convincing Pinots, grown in the cooler, high-altitude regions such as Casablanca, and even from the hotter environs of the Rapel in Colchagua. The style can be a little overripe and heady, but the fruit is there.

## GERMANY

In Germany, they call it Spätburgunder, and it has long been a traditional grape in some of the tiny production of red wines. Typically, they are light as a feather, not much further on from rosé. The southerly region of Baden makes wines with decent fruit, while the northerly Ahr has somehow built a reputation for reds. The odd one, made at the northern limits of world wine-growing, shows true complexity.

*A vineyard in the Bannockburn district of Central Otago (above), one of New Zealand's premier regions for growing Pinot Noir.*

*Hand-plunging the grape skin cap on a tank of Pinot Noir (left) at the Yarra Yering winery in Victoria.*

# SEMILLON

*To many producers, Sémillon suffers a lack of individuality that has destined it to be blended with more fashionable varieties. Yet as the source of rich, golden, honeyed Sauternes, and the unique, aged dry white of Australia, Sémillon is second to none.*

WHILE IT IS undoubtedly one of the world's foremost grape varieties, Sémillon has a surprisingly low profile. In the northern hemisphere, it was traditionally not seen very much as an unblended varietal wine. This is largely because, in its native Bordeaux, it is always mixed with Sauvignon Blanc.

However, its highly prized susceptibility in the right conditions to botrytis, the so-called noble rot that concentrates the sugars of overripe grapes by shrivelling them on the vine, makes Sémillon a surefire bet as a dessert-wine producer. The lofty reputation enjoyed by sweet Sauternes and Barsac – in which Sémillon typically represents around four-fifths or more of the blend – has been such that the grape's role in the production of dry white wine has been largely eclipsed.

In Bordeaux today, producers of dry white wine are in the business of pulling out a lot of their Sémillon vines and replacing them with further plantings of its partner Sauvignon. (As we saw when we looked at Sauvignon Blanc, some of the trendiest dry whites of Bordeaux use no Sémillon at all.) That said, it still accounts for far more acreage in the vineyards than Sauvignon, so if it is in decline, the process will be a lengthy one. Many producers frankly consider it to have far less character than its brasher stablemate, being short of aromatic appeal and general *joie-de-vivre*.

To which one can only reply, tell that to the Australians. Semillon (as it is commonly spelt outside France) has been used to produce a varietal dry wine in southern Australia since the 19th century. Its homeland Down Under is the Hunter Valley in New South Wales. True, many growers weren't sure what the variety was, and its traditional (and misleading) name was Hunter Riesling. It does share some of the aromatic characteristics of real Riesling, most notably a minerally aroma of lime-zest, but it almost always gives a fatter, oilier wine than Riesling.

The most peculiar trait a dry Sémillon wine can have is to smell and taste as if it has been wood-matured when it hasn't. Often, there is a distinctly toasty quality to the wine that becomes steadily more pronounced as it ages. Its colour darkens rapidly too, making old Hunter Semillon one of the strangest but most memorable experiences in the world of white wine.

In areas where a lot of cheap bulk wine is produced, Sémillon's easy-going temperament in the vineyard has made it the grape of choice for those who haven't yet caught the Chardonnay bug. Much of South America's vineland, especially in Chile, is carpeted with the variety. An indication of the status in which it is held here is that these are not the wines Chile chooses to boast about on the export markets.

For many, Sémillon provides a relatively trouble-free source of blending material for more fashionable varieties. Although the Bordeaux precedent is to blend it with Sauvignon, Sauvignon is too much in vogue currently to be thought by many producers to need a partner in the bottle. That is why many winemakers, in Australia particularly, have taken to blending Semillon with Chardonnay.

The resulting wines have become bargain-basement alternatives to neat Chardonnay. The lowish prices of these wines indicate how seriously we are being asked to take them. In a hot vintage, where both grapes have yielded similarly rich, fat, silky-textured wines, it is difficult to see what they are supposed to be doing for each other in a blend.

On the other hand, the Sémillon-Sauvignon partnership is nearly always a happy one. The acidity of the latter gives definition to the textural opulence of the former.

The blend makes particular sense in the production of sweet wines. What makes great Sauternes, Barsac and Monbazillac so sought-after, and so extremely long-lived in the bottle, is that a good balance of sugar and acid is present in the wines to start with. Compared to lesser dessert wines from other wine regions, they are hardly ever cloying, despite their massive, syrupy concentration.

*Sémillon, a golden-coloured grape with markedly deep green leaves (right) is often used to blend with Sauvignon or Chardonnay. When affected by botrytis (noble rot), it creates the world's finest dessert wines.*

**FRENCH ORIGINS**
Bordeaux.

**WHERE ELSE IS IT GROWN?**
Australia, South America, a little in South Africa, the USA and New Zealand, and isolated pockets of southern France.

**TASTING NOTES**
When dry, lime-peel, exotic honey, sometimes has a little of Sauvignon's gooseberry too. Often has a hard mineral purity, even slightly metallic. In the Hunter Valley, deceptive woodiness even when unoaked, turning to burnt toast with age. Blended with Chardonnay, lemon-and-lime squash seems to be the main flavour.When subjected to botrytis for sweet wines, can take on a whole range of exotic fruit characters, but classically has overripe peach or apricot flavour, barley-sugar, honey, allied to a vanilla-custard, *crème brûlée* richness from oak ageing. Australian sweet Semillon can have an emphatically medicinal tinge to it as well.

# Bordeaux



*Sémillon grapes left on the vine that have been affected by botrytis (right). The shrivelled, blackened grapes will yield a lusciously sweet, concentrated juice.*

*The elegant Château La Louvière in Pessac-Léognan, Graves (below), owned by the Lurton family. Dry white Bordeaux from the Graves is often the best of its style.*

Sémillon's most glorious display in its home region is in the wines of Sauternes and Barsac. At the top of the tree, with a classification all to itself, is the legendary Château d'Yquem, the most expensive sweet wine in the world. The late-summer and autumn climate in Bordeaux provides perfect conditions in many years for the development on Sémillon of the noble rot, botrytis, which causes the berries to moulder and dry out on the vines. As the liquid proportion of the grapes drops, so the sugar in them comes to represent an ever higher percentage, and the result is lusciously sweet, alcoholic, viscous wines of enormous longevity.

If the top wines are so expensive, it is in large part because the more conscientious châteaux take great pains over the harvest. They will hand-select only those berries that are fully rotted, so labour costs are accordingly very high. Most of the wines are aged in at least a proportion of new oak, adding further

dimensions of richness to them. Such wines have long been the inspiration for the production of botrytized Sémillon the world over, and deservedly so.

Elsewhere in Bordeaux, in the making of dry wines, Sémillon rather hangs its head these days. The finger of blame for the notoriously flabby, fruitless dry whites the region once turned out by the vatload came to be pointed its way. But this style has waned as fresh young Sauvignon Blanc, with its tangier fruit, began to show it the door in the late 1980s. As a result, consumers may get the idea that Sémillon is incapable of making great dry wine in Bordeaux, but it ain't necessarily so.

In the northern Graves region of Pessac-Léognan, some of Bordeaux's most illustrious names in dry white wine production still use a greater percentage of Sémillon than Sauvignon in their wines. These include Châteaux Laville-Haut-Brion, Olivier and Latour-Martillac. The results can be breathtaking, the wines having more solidity and savoury concentration than the solo Sauvignon.

# Australia

Dry Semillon is one of a handful of unique styles of wine that Australia has contributed to the world. Nor is it a product of some antipodean search for novelty, conceived in a struggle to find ways of doing things that escape the eternal French archetypes. Australia was making Semillons like this in the late 19th century, even though it may have been calling them Hunter Riesling or – even less convincingly – White Burgundy.

The classic Hunter Valley style can be quite austere, as typified by the wines of Tyrrells. Crisp and acerbic in youth, they age to a wonderful roasted-nuts complexity, all achieved without recourse to the expense of oak barrels. Some producers do actually use a modicum of oak to emphasize that natural toastiness. With the tendency now for consumers to drink most wines young, greater stress is being laid on primary fruit flavours – sharp green fruits, usually lime, being the main reference point. Other good Hunter producers are Rothbury, Brokenwood and Lindeman's.

The grape pops up in most Australian regions, though, and fares equally well in areas that are considerably cooler than the Hunter. In the Clare Valley, for instance, Semillon produces a less oily version. As a rough guide, producers who make good Riesling are likely to be reliable for Semillon too: in a cool part of the Clare called Lenswood, Tim Knappstein makes fine, bracingly tart but certainly ageworthy wines.

Western Australia's Margaret River region makes some generously fruity, distinctly smoky Semillons in a style hugely reminiscent of Sauvignon. Evans & Tate is a prime example here.

Although unblended Sauvignon can too often be a disappointment from many parts of Australia, when it is blended with Semillon in the Bordeaux fashion it can produce impressively ripe-fruited wines capable of gaining real complexity with ageing. Cape Mentelle in Margaret River and even St Hallett, in the broiling Barossa Valley region of South Australia, make good blends.

Botrytized, or noble-rotted, Semillon has a long and distinguished tradition here, too. The style may be big and obvious when compared with the top wines of Sauternes, but then there is no particular reason to compare them to Sauternes. De Bortoli in New South Wales was among those who blazed this particular trail, while Peter Lehmann makes a textbook orange-barley-sugar version in the Barossa.

*The de Bortoli winery in New South Wales, Australia (below), complete with irrigation canal.*

*The verdant landscape of South Australia's Clare Valley (below), with Lenswood Vineyard in the foreground. A cool upland district, it can produce bracingly tart but ageworthy Semillons.*

# S YRAH

*Whether recognized as the French grape of the northern Rhône, Syrah, or in its popular guise as Shiraz, in Australia, this grape remains one of the noblest red varieties, fabled for its ability to age majestically for decades.*

*The vibrant blue of the Syrah grape variety (right). Syrah has a unique character most often described as 'peppery', and responds well to oak. In its classic form as the grape of northern Rhône's finest reds, and in Australia as Shiraz, it can make wines that will age for decades.*

S UCH IS the success of this grape in Australia that many may know it only by its southern hemisphere name of Shiraz. More of it is grown in Australia than of any other red wine grape, and it appears varietally, as well as in blends with Cabernet Sauvignon and Merlot.

At the pinnacle of its achievements, it shows why it thoroughly deserves its place among the first division of international grape varieties. Australia's most feted red wine, Penfold's Grange, is overwhelmingly composed of Shiraz, usually with only the merest dash of Cabernet as seasoning. In France, it produces some of the most highly prized single-vineyard wines in Europe, wines made in tiny quantities that are sold on allocation to a lucky few favoured customers.

Shiraz produces some of the world's deepest, darkest, most intense red wines, full of black-fruit richness, hot spice and alcoholic power. Then again, it can be used to make the kind of sweetly jammy, oak-smoothed nursery wine that can lure confirmed white wine drinkers on to a bottle of red once in a while.

Syrah, as we should call it when in France, blends well with a number of other grapes, and hangs out with a whole crowd of assorted pals in the wines of the southern Rhône and Languedoc-Roussillon.

The Rhône valley is the ancestral home of Syrah. In viticultural terms, the valley divides into two zones – northern and southern – and represents two very different approaches to the grape. In the south, it makes its way among a large coterie of mostly minor varieties, from the everyday wines of the Côtes du Rhône and Côtes du Ventoux up to the giddy heights of Châteauneuf-du-Pape and its understudy Gigondas. Up to thirteen varieties are permitted in Châteauneuf, of which Syrah generally plays second or third fiddle alongside Mourvèdre, with Grenache playing lead.

It's in the northern Rhône that Syrah really comes into its own. Here, it is the sole red grape, appearing in wines from Hermitage and Côte-Rôtie at the top of the scale to Crozes-Hermitage at the affordable (but still highly reliable) end. The former two can be monumental classic reds that age for at least as long as the very greatest Bordeaux, on account of their precise and complex balance of hugely concentrated fruit, acidity and massive tannic extract. Clenched and surly in youth, they gradually uncoil into the exotically seductive beauties they can be. A topnote of violets frequently adds to the charm.

One of the most commonly encountered descriptions of Rhône Syrah is 'peppery', and even a simple Crozes-Hermitage from a cooperative can display something of that characteristic, although it may vary in intensity from a mild suggestion of spiciness at the back of the throat to the exact and inescapable scent of freshly milled black peppercorns, quite as though the grower had given the wine a few twists of the grinder before sealing the bottle.

Some debate has been occasioned as to whether the famous pepperiness is a varietal property, or whether it isn't at least partly caused by Syrah that hasn't quite attained full ripeness. It is a late-ripening variety, and invariably needs time to show its paces, even in one of the hotter environs of southern France. Compare Australian Shiraz, where the pepperiness is distinctly more muted, if indeed it's really there at all.

In Aussie Shiraz, the fruit is sweetly ripe and right upfront, and the wines rarely have that sharp edge of tannin that northern Rhône examples do. In youth, the softer contours of Shiraz are often derived from the overt influence of creamy oak flavours, so the wine can be drunk sooner. It can be surprisingly delicate aromatically from certain regions, offering a refreshing waft of eucalyptus, rather than the leather and tar and blackberry it traditionally rejoices in. That said, the most concentrated wines are black as sin, and need plenty of time to unwind.

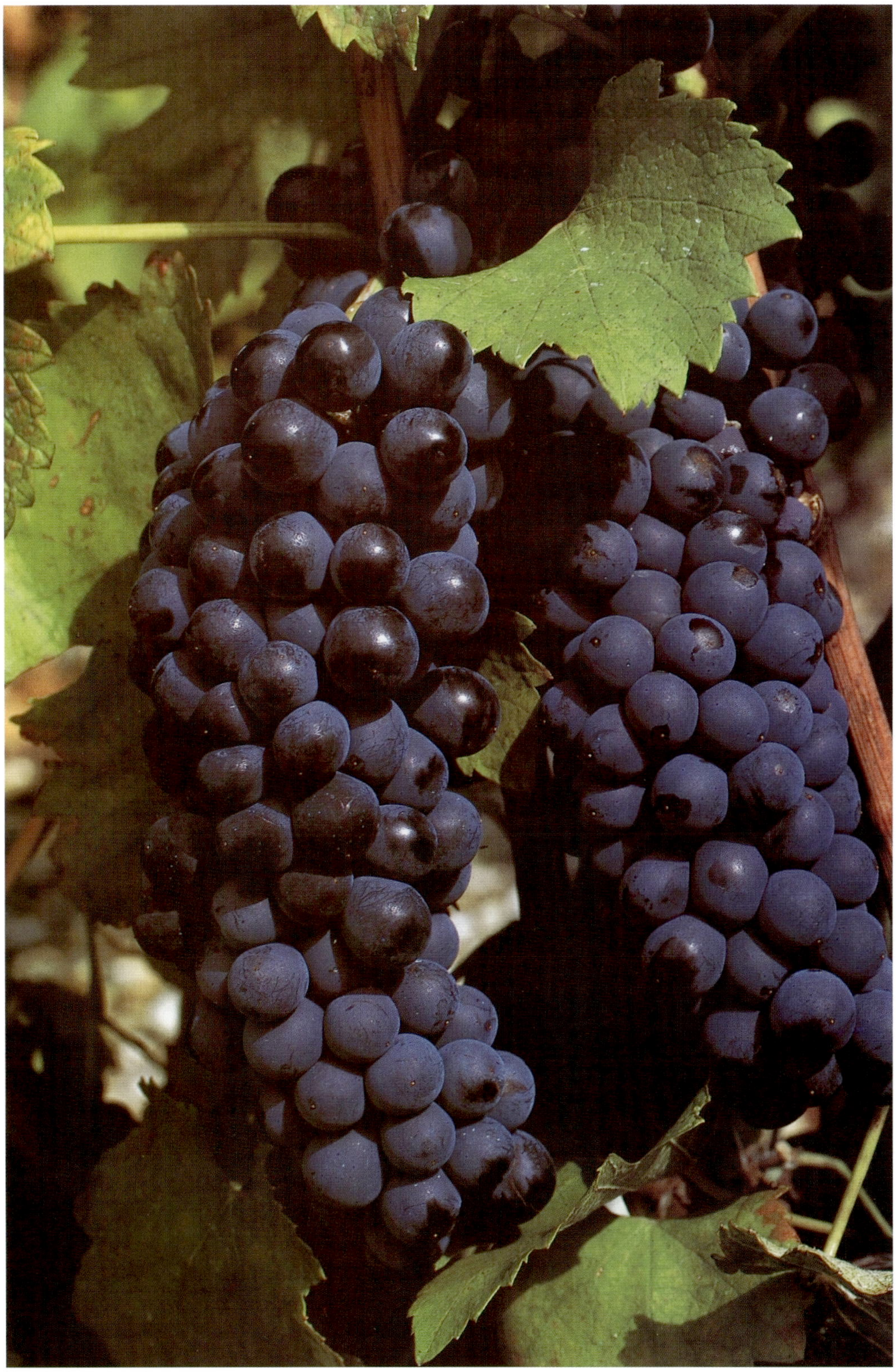

**FRENCH ORIGINS**
Northern Rhône.

**WHERE ELSE IS IT GROWN?**
Australia. Becoming important in the US, South America and South Africa. Traditional in parts of Switzerland.

**TASTING NOTES**
Can smell of almost any dark purple fruit – blackberries, blackcurrants, black cherries, damsons, plums. Freshly ground black pepper in the northern Rhône. Exotic flavours can include liquorice, ginger, dark chocolate, often a distinct floral note, too, like violets. Cool topnote of mint characteristic in parts of South Australia. Aged wines can take on something of the gaminess of old Pinot Noir.

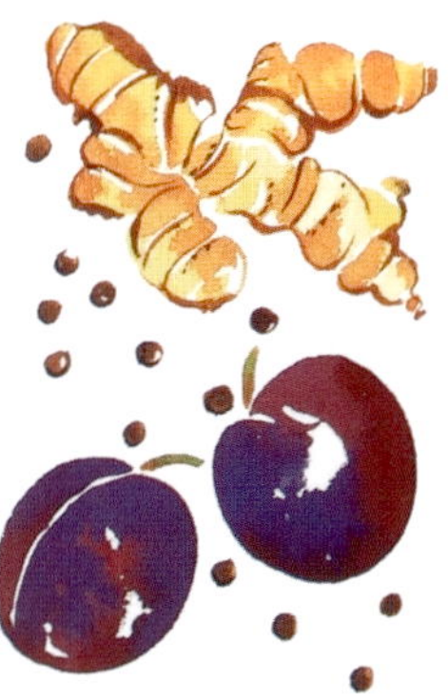

Given that there is so much Shiraz in Australia, it isn't surprising that a lot of it finds its way into very basic wines. A cloyingly sweet, jammy, offputting style is depressingly widespread. On the other hand, its use in thoroughly innovative red sparkling wines in both sweetish and powerfully dry, tannic styles, has been a head-turner. Relinquish any memories of wafer-thin fizzy red Lambrusco. Sparkling Shiraz is a muscled-up blockbuster. I tend to prefer those wines with a little residual sugar, rather than heavy tannic fizz.

# France

The greatest producers in Rhône Syrah are now ranked up with Bordeaux's and Burgundy's finest. This is still, however, a fairly recent phenomenon. While the burly red wines of Hermitage had always had a lofty reputation among British wine enthusiasts, the production of the region as a whole was not held in particularly high regard. When the influential American wine critic Robert Parker began, in the 1980s, to rate some of the best wines of Marcel Guigal (now one of the northern Rhône's superstars) as the equals of the great vintages of Mouton-Rothschild, the international wine trade was persuaded to take notice.

That development inevitably prompted the producers to put up their prices, but it has to be said that the best had certainly been undervalued in the past. These are wines with the same sort of structure and ageing capacity as Cabernet-based clarets (often even more muscularly built, in fact) and their flavours resemble no other red wines in France.

Of the northern Rhône appellations for varietal Syrah, Hermitage is traditionally the biggest and beefiest. Although solidly constructed, the wines are not without grace and elegance, and the fruit flavour can be surprisingly lighter than the reputation – more raspberries than blackberries. At their most immense, though, these are densely textured, ferociously dark stunners, but retaining their primary fruit well into their maturity.

Côte-Rôtie is the appellation that has created all the excitement in recent years, the most frenetic buzz being around Guigal's three single-vineyard wines – La Mouline, La Landonne and La Turque. These are mind-blowingly concentrated expressions of fine Syrah that sell for sky-high prices. Up to 20 per cent of the white grape, Viognier, is permitted in Côte-Rôtie under the appellation regulations, and can add a bewitching note of apricot to Syrah's blackberry.

St-Joseph makes slightly lighter wines, piercingly blackcurrant in the good years, while the bottom-line appellation of Crozes-Hermitage is well worth trying as an introduction to the flavours of Rhône Syrah. I say 'bottom-line', but there are growers now making Crozes as opaque and intense and long-lived as some Hermitage.

The final appellation of the northern Rhône, Cornas, is an odd one, in that its Syrah is the least immediately recognizable. The wines are often rather tough, and lacking the benefit of youthful fruit, or they can simply taste like blended wines from appellations further south such as Châteauneuf-du-Pape. Some growers are working with the grain of Cornas Syrah to make some excitingly individual, if austere, wines. Long bottle-ageing is mandatory.

In the southern Rhône, and down into the Languedoc, Syrah is blended with many other red grapes, among them Grenache, Mourvèdre, Cinsault and Carignan. Unless a producer has used a particularly high percentage of Syrah, the grape may not be individually perceptible in these wines, though it does beef up the structure.

*The chapel and vines on the famous hill of Hermitage (below), overlooking the river Rhône and the towns of Tournon and Tain l'Hermitage.*

# Australia

Shiraz has been the pre-eminent red grape variety in Australia for as long as anyone can remember, but it is only since the 1970s that there has been a significant impetus towards producing world-class wine from it. At its most humdrum, Shiraz is a rather gloopy plum-jam sort of wine with too much heavy oak influence in it, so that the toffeeish sweetness of its aftertaste can be quite sickly. Thankfully, there are more than enough accomplished Shiraz producers to make for a brighter picture overall.

It's all a question, as so often, of microclimate. In the hotter GIs, such as the Hunter and Barossa Valleys, Shiraz is responsible for the thickest, most opulently fruity of all Australia's reds. In the warmer central sector of Victoria, the Goulburn Valley GI is home to some especially concentrated Shirazes of great aromatic intensity.

The red soil of Coonawarra is as distinguished a hotbed of Shiraz as it is of Cabernet Sauvignon, producing subtly spiced wines, as well as accessibly fruit-filled offerings, not all of which use oak.

From old vines in parts of the Barossa Valley, Shiraz results in small amounts of extraordinarily deep, resonant and complex wines that can stand next to top Côte-Rôtie.

*The Hill of Grace vineyard, owned by Henschke (right), in the Barossa Valley, South Australia. The Shiraz vines planted here are over 100 years old.*

# Other Regions

### SOUTH AFRICA

As in Australia, it took a while for Shiraz to persuade its growers that it was worth taking seriously as a variety. Inspired by success elsewhere, some impressive Shiraz is now emerging. It should work after all, given the sultry climatic conditions the grape loves. Stellenbosch and Paarl are among the premier growing regions.

### CALIFORNIA

Despite the West Coast fashion for Rhône grape varieties, Syrah (as it tends to be known here) has been slow to establish itself as an important grape. The trend so far has been to make wines with French levels of acidity and memorably aromatic fruit, but not quite the degree of concentration of the most well-bred Côte-Rôtie. San Luis Obispo has the most extensive plantings, but Santa Barbara and Napa may well be the best regions for it.

### CHILE

Chile started to flex its muscles with Syrah only in the 1990s, with results that are already beginning to intrigue. Rhône comparisons are plentiful, with wines from various sub-zones of Colchagua, together with San Antonio and coastal Casablanca, beginning to look very tasty. The best will age well.

*Orderly rows of Shiraz vines at Franschhoek's Bellingham Vineyards, Paarl, South Africa (above).*

*Vineyards of Joseph Phelps, (left), a trend-setter for quality Syrah in California, in springtime Napa Valley.*

# RIESLING

*Germany's noble white grape variety, Riesling, is a versatile performer. It is prized in northern Europe and the southern hemisphere for its ability to produce classic sweet whites as well as impeccable dry wines.*

THE ONLY FINE wine grape of international importance not to have originated in France, Riesling is the great speciality of German winemaking. Its only base in France is in the Alsace region, a sheltered northeastern enclave between the Vosges mountains and the Rhine valley that has intermittently, usually by force, been a geopolitical part of Germany. Like Sémillon, Riesling is capable of making impeccably dry wines of surprising longevity, as well as lusciously sweet dessert wines affected by the noble rot, botrytis, but unlike Sémillon it also runs the whole gamut of styles in between.

In recent years, Riesling has come to be considered the most underrated of all the top grapes. Why this should be so when it is such a versatile performer might seem a mystery, but is at least partly explicable by the wholly irrational association in many consumers' minds of Riesling with cheap, extraneously sweetened German wine such as Liebfraumilch – the low-alcohol, low-acid introduction to the world of wine that drinkers of my own generation cut our teeth on.

Although Liebfraumilch may not have quite the same purchase on the tastes of young consumers that it once had, it remains infuriatingly confusable with quality German wine. The bottles look the same as top-quality Rhine Rieslings and, even though it's always worth looking for the name of this grape on a German wine label, the good wines turn out to share the same basic characteristics – lightness and often a delicate sweetness (albeit from natural grape sugars) – as the slosh.

How to persuade people that these are in fact much better wines? Only time and tasting practice will tell. For one thing, the clear varietal characters of the grape can be breathtakingly beautiful, a whoosh of citric freshness like squeezing a lime, together with mineral notes and often something like the flesh of a juicy-ripe peach, all suspended in a wine that then belies its apparent fragility by surviving intact in the bottle over many years. There is far more joy in a ten-year-old Riesling of perhaps 7 per cent alcohol than there is in a ten-year-old, 13 per cent Sauvignon.

Because Germany's vineyards are at the northern extremity of where vines can be grown, the country's quality classification system developed along the lines of assessing just how ripe the grapes were when harvested, and therefore how potentially sweet the resulting wines would be. Severely low winter-time temperatures might then arrest the fermentation of the wines, leaving them low in alcohol and retaining a degree of unfermented grape sugar. These were precisely the attributes that aficionados came to treasure in them.

International tastes in wine provoked an experimental movement in Germany in the 1980s and 90s to ferment some of the wines – Rieslings and others – to dryness. Initially, many of these wines were disastrously unbalanced, and the technique appeared to work better with other varieties than Riesling, but more rounded wines have since emerged.

Riesling always gives a high-acid wine, which is perhaps best offset in Germany by some level of natural sweetness, so that even those at the drier end of the spectrum (the styles known as Kabinett and Spätlese) have a softening edge on them. In warmer climes, there is generally enough ripeness and alcohol to balance the high acidity, making for appetizing dry wines that can age well.

This has traditionally been the case in Alsace and the cooler parts of Australia, the world's two best sources of dry Riesling. Other countries have appeared to struggle with the grape. In time, cool-climate New Zealand will doubtless become a reliable producer of outstanding dry Rieslings, but for the time being, there are too many unfocused wines that taste vaguely of boiled sweets. It will not go down well in the Rhine and Mosel valleys to say so, but it may well be that the more success producers outside Europe have with Riesling,

*The Riesling (right) is a hardy, frost-resistant vine, which makes it ideal for the cool vineyards of northern Europe. Riesling can produce long-lived wines of intense aroma and character, ranging in style from bone-dry to lusciously sweet.*

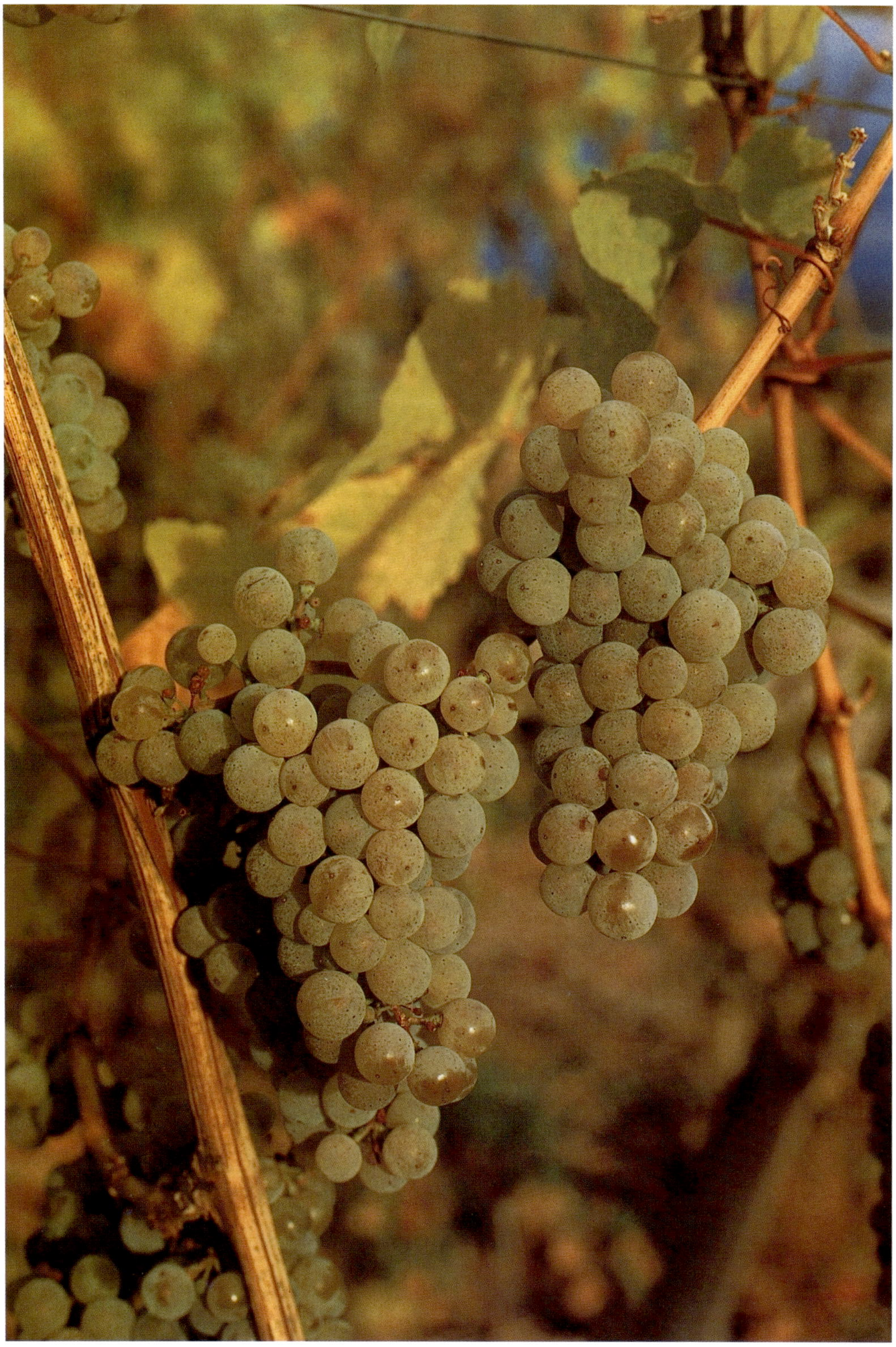

### ORIGINS
Germany.

### WHERE ELSE IS IT GROWN?
Alsace. Australia and New Zealand. Austria and northern Italy. Some in the United States and Canada.

### TASTING NOTES
Nearly always has the scent of lime, whether bitter zests or freshly pressed juice. Riper German ones can have softer fruit like ripe peach or apricot, as well as a gentle floral aroma. In Alsace, there is a very austere mineral quality in the wines and a texture on the palate like sharpened steel. A whiff of petrol (or gasoline) flowing from the pump generally comes with age, although some Australian wines can display it quite young.

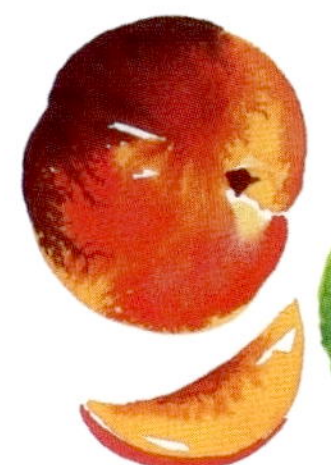

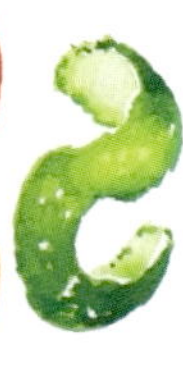

the greater the chance that people may come back to an enjoyment of German wines, freed of the inaccurate preconceptions that still stand in their way.

At the sweetest and richest end of the spectrum, Riesling makes some of the most enticing, and beautifully balanced, botrytized wines in the world. The Beerenauslese and Trockenbeerenauslese offerings of Germany and Austria, as well as the most carefully tended Noble Rieslings of Australia, South Africa and the United States, all combine fresh acidity with layers of honey-soaked, citrus-spiked lusciousness.

# Germany

*The famous steep vineyards of the Mosel region (below) where the Riesling vines tumble down towards the Mosel river. Such steep sites means hand-picking is the only option at harvest-time.*

Riesling is grown in nearly all of the wine regions of Germany, and has since the 1990s been the country's most widely planted variety. It is in many ways particularly well suited to the cold climates it encounters there, because the tough stems of its vines enable them to cope with the worst the winters can throw at them.

The drawback comes at the other end of the annual cycle, when ripening the grapes is something of a gamble against the elements. Picked too early, Riesling can be full of hard, unripe acidity. Waiting for the right levels of ripeness can often mean leaving the bunches hanging into November, when French growers have long since picked, pressed and fermented, and when the weather is so bitter that it can be hard to get a natural fermentation going.

With all that in mind, much effort and funding has gone into crossing Riesling with other German varieties, and even crossing the crosses with Riesling and others. The aim has been to try to perfect a grape that will give the fresh fruit flavours of Riesling, as well as its invaluable susceptibility to botrytis, but with a more reliable ripening pattern. A handful of these have yielded goodish results, but few seriously believe they can take the place of Riesling as Germany's premier performer.

The top classification for German wines, their equivalent of the French *appellation contrôlée*, is *Prädikatswein* (literally, wine with distinction). Within this class, there are five types of wine, measured according to the amount of natural sweetness in them. In ascending order, they are: Kabinett, Spätlese, Auslese, Beerenauslese and Trockenbeerenauslese. The suffix '-lese' means 'picked', and the time of picking is specifically indicated in the prefix, from Spätlese (late-picked, i.e. just after the normal harvesting time) to Trockenbeerenauslese or TBA (meaning berries picked outside – that is, after – the main harvest, which are dried and shrivelled with sugar-concentrating noble rot).

Any of the first three styles may be fermented out to total dryness to become Trocken (dry) wines, or halfway in the case of wines labelled Feinherb. Some super-sweet berries are left on the vines until nearer Christmas, in some vintages even into the new year, and are picked at the crack of dawn when they are half-frozen. During the pressing, some of the crystals of ice that represent the water content of the grapes are removed and the very sweet juice that hasn't frozen is then fermented. This style is known, for obvious reasons, as Eiswein (ice wine).

The fullest, most concentrated Rieslings have traditionally come from the Rheingau, where the vineyard has long been dominated by Riesling plantings. Here, the best producers make wines that are as expressive of their particular vineyard locations as any illustrious Burgundy *grand cru*.

A non-Trocken Riesling from the Rheingau is generally around 10 per cent alcohol, relatively heady in German terms, and there is a rounded, often honeyed feel to the best of them. Legend insists that the Rheingau was the region where the first noble-rotted wines were accidentally produced, many years before the technique became known in Sauternes.

To the west of the Rheingau, the Nahe also has a preponderance of Riesling, although here it is a more recent development as a result of the region's standing having risen considerably in the last few years. There are some very promising young growers here now.

The other two neighbouring Rhine regions are Rheinhessen and Pfalz (the latter originally known in English as the Palatinate). Riesling has made great strides in the Pfalz, where an almost tropical aromatic intensity is the house style of the most talented producers, although the wines are still possessed of that traditionally delicate structure and finesse.

To the northwest, and centred on the city of Trier, the Mosel-Saar-Ruwer region produces the lightest, most exquisitely subtle and refined versions of Riesling made anywhere in the world. Alcohol levels may be as low as 7 per cent, and the aromatic profile of the wines so astonishingly rarefied that a sniff at the glass can be like breathing in pure mountain air. The vineyards are planted on vertiginously steep slopes on either side of the river, so any thought of harvesting with motor vehicles is out of the question. Enforced rigorous hand-picking of carefully selected grapes should go some way to explaining the prices.

*Vineyards looking down to the village of Ungstein, in the Pfalz region of Germany (above). The traditional style of Riesling wines here is both aromatic and tremendously delicate.*

*Schloss Johannisberg, looking down over its Riesling vineyards (left), in the Rheingau. Rheingau Rieslings are traditionally the fullest, most concentrated in style.*

# Alsace

*The 15th-century church in the midst of vineyards at Hunawihr, Alsace (above).*

Anybody familiar with the wines of Alsace may tend more readily to associate them with the highly perfumed, positively decadent flavours of Gewurztraminer and Pinot Gris than with the steely austerity of Riesling. It is, however, an open secret in the region that Riesling is considered the noblest of them all, partly because the acidity levels it usually attains mean that the resulting wines have a good long life ahead of them. The variety has been here since the 15th century, and today comprises over 20 per cent (and counting) of the vineyard land. Everybody loves Riesling.

It is in the hilly Haut-Rhin district of Alsace that most of the Riesling is concentrated. The best plots are those that are protected from the wind so that the ripening of the grapes is not inhibited, although the climate of this sheltered region is generally much more benign than what German growers have to contend with. Unusually for a fine wine grape, the amount of fruit the vines are permitted to yield under the appellation regulations is quite high, without the wines themselves necessarily lacking anything in full-blown aromatic intensity.

Most Alsace Riesling is made in an assertively bone-dry style, with around 12 per cent alcohol and rapier-like acidity. They are the only Alsace wines that are not especially enjoyable if drunk young, most requiring at least five years to begin to settle down. In their youth, they have a highly strung, quite taut feel on the palate, leavened with some bracing citric fruit, comparable to freshly squeezed lime juice.

In addition to the basic dry wines, there are two designations for sweeter styles. The lighter of the two is Vendange Tardive (meaning late harvest); in a warm late summer the grapes are left on the vines to achieve higher sugar levels that convert to a delicately sweet wine. In the right conditions, ie. damp misty mornings giving way to mild sunny daytime weather, Riesling will botrytize, just as it does in Germany. The hugely concentrated syrupy wines that result are called Sélection de Grains Nobles – among the most appealingly balanced noble-rotted dessert wines in all of France.

Certain of the best vineyard sites in Alsace have been designated *grands crus* since the mid-1980s. These wines should have a noticeable extra dimension of intensity in the flavour, and are inevitably sold for higher prices. Prominent among the best of the *grand cru* sites for Riesling are Hengst, Rangen, Schoenenberg and Sommerberg. Lower yields contribute to their unearthly concentration.

*Steeply shelving vineyards form the backdrop to the typically* Alsacien *architecture of Trimbach's premises at Ribeauvillé, Alsace (right).*

# Other Regions

## AUSTRALIA

There was once more Riesling in Australia than there was Chardonnay, which may come as a surprise to those who primarily associate Australian white wine with the sun-drenched oaky flavours of the latter grape. Because it needs a certain amount of acidity to give it sharp definition, Riesling is much more successful in the cooler areas of the country, such as the Clare Valley in South Australia and parts of Western Australia such as Mount Barker.

The Australian style is richer and fatter than the European models. In youth, they have pungent lemon-and-lime fruit and oily texture. Sometimes, most notably in wines from Clare Valley, they also display those heady petrol fumes that German and Alsace Rieslings only tend to take on with bottle-age. Despite their smoother angles, the most sensitively made Australian Rieslings still show good acid balance to maintain that sense of freshness without which Riesling wines are lost.

Many growers are more conscientious about their Riesling than they are about any other variety, ensuring its careful handling every step of the way from harvesting to its treatment in the winery, an approach that is paying off handsomely in the depth and ageing potential the wines now boast.

As well as the dry styles, there are also some extremely fine botrytized Rieslings being made in Australia. Indeed, for many people (myself included), these just have the edge, for

thorough-going complexity and balance, over the country's nobly rotted Semillons. Attaining immense levels of concentration, the wines retain their citric freshness, with a flavour profile like lemon marmalade.

## NEW ZEALAND

New Zealand's cooler climes should be ideally suited to the production of good dry Riesling. In fact, there was a tendency until fairly recently to make an indeterminate medium-dry sort of wine, with a twangy, not-quite-wholesome fruit quality not a million miles from boiled sweets. The South Island has lately led the way in producing some fresh, clean, impeccably limey Rieslings of great promise. When vintage conditions permit, many producers also make a botrytized Riesling.

## NORTH AMERICA

Cooler parts of California and, particularly, Washington State have seen tentative plantings of Riesling, but it's fair to say the grape has not proved the hottest property commercially in the US. Late-picked Washington versions can be sublime, though. Further north, in Canada, Riesling is turning out some convincing wines in the province of Ontario. Some of Canada's fabled Icewines use Riesling; the best can challenge the pick of German Eiswein.

*Harvesting Riesling grapes in the depths of winter (above) in Ontario, Canada. The frozen grapes are destined for Canada's fabled Icewine.*

*Checking the progress of bunches of ripening Riesling (left), in South Australia's Clare Valley, one of the grape's best growing areas.*

# MERLOT

*Historically used in the blended reds of Bordeaux, Merlot's fame is founded on its partnership with Cabernet Sauvignon. Its reputation as a solo performer has been earned more recently.*

FOR WINEMAKERS all over the world, Merlot is the significant other of Cabernet Sauvignon, its truest blending friend and stalwart partner. But whereas Cabernet came to be seen internationally as capable of performing in its own right, Merlot was not generally thought to have the wherewithal to fly solo – at least not at first.

Merlot may have been used unblended for industrial quantities of everyday quaffing wine in northern Italy, but in its homeland of Bordeaux, where it originated, the red wines are always blends. Moreover, the first-growth wines of the Haut-Médoc and Graves are all based on a grape mix in which Cabernet Sauvignon predominates.

And yet, there is far more of Merlot planted in Bordeaux than there is of Cabernet. (It is in fact now the most widely planted grape in France.) While it may be a junior partner on the left bank of the Gironde, though, look to the right bank, and we find the origins of its international reach. In the two best areas here, Pomerol and St-Emilion, Merlot has the starring role.

Some Pomerol properties use virtually all Merlot in their reds; the leader of the pack, Château Pétrus, is nearly all Merlot down to the last five per cent or so of Cabernet Franc. You only have to consider the stratospheric prices commanded by Pétrus to realize that Merlot has no need to hide its light under a bushel of Cabernet Sauvignon. The overall percentage of Merlot in the wines of St-Emilion is a little lower, with proportionately more Cabernet Franc, but it is still the capstone variety, prized for its gentler style.

As in all regions where blended wines are the historical norm, producers will mix and match the proportions of Cabernet and Merlot, depending on vintage conditions. Merlot has the advantage of ripening earlier than Cabernet Sauvignon, meaning that late rain or a sudden cool snap at the end of the growing season,

arriving just in time to spoil the chances of great Cabernet, can be at least partially offset by blending in more of the already-harvested Merlot. Even in the better years (such as 1990), Merlot can often out-perform Cabernet in producing a healthy ripe crop.

Stylistically, what Merlot does for Cabernet in the wines of the Médoc is smooth away some of their harder edges. A claret containing, say,

*The plump, blue Merlot (right), an early-ripening grape, produces soft, rich wines – often described as 'fleshy' – that harmonize well with the more structured Cabernet Sauvignon.*

35 per cent Merlot will have a softer mouth-feel than one where it is limited to a mere 10 per cent. There is an undoubtedly slightly sweeter edge to it than the surlier Cabernet displays.

Outside Bordeaux, Merlot really started to branch out on its own in the California of the 1980s. Varietal Merlot had been produced there prior to this, but the tendency was, as with the Cabernets, to over-extract its tannins. In the latter part of the 80s, softer, gentler Merlots for everyday drinking began to be made. Its role as a red-wine-without-tears saw plantings increase fivefold in the decade from the mid-80s to the mid-90s as Merlot-mania took hold. Washington State also turns out plenty of uncomplicated, velvet-soft Merlot. The result

of that is that knowledgeable wine enthusiasts have stopped treating Merlot as a serious wine. A rethink among producers is now due.

In the southern hemisphere, it has been a conspicuous success in Chile, where the most ambitious Merlots in districts like Rapel are now beginning to rival Pomerol for sumptuous depth of impact. Argentina's plantings are gaining ground too. Outstanding Merlots are cropping up in South Africa, where a spicy, even gamey complexity distinguishes the best.

In Australia, solo Merlot has only lately begun to find its feet. The grape is still more usually seen as a blending partner for Cabernet after the Bordeaux model, an approach common in New Zealand too.

### FRENCH ORIGINS

Bordeaux, especially the Libournais on the right bank of the Gironde, which includes St-Emilion and Pomerol.

### WHERE ELSE IS IT GROWN?

Throughout central and eastern Europe, from Switzerland to Bulgaria. United States. Argentina. Some in Chile, Australia, New Zealand, South Africa.

### TASTING NOTES

At its ripest, soft purple fruits such as blackberries and black plums. In cooler climates, it can have a distinct vegetal streak in it, like French (green) beans or asparagus. If the sun gets to it, there may be a suggestion of dried fruit such as raisins or even fruitcake. Rounded out with oak in the best wines of Pomerol and California, it can also take on a textural richness that has overtones of melted chocolate or possibly Turkish Delight.

# France

*The fairy-tale Château Ausone (above), in St-Emilion, set amid its vines.*

Merlot's French fiefdom is on the right bank in Bordeaux. There, it dominates the communes of Pomerol and St-Emilion. While red wines from the latter district are characteristically composed of around two-thirds Merlot with perhaps just a splash of Cabernet Sauvignon, in Pomerol the proportion may be more like nine-tenths Merlot, with no Cabernet Sauvignon at all.

Differences in character between the wines of the two communes can be quite marked, with the top wines of Pomerol having a seriousness and austerity about them, together with something of the savoury, herbal overtones found in left-bank Cabernet. St-Emilion wines, on the other hand, for all that there may be less Merlot in them, are often softer and more approachable earlier on. Despite the popular assumption that Merlot-based wines mature more quickly than those dominated by Cabernet Sauvignon, St-Emilions and Pomerols can be quite as long-lived as the finest offerings of the Médoc, as witness Château Pétrus.

In 1955, on the centenary of the original Bordeaux classification, St-Emilion endowed itself with a similar league-table of properties. In contrast to the entrenched near-immutability of the left bank, however, the proprietors of St-Emilion undertook to update their classification every ten years. There may be little change from decade to decade, but that is precisely because they know their wines will be

*The legendary Château Pétrus, Pomerol (below). Oil burners are still used in the vineyards as late as May to protect the early-ripening Merlot from frost damage.*

rigorously reassessed, and so the motivation to maintain standards is compelling. Top spot is shared by two châteaux: Cheval Blanc and Ausone.

Alone among the premier communes of Bordeaux, Pomerol has never been subjected to the trials of classification, and there are no plans for one. The legendary Pétrus would no doubt occupy pole position in any such notional system, followed by the likes of Châteaux Clinet, l'Evangile, Le Pin, Lafleur, Vieux-Château-Certan and Trotanoy.

Less illustrious Merlot-based wines come from what are known as the satellite areas of St-Emilion, a group of small communes that form a northeasterly fringe to St-Emilion itself, and are all allowed to append its name to their own – Montagne, Lussac, Puisseguin and St-Georges. In good vintages, when the grander properties can fetch dizzyingly high prices for their wines, some of the satellite wines can represent exemplary value. The most aromatically attractive, for my money, tend to come from Puisseguin and Lussac.

Elsewhere, Merlot has made great inroads among the varietal wines being produced in the Languedoc under the catchall Vin de Pays d'Oc designation, and it also has a part to play in some of the traditional appellations of the southwest. In Cahors, for example, it performs its time-honoured diplomatic role, tempering the sternness of the Auxerrois and Tannat grapes.

# Other Regions

## UNITED STATES

Merlot is the red wine of choice for those California and Washington wine-drinkers who want the richness and structure of a good red, without having to age it until it's soft enough to drink. In that respect, it's very much Cabernet for beginners. The benchmark style is now ripe red fruit with a lick of sweet oak and gentle tannins. Cooler areas of the eastern States, such as the Long Island AVA, are now producing some more complex wines with something of the structure of Bordeaux.

## ITALY

It's fair to say that Merlot doesn't enjoy a particularly exalted reputation in Italy, although large swathes of its wine industry – especially in the northeastern areas of the Veneto, Friuli and Piave – would be lost without it. The tendency is to make a juicy, but light-toned wine, perfectly suited to lunchtime quaffing by the carafe. In hotter years, however, and from producers prepared to limit their yields, there can be a little meaty complexity to the wines.

In the hotbed of viticultural dynamism that is Tuscany, one or two of the smart operators are achieving fine results with Merlot. Producers such as Lodovico Antinori, with his varietal Merlot, Masseto, are showing that the variety can make full-blooded, ageworthy wines that are the equals of the monumental Cabernet and Sangiovese super-Tuscans.

## CHILE

Merlot is now responsible for most of the greatest red wines of Chile. It was for a long time mistaken in the vineyards for another grape, Carmenère (also found in Bordeaux), and wines labelled Merlot often have a percentage of Carmenère in them. The fruit expression in these wines is little short of stunning. They age well, but are also drinkable at barely more than a year old. Merlots from Rapel have just about the best price-quality ratio of any red wines in the southern hemisphere.

## OTHER SOUTHERN HEMISPHERE

The Australasian countries were late starters in the varietal Merlot stakes, the custom having been to blend it traditionally with Cabernet Sauvignon. Hawke's Bay, New Zealand, is responsible for some sharply defined, plummy Merlot now. The Barossa Valley and McLaren Vale are good Australian sources.

In South Africa, especially Stellenbosch, the grape has emerged from its eternal partnership with Cabernet to make some outstandingly complex, full-fleshed wines unblended.

## OTHER EUROPE

Merlot has traditionally been a source of soft, everyday reds throughout eastern Europe (especially Bulgaria and Romania), and it enjoys particular favour in parts of Switzerland, producing mostly light, easy-drinking wines in the Italian-speaking southern canton of Ticino.

*Merlot is the most widely planted red grape variety in Romania (left), making soft, easy-drinking reds.*

*Barrel cellars at Lodovico Antinori (below), Tuscany. Antinori is one of the band of top Tuscan producers creating stunning varietal Merlots.*

# CHENIN BLANC

*Chenin Blanc's wide stylistic repertoire has made it the focal grape variety in the central vineyards of the Loire valley. Put through its paces in Vouvray, it runs the gamut of dry to sweet, and sparkling, wines.*

PERHAPS THE most misunderstood of all the noble grape varieties, Chenin Blanc is the backbone of white winemaking in the Loire valley. While it undoubtedly has a very distinct and recognizable profile in the wines it can produce, it has experienced difficulties in making friends among consumers for two reasons.

One is that, like Riesling, it has a wide stylistic repertoire, ranging all the way from the uncompromisingly bone-dry to luxurious botrytized dessert wines with decades of ageing potential. Nothing wrong with that, except that, in the past, the labelling on Chenin wines from the Loire has been low on information about the style of the wine.

The other hurdle for newcomers to clear is that the drier wines are not over-endowed with the sort of immediately obvious commercial appeal found in young Sauvignon Blanc. Put crudely, they are quite often not very nice. There is an aromatic character to them, but it is composed of rather weird elements – a mixture of brushed steel, old honey and damp. The classic tasting description often heard is 'wet wool'. Add to that the fact that Chenin is nearly always loaded with teeth-grinding acidity, and it is easier to understand why this is not a grape likely to be top of anyone's list of all-time favourites.

Learning to appreciate Chenin requires a more precise knowledge of when to drink the different styles of wines than is the case with most other white wine varieties.

In the Loire, Vouvray is the most important appellation for Chenin. Its wines span the spectrum from dry to sweet, as well as sparkling wine made by the champagne method. The dry wines, increasingly labelled as such (*sec*) these days, can be delicious immediately on release, when they can display exhilarating fruit flavours, and that boldly assertive acid acts as a seasoning in the way that lemon juice does in a fruit coulis. After a year, they seem to lose that fruit and slump into a prolonged sulk;

tasted again at five or six years old, they have developed a honeyed softness that throws that dryness into relief.

In a hotter vintage, the winemaker may choose to leave some of the ripe natural sugars of the grape in the finished wine. This off-dry or medium-dry style is known as *demi-sec*. It can be the most supremely refreshing example of its kind to be found anywhere in France. The delicate note of lingering sweetness tenderizes the prickly acids in a hugely appetizing way.

If the grapes reach a level of sticky-sweet overripeness that the French call *surmaturité*, then the resulting wine is known as *moelleux*. These are not quite the richest dessert wines – they still have that spiky streak of acidity running through them – but they do have a lush coating of honey and caramel.

In years when botrytis has freely developed, some producers may make a fully botrytized wine. This will often be entitled *Sélection*, because it involves selecting only the most extensively shrivelled berries from the vine, for maximum impact. Even then, the layers of concentrated sweetness have a discernible tartness at the centre, so that the overall effect is more toffee-apple than crème brûlée.

Elsewhere in the world, Chenin's malleability has made it something of a workhorse grape. That is certainly the case in the hotter regions of the United States and Australia, where its most widespread use has been as blending fodder, to add a tingle of acid and prevent basic white wines from tasting flabby. It is very extensively planted in South Africa, where it often goes under the alias of Steen. While a lot of it inevitably disappears into the blending vats, some at least is turned into fresh, fruit-filled, even complex whites of almost miraculous crispness, given the climate.

Grapes with naturally high acidity are often a good bet for the production of champagne-method sparkling wine, where a thin, relatively neutral base wine gives the best results. In the Loire, as well as sparkling Vouvray, Saumur is a good source of such fizz, as is the wider regional appellation of Crémant de Loire.

### FRENCH ORIGINS
The central Loire valley –
Anjou-Saumur and Touraine.

### WHERE ELSE IS IT GROWN?
South Africa. Also California,
Australia, New Zealand, and
a little in Argentina.

### TASTING NOTES
When young and dry, tart green
apple and pear, occasionally
something a little more exotic
(passion fruit) in a good year.
Mineral, even metallic, hardness
on the palate, though often with
paradoxical underlying hint of
honey. Can have a dry nuttiness
(walnuts) and an indeterminately
damp smell, like old newspaper
or wet woollens. Sweeter
styles get progressively more
honeyed without losing the
tingly, appley acidity woven
through them.

# Loire

Despite its appearance in many areas outside Europe, no region makes more of Chenin Blanc than does the Loire. It is the most important white grape variety in the two central parts of the valley – Anjou-Saumur to the west, and Touraine in the east.

In Anjou, particularly, cultivating Chenin is something of a challenge. So far north, the grape is a notoriously slow ripener and, as summers in these parts are not exactly torrid, a lot of Anjou Chenin is very acerbic and raw-tasting – not a style that would find many imitators beyond France's borders. Then again, that is exactly how the locals like it to taste.

Autumns, though, are damp and warm enough to permit the regular development of the noble rot, botrytis. It is in Anjou that the premier appellations for botrytized Chenin are found: Coteaux du Layon, which encircles the tiny and very fine enclave of Bonnezeaux (an AOP in its own right), and Quarts de Chaume. In the best years, these wines are fully the equal of great

*An unusually fine summer's day blazes down on the Chenin vines in the tiny AOP of Bonnezeaux in Anjou (below), where some of the Loire's finest botrytized Chenins are produced.*

Sauternes and Barsac, because they have that nerve-centre of acidity that keeps them going into a well-balanced old age.

The lesser-known appellation of Coteaux de l'Aubance makes some reasonably good, though much less rich, sweet wines, from grapes that shrivel on the vines but are only rarely tinged with botrytis. Drink them young.

In the west of Anjou is Savennières, the appellation that many consider to be the highest expression of dry Chenin anywhere in the wine world. In their first flush, these intellectually demanding wines make no concessions to drinkability, tasting hard as nails and tightly clenched. Over maybe seven or eight years, they open out into an austere but profoundly beautiful maturity, full of minerals, bitter apples and bracing Atlantic fresh air. The word 'racy', when applied to wine, might have been coined just for Savennières. Within the appellation is a single-ownership AOP called Coulée-de-Serrant, run along biodynamic principles (see entry, Loire section).

Travelling eastwards into Saumur, we enter fizz territory. Sparkling Saumur is made by fermenting the wine a second time in the bottle to produce carbon dioxide, exactly as for champagne. Made only, or almost entirely, from Chenin, it usually has quite a snap to it, and is dead dry. Served well-chilled on a hot day, it makes an appealing aperitif quaff.

In Touraine, the most important appellation of all for Chenin Blanc is Vouvray. Together with its lesser-known and less distinguished neighbour to the south, Montlouis, Vouvray puts the Chenin through its paces, making it dry, *demi-sec*, *moelleux*, botrytized or fizzy, according to taste. Quality is highly variable, and the wines – as elsewhere – are very vintage-dependent, but when it shines, it really shines.

The wines of the best growers in Vouvray constitute an invaluable introduction to this underestimated grape, with which it is worth persevering. You'll find the odd one that has the mildly vomity smell of dried Parmesan, while others are reminiscent of stale nuts. Then suddenly, there'll be one full of green apple tartness, maybe the sharpness of passion-fruit, with honey lurking underneath, finishing with the taste of freshly shelled walnuts, and you've arrived in Chenin country.

# Other Regions

## SOUTH AFRICA

Chenin, or Steen as it is very often termed, is
put to practically the same sort of versatile use
in South Africa as it is in the Loire. It's even
used in some of the monumental fortified wines
for which the Cape was once famous. Although
plantings have fallen off in recent years, this
is still the country's most widely grown grape.

At one time, the drier styles didn't tend to
be that remarkable, being rather neutral,
uninspiring house-white stuff. These days,
though, that's all changing. Dry Cape Chenin
can now fill the mouth with a gum-cleansing
feel like biting into a just-picked apple. They
have body and definite varietal identity, and
they are full of the sharp aromatic definition
more logically to be expected from the cool
northerly climate of the Loire. Some producers
subject their wines to a modicum of oak, which
they seem to take in their stride.

Fantastic wines are made from noble-rotted
Chenin, when the flavours of tropical fruit,
honey, bitter orange peel and barley-sugar
all seem to mingle in what are some of the
world's most diverting sweet wines.

## AUSTRALIA AND NEW ZEALAND

Not many other non-European producers have
taken Chenin seriously yet as the base for a
varietal wine. There is a tendency to try to make
it too rich for its own good by muffling its
acidity. Plump, oak-enriched examples crop
up in the Swan Valley GI in Western Australia,
although the cool climate of New Zealand is
a more likely setting for successful Chenin.
Some varietal Chenin from the North Island
has looked good, but again the tendency is
towards a high-extract style.

## CALIFORNIA

One or two California wineries have produced
convincing varietal dry Chenin, some of it
oak-aged. The wines articulate the tart fruit
and balancing honey tones of Vouvray, for
all that they are appreciably fatter-textured.
Otherwise, Chenin goes into everyday blended
whites to lend added acidity.

*Chenin Blanc, or Steen, vines
on the Klein Constantia
Estate, South Africa (above).
Chenin has been the
backbone of the country's
white wine production.*

*Widely spaced Chenin
Blanc vines in the Temecula
valley, California (left),
where the variety is still
a minority taste.*

# VIOGNIER

*Viognier's career as an internationally known grape variety has only been very recently established. It is safe to say that, before the early 1990s, the ordinary consumer had probably never heard of it.*

THE RISE TO prominence of Viognier over the past decade has been meteoric. Once a niche variety whose name was rarely seen on labels, it is now everywhere, either on its own, or quite often blended in a double-act with Chardonnay. That last detail is a little ironic, as the chief impetus for everybody suddenly deciding to plant the variety was to fulfil the demands of that section of the market that was getting a little tired of subsisting on an unrelieved diet of Chardonnay.

Its spiritual home is in a small appellation at the northern end of the northern sector of the Rhône, called Condrieu. The wines of Condrieu were once one of the wine world's best-kept secrets, and they owed their opulent, perfumed appeal entirely to the Viognier grape. Most often vinified without oak, these are wines that combine the heady, musky scents of ripe orchard fruits (classically apricots) with some powerful spice tones such as cinnamon and cardamom, backed up by big burly texture and high alcohol.

Elsewhere in the region, it is the only permitted grape in the white wines of a micro-appellation within Condrieu, called Château-Grillet, where the wine is made entirely by one producer. It is also, as we saw when discussing Syrah, entitled to form up to 20 per cent of a blend in the red wines of Côte-Rôtie, to which it can contribute an unearthly, often ravishing, layer of floral scent.

When the revolution in French winemaking of the late 1980s established the Languedoc as the nerve-centre of varietal experimentation, Viognier rapidly became one of the favoured grapes of that region. It wasn't that long a journey after all from the northern Rhône, although Vin de Pays d'Oc Viognier is a much simpler and less elegant wine than Condrieu (as well it might be, given the price differential).

As might be guessed from its location in southern France, the variety prefers a fairly warm climate, which is why it has proved particularly suitable for planting in the southern hemisphere and in the warmer regions of California. The only possible disadvantage to that is that it can lack a little acidity in very warm vintages, which then leaves its fruit flavours tasting slightly mushy. What that in mind, the most conscientious producers pay careful attention to picking times to ensure that the wine retains a freshening lemony streak for balance.

We can perhaps understand why the world was ready for something other than Chardonnay, but why Viognier? The answer to this lies in the immense increase in fashionability that the wines of the Rhône came to enjoy from the 1980s onwards, and which shows no sign of abating. In the northern Rhône especially, Syrah and Viognier played the same pre-eminent role in the vineyards as Cabernet and Chardonnay did elsewhere, and their flavours were seen as usefully distinctive.

Viognier has the structure of the richest Chardonnays, but without needing oak to lend it aromatic personality. It belongs with that category of white wine grapes considered to be naturally aromatic, along with the likes of Gewürztraminer, Riesling and Muscat.

In California, certain quality-conscious producers have achieved results with Viognier that are every bit as gorgeously rich and exotic as the best of Condrieu. There has been a slightly greater tendency to reach for the oak barrel here, but the concentration and extract of the wines is such that they take some judicious wood-ageing in their stride.

The Australians were a little slower off the mark than their American counterparts with Viognier, the variety only starting to become fashionable there in the mid-1990s. Site specification is all. In the hotter districts, the results have been too heavy and clumsy for comfort, but the potential is undoubtedly there, and we can expect to see some more distinguished examples in years to come.

Demand for cuttings of the grape has also rocketed in South America, where both Chile and Argentina are producing convincingly perfumed, unexpectedly subtle Viognier wines with good fruit-acid balance.

*Viognier (right) has become undoubtedly one of the most fashionable white grape varieties on the international scene, producing aromatic, spicy wines everywhere from the south of France to the hotter regions of Australia.*

### FRENCH ORIGINS
Northern Rhône.

### WHERE ELSE IS IT GROWN?
Increasingly important in the
southern Rhône, Languedoc
and Roussillon. Outside Europe,
now fashionable in California,
Australia, Chile and Argentina.

### TASTING NOTES
Its most widely noticed fruit
flavour is apricot, which can
range from the free-flowing
juice and flesh of a fresh
ripe Bergeron fruit to the
concentrated muskiness of
dried Hunzas. Scented white
peach may be in there too, and
ripe aromatic Comice pear.
Supporting that may be subtly
delineated spice notes like
cardamom, cinnamon or ginger,
while the texture of the wine
is close-grained and thick like
clotted cream. From the hotter
regions, it may be distinctly
reminiscent of honey-and-lemon
throat-soothers.

# France

*Château-Grillet (above), in its amphitheatre of vines above the river Rhône at Vérin, is one of the smallest appellations in France.*

*Viognier vines on the Coteau de Vernon (below), from which are made the top wine of Domaine Georges Vernay, long celebrated as one of the most illustrious producers in the whole Condrieu appellation.*

The top wines of Condrieu still probably represent the finest expressions of the Viognier grape variety grown anywhere. Other than in the very best Californian examples, it is only really here that the full complexity locked within the grape blossoms forth. For such a small appellation, there is also an intriguing range of styles.

A handful of producers use a touch of oak to round out the texture of the wine and deepen its aromatic impact. It is certainly true that a lick of vanilla, if sensitively applied, can enhance the natural creamy ripeness of the grape in warm vintages, but over-ageing in wood can muddy the waters.

There are also different schools of thought as to how rich and powerful the wine should naturally be, with some preferring an almost delicate, floral style of Condrieu, while others go down the big and blowsy route, emphasizing big alcohol, dense texture and decadently ripe aromas. There are persuasive examples of Viognier in both camps, and indeed it is this very versatility that makes this one of the most fascinating appellations in the whole Rhône valley.

Wholly enclosed with the Condrieu zone is the separate appellation of Château-Grillet which, like certain Burgundy *grands crus*, is exclusively owned by one producer. The style here is quite distinct from Condrieu, with the wine being cask-aged and only released after the next vintage has been made. As a result, the fruit tones are much more muted, leaving just the heftiness of the wine's texture to appreciate.

Many growers in the bulk-producing region of the southern Rhône are now looking to Viognier to add a little aromatic character to their white wines, which have traditionally been rather neutral in flavour. Even so, it is extremely unusual to come across wines that are made from unblended Viognier.

For solo Viognier at kinder prices, it is necessary to head a little further south to the Languedoc, where this grape has become something of a buzz varietal. The wines here don't attempt anything like the complexity of Condrieu, but then the vines themselves are not nearly as ancient. A mouthful of very fresh, apricotty or peachy white, usually unoaked, is to be expected, along with strong alcohol (typically 13.5 per cent), and an often slightly overdone acidic streak with the pronounced flavour of lemon juice. These wines are generally for drinking young, but can benefit from a little ageing to tone down the acidity. They can make a good, if heady, aperitif.

# Other Regions

## CALIFORNIA

Without a doubt, the best examples of unblended Viognier outside France are being produced in California, specifically in the Napa Valley. Tasted blind, the finest bottlings are all but indistinguishable from best Condrieu, imitating not only the ripe yellow fruits and Indian spices of the Rhône stars, but also their lush, floral, creamy style too. There is also the same debate as to whether oak-ageing suits the wines or not, with exponents of both styles producing some stunning wines. By acclamation, the star winemaker here has been Josh Jensen of Calera, whose small quantities of scintillating wines are as much sought-after (and as hard to find) as the top Condrieus.

At the lower end of the price range, and especially from the northerly Mendocino AVA, there can be a tendency in the wines to that slightly confected honey-and-lemon flavour of proprietary throat-sweets, with all the floral charm and the exotic spice notes missing. However much refined sensibilities may be offended by such tastes, though, these have proved commercially popular wines with the ABC (Anything but Chardonnay) contingent, and plantings of Viognier are on the increase. Quality will undoubtedly continue to improve.

## SOUTH AMERICA

Varietal Viogniers from Argentina and Chile have been making their presence felt in the export markets since the late 1990s. The style tends to be big and alcoholic, as elsewhere, but with a little of the honeysuckle charm of Rhône Viognier in the better efforts. Both countries favour an unoaked style over cask-ageing, but with strength prevailing over grace. A strong lemony note underpins the peachy fruit, and the finish may often be quite spirity. Creditable showings have been made by certain of the volume producers in both countries, and we must expect this to be an important varietal in the future.

## AUSTRALIA

The honey-and-lemon tendency still vitiates too many of Australia's efforts with Viognier, for all that there are plenty of suitable sites for growing it. Top bottlings can have the structure and intensity as those of the Rhône big boys, but without the aromatic finesse or the subtleties to back them up. The McLaren Vale GI has so far been the most promising stamping-ground.

More eye-catching perhaps than varietal Viognier from Australia has been the practice of adding it to Shiraz to produce a southern-hemisphere homage to those Côte-Rôties that have a little Viognier in the blend. There is something peculiar but compelling in finding a waft of clean apricot scent emerging through the inky-dark, blackberry style of strapping Aussie Shiraz. Producers in the Yarra Valley, Victoria, and South Australia's McLaren Vale and Langhorne Creek GIs, have made waves in recent vintages.

*Joseph Phelps Vineyards (above), at St Helena, in Napa County, California, has been among the trailblazers for varietal Viognier in what many now regard as its second home after the Rhône.*

*A gum tree in the Heggies vineyard of Yalumba (left), in the Eden Valley, South Australia. Viogniers from regions as hot as this usually have the structure and alcohol levels of certain Rhône examples, though perhaps don't always have the same aromatic finesse.*

# GEWÜRZTRAMINER

*Unique among the white varieties, Gewürztraminer is very much a love-it-or-hate-it grape. Once tasted, never forgotten, its ostentatious, scented, rich character has made it the grape forever associated with Alsace.*

*The unmistakable livery of the Gewürztraminer grape (right). Unlike the green or golden colour of its fellow white grapes, Gewürz sports a dusky pink skin – a fitting outer expression of its flowery, highly perfumed character.*

WHETHER OR NOT you enjoyed it, your first taste of Gewürztraminer is likely to have made an impression. While a simple Chardonnay may seem shy and retiring in the glass, Gewürz comes screaming out at you with some of the most unearthly and downright bizarre scents and flavours to be found anywhere in the world of wine. So strange can it taste that those encountering it unexpectedly for the first time may wonder whether it has had some other flavouring added to it.

The parent variety seems to be of north Italian extraction, in a grape known simply as Traminer. Its highly scented offshoot, first identified in the 19th century, took its prefix from the German word for 'spice'. By this time, the grape had acquired, by natural mutation, a deep pink skin in place of the green one, and had begun to yield an extraordinarily perfumed juice. Popular in Germany, Gewürz was widely planted in Alsace during the period of the region's absorption into Germany in the late 19th century.

Alsace, now incontrovertibly French, is the variety's first home today. While there are increasingly impressive examples being produced elsewhere, particularly in Germany, they never quite seem to attain the uninhibited aromatic splendour of the greatest Alsace Gewürz. In an especially ripe year, it may combine musky fruit notes like lychee and squishy apricot, with ginger, cloves, talcum powder, and a whole florist's shop of roses, violets and jasmine. It is usually pretty low in acidity, which makes it drinkable quite young, but roaring with alcohol, so that a little – combined with those unsubtle flavours – goes an exhaustingly long way.

Because of its larger-than-life character, Gewürz is constantly in danger of not being taken terribly seriously by those who are used to more restrained flavours in a white wine. In the long dry summers of Alsace, it ripens to a tremendous richness, which accounts for all that alcohol, but even when fermented up to around the 14–15 per cent levels I have seen on some, it still seems to retain a core of residual sugar that leads a lot of consumers to find it too sweet for a supposedly dry wine.

Once the taste is acquired, however, it becomes clear that Gewürztraminer is without doubt one of the classic wine grapes. From a *grand cru* vineyard site owned by one of the top producers in Alsace, its peculiar intensity can be a mightily refreshing antidote to the containerloads of tell-em-apart Chardonnay that the wine market is still awash with. The best Gewürzes will age, although they tend to be the ones that have unusually pronounced acidity to begin with, and there are not too many of these. You can bump up acid levels by picking the grapes earlier, but then you risk losing some of that striking flavour.

The dilemma over picking times is problem enough in Alsace. In warmer climates, it becomes a complete headache. The difficulties of timing it right account for why most efforts outside Alsace have so far failed to match the quality of the best wines produced in this one enclave of northeastern France. That said, some German growers are beginning to achieve convincing results with the variety, especially in the slightly warmer areas of the Pfalz and Baden. New Zealand is giving it its best shot, and there are isolated stars in Chile and the United States. One or two South African examples have been particularly exciting.

For a grape that seems to be telling the winemaker that it wants to be sweet, it comes as no surprise to find that many Alsace and German growers make a late-picked Gewürz in the form of flowery Spätlese and Auslese in Germany, and peach-scented Vendange Tardive in Alsace. When conditions are right, the grape can acquire botrytis, and a fully rotted wine is labelled Sélection de Grains Nobles in Alsace. These are massively dense, opulent dessert wines, tasting like orange and ginger marmalade – one of the great taste experiences. They can age for many years in the bottle.

### ORIGINS
For the Gewürztraminer specifically, possibly Alsace. For its less intoxicatingly scented forebear, Traminer, probably the south Tyrol area of northern Italy.

### WHERE ELSE IS IT GROWN?
Apart from Alsace, it has important bases in Germany and Austria, less so in Spain and eastern Europe. Experimental plantings dotted around the southern hemisphere, and also the United States, particularly the Pacific Northwest.

### TASTING NOTES
The list is well-nigh endless. Fruits are usually an eerily precise imitation of ripely juicy lychees, together with overripe peach or nectarine when the flesh is just starting to turn mushy. Some authorities dispute the spice connection evoked in the German word *Gewürz*, but there is nearly always a good sprinkling of ground ginger and often cinnamon, occasionally the scent of whole cloves and even a dusting of white pepper. Flowers are very much in evidence too – violets and rose-petals (often reminiscent of attar of roses, as in Turkish Delight) – and then there is a whole range of scented bathroom products – aromatic bath salts, perfumed soap, talcum powder. Gewürz from regions other than Alsace may present a toned-down version of all that, which may come as a relief to some.

# Alsace

Gewurztraminer (spelt without the *umlaut* in France) accounts for just under a fifth of total vineyard plantings in Alsace. It is one of the favoured grapes permitted in the designated *grand cru* areas. Although Riesling is unofficially thought of as the first among this top division by the growers themselves, Gewurz is cherished for the forthright character that has made it the grape most ineradicably associated in consumers' minds with the region as a whole. Blowsy, spicy, exotic Gewurz just is the taste of Alsace.

The grape does exceptionally well on the often rather claggy clay-based soils found in the Haut-Rhin area of Alsace. Its willingness to ripen well in the generally dry vintages of this very sheltered region allows its personality to shine through in the finished wine. In many ways, it is the antithesis in Alsace of the Riesling we looked at earlier, giving more alcohol and less acidity, resulting in a considerably more forward style of wine.

Another quality that marks Gewurz wines out from their counterparts is their very deep colour. They usually have a richly burnished golden tone, not dissimilar to the most heavily oaked Chardonnays, a characteristic derived in Gewurz's case not from wooden barrels but from the distinctive pigmentation of the grapeskin. Whereas most white varieties come in conventional shades of green, Gewurz, as befits its gaudy nature, is turned out in a deep pink livery that lends some of its blush to the wine itself, very occasionally showing even as a faint pinkish tinge behind the deep yellow.

In the cooler years in Alsace, Gewurztraminer can seem a rather pale imitation of itself, both in terms of colour and flavours. The vintage of 2001 wasn't particularly good, for example, and the wines' resulting balance was seriously skewed, leaving an overall impression of weight, but without the depth of flavour to carry it off with any grace.

The classification of the *grand cru* sites came into effect in Alsace in the 1980s. While dogged inevitably by controversy over what should be included and what not, it has since emerged

*The Clos Windsbuhl vineyard at Hunawihr, owned by Zind-Humbrecht (below). The Gewurztraminer from this site is one of the finest examples of what Alsace Gewurz can achieve.*

that much of the land that has been incorporated is of sufficient quality to inspire the producers to their greatest efforts. Of the 51 sites, some of the best for Gewurztraminer are Brand, Goldert, Hengst, Kessler, Sporen, Steinert and Zotzenberg, but there are many more.

Wines with those names on the label are undoubtedly worth the extra cost over a bottle of everyday Gewurz. Many producers are in the habit of labelling their wines Cuvée Réserve or something similar, supposedly indicating notably successful batches of a particular vintage, but these terms, unlike *grand cru*, have no legal force.

What is probably more important than anything pertaining to labelling in Alsace is the grape yields. Almost without exception, the best wines, whatever their designation, are sourced from older, lower-yielding vines. Much more

than about 50 hectolitres per hectare, and you're liable to produce a wine that lacks true focus, while some of the finest wines are being vinified off barely more than 25 hl/ha. It may cost twice as much, but then you're buying twice the concentration, and concentrated flavours are what Alsace is all about.

Cooperatives are an important part of the wine scene in Alsace, and vary enormously in quality, but one of the most commercially significant, exporting substantial quantities – the Caves de Turckheim – is one of the most reliable. At the stratospheric end of the spectrum, wines from some of the old-established family vineyards, particularly some of the Vendange Tardive bottlings from *grand cru* sites like Hengst and Goldert, are unutterably exquisite, powerful essences of this most ostentatious grape.

*Gewurztraminer grapes left on the vine until November (above), destined for the peach-scented style of Alsace Vendange Tardive.*

# Other Regions

## GERMANY

Although plantings of Gewürztraminer in Germany are by no means extensive, some German growers have achieved notable successes with it in the light-textured, low-alcohol styles for which the country is renowned. It fares better in the warmer regions such as Baden in the south, and the Pfalz, where its best manifestations are brimful of expressive ripe fruit.

## UNITED STATES

As others of the Alsace grapes, such as Riesling and Pinot Gris, have thrived in the states of the Pacific Northwest, so Gewürz has also done its bit. Success has come patchily, and the results are not as yet much exported. There are some reasonably tasty examples in Washington State, including a handful of delicate but attractive late-harvest versions.

## NEW ZEALAND AND AUSTRALIA

The cooler climate of New Zealand is better for Gewürz than most of Australia (where the grape has often been used simply as blending material for dry Riesling). The North Island regions of Gisborne and Auckland, as well as Central Otago on the South Island, have produced some convincing attempts, but the weight is often lacking, and the perfume more fugitive.

## ELSEWHERE

The occasional quietly impressive Gewürz does crop up in other countries, for all that we don't really want Gewürz to be quiet. Chile has some properly scented wines, and one or two South African growers are getting the hang of it rather impressively. It has proved to be a useful blender with Muscat in Penedés in northeastern Spain, especially from Torres.

*Matua Valley Winery, set amid its vineyards in the Auckland area of New Zealand's North Island (above). Matua Valley is one of New Zealand's most notable producers of characterful Gewürztraminer.*

# GAMAY

*The one classic grape variety that has stayed close to home, Gamay is synonymous with Beaujolais, that light, fresh, strawberry-fruity red that is mostly designed to be drunk young and lively, but whose best wines will age.*

LOOKING AT a map of the world distribution of grape varieties might seem to suggest that Gamay is something of an interloper among our exalted company of 12 noble grapes. A red blob shows a significant concentration of it in eastern France, with only the skimpiest of traces anywhere else. In fact, it gets in because that red blob constitutes one of the world's most individualistic red wine styles – Beaujolais.

Gamay is the only grape used in the making of (red) Beaujolais. Some of it is also grown further north, in the southern stretch of Burgundy known as the Mâconnais, where it's responsible for usually rather indifferent wines bottled as Mâcon Rouge. Elsewhere, it may be blended in a proportion of up to two-thirds with Pinot Noir to make Bourgogne Passetoutgrains. A fair bit is grown in the Loire valley to the west, some as Touraine Gamay, some used in Crémant de Loire pink fizz. On the western flank of the central Rhône, in the Coteaux de l'Ardèche, it makes spicy reds to rival the Grenache-based wines of Côtes du Rhône.

It is on the stern granite hillsides of Beaujolais, however, that Gamay really comes into its own. In addition to basic Beaujolais and Beaujolais-Villages, there are ten villages that are theoretically capable of making the best wine (known as *cru* Beaujolais), and which have their their own appellations within the region. Running north to south, these are: St-Amour, Juliénas, Chénas, Moulin-à-Vent, Fleurie, Chiroubles, Morgon, Régnié, Brouilly and Côte de Brouilly. The last is a peculiar little hill of blue granite that pops up in the middle of the larger Brouilly appellation.

There are some subtle stylistic differences among these ten, but what links them is more important than what distinguishes them, and that is the sunny-natured Gamay grape. Gamay offers the lightest possible style of red wine, full of simple strawberry fruit, fresh sappy acids,

and little or no tannin. Although the best growers do achieve a certain measure of complexity in their wines, and some of the best *cru* Beaujolais can age well for five or six years, most producers are content to turn out oceans of straightforward quaffing wine that reacts appetizingly to chilling for summer drinking.

The light texture of Beaujolais derives from a method of vinification called carbonic maceration, to which Gamay is especially suited. Instead of being crushed in the normal way, which extracts some tannin from the skins and pips along with the juice, the grapes are tipped whole into fermenters from which the air has been driven out with carbon dioxide. The juice starts to ferment inside the whole grapes, until the skins burst from the build-up of gas within them. The grapes at the bottom of the heap are punctured by the weight of those on top, and ferment in the normal way, but that is still gentler than most assisted forms of pressing.

Gamay's suitability for producing cheap, early-drinking, featherweight reds is what inspired the marketing of Beaujolais Nouveau, which continues to this day. Those who feel like imbibing quantities of embryonic, just-fermented, acid-tingling red from the very latest vintage can indulge their passion freely in the third week of November.

There is a movement afoot in the region to introduce greater depth into the wines in an attempt to throw the happy-go-lucky, knock-it-back image of Beaujolais into some sort of relief. Some are using a proportion of normally fermented juice in order to inject a little tannic kick; others are ageing in new oak barrels in a region where such a thing was once anathema. Such courageous swimming against the tide has resulted in top *cuvées* of *cru* Beaujolais that have the gingery, brambly concentration of northern Rhône Syrah (no, really).

External markets are still dominated by the wines of the powerful bulk producer Georges Duboeuf. For once, quantity does not preclude quality because most of the company's wines are good, and easily recognizable by their distinctive flower labels.

*Gamay (right) offers the lightest style of red wine, full of simple strawberry fruit, fresh, sappy acids and very little tannin.*

About 10 per cent of the vineyard land in Switzerland is planted with Gamay, where it is often blended with the far more widely grown Pinot Noir, and there are one or two producers in California doing their best with it, and achieving reasonable approximations of the style of young *cru* Beaujolais.

By and large, however, Gamay hasn't performed well on soils different to those of its native region. Coupled with the fact that the style of wine it is happiest producing has not been a noticeably fashionable one for red wines in recent years, there isn't the incentive that there is with a variety like Pinot Noir to compete with the best of France. All of which is a shame because, when on song, Gamay is among the most effortlessly charming styles of young red wine. (Its rosés, by contrast, are probably best passed over in silence.)

*Misty autumnal scene in Brouilly (left), one of the ten* crus *of the Beaujolais region.*

### FRENCH ORIGINS
Beaujolais.

### WHERE ELSE IS IT GROWN?
Burgundy, Loire, Rhône. Switzerland and other central European countries. Minute amounts in California.

### TASTING NOTES
At its deliriously ripest, fistfuls of pulpy wild strawberries. When very young (as Nouveau, particularly) it can have a synthetic smell like boiled sweets, reinforced by the crunchiness of its acidity in the mouth. That, and related aromas like peardrops (pear candy), banana flavouring and bubblegum, are all fermentation smells accentuated by the fact that no air gets into it while it is vinifying. Some of the richer, meatier *cru* wines can take on the attributes of mature Pinot Noir after five or six years.

# OTHER GRAPE VARIETIES

*In the 21st century, a roll call of prominent grape varieties would not be complete without crediting some of the once lesser-known grapes that have become familiar through classic styles made mostly outside France.*

FOR A WHILE at the end of the 20th century, it looked as though the greater part of the world's wine would end up being made from one or more of the so-called international varieties this section deals with. What has happened since, though, has gone a long way to restoring the faith of wine drinkers everywhere. Other grapes have emerged from the margins of European viticulture, and enjoyed their share in the spotlight, broadening the spectrum of flavours and styles available to us.

There is often no particular reason that a grape variety suddenly finds itself on everybody's lips, in every sense of the phrase. Astute marketing, audacious labelling and adventurous drinking combine to produce brand recognition of what were once unfamiliar names and tastes. If Viognier could become an internationally known variety, pretty much anything could.

*Malbec grapes (above) ripening in their new spiritual homeland of Mendoza, Argentina.*

*Albariño (right) growing in a vineyard at Rías Baixas, in the Galicia region of Spain.*

## MALBEC

Long one of the supporting cast – and a fairly minor one at that – in Bordeaux, Malbec has traditionally been front and centre of the blend in the wines of Cahors, where they know it as Auxerrois. Its rise to prominence is almost entirely to the credit of the wine industry of Argentina, where it was introduced in the mid-19th century, and where it is now the most widely planted grape, most of its vineyard land being in the hive of productivity that is the Mendoza region. While neighbouring Chile stuck for a long time to the more recognizable French varieties, Argentina's winemakers bet the house on Malbec. It probably helps that its name is simpler to say than Cabernet Sauvignon.

The grape produces full-bodied, richly textured reds that are never short of ripeness and develop well in the bottle. Even when young, its wines rarely have forbidding levels of tannin, but there is a bundle of juicy purple fruit in every glass. There was a period around the turn of the millennium when quite a few examples were clumsily over-oaked, but that problem has been largely consigned to history now. The alcohol levels can be high, but somehow, even in those wines that come in at 14 per cent, their natural potency is hardly ever detrimental to their overall balance.

## ALBARIÑO

A white variety that was once confined to Galicia in the northwest corner of Spain, and (as Alvarinho) to the Vinho Verde region of Portugal, Albariño has begun to extend its reach in both hemispheres. Its naturally thick skins enable it to weather any damp conditions remarkably well, and plenty of sun during the ripening season brings out bushels of rich, ripe fruit – peach, guava, a little Viognier-adjacent apricot – with hardly anything in the way of bitter acidity to confound it. Its ancestral denomination in Galicia is Rías Baixas, but there are Albariños now in La Mancha, California and the Pacific Northwest of the USA, South America and Australia. The

Portuguese version is quite different, much more taut and astringent on the palate, with higher acidity and a savoury-salty quality.

## PICPOUL

Picpoul Blanc, to give it its full name, was once one of the miscellaneous basket of white grapes that went into the fairly workaday white wines of the Languedoc in southern France. The pic- part of its name, originally pique-, is derived from the verb *piquer*, to sting, indicating its reputation for coruscating acidity. It enjoyed a little very modest local fame around a village near the saltwater lagoon of the Etang de Thau, where it received its own billing as Picpoul de Pinet within the larger Coteaux du Languedoc designation. It finally attained its own AOP in 2013, since which it has forged a reputation for snappy wines with bracing but ripe lemon character and assertive acids. It isn't so far as well travelled as Albariño, but it is being tried in vineyard patches across the USA from California to Arizona, and in Australia too, always in the kind of hard-edged, bone-dry style that makes it perfect with shellfish.

## TORRONTES

Returning to Argentina, we find another of the great one-offs among the world's white grapes. If you thought Alsace Gewurztraminer was assertively aromatic, try Torrontes. Even at the most basic level, its wines are hauntingly floral, while at its most intense, it has unearthly depths of piercing rose-petal and bergamot, so that putting your nose in the glass is very similar to opening a box of scented lokum (Turkish Delight). Its acidity is quite pronounced, though gently nippy rather than anything too aggressive, and its fruit tends to the peachy-grapey end of the spectrum. There are three sub-varieties of it in Argentina, known as Riojano, Sanjuanino and Mendocino, the first of which tends to be the most seductively perfumed. Torrontes was once thought to be related to a grape known by the same name in Galicia, but this has turned out to be a bit of over-deduction.

## PINOT GRIS/GRIGIO

There were once essentially two manifestations of this grape. One, known by the French name Pinot Gris, was grown in Alsace, where it was one of the range of remarkably spicy, florally perfumed grapes in which that region

*The high-altitude vineyards of northwest Argentina's Cafayate region (left) are perfectly suited to growing perfumed Torrontes.*

*The Languedoc AOP Picpoul de Pinet (above) has helped put this quality grape on the map.*

specializes, and the other was Italian Pinot Grigio. The latter was much more of a dullard, overcropped, light and thin, often quite acidic and displaying hardly any fruit character at all. For reasons that remain obscure, it was the Italian version that was to become widely known. Not many consumers made the link with the quality Pinot Gris that was being assiduously cultivated by producers in America's Pacific Northwest, Canada, New Zealand and Australia. The answer to this has been to rename these wines with the Italian designation, making them more familiar and thereby improving the reputation of Grigio into the bargain. It is increasingly widely grown in central and eastern Europe, and in Chile. It has always been one of the minority grapes of German viticulture, where they call it Grauburgunder.

By the turn of the millennium, when it was well on its way to becoming as familiar to white wine drinkers as Chardonnay had been before it, too much Pinot Grigio was a watery travesty of the grape's innate characteristics – just as we thought we had left anonymous, personality-free dry white wine behind forever. These days, the overall picture is much improved, and something of the fat-textured, musky, peachy-pear and citric quality it has long shown off in Alsace is coming to the fore. It doesn't suit the massively high alcohol that grapes grown in the hotter countries are turning out, but since it is relatively low in acidity, it can afford to be picked earlier to avoid over-ripeness.

*The pinkish hue of the skin of some variants of Pinot Gris (above) make it that rare thing – a white grape that can produce rosé wines, the marketing manager's dream.*

FRANCE

1994
GALET
VINEYARDS
Merlot
PRODUIT DE FRANCE
VIN DE PAYS D'OC
VINIFIÉ ET MIS EN BOUTEILLE PAR
GABRIEL MEFFRE, 84190 FRANCE
GABRIEL MEFFRE
75cl e

*The Loire valley region is famed for its many riverside châteaux of great opulence, like this one (above) at Azay-le-Rideau, on the Indre tributary, southwest of Tours.*

The historical pre-eminence of France as the world's foremost wine-producing nation is under threat as never before. As consumers over the past quarter-century have discovered the wines of sunnier climes, with their easily comprehensible labels, pronounceable names, and big, ripe, readily accessible fruit flavours, the country that once lorded it over the whole viticultural world has been left in crisis.

Not only is French wine struggling for market share among what were once its most reliable customers (its slice of the UK retail action finally dropped below 15 per cent at the beginning of the 2010s), but the French wine industry itself has become prone to outbreaks of panic. Internecine arguments about quality control, a hostile, even xenophobic, attitude in some quarters to incoming winemakers from abroad, and the clenched-teeth refusal more widely of any acknowledgement that the produce of other wine countries might compare to it, has led its wine industry into a period of sullen retrenchment that can only be wholly self-defeating. Something has to change.

The first straw in the wind came as long ago as 1976, when a young English wine merchant with a business in Paris staged a comparative blind tasting of premium wines from France and California. The American wines, sun-soaked Cabernet Sauvignons and Chardonnays chancing their arms against the French viticultural aristocracy of Bordeaux and Burgundy, emerged as the overwhelming winners, the victory all the sweeter for the fact that the greater part of the tasting panel was composed of French experts. News of the results received very short shrift in the French media (where they were reported at all, that is), but the storm-cones had been hoisted.

In one sense at least, it isn't hard to feel sympathetic to those French *vignerons* who are tired of being reminded of the findings of this tasting, and many thousands of others like it in the years since. They are not intentionally making wines to compete with, rival, imitate or outclass the products of other cultures. Their wines have their own specific identities; they are, at their best, highly individual expressions of their environments, and the practices and

*France's* appellation contrôlée *regions (right), from the cool vineyards of Champagne to the hotter regions of the Midi in the south.*

1. BORDEAUX
2. LOIRE
3. CHAMPAGNE
4. ALSACE
5. BURGUNDY
6. RHÔNE
7. PROVENCE
8. LANGUEDOC-ROUSSILLON
9. GASCONY & SOUTHWEST
10. JURA
11. SAVOIE & BUGEY
12. CORSICA

philosophies of the winemakers. Then again, it's hard to argue with the miserable brute fact of plummeting market share.

Sooner or later, all what-is-to-be-done? arguments about the French wine crisis get round to raising the question of the AOP system. This is the framework by which the country's wines are graded in quality, with the highest designation – *appellation d'origine protégée* – sitting above the progressively humbler *vin de pays* or IGP (*indication géographique protégée*) regional wines and, since 2009, *vins de France*, wines that can be blended from different regions. It's all so complicated, so bureaucratic, and allegedly operates too much like a cartel.

We can safely dispense with this line of argument for a number of reasons. The AOP regulations have been overwhelmingly a force for good since they began to be formulated in the 1930s. They have given legal standing, institutional integrity and binding definition to the best wines of France, in many cases ratifying the status of already celebrated wines, in many others making possible the elevation of the overall quality of a previously humdrum region's production. The system is flexible in that it allows for promotions (from *vin de pays* to AOP, for example), and it is based on empirical observations of which grapes work best in which soils, how they should be vinified, and so forth.

Yes, the system is complicated in the sense that there are hundreds of wine regions to classify, but what's the alternative? Dividing the whole of France into North, South, East and West, and leaving it at that? How is that going to enlighten the consumer? I'm not for a minute suggesting the framework is infallible, and indeed far too many sub-standard wines do slip through the assessments of the regional tasting panels, but the challenge is to make the system work better, not abandon it altogether, as many external commentators (and even some within the French industry itself) keep naively insisting.

There is, moreover, no better argument for the logical force and benign impact of a system of controlled appellations than the fact that every wine-producing country on the planet has either introduced one, or is in the process of doing so. Certainly, the regulations may be looser in Australia, say, than in France, but the geographical principle – the idea that wine is at its best when it tastes as though as it comes from Somewhere rather than Anywhere – has been accepted as a spur to quality all over the viticultural world.

Where I think France is in difficulties at present is the too often uncomfortable gap that exists between the best and the least impressive wines of each area. To its credit, the Bordeaux region, responsible for the lion's share of the country's finest reds, began to look seriously in the 1990s at its often frankly disastrous performance at the lower end of the quality scale, where it has been decisively elbowed aside by riper, fruitier wines from the southern hemisphere. Gradually, the picture here has improved.

What too many consumers find, however, is that when they venture into the market to try one of the many appellation wines, they find themselves choosing between dull generic wines made or bottled by big companies and the almost invariably unaffordable, and much rarer, wines of the most celebrated growers. That creates more of a toxic sense of commercial apartheid than is generated by any of the New World countries.

I remain, indomitably, unrepentantly, a Francophile. When they perform at the top of their game, French wines are regularly among the most exciting in the world. That they should have had to surrender the limelight to other wine countries was always inevitable – and right. But if they become hopelessly marginalized by a combination of implacable indifference on one side of the counter and consumer prejudice on the other, we will have lost one of the Western world's outstanding cultural achievements.

*Dusk descends over vineyards in Corbières, in the Languedoc (above).*

*Ancient presses in the underground cellars at Gaston Huët (above), producer of fine sparkling Saumur, Loire.*

# BORDEAUX–RED

*Occupying a position at the pinnacle of world winemaking, the grand châteaux of Bordeaux produce fine clarets and sweet whites in a landscape that could not have been better designed for growing vines.*

**BORDEAUX–RED**

*GRAPES: Cabernet Sauvignon, Merlot, Carmenère, Cabernet Franc, Malbec, Petit Verdot*

*The Bordeaux region lies within the Gironde* département. *The Médoc is a narrow strip on the left bank of the Gironde estuary. Upstream, the river Garonne provides the damp climate so suitable for the botrytized wines of Sauternes.*

THE RED WINES OF Bordeaux – or clarets, as they are known in the English-speaking world – have long been synonymous with the popular image of fine wine. If the region's profile has tended to be higher than that of its great rival, Burgundy, that is partly because the trade in fine red Bordeaux has been of paramount international significance, and also because there is just hugely more wine produced in Bordeaux than there is in Burgundy.

At the top of the tree sit the wines enshrined in the 1855 regional classification (more of which below), as well as those from districts considered their equals, notably Pomerol and St-Emilion. It is these that provide the archetype for the notion that red wines improve with age, as they go on developing in the bottle, sometimes for decades, occasionally emerging in parcels from private cellars to be sold at auction, and realizing a tidy profit for the investor.

Say you don't have a private cellar, though (neither do I). In that case, you can either start your own little collection in the garage, or else buy from one of the many independent wine merchants who specialize in occasional purchases of good mature vintages. But either way, you can't avoid the crucial issue, which is that the overwhelming majority of Bordeaux reds need ageing. Ten years isn't a bad rule of thumb for most; the best may well need considerably longer than that.

During the economic boom-time of the 1980s, a trend for buying claret directly from the château in the spring following the vintage, before it's even been bottled, for delivery at a later date – a deal known as buying *en primeur* – became the smart way to invest. It's certainly cheaper in the long run than waiting until the retailers have bought the wine themselves, and then paying their mark-ups. It is now increasingly coming under fire from within the region for its tendency to provoke winemakers to produce overly forward, upfront wines that will taste good enough to buy at six months old, which is not at all what fine Bordeaux is traditionally about.

Drunk in its youth, a good claret is really wasted. It will be tight and tough in texture, and rigid with tannin. After around five or six years, it can begin to soften up a bit and allow some of the blackcurrant or plum fruit of Cabernet or Merlot grapes to shine forth. Then, in a curious, little-understood development, it will seem to withdraw into a sulky state (known in the lingo as 'dumb'), only blossoming again a few years later, with its fruit still intact, but now deepened with all sorts of complex additional (or 'secondary') scents and flavours.

Great if you can afford it. But if you can't?

That leaves the rest of the market to be mopped up by the everyday produce of the big wine companies, and here is where the problem has traditionally started. Cheap generic Bordeaux can be unattractive at best. Produced from underripe, over-cropped grapes and churned out in bulk for the mass market, it can be vile. That said, the Bordelais have

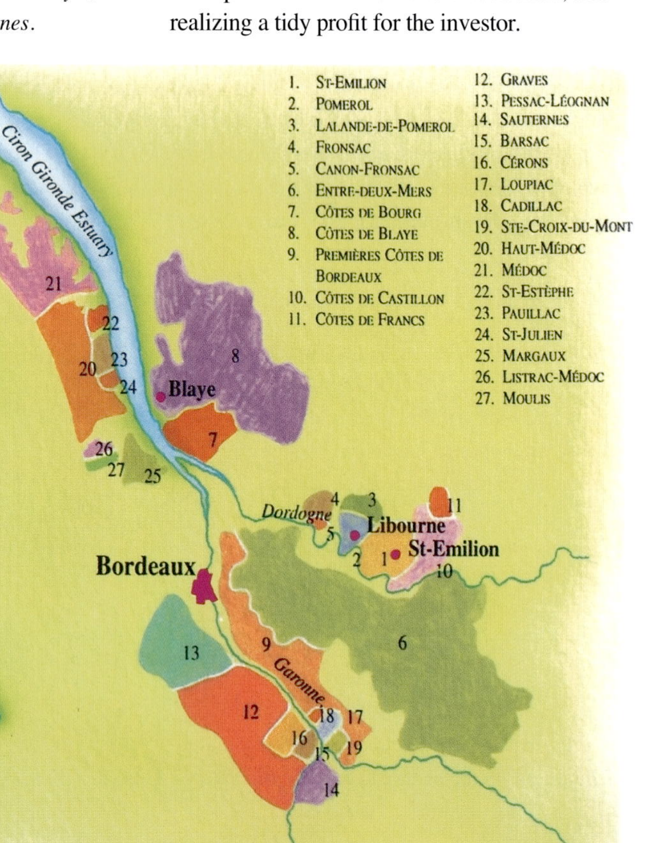

been looking to their laurels since the 1990s, reducing overall production in the region, and even – *quelle horreur!* – studying the Cabernet and Merlot wines of their non-European rivals to see what they might do better.

The Bordeaux classification formulated for the Paris Exhibition of 1855 is a five-tier hierarchy based on the commercial value of the properties listed at the time. It covers only the Haut-Médoc, plus Château Haut-Brion in the Graves. The Graves itself was classified in the 1950s, along with St-Emilion, but Pomerol has never been classified.

To a surprising degree, much of the classification holds good, but properties change hands, expand into new vineyard land, employ new winemakers, and find their standards inevitably fluctuating with the vagaries of successive vintages.

That leaves the individual consumer in the happy position of offering his or her own periodic reassessments. I've rated the properties in the 1855 table below in accordance with the general consensus as to their relative performances over the past 40 years, a period that ranges from difficult vintages like 1984, 1991 and 2002 to the out-and-out stunners like 1982, 1990, 2000, 2005, 2010 and 2016.

## 1855 AND ALL THAT

(Appellation shown in brackets – P = Pauillac, M = Margaux, P-L = Pessac-Léognan, *formerly Graves,* S-J = St-Julien, S-E = St-Estèphe, H-M = Haut-Médoc)

**First Growth/1er cru**

Lafite-Rothschild (P) ***** Margaux (M) ***** Latour (P) ***** Haut-Brion (P-L) ***** Mouton-Rothschild (P) *****

**Second Growth/2ème cru**

Rauzan-Ségla, *formerly Rausan-Ségla* (M) **** Rauzan-Gassies (M) ** Léoville-Las Cases (S-J) ***** Léoville-Poyferré (S-J) **** Léoville-Barton (S-J) **** Durfort-Vivens (M) *** Lascombes (M) *** Brane-Cantenac (M) *** Pichon-Longueville, *formerly Pichon-Longueville Baron* (P) ***** Pichon-Longueville Comtesse de Lalande, *formerly Pichon-Lalande* (P) ***** Ducru-Beaucaillou (S-J) **** Cos d'Estournel (S-E) ***** Montrose (S-E) **** Gruaud-Larose (S-J) ****

**Third Growth/3ème cru**

Kirwan (M) *** d'Issan (M) *** Lagrange (S-J) **** Langoa-Barton (S-J) ****

Giscours (M)*** Malescot St-Exupéry (M) *** Boyd-Cantenac (M) *** Cantenac-Brown (M) *** Palmer (M) **** La Lagune (H-M) **** Desmirail (M) *** Calon-Ségur (S-E) **** Ferrière, *not generally available outside France* (M) ** Marquis d'Alesme Becker (M) **

**Fourth Growth/4ème cru**

St-Pierre (S-J) *** Talbot (S-J) *** Branaire-Ducru (S-J) *** Duhart-Milon-Rothschild (P) *** Pouget (M) ** La Tour-Carnet (H-M) ** Lafon-Rochet (S-E) *** Beychevelle (S-J) **** Prieuré-Lichine (M) *** Marquis-de-Terme (M) ***

**Fifth Growth/5ème cru**

Pontet-Canet (P) *** Batailley (P) *** Haut-Batailley (P) *** Grand-Puy-Lacoste (P) **** Grand-Puy-Ducasse (P) *** Lynch-Bages (P) ***** Lynch-Moussas (P) * Dauzac (M) * d'Armailhac, *formerly Mouton-Baronne-Philippe* (P) *** du Tertre (M) *** Haut-Bages-Libéral (P) *** Pédesclaux (P) ** Belgrave (H-M) *** de Camensac (H-M) ** Cos-Labory (S-E) *** Clerc-Milon (P) *** Croizet-Bages (P) * Cantemerle (H-M) ***

*The hard way of transporting a barrel through the extensive* chai, *or cellar, of first-growth Château Margaux (above).*

*Ripe Cabernet Sauvignon grapes being harvested for first-growth Château Latour in Pauillac (below).*

## GRAVES, ST-EMILION AND POMEROL

**Graves** This extensive sub-region, lying mostly south of the city of Bordeaux on the west bank of the river Garonne, is named after the gravelly soils that predominate there. Many tasters insist that there is a gravelly, earthy taste in the red wines themselves, and certainly they tend to come clothed in much more austere garb than the lavish finery of the Médoc wines. However, they are quite as capable of ageing, notwithstanding the fact that many producers are attempting to make a more easy-going, early-drinking style of red.

The Graves was classified in 1959, for both red and dry white wines (whereas 1855 applies only to reds). A château is either *cru classé* or it isn't; it's as simple as that. A superior swathe of land in the north of the district was separately demarcated as Pessac-Léognan in 1987, all of the classed growths of 1959 falling within that appellation. (Haut-Brion is the only property whose red also falls within the 1855 classification.) For the reds, they are:

Bouscaut ** Haut-Bailly **** Carbonnieux *** Domaine de Chevalier ***** de Fieuzal *** d'Olivier ** Malartic-Lagravière *** La Tour-Martillac ** Smith-Haut-Lafitte *** Haut-Brion ***** La Mission-Haut-Brion **** Pape-Clément **** La Tour-Haut-Brion ***

**St-Emilion** Situated on the right bank of the river Dordogne, this is predominantly Merlot country – although not quite to the same degree as Pomerol. The reds are supplemented by the lighter, grassier Cabernet Franc, with only a dash of Cabernet Sauvignon. The style is consequently leaner than in the Médoc, but sharpened by that Cabernet Franc. Ordinary St-Emilion is not that distinguished – many producers have been guilty of over-production – but the top names are worth the premium.

The classification of St-Emilion's reds was drawn up in 1955, but is healthily subject to revision every decade. At the humblest level, Grand Cru is so inclusive as to be all but meaningless. A step up is Grand Cru Classé with around five dozen properties (among which Canon-la-Gaffelière and Clos de l'Oratoire stand out as worthy of ****), and at the top is Premier Grand Cru Classé, subdivided rather prosaically into A and B. Class A consists of just two properties:

Ausone **** Cheval Blanc *****

As of 2006, Class B contains 13:

Angélus **** Beau-Séjour Bécot **** Beauséjour (Duffau-Lagarrosse) **** Bélair-Monange **** Canon ***** Figeac **** Clos Fourtet *** La Gaffelière **** Magdeleine **** Pavie **** Pavie-Macquin **** Troplong-Mondot **** Trottevieille ***

**Pomerol** Immediately to the north of
St-Emilion, and the only one of the top
Bordeaux districts never to have been classified,
Pomerol's reds are as close to varietal Merlot
as Bordeaux gets. Many have simply the merest
seasoning of Cabernet Franc to add an edge
of ageworthy sternness to what is essentially
pure velvet-soft opulence, the sweetness of
prunes coated in dark chocolate, leading to
a gorgeously creamy finish.

Anybody setting out to play the Pomerol
classification parlour-game for themselves
would have to start out with the hyper-
expensive Pétrus ***** at the top, probably
joined by Lafleur ***** and Le Pin *****.
In the next rank (****) would come Bon
Pasteur, Certan de May, Clinet, La Conseillante,
La Croix de Gay, L'Eglise-Clinet, L'Evangile,
Le Fleur de Gay, La Fleur-Pétrus, Le Gay,
Latour à Pomerol, Petit-Village, Trotanoy
and Vieux-Château-Certan.

## CRUS BOURGEOIS/PETITS CHATEAUX/ SECOND WINES

**Crus Bourgeois** Immediately below the five
layers of Médoc *crus classés* are a group of
wines known, in an echo of 18th-century
social stratification, as the *crus bourgeois*.
For the purposes of this category, not only the
Haut-Médoc but also the bottom-line Médoc
area to the north of St-Estèphe comes into
consideration. Many of these properties would
now be included in any redraft of the 1855
classification, including a fair handful from
the less well-known commune of Moulis.

Reliably excellent wines have been produced
in recent years by the following (****):
d'Angludet (M), Chasse-Spleen (Moulis),
la Gurgue (M), Haut-Marbuzet (S-E), Gressier-
Grand-Poujeaux (Moulis), Labégorce-Zédé
(M), Lanessan (H-M), Maucaillou (Moulis),
Meyney (S-E), Monbrison (M), de Pez (S-E),
Potensac (Médoc), Poujeaux (Moulis) and
Sociando-Mallet (H-M).

Next best (***) would be: Patache d'Aux
(Médoc), Ramage-la-Batisse (H-M), Sénéjac
(H-M), la Tour-de-By (Médoc) and la Tour-du-
Haut-Moulin (H-M).

**Petits châteaux and other districts** Other
important quality districts (with good
unclassified properties known as *petits
châteaux*) are Lalande-de-Pomerol, adjoining
Pomerol to the northeast (Bel-Air, Bertineau
St-Vincent), Fronsac and Canon-Fronsac to the

west of Pomerol (Dalem, Mazeris, La Truffière)
and the various satellite villages to the northeast
of St-Emilion, such as Lussac (Lyonnat),
Puisseguin and St-Georges. Discovering the
best of these lesser-known properties has made
for much happy exploration in recent years.

The huge area of the Entre-deux-Mers
between the Garonne and Dordogne rivers
tends to produce pretty rough-and-ready reds
under the most basic appelations, Bordeaux and
Bordeaux Supérieur. On the right bank of the
Gironde, directly opposite the *cru classé*

*Many of the châteaux of
Bordeaux have idiosyncratic
architectural features, such
as the pointed turret (above)
after which Château la
Tour-de-By is named.*

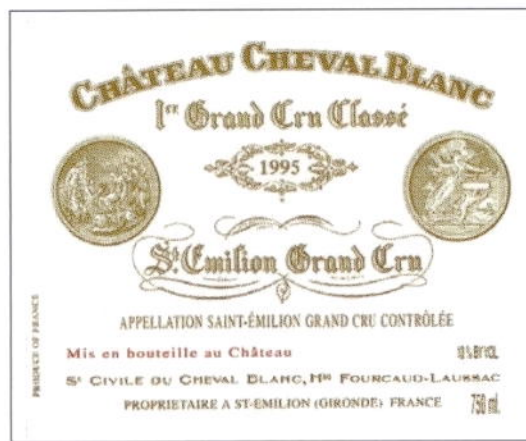

*Looking over the medieval rooftops of the City of St-Emilion (below) out towards the vineyards.*

enclaves of the Haut-Médoc, are the Côtes de Blaye and Côtes de Bourg areas. The best vineyards of the former are entitled to the designation Premières Côtes de Blaye, while the much smaller Bourg district is home to some exciting innovators (Civrac's wines have big, concentrated fruit and new oak). The long strip on the right bank of the Garonne, the Premières Côtes de Bordeaux, is responsible for some increasingly satisfying, firm-textured reds.

To the east of St-Emilion are two areas that are among the most unsung (and therefore good-value) sources of classy wine in the whole region: the Côtes de Castillon and Côtes de Francs. Cabernet Franc plays a significant role in the Merlot-based wines, making for some attractive lighter clarets, but there are also wines of impressive intensity from Pitray, d'Aiguilhe, Robin, Grand-Peyrou, Parenchère, Belcier and Moulin-Rouge in Castillon, and Puygueraud, La Prade, de Francs and Marsau in the Francs. Many of these wines will go the distance in the cellar.

**Second wines** When the prices of Bordeaux began seriously inflating in the 1980s, much attention came to be focused on the second wines of the principal châteaux. Most producers make a subsidiary wine to their main offering (the *grand vin*), to use grapes that were not thought quite good enough for the flagship wine, or came from vines that were still too young to yield thoroughly concentrated fruit.

A ready market emerged for those who may not have been able to afford the *crus classés*, but wanted to gain at least a partial glimpse of their style, and these can be highly rewarding.

The point to remember when considering buying a second wine is only to buy from the best vintages. Top châteaux may be able to make a silk purse out of the sow's ear of an off-vintage, and it should be correspondingly cheaper, so you don't need the second wine. In a super-ripe vintage like 2005, however, when the *grand vin* prices soar out of sight, the second wines represent an affordable alternative.

The following are regularly some of the best (with the main château name shown in brackets):

Les Forts de Latour (Latour), Carruades de Lafite (Lafite-Rothschild), Pavillon Rouge du Château Margaux (Margaux), Bahans Haut-Brion (Haut-Brion), Clos du Marquis (Léoville-Las Cases), Réserve de la Comtesse (Pichon-Longueville Comtesse de Lalande), Marbuzet (Cos d'Estournel), La Dame de Montrose (Montrose), Sarget de Gruaud-Larose (Gruaud-Larose), Lady Langoa (Langoa-Barton), Réserve du Général (Palmer), Haut-Bages-Avérous (Lynch-Bages), La Parde de Haut-Bailly (Haut-Bailly), Grangeneuve de Figeac (Figeac), La Gravette de Certan (Vieux-Château-Certan), La Petite Eglise (l'Eglise-Clinet).

## VINTAGE GUIDE

Below is a broad overview of the most recent vintages, as represented by the better wines of each year, plus some earlier stars.

*2024* *** A patchy vintage of generally lighter wines.

*2023* **** Encouraging quality from the better estates. A vintage that will mature relatively quickly.

*2022* ***** Exciting wines with great opulence and expressive fruit. One to keep.

*2021* *** Generally rather uninspiring.

*2020* **** One of the few good things to come out of the pandemic year. Wines of exemplary balance and charm.

*2019* **** Very attractive, beautifully balanced wines for the long haul.

*2018* ***** Glorious. Probably the best vintage of the decade. Big but graceful wines across the board.

*2017* *** Lighter wines, often lacking the structure to go the distance.

*2016* ***** Ripe, seductive, deeply eloquent clarets for cellaring.

*2015* **** Convincing year for solidly built, sturdy wines.

*2014* **** Classic earthy Bordeaux, especially from the Haut-Médoc.

*2013* ** Oh dear, no.

*2012* *** Only the very best estates made silk purses for 2012.

*2011* ** See 2013.

*2010* ***** Excellent, scintillating, age-worthy wines that would grace any cellar or table.

*2009* ***** The new century's first decade closed with an absolute stunner. Levels of ripeness, depth and concentration are superb, and the overall balance is well-nigh flawless. Investors (and drinkers too), take note.

*2008* *** A difficult growing season with much late picking resulted in a generally patchy picture. Not a classic.

*2007* *** Not dissimilar to 2008, with a poor summer undermining the chances of greatness. Gently priced wines should provide good earlyish drinking.

*2006* **** Not great for the Merlot wines of the right bank, but Cabernet-based Médoc is generally looking good.

*2005* ***** A beautiful vintage of ripe, intense, well-balanced wines that will go the distance for those prepared to keep them.

*2004* **** Late picking resulted in big, tannic wines with plenty of alcohol.

*2003* ***** The heatwave summer produced a humdinger of a vintage. Not one for purists, maybe, with its colossal alcohol and fruit-preserve intensity, but definitely one for the cellar.

*2002* *** A good showing on the left bank, but much of the right bank failed to ripen well.

*2001* **** Harvest rains spoiled the chances of some, but this vintage has turned out better than expected, especially in St-Emilion.

*2000* ***** A fabulous vintage that has already passed into legend.

*1999* ** Very dull (although Mouton is good).

*1998* *** Pretty good, though not outstanding.

*1997* ** A little better than feared, but basically mediocre.

*1996* **** Some classic, austere, ageworthy wines in the Médoc.

*1995* **** A very ripe, attractive year, particularly for Cabernet.

*1990* ***** Brilliant across the board, with Pomerol the best.

*1989* **** Classic claret vintage of well-balanced wines that showed their charms early.

*1988* **** Deeply classical wines with intensely ripe fruit and solid structure.

Pick of the older vintages: *1986* ****
*1983* ****   *1982* *****   *1978* ****
*1970* ****   *1966* ****   *1961* *****
*1959* ****   *1955* ****   *1953* ****   *1949* ****
*1947* ****   *1945* ****   *1970* ****
*1955* ****   *1953* ****   *1949* ****   *1947* ****
*1945* *****

*Despite its venerable history, Domaine de Chevalier, one of the Graves crus classés, has always kept abreast of the times, as witness its state-of-the-art cellars at Pessac-Léognan (above).*

# BORDEAUX–DRY WHITE/ROSÉ

*The dry white wines of Bordeaux have enjoyed a remarkable renaissance in recent years, shaking off their image of being poorly made and dull, and emerging with the kinds of flavours normally only found in America's finest.*

***BORDEAUX–DRY WHITE/ROSÉ***

*GRAPES: Sémillon, Sauvignon Blanc, Muscadelle*

***BORDEAUX-ROSÉ***

*GRAPES: Cabernet Sauvignon, Merlot, Carmenère, Cabernet Franc, Malbec, Petit Verdot*

THE PAST 30 YEARS have seen a winemaking upheaval in the dry whites of Bordeaux, and one that was sorely overdue. Certain properties, such as Domaine de Chevalier, have always been highly valued for their white wines, and one of the 1855 *crus classés*, Haut-Brion, showed itself as adept at white as at red. The generality, though, for a long time was a rather aimless, unfocused style in the middle rank, and a tidal wave of fruitless, stale-tasting rubbish at the bottom end. These were the least impressive dry whites produced in any of France's classic regions.

The upturn came about via a handful of winemakers – Denis Dubourdieu, André Lurton and Peter Vinding-Diers among them – who began, in the early 1980s, to incorporate a more modern approach to white wine. Better grape selection during harvest, fermenting at controlled temperatures in stainless steel, and considered experimentation with oak-ageing to add an extra dimension to the wines' flavours all paid handsome dividends.

Most importantly of all, the innovators took a long hard look at their grape varieties. Much of the dullness of the bad old days came from overcropped Sémillon being used as a workhorse grape. Some of the most interesting wines have been made from unblended Sauvignon Blanc, but there are exemplary wines now that use both varieties in impressive balance. Look to Pessac-Léognan, and the wider

Graves area, for the best, but even the sprawling Entre-Deux-Mers is brushing up its act these days, and nobody saw that coming.

Occasionally, the wines can taste a little too nervy to me, especially in their youth, and there is often a bit too much oak to suit them. Otherwise, it's all good. A pronounced petrolly pungency characterizes some of the top wines, and the fruit flavours on them, which can mix tropical melon with the apple and lemon scents of Sauvignon, can be astonishing.

Only the Graves has a classification for dry whites, drawn up in 1959. As with its red wines, all of the properties are in Pessac-Léognan, but there are only nine of them:

Bouscaut ** Carbonnieux *** Domaine de Chevalier ***** Couhins ** Couhins-Lurton **** Latour-Martillac **** Laville Haut-Brion ***** Malartic-Lagravière *** Olivier ***

Unclassified fine dry whites from the Graves include: Haut-Brion ***** de Fieuzal ***** Pape-Clement **** Clos Floridène **** La Louvière **** Tour Léognan ****

In the Entre-deux-Mers, the best property without a doubt is Thieuley (****). Elsewhere, the catchall of Bordeaux Blanc applies, and quality is still all over the place, but notably fresh, zippy white is made at de Parenchère (***). Some branded wines, blended from grapes sourced throughout the region, can be fresh and innocent enough (look for Dourthe or Yvon Mau on the label).

Down in the Sauternes region, the top sweet wine producers offer dry whites made from grapes not suitable for Sauternes itself, bottled as Bordeaux Blanc but unofficially thought of as dry Sauternes. Named after the initial letter of the château, they include R (Rieussec), G (Guiraud) and – best of all – Y (Yquem), majestically austere wines with commanding presence on the palate.

The rosé wines of Bordeaux are also much improved, as well they might be since both Cabernet Sauvignon and Merlot make good pink wine. There is more body and riper fruit on them than a lot of rosés from further north. Look out for Méaume, de Bel, de Sours, Clos Fourtet and Roc de Minvielle.

## VINTAGE GUIDE

The simpler whites that use a high percentage of Sauvignon are best drunk on release. The top *crus classés* are intended for longer ageing. The fact that there hasn't been an out-and-out disaster in Bordeaux's dry white wines in any of the most recent years is testament to the advanced state of viticultural know-how and the quality-conscious approach among the region's growers. This represents a huge advance on what things looked like as recently as the 1990s.

*2024* **** Fresh fruit and invigorating acidity make this a particularly appealing prospect.

*2023* **** A lengthy harvest produced wines with good ripeness and lovely fruit.

*2022* **** A steaming-hot vintage, but the best growers retained enough fresh acidity in the wines to equip them for ageing.

*2021* ***** Outstanding wines across the region, despite an assortment of challenges during the growing season.

*2020* ***** The pandemic year saw another hot summer, but the wines have turned out to be very impressively balanced, with plenty of ageing potential.

*2019* **** Another finely honed vintage, now displaying complex maturity.

*An ancient windmill presides over vineyards at Gornac, in the Entre-deux-Mers (above).*

*The gently sloping vineyards of Château Benauge on the border between the Entre-deux-Mers and Premières Côtes de Bordeaux regions (left). Many of the dry whites made in these regions are now much improved.*

# BORDEAUX–SWEET WINE

*Its lofty reputation founded on botrytis, a fungal disease that attacks ripened grapes in late summer and early autumn, the long-lived and intensely rich sweet wine of Bordeaux is the most celebrated of its kind in the world.*

***BORDEAUX–SWEET WHITE***

*GRAPES: Sémillon, Sauvignon Blanc, Muscadelle*

*The Sauternes region of Bordeaux contains some of the most valuable land in the world for producing sweet wines, none more so than at Château d'Yquem (below).*

THE FINEST DESSERT wines in the world, whether in Bordeaux or elsewhere, are made from grapes infected by a strain of fungus called *Botrytis cinerea*, widely known as noble rot. Rot normally develops on grapes if the weather turns wet towards harvest-time. This grey rot is the decidedly ignoble sort and, particularly with red grapes, can torpedo any hopes of making great wines. Botrytis, on the other hand, occurs in damp rather than drenching conditions.

Because of its proximity to the Atlantic Ocean, Bordeaux experiences increasingly humid, misty mornings as the autumn comes on, relieved by gentle sunshine during the day. This delicate process of dampening and drying off is the ideal climatic pattern for the encouragement of botrytis on Sémillon grapes. As the berries shrivel on the vine, they lose moisture, meaning that their natural sugars become densely concentrated.

The most celebrated sweet wines on earth come from the southern Bordeaux communes of Sauternes and Barsac. Although the technique was almost certainly discovered in Germany – by accident, of course, like many of the best inventions – it is here that it has been put to the most highly reputed use. Not every vintage produces the right conditions, and the more quality-conscious châteaux simply don't bother making a wine in the off-years.

Quality depends on making painstaking selections of only the most thoroughly rotted grapes. In many cases, proprietors have decided the only way of doing that is by individual hand-sorting, picking only those berries that are completely shrivelled, and leaving the others to moulder a little further on the vine being going through the vineyard again. Several such turns (or *tries* in French) may be necessary to make the most concentrated wines possible. That, together with the long maturation in oak casks that the wines are generally accorded, explains the drop-dead prices that classic Sauternes sells for. It is an immensely labour-intensive wine.

A group of five villages in the southern Graves famous for their botrytized wines – Sauternes, Barsac, Bommes, Preignac and Fargues – was included in the 1855 classification. Together, they now constitute the Sauternes appellation, although Barsac can carry its own appellation as well, if an individual property so chooses. (Just for good measure, it can also be AOP Sauternes-Barsac, if it wants the best of both worlds.)

At the top of the classification, and with a category to itself, rather like the duck-billed platypus, is the legendary Château d'Yquem, for many the supreme achievement in botrytized wine. Fantastically expensive and fabulously rich, its best vintages can last for over a century.

**Grand first growth/1er grand cru**
Yquem *****
**First growth/1er cru**
La Tour Blanche ****   Lafaurie-Peyraguey ****
Clos Haut-Peyraguey **   Rayne-Vigneau ***
Suduiraut ****   Coutet ****   Climens *****
Guiraud ****   Rieussec *****   Rabaud-Promis
***   Sigalas-Rabaud ***
**Second growth/2ème cru**
de Myrat ****, *began replanting in 1988 after
coming close to total extinction*   Doisy-Daëne
***   Doisy-Dubroca ****   Doisy-Védrines
***   d'Arche **   Filhot ***   Broustet ***
Nairac **   Caillou ***   Suau **   de Malle ***
Romer-du-Hayot **   Lamothe-Despujols *
Lamothe-Guignard ***

Other good properties in Sauternes-Barsac,
but outside the classification, are:
Raymond-Lafon ****   Gilette ****
Bastor-Lamontagne ***

In the immediate vicinity of Sauternes are
four less well-known AOPs for botrytis-affected
wines. When the vintage is propitious, they
can produce wines that show something of the
flavours of their more exalted neighbours, while
lacking those final layers of richness that make
Sauternes so fabled. Given that, they are much
more humanely priced. They are Cérons,
Loupiac, Cadillac and Ste-Croix-du-Mont.
Of these, all but Cérons, to the northwest
of Barsac, are on the opposite bank of the
river Garonne to Sauternes. Best properties
are Cérons and Archambeau in Cérons, and
Loupiac-Gaudiet in Loupiac.

Sweet wines from the Premières Côtes de
Bordeaux region, along the eastern side of the
Garonne, are not invariably fully botrytized.
One exception that has provided excellent value
for money in recent years is de Berbec.

## VINTAGE GUIDE

If a sweet white Bordeaux has been
conscientiously made, it can easily last a good
20–30 years, and the very top ones are virtually
indestructible. They turn from rich yellow to
burnished orange, and then the distinguished
deep brown of dark sherry, as they age, and
go on selling for phenomenal sums.
*2015* ***** Exceptional Sauternes with all the
elements pulling together – aromatic beauty,
nippy acidity and lashings of honeyed richness.
*2011* **** Highly attractive sweet wines with
very focused fruit and good acids.
*2010* **** Gentler style. Not as flashy as some

vintages, but still very impressive. They will be
ready for drinking a little earlier than the above
two years.
*2009* ***** Abundant botrytis from late
September on produced wines of staggering
richness, balanced by exemplary acidity.
As close to perfection as sweet wine gets.
*2007* **** Superb Sauternes. Colossal extract
and deep honeyed richness, matched by fresh
acidity. Needs keeping for ages yet.
*2003* ***** A sensational vintage of fully rotted
wines with long lives ahead of them.
*2002* **** Sandwiched between two legends,
but full of elegance.
*2001* ***** Brilliant, complex, hauntingly
beautiful wines. The best since 1990.
*1990* ***** Virtual perfection. Unbelievable
levels of concentration and intensity.
PICK OF THE OLDER VINTAGES: *1989* ****
*1988* ****   *1986* ****   *1983* ****   *1976* ****
*1967* *****   *1959* *****   *1945* *****   *1937*
*****   *1929* *****   *1921* *****   *1900* *****

*Autumn vines resplendent
beneath a clear blue sky at
Château Rieussec (above),
one of the best first-growth
properties in Sauternes.*

# LOIRE

*The river Loire flows through five wine-producing areas, from the Pays Nantais in the west, far inland to Sancerre in the east, each of them boasting very different styles of wine, and offering much good value along the way.*

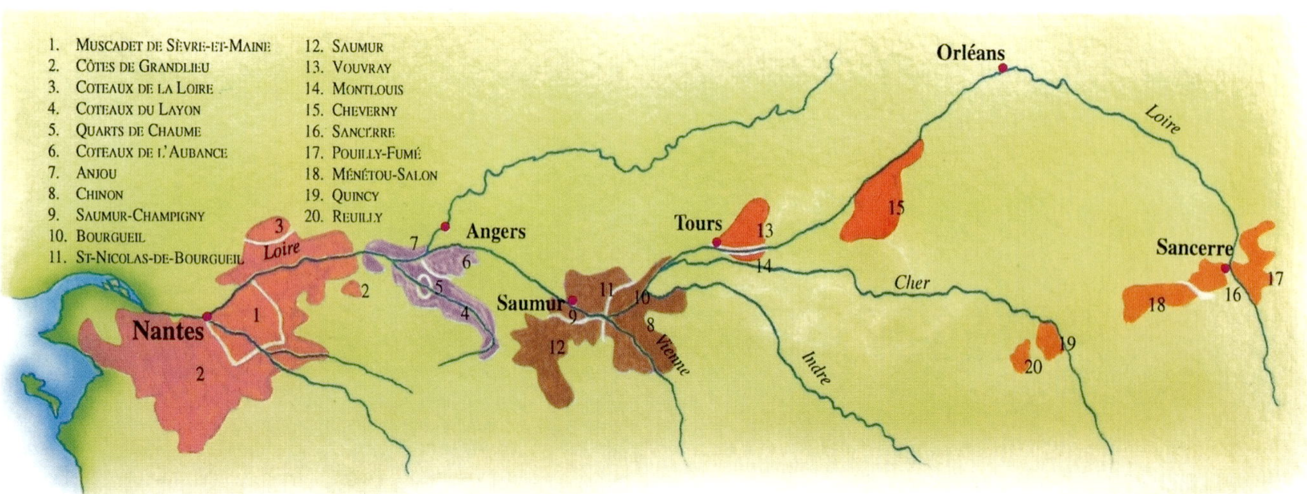

*Château de Nozet (above) set in the upper Loire, where Pouilly-Fumé is produced.*

***PAYS NANTAIS***
*GRAPES: Melon de Bourgogne (Muscadet), Folle Blanche (Gros Plant).*

*The five wine regions of the Loire valley (below) lie along the banks of the river Loire.*

THE LOIRE VALLEY in northern France is a hugely diverse region, encompassing a very broad range of wine styles. Crisp dry whites are usually seen as its strongest suit, but there are medium-dry and lusciously sweet whites, a host of refreshing light reds and rosés, and some of the better sparkling wines made outside Champagne. The Loire is the nation's longest river, rising in central France and disgorging into the Atlantic west of Nantes. To get a coherent view of it as a wine region, it makes sense to subdivide it into five areas, running from west to east.

## PAYS NANTAIS

**Muscadet** The main business of the area around the city of Nantes is Muscadet, which has by far the largest volume of production of any Loire AOP. Made from a single grape variety, Melon de Bourgogne, it is the epitome of a bone-dry, crisp, neutral-tasting white wine. The grape was once grown in Burgundy, as its name suggests, but was imported into Brittany in the early 18th century for its ability to survive frosts.

There are four appellations. Muscadet de Sèvre-et-Maine, in the centre of the region, makes about 75 per cent of all Muscadet, and is generally considered to produce the wines with the most character. Growers with land on the granite hills around St-Fiacre, or in the clay-based soils around Vallet, are good bets for the most interesting offerings. Muscadet Côtes de Grandlieu, centred on a large lake of that name, was demarcated in 1994, and contains a fair amount of sandy soil, which imparts its own aromatic personality to the wines.

The small, more northerly district of Muscadet des Coteaux de la Loire turns out a negligible quantity of undistinguished wine, and the rest is basic AOP Muscadet, not by and large worth dwelling on.

About half of all Muscadets include the words *sur lie* on the label. What this means is that the finished wine was left on its lees (the dead yeast cells left over from fermentation) for up to 12 months. Just as lees-ageing imparts a softer, creamier feel to champagne, so in Muscadet it adds a valuable dimension of textural complexity and some depth of flavour. Always choose a *sur lie* wine. Some producers mature their wines in oak, a high-risk technique for such a light wine, but there are successful examples.

At best, Muscadet has a taut, nervy, high-acid freshness, occasionally with a little fruit (tart green apple, grapefruit) and sometimes a wisp of anise. The bulk-produced stuff smells and tastes of nothing whatsoever. The better ones, believe it or not, will age, taking on a cabbagey, but not unattractive, secondary aroma, while the youthful acidity softens out.

PRODUCERS: Sauvion, Luneau-Papin, Métaireau, Dom. de l'Ecu, Ch. de la Ragotière, Landron.
**Gros Plant du Pays Nantais** The archetypal French local wine, much beloved of the Nantais themselves, but hardly at all exported. Its grape, Folle Blanche, is mostly grown elsewhere for brandy distillation, but appears here in vinified form. Expect highly pronounced (oh all right then, excruciating) levels of acidity in a dead-neutral, squeaky-clean style. Served bone-chillingly cold with the local shellfish, it's a zinger. Look for a *sur lie* wine made by one of the Muscadet growers, such as the reliably good Guy Bossard at Dom. de l'Ecu.

## ANJOU

The area south of Angers is the start of Chenin Blanc country, and it's here that some of the great sweet wines of the Loire are made. Chenin submits to botrytis with obliging regularity in these districts, producing finely balanced dessert wines, full of mouth-coating marmalade flavours, but thrown into a state of nervous excitement by a lemony streak of acidity.
**Coteaux du Layon** The largest AOP for sweet wines regularly produces liquorous but refreshing examples of rotted Chenin. Even in years when there is a lower concentration of botrytis, and the resulting wines are a little less intense, these are generally pretty reliable. Best are labelled Sélection de Grains Nobles. Within the Coteaux du Layon are three separately demarcated AOPs: **Bonnezeaux** to the east, and **Chaume Premier Cru** to the northwest. Within the latter, the enclave of **Quarts de Chaume** can justly be considered a Grand Cru wine, mostly made only when botrytis is sufficiently widespread that only fully rotted grapes need be used. These are exquisitely intense sweet Chenin, with all the majesty of top-flight Sauternes.
PRODUCERS: Ch. de Breuil, Dom. de la Soucherie, Baumard, Ch. Pierre-Bise, Delesvaux, Ogereau.
**Coteaux de l'Aubance** Northeast of Chaume, this larger AOP produces generally lighter, often non-botrytized sweet wines, but when rot does set in, they may be labelled Sélection de Grains Nobles.
**Savennières** The best dry white of Anjou is a long-lived, memorably intense Chenin Blanc, brittle in youth, full of mineral purity, but ageing into a stately maturity in the best vintages. They need at least seven or eight

years. Within the appellation are a pair of super-fine enclaves with their own AOPs, **La Roche-aux-Moines** (look for the wines of Soulez) and **La Coulée-de-Serrant**, wholly owned by Nicolas Joly. The latter was one of the pioneers of biodynamic winemaking in France, and the wines are shatteringly pure and concentrated.
OTHER PRODUCERS: Baumard, Pierre-Bise, Ch. d'Epire, Dom. du Closel.
**Anjou Blanc Sec** The bottom-line AOP for everyday dry white. It is allowed to mix in some Chardonnay and/or Sauvignon with the Chenin, but some opulent straight Chenin is produced in the South African style by fermenting in oak, as at Dom. de Bablut.
**Anjou-Villages** The better village sites make passable reds from Cabernets Sauvignon and Franc. **Anjou-Villages Brissac** has its own appellation for these in the Aubance.
**Anjou Rouge** Overlapping into Saumur, these are allowed to use the Beaujolais grape Gamay as well as the Cabernet duo. The Gamays can be charming enough.
**Cabernet d'Anjou** The best of the AOPs for the considerable quantities of rosé made in the Loire, these can be made from both Cabernets, and tend to be acerbically dry, but with good blackcurrant fruit.
**Rosé d'Anjou** Made primarily from a local grape, Groslot, often in a demi-sec style, these used to be bog-standard rosés, but some producers (Ch. de Fesles) are now making more attractive, summer-fruited wines to capitalize on the rosé boom. Worth a punt.

*Poplar trees break the skyline in vineyards near Vallet (above), Muscadet de Sèvre-et-Maine.*

***ANJOU***
*GRAPE: Chenin Blanc (whites)*

*Harvesting Muscadet grapes at Clisson (above), in the Sèvre-et-Maine AOP.*

*The soaring turrets of Château Saumur (above), overlooking the Loire in Saumur.*

***SAUMUR***

*GRAPES: Cabernet Franc (reds); Chenin Blanc (whites)*

***SPARKLING SAUMUR***

*GRAPES: Chenin Blanc, Chardonnay, Sauvignon Blanc*

***TOURAINE***

*GRAPES: Cabernet Franc, Gamay (reds); Chenin Blanc, Sauvignon Blanc, Chardonnay, Romorantin (whites)*

## SAUMUR

Two types of wine are important in Saumur – reds and sparklers. This district and Touraine make a speciality of the Cabernet Franc grape, one of the lesser players in red Bordeaux, in the principal red AOPs. In warm vintages, these wines have pleasant blackcurranty fruit, a lightish feel in the mouth (although by no means as light as, say, Beaujolais), and gentle tannins. They can mature agreeably for several years. In less ripe years, though, they can be pretty depressing, full of bitter green tannin and hard acid.

**Saumur-Champigny** Saumur's best reds are attractive, juicy-fruited wines, their upfront flavours of summer berries underpinned by considerable structure. In the good years, they are worth ageing.

PRODUCERS: Dom. des Roches Neuves, Ch. du Hureau, Ch. de Villeneuve, Clos Rougeard.

**Saumur** The less distinguished area around Saumur-Champigny. Reds are drier and more astringent, but occasionally summer-ripe (Filliatreau's are good). One area, **Saumur Puy-Notre-Dame**, received its own AOP for reds in 2006. Whites are mainly Chenin with up to 20 per cent Chardonnay to smooth them (look for Les Andides).

**Coteaux de Saumur** Sweet Chenin wines made in the better years.

**Cabernet de Saumur** Simple, grassy rosés.

**Saumur Mousseux** Sparkling Saumur is made by the same method as champagne, and is mainly Chenin Blanc, with occasional additions of softening Chardonnay. From good producers, such as Gratien & Meyer (who also make a sparkling rosé from Cabernet Franc), or Bouvet-Ladubay, they have a tart but refreshing crispness.

## TOURAINE

In the west of Touraine, the Loire's most fascinating, complex reds are made from Cabernet Franc in three celebrated appellations.

**Chinon** The best of the three for structure, balance and ageability, Chinon has been famed ever since the time of Rabelais. Up to 10 per cent Cabernet Sauvignon is permitted. Appealing, complex aromas of raspberries and anise, with underlying woody notes.

PRODUCERS: Baudry, Couly-Dutheil, Druet.

**Bourgueil** Rapidly improving from a rough-and-ready past, these now have good red fruit along with their earthiness.

PRODUCERS: Druet, Dom. de la Butte, Audebert.

**St-Nicolas-de-Bourgueil** An enclave within Bourgueil, the wines are similar in style, ageworthy in the ripe years, with perhaps deeper, plummier fruit.

PRODUCERS: Pavillon du Grand Clos, Taluau. Chenin continues its sway into the area east of Tours, where its principal stamping-ground is one of the Loire's world-famous wines.

**Vouvray** The AOP covers almost every stylistic manifestation that white wine can adopt – dry, medium-dry, semi-sweet, botrytized and sparkling. Despite being very vintage-sensitive, Vouvray is capable of making some of the most appetizing Chenin wines in all the Loire. Labelling is more precise than it used to be, ranging through Sec (dry), Demi-Sec (medium-dry), Moelleux (sweet) and Sélection (noble-rotted). Dry wines are nutty, honeyish but austere at the same time, while the demi-sec is peachier, gently sugared but beautifully balanced. Moelleux have the unctuousness of fruit syrups, while the rotted wines are all spangling, marmaladey intensity. Even the dry wines benefit from keeping.

PRODUCERS: Champalou, Dom. des Aubuisières, Clos Naudin, Pichot, Dom. de la Fontainerie. Huët makes by far the best Vouvray fizz, a wine as deeply, yeastily rich and complex as good champagne.

**Montlouis** To the south of Vouvray, on the other side of the river. Chenin wines in the same repertoire of styles as its more famous neighbour, but with less finesse.

**Cheverny** In northeastern Touraine, Cheverny whites may use Chardonnay, Sauvignon or Chenin, but there is also a separate AOP – **Cour Cheverny** – for wines made from residual plantings of a high-acid local grape, Romarantin. The crisp-edged Cheverny reds may use Cabernet Franc, Gamay or Pinot Noir. There is also some sparkling wine with bite.

**Touraine** The regional AOP is for other reds and whites, usually labelled with the variety. Gamay reds are pleasantly light, those made from the Cabernets have a little more stuffing. Sauvignon whites can be splashed with glorious gooseberry fruit.

## UPPER LOIRE

Here, at the eastern end of the Loire, in almost the dead centre of France, Sauvignon Blanc comes into its own for some of the most fashionable of all dry whites.

**Sancerre** On the left bank, the name that has come to be the reference-point for Sauvignon the world over. They can be intriguing wines indeed, full of intense green flavours of apple, gooseberry, nettles, asparagus and parsley, as well as wisps of beguiling smoke. Best drunk within two years of the vintage. There are also reds and rosés here, made from Pinot Noir, wines that I still struggle to see the point of even in the ripest vintages. The reds are typically very thin and grassy, the rosés barely more than a mouthful of fresh air.
PRODUCERS: Bourgeois, Vacheron, Cotat, Mellot, Pinard, Vatan, Gitton, Bailly-Reverdy.

**Pouilly-Fumé** Facing Sancerre on the right bank of the Loire, Pouilly's wines are made in an almost identical style, perhaps emphasizing that smokiness (as befits the name) a little more in the very best. Some of the most exciting are grown on a type of flint soil called Silex (look for that word on the label), and emphasize stark minerality rather than fruit. The very best are thinner on the ground than they ought to be, given the prices. For the time being, Sancerre is usually a safer bet.
PRODUCERS: Bourgeois, Ch. de Tracy, de Ladoucette, Chatelain.

**Menetou-Salon** West of Sancerre, this AOP offers great crunchy Sauvignon with as much class as decent Sancerre from the best.

Also Pinot reds and rosés.
PRODUCERS: Pellé, Roger, Mellot.

**Reuilly** Across the river Cher, these are lighter, much less piquant Sauvignon whites, with Pinot Noir reds and (an oddity, this) gentle rosé from pink-skinned Pinot Gris.

**Quincy** Whites only from Sauvignon, the least distinguished of the Sancerre understudies, but still fresh and sappy when caught young.

**Pouilly-sur-Loire** A little-seen dry white made from the humdrum Chasselas grape.

## OTHER WINES

**Haut-Poitou** South of the Loire, but north of the ancient town of Poitiers, the Haut-Poitou produces good, simple Sauvignon and Chardonnay whites and Gamay reds.

**Crémant de Loire** Often impressive champagne-method fizz is made under this designation in Anjou and Touraine from Chenin and Chardonnay, with Cabernet Franc and Gamay for the rosés.

**Vin de Pays du Jardin de la France** Regional wines made outside the demarcated AOPs, or using non-permitted grapes (often fair quality Sauvignon, Chardonnay, Chenin or Gamay).

## VINTAGE GUIDE

Most dry whites are best drunk young. *2022* was good across the board, from Muscadet to the Upper Loire. The best recent vintages for reds have been *2022*, *2020* and *2015*. As with Sauternes, the Loire's best dessert wines last for aeons. Greatest recent vintages are *2020*, *2018* and *2016*.

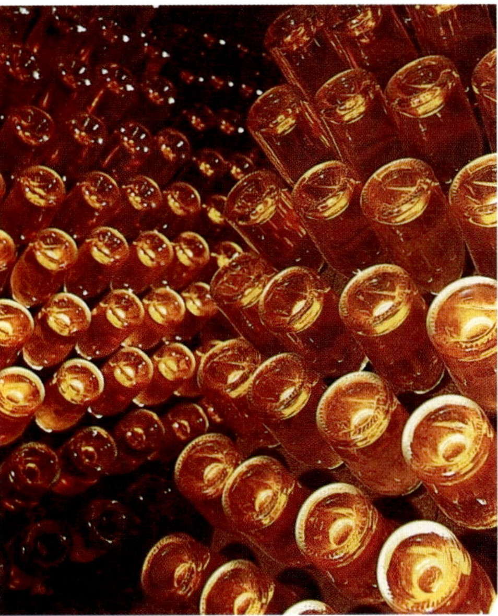

*Sparkling rosé, made from Cabernet Franc (left), resting in pupîtres at Gratien et Meyer, Saumur.*

***UPPER LOIRE***
*GRAPE: Sauvignon Blanc (whites)*
***SANCERRE, MENETOU-SALON AND REUILLY***
*GRAPES: Pinot Noir, Gamay (reds/rosés)*

# CHAMPAGNE

*The name alone conjures an image of celebration, of romance. The most northerly of France's fine wine regions, Champagne is the source of the world's greatest and most seductive sparkling wines.*

NO OTHER WINE in the world comes with quite such an inbuilt, ready-made aura as champagne. With its smart packaging, its world-famous names and the foaming luxuriance of its bubbles, it is the very image of celebration and of luxury. It marks the arrival of good news and the stroke of the new year; it crowns birthdays, anniversaries and weddings. It can alleviate the spirits of the downhearted, and arouse hope at the outset of a grand venture. As Sir Winston Churchill, one of its doughtiest admirers and consumers put it, 'In victory, we deserve it; in defeat, we need it.'

The wines that are produced in France's most northerly vineyard region have, for the better part of the past three centuries been the worldwide reference-point for sparkling wine. Indeed, with the exception of Spanish cava, virtually all other producers of fizz began by referring to their wines as champagne, ciampagna, champanski, or some such. Much tireless litigation has taken place in the Champagne region in recent years to prevent its name from so much as being whispered in the same breath as any other product. Thus there may be no English elderflower 'champagne', no perfumes of that name, not even any official reference to what was once known as the 'champagne method' on the labels of other bottles, even if they were produced in exactly the same way with the same grape varieties. Champagne is a region of northern France, and so it will inimitably stay on pain of litigation.

While consumers go on innocently referring to all sparkling wines as 'champagne', the efforts of the *champenois* to protect their brand are understandable. If an appellation system is to mean anything, it has to define the geographical origin in which a wine may be produced. (An anomaly of the regulations, ironically, is that Champagne is the only AOP that doesn't have to state itself on the label, many producers settling for simply having the C-word in suitably prominent lettering all over it.)

One of the problems that comes with having such an exalted image, though, is that your product is much more hawkishly scrutinized than its humbler competitors are. And

*The four vineyard areas of the Champagne region (below), with the warmer Aube valley tucked away to the south.*

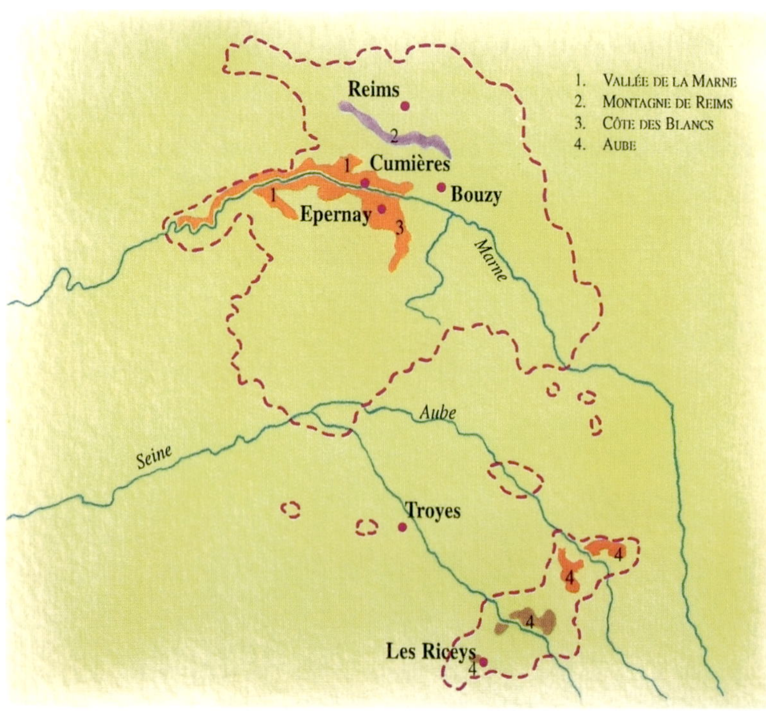

champagne, more than any other French wine, periodically finds itself at the centre of hot political controversy. Most of that controversy in the past 30 years or so has turned on quality, and who has the right to drink champagne.

With the coming of prosperity after the second world war, champagne began very gradually to trickle down the social scale. The industry lost its way somewhat in the 1980s, when consumption in the UK (its premier market) reached unprecedented levels to coincide with a transient economic boom. Some members of the CIVC, its controlling body, felt that the wine was in danger of losing its aura of elite unaffordability. A more or less explicit attempt to ration consumption, using the sledgehammer of price inflation, was just beginning to work when the coming of severe recession did the job for them.

What was so galling about this was that there was suddenly an awful lot of poor champagne out there. After much publicly acrimonious debate, the introduction of a new quality charter in the 1990s set about restoring the region's reputation. An attempt to pretend that there might not be enough champagne to supply the millennium celebrations at the end of 1999 was soon enough rumbled, but contributed to the malign impression that whatever official pronouncements emerge from the regional committee are worth taking with a pinch of salt.

*Barrels holding unblended grape must (above). The markings show which area the grapes came from – VZY stands for Verzenay, on the Montagne de Reims.*

*A blanket of snow covers the walled Clos du Mesnil vineyard owned by Krug (left), planted solely with Chardonnay grapes destined for its prestige* blanc de blancs.

*Pinot Noir vines on the slopes of the Montagne de Reims (above). That puff of smoke in the distance is the prunings being burned.*

*Champagne going through the* remuage *process (below) in traditional* pupîtres, *twisted and tipped by hand over many weeks.*

All of this is something of a storm in a champagne flute when set against the Number One problem the champagne producers now face, which is the seriousness and credibility of the challenge from elsewhere. The days when other sparkling wines could be considered as at best courageous, if flawed, attempts to mimic the elegance of the real thing are now irrevocably in the past, whatever certain of the big champagne houses continue to believe. There are excellent, conscientiously made sparkling wines being produced by what we now call the traditional method all over the world, from southern England to South Africa. I recently tasted an impressive Chardonnay sparkler made in Malta.

With western economies set to remain for the forseeable future on the giddying switchback ride set in motion by the global banking crisis of 2008–9, an expensive product like champagne needs all the friends it can get. Supplying own-brand champagnes of decent quality and restrained prices to the major supermarket retailers has been one way of maintaining a presence at the affordable end of the market, but when the champagne industry is permanently convinced that its product is losing market value relative to average incomes, then it's hard to be

boundlessly sympathetic. Do they want us to drink it or not? And do we always have to feel privileged when we do?

The taste for sparkling wine arose in England in the mid-17th century. It happened quite by chance, but became a habit that stuck. Prior to that point, wine wasn't supposed to fizz. Re-fermentation was a natural hazard to be avoided as much as possible in the northerly climate of a region like Champagne, where the onset of cold weather might arrest the initial transformation of grape juice into alcohol. A wine that turned out the following spring to have resumed fermenting was a failure.

Much of the highly regarded still wine of Champagne was exported to Britain at this time. It was shipped in cask and would be bottled by the London merchants soon after its arrival. The British trade had for some time been used to adding brandy and a little sugar to imported wines before the long sea voyages they had to endure, to stop them turning rank. Although the white wines of Champagne didn't have to travel far enough to need such treatment, they were nonetheless also subjected to it, to cater for what had become the marked English predilection for sweetness and potency in a wine.

Given the fact that many of these wines were biologically unstable to begin with, this treatment, followed promptly by bottling, would have virtually assured anything from a light purling to volcanic eruption when the bottle was broached. Indeed, explosions in the cellars were an occupational hazard for a London wine-merchant, and the injuries sustained thereby were viewed as just deserts for what quickly became the latest preposterous English fad. Not ones to be deterred by a bit of flying glass, the English responded by inventing stronger bottles.

In due course, the *champenois* themselves rose to the challenge, acquired the English taste and began refining techniques for producing wines that were intentionally bubbly. So extensively did these technological developments reach that recorded history came to believe that it was they themselves who had invented sparkling wine, legendarily in the figure of Dom Pérignon, treasurer of the abbey at Hautvillers from 1668 onwards.

Even if he isn't the true progenitor of sparkling champagne, Brother Pérignon was a tireless innovator, to whose credit we can chalk up the perfecting of a means for making white wine from red grapes, advances in clarification

treatments, and the refinement of the art of blending wines from different vineyards in the region to obtain an optimum product.

Chanpagne begins as a thin, acidic, low-alcohol, light white wine. After its initial fermentation is complete, a further quantity of sugar is added to it and the bottle re-sealed with a crown cap. As the yeasts begin to feed on this new supply, they generate more alcohol and carbon dioxide in the normal way, but because the bottle is sealed, the prickly gas has nowhere to escape, and so it remains present in the wine.

As the wine undergoes this second fermentation in the bottle, it also generates a deposit of dead yeast cells. Much as happens with certain cask-conditioned ales, the wine gains extra complexity and rounder texture from its extended contact with these yeast lees, in a process known as autolysis. Basically, the longer you can afford to age your chamapagne on its lees (the legal minimum is 15 months for non-vintage wines, and three years for vintage), the richer, softer and more complex the final wine will be.

That yeast gunge has to be removed, of course, before the wine is sold. This is achieved by a process known as *remuage* (removal), in which the bottles are gradually turned and tilted until the sediment has all collected on the underside of the cap. Most champagne houses now use automated equipment, with the bottles packed in huge crates, to achieve this, but many still rely on the traditional method first developed by the house of Veuve Clicquot in the late 18th century, in which the bottles are stuck neck-first into wooden racks and painstakingly turned by hand.

When the champagne is ready to undergo its *dégorgement* (disgorgement), the necks of the bottles are dipped in a freezing salt solution, so the portion of the wine containing the sediment is flash-frozen. When the metal cap is knocked away (a minority of artisanal producers still do this too by hand), the deposit flies out with it, the bottle is topped up with a sugar solution that determines the final style of the wine along the dry to sweet (or, properly, Brut to Doux) spectrum, and the traditional champagne cork goes in. It will soon be ready for release.

## THE WINES

Champagne production is dominated by members of the Club des Grandes Marques, the big houses such as Moët & Chandon, Bollinger,

Mumm, Taittinger, Veuve Clicquot and Pol Roger. They have the highest profiles and their wines, in the main, sell for the highest prices. Additionally, there are a number of important cooperatives in the region, who often make the own-brand champagnes for the high-street chains in the export markets. Most excitingly, there is a growing movement of go-it-alone growers who are making their own highly impressive wines on a small scale.

The region divides into five broad areas: the Vallée de la Marne nearest to the river that runs through the region; the Montagne de Reims, a large hill where most of the Pinot Noir is grown, overlooking the region's principal city to the north; the Côte des Blancs to the south of the industry's nerve-centre at Epernay, where the concentrations of Chardonnay are found; the Côte de Sézanne, further south; and the Aube valley, quite detached from the rest of the region to the southeast, and which tends to produce the most rustic wines. Throughout the region, the chalky soils are held to endow champagne with much of its finesse.

While most of the big houses own some vineyard land, they nearly all rely on buying grapes in from contract growers in the various vineyards, who are free to negotiate what they can get for their crops. Some houses possess no land at all. Others make special *cuvées* from individual plots they own, the most illustrious example being the fabulously rare wine of the tiny Clos du Mesnil vineyard owned by Krug. The small growers, on the other hand, may produce exclusively from their own holdings, notably in the Sézanne and the Aube.

*Summer at Verzenay, on the Montagne de Reims (above). The sunny slopes of the Montagne are planted mainly with Pinot Noir.*

### CHAMPAGNE

*GRAPES: Pinot Noir, Pinot Meunier, Chardonnay*

*Hand-harvesting ripe Pinot Noir grapes at Mailly on the Montagne (above).*

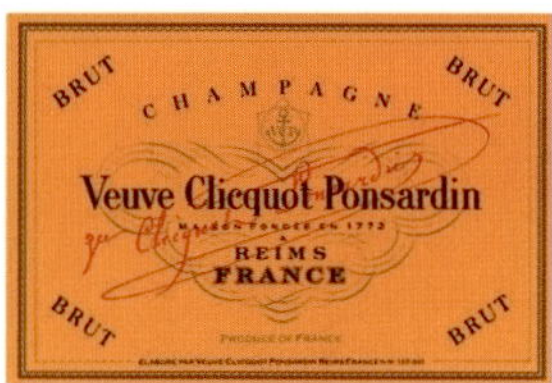

*Pruning vines in early March (above), and burning the cuttings on a portable fire in the vineyard.*

Of the three grapes permitted in the wine, two are red, although most champagne is white. Pinot Noir brings weight and richness to a blend and helps it to age productively, while those who use a greater percentage of Chardonnay value it for the elegance and gracefully lighter feel it can impart.

Pinot Meunier is a less distinguished grape in itself, but does lend a distinct fruity immediacy to many blends. Some houses play down the influence of this grape; others (including Krug) openly celebrate the function it serves. (Its image isn't helped by the fact that it cannot be planted on the best vineyard sites, designated *grand cru*.)

The aim for quality enshrined in the Chartre de Qualité in the 1990s stipulates that only the first free-run juice of the harvested grapes, followed by the juice of one subsequent gentle pressing, may now be used in the wines of the charter's signatories. (Previously, the harsher, more astringent juice of a second pressing went in as well, and did a lot to coarsen the taste of too many champagnes.)

Most champagne is labelled Brut, which is the standard bone-dry style. The style of a champagne is determined at the last moment, before the cork goes in, when a quantity of sugar in solution known as the *dosage* is added to create the final taste. Even Brut contains some sugar, since unadorned champagne is a naturally very acidic wine. A very few wines receive no *dosage* at all, and may be labelled Brut Zéro. These always taste somehow like unseasoned food to me, although Laurent-Perrier makes an acceptable one.

Alternatively, an above-average amount of sugar can be added to create a sweeter style – either medium-dry, labelled Demi-Sec, or positively sweet, and labelled either Doux or, sometimes, Rich. Louis Roederer makes a nicely balanced Rich.

**Non-vintage (NV)** The benchmark style, and the wine that the reputations of the houses live or die by, is the non-vintage blend. Each year, a quantity of base wine is held back in reserve, and small amounts of this older, maturer wine are used to give a softer feel and more complex flavour to what would be otherwise be very raw, acidic wine. When there has been a run of good vintages, the quality of the NV goes up significantly. Styles vary enormously from one producer to the next. What unites the best are good balance, roundness of texture and depth of flavour leading to a long finish. Squirrel away one or two NVs for six months to a year. You'll be surprised how much it can improve.

BEST HOUSES: Charles Heidsieck, Pol Roger, Bollinger, Veuve Clicquot, Billecart-Salmon, Taittinger, Louis Roederer.

**Vintage** This is the produce of a single year's harvest, with the year stated on the label, aged for a minimum of three years on its lees (although the better houses will give it longer). Like port, vintage wine should theoretically only be made in the best years, maybe three or four times a decade, but it seemingly takes a spectacularly rotten vintage to dissuade everybody from producing a vintage wine.

On average, vintage wines are released at around five years old (but barely more than three is not unknown, sadly). They don't really come into their own until after eight to ten years. Bear this in mind when you buy it; these wines are too expensive to waste by drinking them immature. The reward is deep, richly complex, honeyed wines, often having the aroma of freshly baked bread or brioche, the best suitable for drinking with food.

BEST VINTAGE PRODUCERS: Taittinger, Bollinger, Moët & Chandon, Lanson, Veuve Clicquot, H Blin, de Venoge, Henriot.

**Rosé** Most rosé is made by adding a little still red wine from the locale to the white champagne (a practice not permitted anywhere else in France). A very small amount, perhaps two per cent, is made by staining the white juice by allowing the red grapeskins to soak in it for a short while. At their best, rosé champagnes have an exhilarating strawberry or raspberry fruit that makes them glorious for summer drinking. Colours vary hugely, from Hollywood-starlet lipstick to a faint brownish tinge ('onion-skin' is the technical term) for those given the briefest maceration.

BEST: Pol Roger, Veuve Clicquot, Ruinart, Bollinger, Gosset, Billecart-Salmon, Jacquart and – at the expensive end – Perrier-Jouët Belle Epoque, Roederer Cristal and Veuve Clicquot La Grande Dame.

**Blanc de Blancs** Champagne from the Chardonnay grape only. These are, on release, the lightest and most graceful wines of the lot, but properly aged vintage examples take on a gorgeous toasty richness that quite belies the lightness argument. My personal favourite style, if you're buying.

BEST: Salon, Ruinart, Nicolas Feuillatte, Billecart-Salmon, Drappier, Taittinger Comtes de Champagne, Krug Clos de Mesnil.

**Blanc de Noirs** White champagne made from the black grapes, Pinot Noir and Pinot Meunier, usually with a noticeably darker tone to it, although it's never pink. They can be rather heavy and lumpish, certainly not beginner's champagne, but when good, their richer style can be impressive. Good champagnes to accompany food.

BEST: Bollinger Vieilles Vignes, de Venoge, Billiot, Serge Mathieu, Alexandre Bonnet.

**Prestige Cuvée** Most of the big houses make a top-drawer special bottling. These are usually – but not always – a vintage wine, produced just to show how good they can really get. They are aged for longer than ordinary vintage wine, or come from particularly favoured parcels of vineyard land. The packaging is often quite diverting, as witness Belle Epoque in its flower-painted bottle, or the multi-faceted crystal cffcct of Nicolas Feuillatte's Palmes d'Or. Even more than straight vintage wines, these champagnes have to be aged properly. If it's cost you a day's wages, the incentive should be there.

BEST: Roederer Cristal, Pol Roger Cuvée Sir Winston Churchill, Dom Pérignon, Krug Grande Cuvée, Veuve Clicquot La Grande Dame, Bollinger RD, Perrier-Jouët Belle Epoque, Gosset Grande Réserve, Mumm René Lalou, Pommery Cuvée Louise, Laurent-Perrier Grand Siècle, Nicolas Feuillatte Palmes d'Or.

## VINTAGE GUIDE

*2019* ***** These will be excellent on release, with concentrated flavours and true ripeness.

*2014* **** Looking good, with harmonious, attractive wines in abundance.

*2013* **** A slightly underrated vintage of leaner, but still distinctive wines.

*2012* ***** Glorious quality from all over the region. Long-lived champagnes of tremendous depth.

*2009* ***** A fabulous year of many opulent wines.

*2008* **** Lovely balance, good acid definition and rich fruit tones.

*2004* **** Good vintage of mostly quite gentle wines.

*1998* **** Many wines now showing imprcssive maturity.

*1996* ***** Intensely lush, honeyed wines that matured sooner than the 95s.

*1995* **** A great vintage of rich, structured wines.

Earlier vintages worth trying from houses that specialize in late disgorgement of old stocks are: *1990* ****   *1989* *****   *1988* **** *1985* ****   *1982* *****

*Autumnal glow of the Champagne region (below) with the golden-coloured vineyards spreading across the hills.*

# ALSACE

*A richly endowed wine region that deserves greater recognition, Alsace is a unique blend of the best of Germanic and French culture and grape varieties, and offers some of France's most idiosyncratic wine styles.*

*The village of Hunawihr, Alsace (above), with its 15th-century church, and the* grand cru *vineyard of Rosacker on the slope beyond.*

OF ALL FRANCE'S principal wine regions, Alsace is the one that has had politically the most chequered history. Twice absorbed into Germany by act of aggression in the last 150 years, it is now proudly, incontrovertibly French, for all that its inhabitants may well have Germanic names. Sheltered between the Vosges mountains and the river Rhine, the region grows French and German grape varieties.

The wine it produces have no precise equivalents, however, in either the rest of France or Germany. They are instead among the most idiosyncratic styles made anywhere. Their problem has always been that less informed consumers mistake the wines for German, and if their only association for German wine is with cheap, sugared-up products like Liebfraumilch, as it once was, that isn't going to help. One glance at the bottle, a tall Germanic flute, its label perhaps declaring it to be from a vineyard with a name like Pfingstberg, the grape variety possibly Riesling, and its fate is sealed. This is surely a sweet German wine. No, thank you.

The pity of this is that Alsace should be one of the easiest French regions to understand, in that it's the only part of France where the wines are named after their grape varieties, as opposed to their villages or châteaux, within one overriding regional appellation, AOP Alsace.

What has happened to complicate that picture was the introduction in the 1980s of a system of demarcations for the best vineyard sites, the Grands Crus. There are now 51 of these. Originally, only four grapes were permitted in Alsace Grand Cru – Gewurztraminer, Riesling, Pinot Gris and Muscat – but the rules have now been stretched to include Sylvaner in the *grand cru* of Zotzenberg, and Pinot Noir is expected to be elevated into the noble company in due course.

The *grands crus* account for less than five per cent of the total regional production, and are of course the more expensive wines, but it's fair to say that most consumers (even within the region itself) remain in the dark about what distinguishes the individual *crus* from each other. The ancestral family firm of Hugel cheerfully ignores the whole system, declining to label its wines with *cru* names, even where they qualify for the designation.

Although Alsace is a relatively northern area, its sheltered position makes it particularly dry, giving it as little annual rainfall as parts of the broiling Midi down south. That means that, when a harvest has been rather poor in much of the rest of France, Alsace tends not to take quite the caning that other regions might suffer.

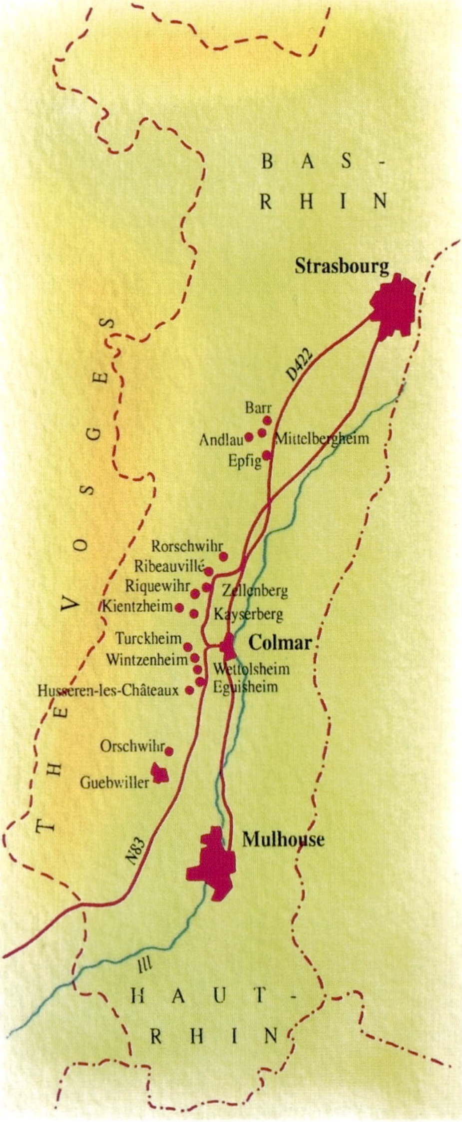


*Alsace, bordered by the Vosges mountains and the river Rhine (right), has one overall AOP, with specified* grand cru *vineyards. The marked villages are where the cellars of most of the region's top producers are located.*

It is in these sometimes too arid conditions that clay-based soils, such as Alsace has in some of its lower-lying vineyards, are beneficial. Clay absorbs moisture during wet spells, and doesn't allow it to drain away as freely as other soil types do – a precious asset when summer drought is a real possibility.

The mental block that consumers have shown about Alsace wines means that many high-street outlets only list the lowest-common-denominator produce of the region's many cooperatives. Much of this is perfectly reliable and not to be scorned, but for the true glory that Alsace is capable of, it nearly always pays to try one of the wines of the region's individual growers, many of which are made from low-yielding vines that produce sublimely concentrated, hauntingly perfumed wines.

## THE WINES

Nearly all Alsace wine is dry to medium-dry varietal white, produced from one of the following varieties, with Pinot Noir the only exception. The first four listed here are the only ones permitted in the great majority of the *grands crus*.

**Gewurztraminer** This is the variety most readily associated in people's minds with the region's wines. Intensely aromatic, with a range of musky floral scents, underpinned with ripe orchard or citrus fruits and sweet spice, Gewurztraminer is usually a deeply coloured wine with low acidity and rumbustious levels of alcohol. Despite its headstrong personality, it is a sympathetic partner to many foods, including the richly flavoured pâtés and terrines for which Alsace is famous, as well as east Asian cuisines such as Chinese and Thai. The wines can benefit from some bottle-ageing, although in very ripe years, such as 2003, the acidity level in the finished wine may be so low that prolonged ageing will only turn it mushy. PRODUCERS: Zind-Humbrecht, Hugel, Trimbach, Kuentz-Bas, Weinbach, Adam, Willm, the Turckheim and Pfaffenheim co-ops.

**Riesling** The starkest, most unnervingly pure dry Rieslings in the world come from Alsace. They are almost painfully austere in youth, and a period of bottle-ageing is mandatory for most examples. The fruit flavours are acerbic lime-peel and grapefruit, held together by exemplary levels of steely acid, and with more alcohol than Germany's Rieslings. They make an appetizing accompaniment to simply prepared fish dishes

and Thai food. In their maturity, they can be overcome with a bewitching fume of petrol and damp earth, but never quite losing the outline of that nervy acidity. The buzzword for them is 'racy', and you can see why. PRODUCERS: Weinbach, Trimbach, Schlumberger, Josmeyer, Sipp, Adam, Zind-Humbrecht, Beyer.

**Pinot Gris** A much misunderstood variety, Pinot Gris can have all the spicy pungency of Gewurztraminer, with the fruit just a little sharper – orange perhaps, rather than the ripe peach of Gewurz. Then again, it can have a fat buttery texture to it, together with a layer of honey, which can make it seem curiously like a particularly aromatic Chardonnay. Like Gewurz, the acidity is generally fairly low, and that should be taken into account when deciding how long to age a Pinot Gris. Banish all thought of mass-produced Italian Pinot Grigio (the same grape); these are the real deal. PRODUCERS: Zind-Humbrecht, Schlumberger, Kreydenweiss, Beyer, Albrecht.

*Husseren-les-Châteaux, a typical Alsace village, surrounded by vineyards (above), with the three ruined towers on the hill behind.*

*The steeply sloping* grand cru *Rangen vineyard at the village of Thann (right), Alsace's most southerly* grand cru.

**Muscat** Muscat is the name of one of the oldest known grape varieties, in fact a many-membered family as opposed to a single variety. Two of the scions are present in Alsace, one of them not surprisingly known as Muscat d'Alsace and the other Muscat Ottonel. No distinction is made between them on the labels. Muscat is one of the great sweet wine grapes, the only one by consensus to actually smell and taste of grapes. Vinified dry, it can be bracingly tart and much thinner in texture than the three varieties listed above. There is very little of it planted compared to the others, but in a good year, from low-yielding vines, it can make a pleasantly sharp, refreshing white with some of the musky spice the region rejoices in.
PRODUCERS: Trimbach, Rolly-Gassmann, Weinbach, Schleret.

**Pinot Blanc** Not an especially aromatic grape, but definitely an underrated one. Pinot Blanc makes a creamy, slightly appley wine that provides an unstartling introduction to the region for those nervous of plunging headlong into the giddy waters of Gewurz. Sometimes, in ripe vintages, it might have a suggestion of peach to it. Drunk young, these have far more character than many another unoaked dry white. Not for long ageing. (One of its permitted pseudonyms in Alsace is Klevner or Clevner.)
PRODUCERS: Rolly-Gassmann, Hugel, Mann, Zind-Humbrecht, Trimbach, Weinbach, Deiss.

**Sylvaner** The speciality grape of Franken in western Germany makes a pungently vegetal, often distinctly cabbagey wine in Alsace. Not the most attractive flavour in the world, but the odd one can have a honeyed quality and unexpected richness. In 2006, it was allowed into the *grand cru* of Zotzenberg, elbowing out Muscat in the process.
PRODUCERS: Zind-Humbrecht, Becker, Weinbach, Ostertag, Seltz.

**Auxerrois** This is the grape that nobody really talks about, although there is still plenty of it about. Related to Chardonnay, it has tended to be treated interchangeably with Pinot Blanc in Alsace, so that a wine labelled with that latter grape may be blended with Auxerrois (or indeed be nothing but). By itself, it gives very simple, though fairly full-textured wines with a vaguely soapy flavour. (Not to be confused with the red Auxerrois, aka Malbec, of southern France.)
PRODUCERS: Mann, Rolly-Gassmann.

**Chasselas** Very rarely seen on labels, this undistinguished grape makes extremely light, neutral-tasting wine. Schoffit works miracles with it to produce an impressively lush-textured wine from old vines – worth trying.

**Edelzwicker** The name used for blends of any of the above grapes (with the exception of Pinot Blanc and Auxerrois). They may be appealing enough, but since the varietals are generally so sharply delineated, there seems little point in drinking one of these if you can have a single-grape wine.

**Pinot Noir** The only red grape in Alsace makes some mostly very light reds and tiny amounts of rosé. In recent years, it has begun to show some pedigree, nothing like burgundy, to be sure, but still encouraging. There is usually some sharp cherry fruit in it, together with a rustic earthiness, but proper roundness too in the warmer years. When fully concentrated, it can take some oak-ageing.
PRODUCERS: Deiss, Adam, Weinbach, Hugel.

**Crémant d'Alsace** Alsace makes some of the most impressive sparkling wine in France outside the Champagne region – often a better bet than the Crémants of Burgundy or the Loire. The principal grape used is Pinot Blanc, usually mixed with Pinot Gris, but the small plantings of Chardonnay found in the region go into the sparklers too. The method is the same as that used for champagne, with a second fermentation taking place in the bottle. The result is often attractively nutty, full-flavoured wines of considerable depth. There is also some featherlight Pinot Noir rosé.

PRODUCERS: Dopff au Moulin, Adam, Albrecht, Blanck, Turckheim.

**Vendange Tardive** This is the less rich of the two sweeter styles of Alsace wine. The name means 'late harvest', to denote grapes that have been left on the vine to overripen, and thereby achieve higher levels of natural sugar. The designation applies only to the first four grapes listed above. They can be utterly delicious, perfectly balanced between the tang of ripe fruits and the lightest trickling of spicy syrup. In the great vintages of 2005 and 2009, they were particularly rich, honeyed and decadently creamy. In lesser years, they can be pretty close to the dry wines, but with a just perceptible extra depth to the texture.

**Sélection de Grains Nobles** The 'noble' in the name of this category refers to the noble rot, botrytis, which stalks the vineyards in some years and allows the growers to make Alsace's richest and most unctuous wines. They are powerfully alcoholic and glutinously sweet, and should theoretically age beautifully. The only slight vitiating factor is that, particularly in Gewurz and Pinot Gris, the acidity – low enough in the dry wines – can drop even further when the rotted berries are left on the vine for so long. Once again, only the big four grapes can be used, with Muscat by far the rarest.

**Alsace Grand Cru** The only other AOP in the region, apart from straight Alsace. It has, since 1983, covered the most prestigious vineyard sites, of which 51 have now been demarcated. Maximum yields permitted are 66 hectolitres per hectare, although the better wines are made from crops that are significantly smaller than this. Riesling, Gewurztraminer, Pinot Gris and Muscat are the privileged quartet allowed on most of the specified sites (with Sylvaner getting the nod too in Zotzenberg). Since the individual vineyards are quite distinct from each other in terms of soil, exposure and microclimate, the *grand cru* wines should give

us a beguiling insight into the versatility that Alsace is unquestionably capable of, but they remain for the time being far less fixed in even knowledgeable consumers' minds than the *crus* of Burgundy. Perceptions shift slowly.

## VINTAGE GUIDE

Vintages in Alsace remain remarkably even, with the first two decades of the 21st century delivering a sequence of very good to great years. *2023 ****** was a superb year for concentrated, explosively aromatic wines. *2022 ***** was almost as good. *2020 ***** had great Riesling and lusciously ripe Pinot Noir reds. *2015 ****** was sensational across all varieties, from dry to noble-rotted. Buy these recent vintages with confidence. Of the earlier ones, *2009* and *2005* were both worth *******, as were *1990* and *1985*. The raging hot *2003 ***** was especially good for the sweet dessert wines, less so for the drier varietals.

*The village of Riquewihr, dominated by its church spire (above), seen from the Schoenenburg grand cru.*

*Half-timbered Alsace building (below), Hugel's cellars in Riquewihr.*

# BURGUNDY

*Lovers of great Pinot Noir and classic Chardonnay speak the name with reverence. Burgundy's vinous history dates back for centuries, tied up in the division of land and the role of the négociant.*

*The autumnal colours of the Charmes vineyard at Gevrey-Chambertin on the Côte de Nuits (above).*

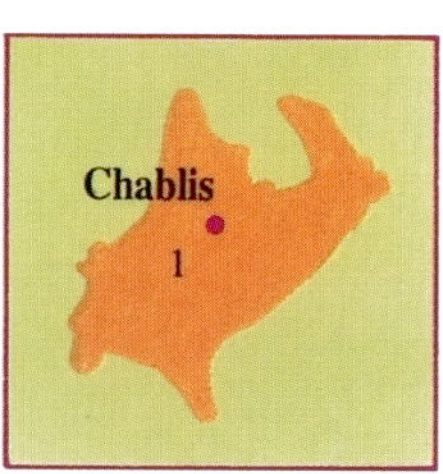

*The great names of Burgundy (right) are concentrated in a line north-south between the towns of Dijon and Lyon; Chablis lies alone to the north.*

B URGUNDY HAS ALWAYS been the consort to Bordeaux's monarch among the French wine regions. Its red wines in particular have their diehard devotees, just as fine claret does, and there has always been a romanticized comparison between the two. If the claret aficionado is an old-school connoisseur, fastidious, cerebral and contemplative in his approach to wine, the burgundy-lover was more of a wild child, a devotee of hedonistic sensuality, free-spirited and closer to nature.

Passionate controversies have raged and still rage about burgundy, to a degree because of the uncertain quality of so many of the wines. What

makes the debate all the more poignant is that the annual production of fine burgundy is microscopically small compared with the output of Bordeaux. Its premium *grand cru* and *premier cru* wines (the rough equivalent of the classed growths of Bordeaux) come almost entirely from the narrow limestone ridge of the Côte d'Or, less than 30 miles from north to south, and not more than five miles across at its widest point. (Compare that with the oceans of unsold claret that regularly build up in the cellars of the Bordelais.)

The land in Burgundy, which constitutes some of the most costly real estate on the face of the earth, was ruthlessly subdivided over the generations, in accordance with a legal code enacted under Napoleon Bonaparte, which stated that the property of a landowner was to be divided equally among his offspring on his death. Many of these tiny smallholdings are today responsible for producing Burgundy's greatest wines.

They are not, however, the only game in town. Dominating the scene are the large merchant houses, known as négociants, who buy in grapes, and even finished wine, blending them for their own bottlings. If certain of these companies, whose commercial clout after all did much to establish the reputation of the region as a whole in times gone by, are bywords for reasonably good – occasionally scintillating – wines, they can almost never compete with the efforts of the most quality-conscious small growers. Indeed, they rarely try to.

A mood of change has come over Burgundy in the most recent generation, with the result that the wines (the reds especially) are more conscientiously thought about than any other wines in France. There is anything but a consensus as to what the most natural style of Pinot Noir should be here. Some growers emphasize lightness, fruit and charm; others aim for a more dark and brooding style, the kind of wine that delights in making you work hard to become friends with it. There are definite stylistic differences among the various appellations, but the producer's own style is even more crucial.

The white wines of the region are generally more reliable across the board than the reds, not least because Chardonnay behaves more obligingly in most years than Pinot does. If there has been a perceptible shift in philosophies here, it has been to produce more delicate, leaner wines with less overt oak influence, which, in the classiest appellations, I find rather a pity.

To the burgundy-lover (and I am one), there is more of a sense of the soil, of the place the wine comes from, in a good Côte d'Or Pinot or Chardonnay than there is in almost any other wine in the world. It can be heartbreaking to taste the uninspiring generic wines of big companies trading only on the cachet of the famous village names, and even more upsetting that these are likely to be the only wines within reach of the average pocket. It absolutely pays to know who are the better producers, which are the better vintages and – to a lesser extent – which are the better appellations.

This chapter moves from north to south, making its way down through the fabled Côte d'Or towards the large district of the Mâconnais, but beginning – as so many of the best evenings do – with a glass of Chablis.

## CHABLIS

Although historically considered to be a viticultural part of Burgundy, the Chablis vineyards lie to the northwest of the main region in the *département* of the Yonne, geographically closer to the southern end of Champagne than they are to the Côte d'Or. As such, they represent one of the most northerly outposts of still Chardonnay wine in the world. Not surprisingly, the style that came to be associated with the area was one of light-textured wines with scything acidity and either complete absence of oak, or only a very restrained use of it.

The appellation's claim to fame is a geological formation of limestone and clay, which it shares with parts of southern England, and which is known as Kimmeridgian (after the Dorset village of Kimmeridge). This is held to endow the wines with their celebrated minerality, an austere hardness that makes them worth ageing for a few years.

The class structure of the wines of Chablis is much the same as in the rest of Burgundy. The top vineyard sites are designated *grand cru*, the next best *premier cru*, and then come the wines of the basic appellation. In Chablis, this hierarchy is supplemented by a basement category of Petit Chablis, made from land outside the heartland of the appellation, or from vines within it that have not yet attained the minimum age required for Chablis proper.

One of the debates that has consumed the Chablis universe in recent years concerns the question of machine-harvesting. When most or all of your effort is concentrated on making one style of wine, it pays to get it right. And the inherent delicacy of Chablis is such that it benefits hugely from careful hand-picking of only the ripest bunches. Mechanical harvesting for the *grand cru* and *premier cru* wines in particular ought probably to be outlawed altogether.

**CHABLIS**
*GRAPE: Chardonnay*

*Four of Chablis's seven grand cru vineyards (below): looking from Grenouilles towards Vaudésir, Preuses and Bougros beyond.*

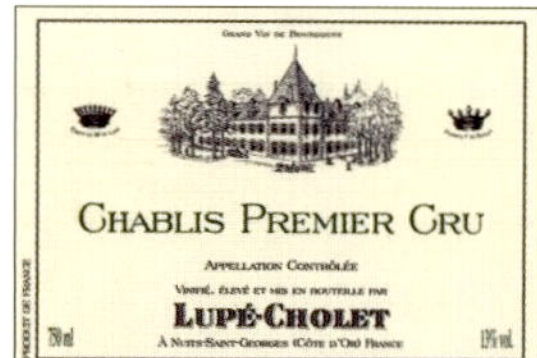





**CÔTE DE NUITS**

*GRAPES: Red – Pinot Noir; White – Chardonnay, small amount of Pinot Blanc*

**Chablis** The basic appellation is the most extensive area of the total vineyard. In its classical idiom, it is taut and tense in youth, often showing no aromatic personality beyond a tart appley or lemony quality, but then softening beguilingly in the bottle, so that after around three or four years, it takes on a creamy feel, hinting at some imaginary oak influence, and acquires a gentle vegetal aroma, like green beans or leeks tossed in melted butter. Some producers do actually use a little oak to round out the texture, but it should never taste like an oaky wine. Nor should be good Chablis ever be bitter or green. Overcropped, it may taste tart and watery, like bad Pinot Grigio. A tendency to play down its youthful acids with longer hang-times on the vine is becoming more widespread in the region. Such wines will age less well. PRODUCERS: Raveneau, R&V Dauvissat, A&F Boudin, Vocoret, Michel, Durup, Defaix, Lupé-Cholet, Leflaive, Brocard, Fèvre (for the best of the oak-influenced Chablis), la Chablisienne.

**Chablis Premier Cru** Forty vineyards are entitled to the designation *premier cru*, representing around 25 per cent of the total production, although many of them shelter under larger collective names. Of the 17 such recognized names, the best are Vaillons, Fourchaume, Beauroy, Montée de Tonnerre, Mont de Milieu, Montmains and Vaucoupin. The campaign to have certain vineyards promoted from straight Chablis has been virtually unceasing, and some of the promotions haven't really been merited, with the result that too much Chablis Premier Cru used to taste no different to ordinary Chablis. That picture has now improved, and there are many wines that show the perceptibly greater richness and density that the extra outlay should be buying.

**Chablis Grand Cru** There are seven of these, all located on the same southwest-facing slope just to the north of the town of Chablis itself, and accounting for a mere three per cent of the regional output. They are Bougros, Les Preuses, Vaudésir, Grenouilles, Valmur, Les Clos and Blanchots. An eighth, La Moutonne, can be considered *grand cru*, although it officially isn't, because it overlaps Les Preuses and Vaudésir and therefore escapes the classification. These are the richest and weightiest Chablis, usually aged in oak barrels to underpin their creamy concentration, and quality is by and large very fine. They should be left at least five years from the vintage before drinking, when they become as honey-rich as Côte d'Or Chardonnay but without losing their core of flinty minerality.

**Petit Chablis** Just as a lot of simple Chablis was elevated to *premier cru*, so a lot of Petit Chablis has miraculously become Chablis, with the result that less of a quarter of the land in the remaining Petit Chablis designation is planted. The wines generally lack concentration and breeding, making the narrowing of the price differential with Chablis itself hard to swallow, though there is the very occasional shining exception (look for the wines of Séguinot-Bordet).

## CÔTE DE NUITS

The northern half of the Côte d'Or, starting just south of Dijon, is the Côte de Nuits. This area is particularly important for its red wines, although a small amount of white is produced in some appellations. For many aspirant red wine makers around the world, the Côte de Nuits is the true heartland of Pinot Noir. The majestic intensity (and scarcity) of the wines makes the highest among them – the legendary *grands crus* – among the most sought-after and highly valued red wines on the planet.

This guide to the appellations runs from north to south. Some of the villages have individually designated vineyard sites within their appellations, the *grands* and *premiers crus*. Listed after each AOP, where appropriate, are the names of its *grands crus* (GC), with the number of *premiers crus* (pc) in brackets.

**Marsannay** An AOP since 1987, Marsannay was long famed for its light, strawberryish rosé, but it can come in all three colours. The reds are seriously improving. Good value. PRODUCERS: B Clair, Mortet, Trapet, Jadot.

**Fixin** Meaty reds with considerable depth and structure, if not often great finesse. Some ordinary white. (5 pc.) PRODUCERS: Joliet, Charlopin, Guyard.

**Gevrey-Chambertin** The first of the great appellations (reds only). Powerful, strongly scented, beefy wines with richness and ageability at their best. Tough and lacking fruit if not. GC: Charmes-Chambertin, Chambertin Clos-de-Bèze, Le Chambertin, Mazis-Chambertin, Latricières-Chambertin, Chapelle-Chambertin, Ruchottes-Chambertin, Griotte-Chambertin. (26 pc.) PRODUCERS: Rousseau, Dugat, Mortet, Rossignol-Trapet, Roty, Dujac, Sérafin, Faiveley, Jadot.

**Morey-St-Denis** Somewhat lighter than Gevrey, but still full of beefy, savoury character over dark-skinned plum fruit. Tiny amounts of impressive white. GC: Clos de la Roche, Clos des Lambrays, Clos de Tart (wholly owned by Mommessin), Clos St-Denis, Bonnes Mares (shared with Chambolle-Musigny). (20 pc.) PRODUCERS: Dujac, H Lignier, Lignier-Michelot, Roumier, Rousseau, Ponsot, Dom. des Lambrays.

**Chambolle-Musigny** Lighter reds with sweet strawberry fruit, atypical for the Nuits. Increasingly good from small growers. GC: Bonnes Mares (overlapping with the above), Le Musigny (which, unlike the main AOP, can also be white). (25 pc.) PRODUCERS: Roumier, Dujac, Leroy, Rion, Mugnier, Vogüe, Drouhin.

**Vougeot** Small production of sound wines from the village AOP, totally overshadowed by the acclaimed *grand cru* for its wines of stunning intensity and longevity. Also some fair whites. GC: Clos de Vougeot. (4 pc.) PRODUCERS: Leroy, Méo-Camuzet, Mugneret-Gibourg, Gros, Grivot, Mortet, Confuron.

**Vosne-Romanée** Superbly aromatic, gamey Pinot, intense raspberry fruit and huge structure. Demands ageing. The *grands crus*, famously from the ancestral Romanée-Conti estate, are the finest reds in Burgundy, made in tiny quantities at prices to induce a blackout. The neighbouring commune of Flagey-Echézeaux has two *grands crus*, but its village wine is labelled Vosne-Romanée. GC: Grands Echézeaux, Echézeaux, Richebourg, Romanée-St-Vivant, Romanée-Conti, La Romanée, La Grande Rue, La Tâche. (15 pc.) PRODUCERS: Dom. de la Romanée-Conti, Leroy, Méo-Camuzet, Liger-Belair, Lamarche, Arnoux, Grivot, M Gros, Rouget, Cathiard.

**Nuits-St-Georges** At best, classically meaty, cherryish reds with depth and complexity, but has become very patchy. The lack of a *grand cru* is keenly felt. Rather solid whites. (41 pc.) PRODUCERS: Gouges, l'Arlot, Chevillon, Rion, Grivot, Arnoux, Chauvenet, Confuron, Jayer-Gilles, Faiveley.

**Hautes-Côtes-de-Nuits** A group of little village in the hills to the west of the Côte de Nuits is bunched together under this appellation, a reliable starting-point for those wanting a gentle run-up to the more extravagant stuff. Raspberry-ripe reds, with some sinewy structure. Soft, nutty, everyday whites.

The château of Gevrey-Chambertin (above), the first of the great red Burgundy appellations in the Côte de Nuits.

PRODUCERS: Jayer-Gilles, Caves des Hautes-Côtes, Verdet.

**Côtes de Nuits-Villages** An AOP that gathers in a handful of villages from the extreme northern and southern ends of the Nuits. Usually well-made, if lightish, reds and whites with a little modest ageing potential. PRODUCERS: Chopin-Groffier, Bachelet, Jourdan.

## CÔTE DE BEAUNE

This is the southern stretch of the Côte d'Or, an area particularly famed for its white wines, although there are many good reds too. Burgundy's benchmark oak-aged Chardonnays come mainly from the southern end of the Côte de Beaune, while the best reds from further north are fully the equals of those from the Côte de Nuits. They tend to be slightly softer and more immediately approachable, however, emphasizing red fruit flavours first and the classic Burgundian meatiness second.

Once again, we travel north to south.

*COTE DE BEAUNE*
*GRAPES: Red – Pinot Noir; White – Chardonnay, some Pinot Blanc and Aligoté*

*The famous Hôtel de Dieu (above), glimpsed through the entrance to the Hospices de Beaune in the village of Beaune.*

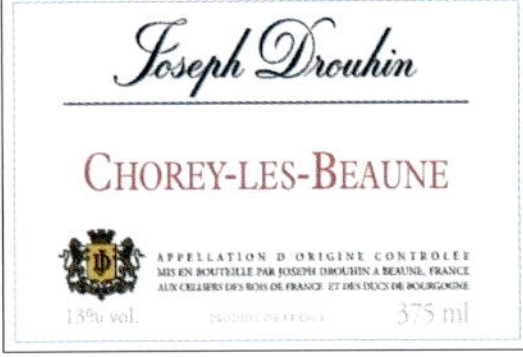

**Pernand-Vergelesses** Delicate whites and slimline reds can both be very attractive when a lighter style is required, but this is not generally the appellation to choose for the full-throttle Burgundy experience. GC: about a quarter of the *grand cru* Corton-Charlemagne lies within this AOP. (8 pc.)
PRODUCERS: Chandon de Briailles, Pavelot, Rollin, Rapet, Laleure-Piot.

**Bourgogne Aligoté** Some of Burgundy's unsung alternative white wine, Aligoté (from the grape of that name) comes from around Pernand. Expect lemon-sharp acids and spritzy freshness over a softer sour-cream base. (See also Bourgogne Aligoté de Bouzeron, Côte Chalonnaise.)

**Ladoix** Rarely seen AOP of the village of Ladoix-Serrigny, almost all lean, simple red. Now for the confusing part. GC: about one-eighth of Le Corton (nearly all red) and a tiny part of Corton-Charlemagne (white only) lie within Ladoix, although they are officially the *grands crus* of Aloxe-Corton (see below). Similarly, some of Ladoix's *premiers crus* are claimed by Aloxe, leaving it with 11 pc to call its own.
PRODUCERS: Chevalier, E Cornu, Loichet.

**Aloxe-Corton** Good muscular reds from the village appellation and a minuscule quantity of underwhelming white. GC: Le Corton (the only *grand cru* for red wines on the Côte de Beaune) may have any one of up to 21 vineyard names attached to it, e.g. Corton-Bressandes, Perrières, Clos du Roi, etc. Corton-Charlemagne (the *grand cru* for whites only) is shared, as above, with Ladoix and Pernand-Vergelesses. (15 pc, some technically in the village of Ladoix.)
PRODUCERS: Tollot-Beaut, Chandon de Briailles, Bonneau du Martray, Méo-Camuzet, Girardin, Coche-Dury, Rapet, Louis Latour.

**Savigny-lès-Beaune** On the western side of the Côte, this was once considered rather rustic and forgettable, but is now much improved. Still relatively sanely priced. Good red-fruit Pinot, a very little decent white. (21 pc.)
PRODUCERS: Tollot-Beaut, Leroy, Pavelot, Jacob.

**Chorey-lès-Beaune** Underrated, and therefore generally affordable, reds (and a dash of white). The best have the soft red fruit of good Beaune Pinot, with some depth and ageability to boot.
PRODUCERS: Maillard, Arnoux, Drouhin.

**Beaune** The village that gives its name to this sector of the Côte. Famous for soft, strawberry-scented reds of great elegance. Also some initially hard, but eventually impressive Chardonnay. (42 pc.)

PRODUCERS: Lafarge, Tollot-Beaut, de Montille, Morot, Drouhin, Champy.

**Pommard** Classy, long-lived red wines with as much authoritative weight as some Côte de Nuits reds. In the wrong hands, can be a bit heavy, and always expensive for the quality. (27 pc.)
PRODUCERS: Comte Armand, Boillot, de Montille, Lafarge, Girardin, Courcel.

**Volnay** Top-drawer Beaune Pinot, at best perfectly capturing the combination of creamy red fruit (raspberries, loganberries) with underlying savoury depth. Arguably the finest red of the Côte de Beaune. Expensive, but mostly very fine. (35 pc, five in Meursault.)
PRODUCERS: Comte Lafon, de Montille, Lafarge, Ampeau, Matrot, Potel, Voillot.

**Monthélie** Suffers from its position between Volnay and Meursault, both of which are better-known, but this is nonetheless a good mainly red village for sturdy, if not noticeably elegant wines. (15 pc.)
PRODUCERS: Comte Lafon, Roulot, Jobard.

**St-Romain** On the western flank of the Côte, St-Romain makes both white and red, its earthily dry Chardonnays distinctly better than its light, often inconsequential Pinots.
PRODUCERS: Chassorney, Gras, Verget.

**Auxey-Duresses** A period of instability has been rectified with some gentle, strawberryish Pinots and pleasantly buttery Chardonnays. (9 pc.)
PRODUCERS: Leroy, Diconne, Ampeau, Prunier, Comte Armand.

**Meursault** First of the five-star white wine villages, and the only one with no *grand cru*. Meursault used to be hugely fat and rich, intensely oaky golden wine full of honey and butterscotch. These days, it's much leaner and more restrained, part of which is owing to over-production. Inexpensive-looking Meursault is likely to be poor value. (19 pc, two of which – Blagny and Santenots – are also for red wine, in which case they don't mention the name Meursault. Santenots then counts as a *premier cru* of Volnay.)
PRODUCERS: Comte Lafon, Coche-Dury, Roulot, Jobard, Ente, Girardin, Bouzereau, Fichet, Jadot.

**Puligny-Montrachet** The village wines are typically leaner than Meursault, but can be beautifully balanced, creamy and hazelnutty Chardonnay, supported by spicy, toasty new oak. From here on in, all the wines bask to some degree in the reflected glory of the greatest white burgundy of them all, the *grand cru* Le Montrachet, which makes hauntingly powerful,

smoky, almondy, mouth-filling Chardonnay at second-mortgage prices. There is a little fairly dull red Puligny. GC: Le Montrachet, Bâtard-Montrachet (both shared with Chassagne-Montrachet – see below), Chevalier-Montrachet and Bienvenues-Bâtard-Montrachet. (17 pc.)
PRODUCERS: Sauzet, Leflaive, Carillon, Ente, Ramonet, Larue. For *grands crus*: Dom. de la Romanée-Conti, Colin, Bouchard, Lafon, Leroy, Drouhin's Montrachet Laguiche.
**St-Aubin** Out west, this emergent AOP is making some fine, smoky, pedigree Chardonnay, and a smaller quantity of light, strawberry Pinot at very attractive prices. Most of the appellation is *premier cru*. (20 pc.)
PRODUCERS: Bachelet, H Lamy, Thomas, Larue.
**Chassagne-Montrachet** Last of the great whites, perhaps the least spectacular for its basic village wines, though they still have the imprint of fine Burgundian Chardonnay, but producing some memorable *grands crus*. Reds are pretty much run-of-the-mill. GC: Le Montrachet, Bâtard-Montrachet (both shared with Puligny-Montrachet), Criots-Bâtard-Montrachet. (50 pc.)
PRODUCERS: Blain-Gagnard, Ramonet, Colin, B Morey, M Morey, Niellon, Verget.
**Santenay** In the south of the Côte, Santenay produces mainly reds of no conspicuous finesse, but can be a satisfying glass of hearty Pinot from the better growers. Good savoury whites. (12 pc.)
PRODUCERS: Girardin, Vincent, Muzard, Belland.
**Maranges** Created in 1988, the AOP unites three villages – Dezize, Sampigny and Cheilly – each followed by the appellation suffix (Dezize-lès-Maranges, etc.), though they may also be labelled simply Maranges. Overwhelmingly red, fairly rustic, but kindly priced. (7 pc.)
PRODUCERS: Bachelet, Girardin, Charleux.
**Hautes-Côtes-de-Beaune** As in the Nuits, there is a scattering of villages among the hills to the west of the sector that take this appellation. Quality is generally good, notably for the soft, cherry-fruited reds.
PRODUCERS: Joillot, Jacob, Ch. de Mercey, Caves des Hautes-Côtes.
**Côte de Beaune-Villages** Red wine appellation that covers most of the Côte, and may be used by any of the individual villages (with the big four exceptions of Aloxe-Corton, Beaune, Pommard and Volnay) or for any wine blended from two or more villages, a practice not much in evidence now.
PRODUCERS: Drouhin, Jadot, Lupé-Cholet.

**Côte de Beaune** The simplest appellation in the area takes in vineyards on the hill overlooking the village of Beaune itself – but not from anywhere else on the Côte, perplexingly. Undistinguished reds and whites.

## CÔTE CHALONNAISE

The large bulk-producing area in the south of Burgundy, the Mâconnais, is separated from the Côte d'Or by a strip of vineyard called the Côte Chalonnaise, which takes its name from the town of Chalon-sur-Saône. As well as producing some basic AOP Bourgogne Rouge and Blanc, there are five important village appellations here. Because their reputations are nothing like as exalted as the villages of the Côte d'Or, these generally represent good value, although they don't have quite the same class. From north to south:

**Bouzeron** An AOP since 1998, this village appellation is considered the best for the second-string white grape of Burgundy, Aligoté. They should be drunk fairly young to capture their challenging lemon-and-crème-fraîche character.
PRODUCERS: de Villaine, Goisot, Mortet, Ente.
**Rully** The whites and reds of this village have now eclipsed its erstwhile reputation as a source of cheap and cheerful fizz. Its whites are lighter and drier than from the Côte de Beaune, but well-made by and large, as are its simple, plummy reds. (23 pc.)
PRODUCERS: Jacqueson, Dureuil-Janthial, Briday, Jadot, Girardin.
**Mercurey** The lion's share of Chalonnaise production comes from this village, which is

*CôTE CHALONNAISE*
*GRAPES: White –*
*Chardonnay, Aligoté;*
*Red – Pinot Noir*

*Dusk falls over the vineyards of the Hautes-Côtes-de-Nuits AOP, in the hills of the Côte d'Or (below).*

*Chardonnay grapes arriving
at the Caves de Buxy
cooperative (below)
in the Montagny AOP,
Côte Chalonnaise.*

why you will sometimes see the whole sub-region referred to as the Région de Mercurey. Mostly, well-balanced, concentrated reds, though whites are much improved, and can be surprisingly rich. (30 pc.)
PRODUCERS: Ch. de Chamirey, Juillot, de Suremain, Lorenzon, Raquillet, Faiveley.
**Givry** Predominantly red wines in an impressively scented raspberry style, with good structure. Small amount of intriguingly spicy white. (17 pc.)
PRODUCERS: Chofflet-Valdenaire, Joblot, F Lumpp, Sarrazin.
**Montagny** Quality in this whites-only appellation is decidedly patchy. Some possess convincing intensity; many taste pretty similar to anonymous Mâcon Blanc-Villages. Absurdly enough, fully half of the land planted qualifies as *premier cru*. (49 pc.)
PRODUCERS: Aladame, Vachet, Roy, Louis Latour, Caves de Buxy.

## MACONNAIS

The southernmost district of Burgundy, opposite the town of Mâcon, is in many ways the commercial hub of the region. The majority of Burgundy's cooperatives are found here, and in Beaujolais to the south. Predominantly everyday whites, with one or two stars, the production is very much geared to volume markets, and is easily outshone in many instances by low-priced Chardonnay from elsewhere in the world.
**Pouilly-Fuissé** A whites-only appellation that carries the quality torch for the Mâconnais as a whole, pricing its wines in accordance with its

ambition. At their classiest, they are richly oaked and fleshy, and do display some elegance. Neighbouring appellations of Pouilly-Vinzelles and Pouilly-Loché are not quite in the same class.
PRODUCERS: Château-Fuissé, Guffens-Heynen, Ch. de Rontets, Valette, Ferret, Robert-Denogent, Lassarat, Merlin, Jadot.
**St-Véran** In the dead south of the Mâconnais, overlapping into Beaujolais and wholly enclosing the Pouilly-Fuissé AOP, St-Véran is a somewhat underrated source of dry, chalky Chardonnay wines with a certain amount of Burgundian flair.
PRODUCERS: Thévenet, Lassarat, Deux Roches, Corsin, Gerbeaux, Jadot.
**Viré-Clessé** These two villages in the far north of the region were plucked from the humdrum mélange of the Mâcon-Villages in 1999 to form their own AOP. It's Chardonnay only once again, and there are some bravura wines with a deal of showoff oak on them being produced.
PRODUCERS: Bonhomme, Michel, Ch. de Viré.
**Mâcon-Villages** The umbrella AOP covers a total of 26 villages making white wines, all of which have the right to append their names to the word Mâcon on the label. Some of the better quality are Lugny, La Roche-Vineuse, Montbellet, Uchizy and – tantalizingly – Chardonnay. Prissé has its own AOP.
PRODUCERS: Thévenet, Merlin, Manciat, Barraud, Bret Brothers, Bonhomme.
Below Mâcon-Villages are the basic appellations of Mâcon Supérieur (reds and whites) and simple Mâcon (reds only, mostly from Gamay).

## OTHER WINES

The basic appellation for the whole region, top to bottom, is AOP **Bourgogne** – Blanc, Rouge or Rosé. Increasingly, producers are using this to make eye-catching decent varietal wines to hone Burgundy's competitiveness at the affordable end of the market. The whites are often given a little oak, the reds properly endowed with fruit, and the rosés are usually light and evanescently fruity.

Some of the more northerly villages, notably those from the Auxerre region near Chablis – **Chitry**, **Irancy** and **Epineuil** – now have the right to add their names to the Bourgogne designation. In the whites, Chardonnay may be joined by leavenings of Pinots Blanc and Gris, while reds may add Gamay to the Pinot Noir, together with a pair of historical oddities from near Chablis – César and Tressot.

**Bourgogne Passetoutgrains** is a regional AOP for a blend of Pinot Noir and Gamay, in which the former should account for not less than a third of the assemblage.

**Crémant de Bourgogne** The traditional-method sparkling wine can be made from any of the region's grapes, but is principally Chardonnay and Pinot Noir. It can be crisp, palate-cleansing stuff, sometimes with a little depth. The terms Blanc de Blancs and Blanc de Noirs may be used for white wines made from all white grapes or all black grapes respectively. There is also some pleasant Crémant rosé.

## VINTAGE GUIDE

Vintage conditions in Burgundy affect the red wines far more than the whites. An off-year for Chardonnay may result in less substantial but perfectly drinkable wines, whereas unripe Pinot Noir may be feeble in colour, flimsy in texture and hopelessly lacking fruit.

## REDS

*2022* **** A little rainfall in June kept things fresh before a long, hot summer, resulting in charming Pinots with plenty of red fruit and good structure.

*2021* ** Not worth dwelling on, by and large.

*2020* **** The pandemic year produced an excellent Pinot harvest, with attractive balance in the best wines, and plenty of ripe fruit at all levels.

*2019* **** Appealing vintage with lots of silky-textured, fruit-forward wines. Particularly good on the Côte de Nuits.

2018 *** Problems with overripeness spoiled the chances of many wines, but the Côte de Beaune villages produced some impressive showings.

2015 ***** Buy these if you see any. It was a fabled vintage of sensational, long-lasting Pinots.

2010 ***** Every bit as good as the 2015 for big, complex, robustly constructed wines made to last.

2009 ***** A great vintage of intensely concentrated wines with glorious fruit. Perfect for laying down.

EARLIER HIGHLIGHTS: *2005* *****  *2002* ****
*1999*  ****   *1990* *****   *1989* *****
*1988* ****

## WHITES

BEST RECENT VINTAGES: *2023, 2022, 2020, 2019, 2017, 2014.*

*The rock of Vergisson (above) towers over the Pouilly-Fuissé vineyards, source of Mâconnais's finest white burgundies.*

*Barrels awaiting the new vintage (left) at Louis Latour's cellars in Aloxe-Corton, Côte de Beaune.*

# BEAUJOLAIS

*Burgundy's southernmost wine region, the huge Beaujolais area, is devoted to the red grape Gamay and one of the winemaking world's most individual red wine styles. The winemakers here offer much more than just Nouveau.*

*The hilly Beaujolais region (above), the most southerly of Burgundy's wine areas.*

**BEAUJOLAIS**
GRAPES: *Red – Gamay; White – Chardonnay*

IT IS THE FATE OF Beaujolais never to be taken quite seriously. It is mostly such a lightweight wine that few bother to age it, and most retailers are keen to get rid of last year's stocks before the new vintage arrives. You could sympathize with the region's négociants and growers until you are reminded that they pump out about a third of the entire production every year as Beaujolais Nouveau, which hardly transmits the message that this is a wine worth dwelling on. It remains, I suspect, for a great number of consumers, one of those wines that you might drink one bottle of in any given year.

All this is something of a shame because the wines of many of the *cru* villages age well, but neither their producers nor much of the wine commentariat seem to want you to know that. Admittedly, in its youth – say, six months to a year from the vintage – it can be an incomparably charming wine, its lightness of texture and lack of tannin compensated for by its alcoholic weight (typically around 13 per cent) and the easy, accessible ripeness of its juicy strawberry fruit. But what most Beaujolais lacks in tannin, it more than makes up for in acidity, and it's that raw, crunching tartness – like biting into what you hoped was going to be a nice juicy pear, and finding it as hard as an onion – that too often spoils the enjoyment.

There are moves from some growers to give the *cru* wines more depth and power by varying the vinification method (traditionally carbonic maceration, in which the fermentation takes place within the grape) to allow a little tannin into the wines. Those used to the happy-go-lucky reds of summer may find these wines, which are also sometimes aged in oak, normally a foreign substance in Beaujolais, something of a shock to the system, but they have been among the region's more notable successes.

By and large, though, Beaujolais remains pre-eminently an unchallenging summer tipple, easily made, bottled early and drunk chilled. Most of it is too expensive for what it is, but when growers in the *cru* villages are presented with a ripe vintage of wines that are capable of deepening over six or seven years into a complex,

gamey maturity, then I don't mind the price of admission. Négociants dominate the Beaujolais scene, with the old and reputable house of Georges Duboeuf in the vanguard, but there are many fine small growers to look out for too.

The more basic the quality and the younger it is, the colder Beaujolais should be drunk. Keep the best *cru* wines for longer, and don't chill them at all. These come from ten villages identified as having the best vineyard sites. From north to south, they are:

**St-Amour** Traditionally drunk on Valentine's Day, of course. Intensely fragrant, but with a hint of Burgundian structure to it as well. It is often one of the best-balanced of the *cru* Beaujolais. PRODUCERS: des Ducs, des Billards, Côtes de la Roche.

**Juliénas** One of the less charming wines, often rather hard and insufficiently endowed with fruit, but made in a softer style by some. PRODUCERS: Ch. de Juliénas, Pelletier, Tête, Duboeuf Ch. des Capitans.

**Chénas** At this point, the *cru* wines start becoming bolder and sturdier. These are prime candidates for ageing, being clenched and dour in their first flush of youth, but ageing to a meaty, sinewy richness. PRODUCERS: Champagnon, Lapierre, Piron & Lafont Quartz, Santé.

**Moulin-à-Vent** The Beaujolais that seems to think it's a Rhône wine, Moulin-à-Vent is always the biggest and burliest of the *crus*. From a good producer, the wines can take ten years' ageing in their stride, but they can be just as enjoyable at three or four years, with ripe blackberry fruit and often a fair bit of tannin. PRODUCERS: Janodet, Ch. des Jacques, Duboeuf Tour du Bief, Santé, Champagnon.

**Fleurie** Still the best-loved of the *crus* – and therefore often the most expensive. Classic Fleurie is summer-scented with strawberries and roses, light-textured and creamy and soft. A lot isn't. Guy Depardon's atypical wines will shock the purists, but are masterpieces of violetty, gingery, Turkish Delight seductiveness, rounded with barrel-ageing, and needing a decade in the bottle.

PRODUCERS: G Depardon, Verpoix, Chignard, Berrod, Clos de la Roilette, Duboeuf La Madone and Quatre Vents.

**Chiroubles** Light and attractive wines, not much seen outside France, but worth trying if you come across one.

PRODUCERS: Cheysson, Desvignes, Passot, la Combe au Loup.

**Morgon** Morgon's wines are famous for their capacity to age very quickly into a light but interestingly meaty Burgundian maturity, an experience worth seeking out. To capitalize on this, some is released with the designation Morgon Agé; it's cellared for 18 months before it hits the market. Even in youth, there is a savouriness to them, and the fruit is often more blackcurrant than strawberry. Best come from a hillside called the Côte du Py, which will be named on the label.

PRODUCERS: Janodet, Desvignes, Aucoeur, Lapierre, Foillard, Duboeuf Jean Descombes.

**Régnié** The newest *cru*, created in 1988, and it can consider itself very lucky. These are the lightest of the light.

PRODUCERS: Rampon, Durand, Duboeuf des Buyats.

**Brouilly** Silky-soft, cherry-fruited charmers at their best, the wines of Brouilly are the most approachable of the *crus*. They don't generally need ageing, as their youthful fruit is so exuberant. By far the biggest production of the ten.

PRODUCERS: Ch. Thivin, Ch. de la Chaize, Lapalu, Michaud, Duboeuf Ch. de Nevers and Dom. de Combillaty.

**Côte de Brouilly** Hillside vineyards in the middle of Brouilly, but possessing their own blue-granite soil and exposure, consequently making distinctive wine. Deeper cherry fruit and richer texture than Brouilly itself, often with a touch of ginger. Underrated and not much exported.

PRODUCERS: Ch. Thivin, Pavillon de Chavannes, Viornery, Ravier.

Wines from any of 39 villages in the northern part of the region may be sold as **Beaujolais-Villages**, with the village name mentioned if the wine comes solely from that vineyard. These can be delightful, fruity reds for quaffing young. The rest is basic **Beaujolais**, and represents a significant drop in quality. Buy a Villages wine if you're not in the market for a *cru*. There are small amounts of ethereally light **Beaujolais Rosé**, and a smidgen of often pretty impressive, if austere, **Beaujolais Blanc** made from Chardonnay.

As to **Nouveau**, it is the wine of the new vintage, released on the third Thursday of November. In occasional years, it can have a chewy-candy charm, but it mostly stinks of fermentation and is piled with stomach-provoking acids. Yum.

BEST RECENT VINTAGES (but note that Beaujolais rarely has complete disasters): *2023, 2022, 2020, 2019.*

*Gamay vines under an autumnal mist in the village of Juliénas (below), one of the more northerly of the Beaujolais cru villages.*

# RHÔNE

*Overshadowed for centuries by Bordeaux and Burgundy, the Rhône valley is
nonetheless the source of formidable spicy, rich reds and intriguing whites from its
two distinct areas – the Syrah-dominated north and the mixed culture of the south.*

THE RHONE VALLEY consists of two quite
distinct viticultural sectors about
30 miles apart, running from Vienne down to
Avignon, and referred to simply as Northern and
Southern Rhône. Production is predominantly
of red wines, and the styles are typically big,
hefty, spicy creations that mature as excitingly
as the best Bordeaux.

The last 30 years or so have seen a
transformation in the Rhône's fortunes. Where
once only Hermitage and Châteauneuf-du-Pape
were known at all well outside its confines, its
many other fine appellations have had the world
beating a path to its door. They have also inspired
winemakers elsewhere to try their hands with
the indigenous Rhône grape varieties, Syrah,
Mourvèdre, Grenache, and the white Viognier.

Prices for the top wines have accordingly
ascended into the stratosphere, but the good
news is that, far more than in Bordeaux or
Burgundy, the more gently priced everyday
wines are thoroughly reliable. The Rhône thus
remains a democratic wine region, where the
ordinary customer is far less likely to be fobbed
off with undrinkable tat than in the hallowed
environs of the Médoc or the Côte d'Or.

*NORTHERN RHONE*

*GRAPES: Red – Syrah;
White – Viognier,
Marsanne, Roussanne*

*The Rhône river lends its
name to the long stretch
of the Rhône valley wine
region (below), divided into
two distinct viticultural
districts – northern and
southern Rhône.*

## NORTHERN RHÔNE
(from north to south)

**Côte-Rôtie** What distinguishes the reds of the
north from those of the south is that they are
made from one red grape, Syrah, whereas the
southern wines are always a mix, with Syrah
usually a fairly junior partner in the blend.
Having said that, Côte-Rôtie is permitted to
include up to 20 per cent of the white grape
Viognier (see Condrieu below). Not all producers
use it, but those who do add a little – and it
is hardly ever the full 20 per cent – produce
perfumed wines of astonishing intensity.

The AOP name, the 'roasted hillside', refers
to its steep, southeasterly exposure on the left
bank of the river, where the vines are sheltered
from the worst the weather can do, enjoying
their own little sun-trap. In the hotter years,
Côte-Rôtie is an uncommonly concentrated
wine, crammed full of blackberry fruit and
tannin, but with layers of spice and chocolate
underneath, just waiting for a decade's maturation.
It is arguably even more highly prized than
Hermitage itself these days, with the inevitable
consequence that prices for the wines of the
best growers have shot through the roof. At the
pinnacle of achievement are the wines of Marcel
Guigal, who makes not only straight Côte-
Rôtie, but also three exemplary wines from
single vineyards (La Landonne, La Mouline and
La Turque), for which he charges the earth.
PRODUCERS: Guigal, Jamet, Jasmin, Delas,
Rostaing, Cuilleron, Bonnefond, Vidal-Fleury,
Duclaux, Gérin, Ogier.

**Condrieu** The sole grape of this white-wine
appellation is Viognier, suddenly internationally
fashionable in recent years as an alternative to
Chardonnay. Condrieu is its true home, making
wines that continue to set the pace for all other
growers of the variety. The wines initially seem
rather heavy and creamy on the nose, but then
a wonderfully musky scent of puréed ripe
apricots comes through, followed by subtle
spice notes often reminiscent of Indian cooking
– ground coriander, sticks of cinnamon, ginger
root – but all bound by that thick, clotted-cream
feel. Many producers achieve this, moreover,

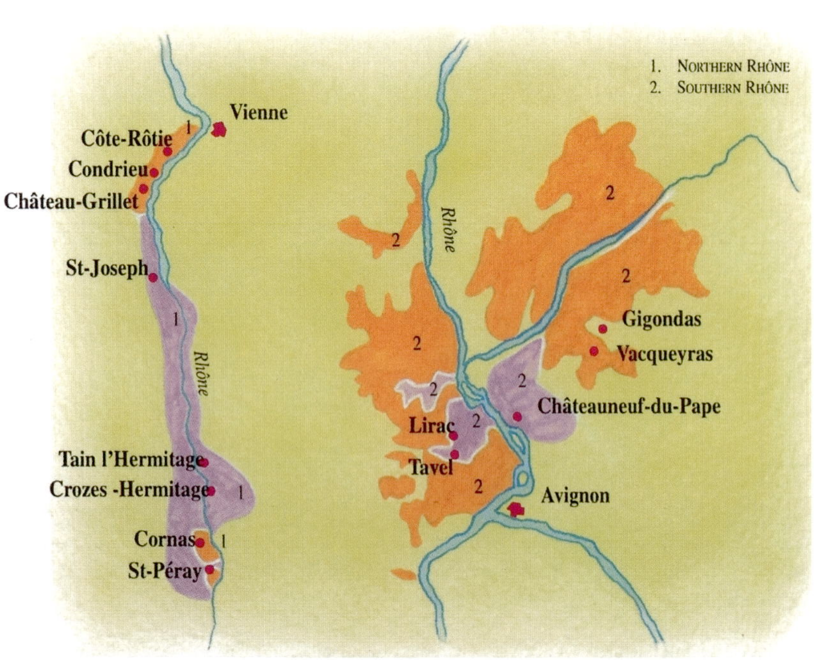

without resorting to oak. Opinion tends to divide on the best moment to drink these wines. I think they are at their best fairly young, up to two years old. Once again, they are expensive, but worth trying at least once. A small amount of sweeter late-harvest wine is made.

PRODUCERS: Vernay, Guigal, Cuilleron, Perret, Villard, Colombo, Monteillet, Pichon, Gaillard.

**Château-Grillet** Single-vineyard enclave of four hectares within Condrieu, wholly owned by the Neyret-Gachet family and awarded an appellation all of its own. The wine is aged in cask, and is intended to be far longer-lived than Condrieu. At five to ten years, it is full of orange and apricot scents against a mineral background, with notes of golden raisins on the finish.

**St-Joseph** Red and white wines. The reds may be less distinguished than those of Côte-Rôtie, but do have a raspberry-fruited immediacy to them and some definite ageing potential. Some producers make a practically Beaujolais-like lighter red, but even the heavier ones are nothing like as dense as other northern Rhône reds. Whites are made from a pair of grapes often found together in these parts – the twin sisters Marsanne and Roussanne. There isn't much made in St-Joseph, but what there is is fairly chunky, walnut-dry, but spice-tinged.

PRODUCERS: Chave, Gripa, Coursodon, Graillot, Durand, Jaboulet's Le Grand Pompée.

**Crozes-Hermitage** The largest output, mostly of red wines, of the north comes from this AOC. Usually considered to be the first rung of the quality ladder, but in fact its wines are remarkably well-made, even at cooperative level, and can therefore represent outstanding value. Peppery, gingery, plummy and firm-textured, they are capable of a few years' ageing. Up to 15 per cent white grapes (Marsanne and Roussanne) may be added to them, though rarely are. The white wines themselves are florally scented, but quite solid and lumpish in texture.

PRODUCERS: Graillot, Ferraton, Fayolle, Combier, Pochon, Les Bruyères, Dom. des Grands Chemins, Darnaud, Cave des Clairmonts.

**Hermitage** The great hill of Hermitage pops up in the middle of the Crozes appellation, its steeply shelving vineyards forming the AOP of Hermitage itself. Often among the most majestically proportioned red wines made anywhere in France, they are huge, powerfully concentrated, full-on Syrah, with tannin and extract to spare, and demanding the best part

of a decade to begin to unwind. When they do, their fruit remains as vibrantly fresh as the day they were bottled, so that even at 12 years old, they can gush forth blackberries and raspberries in abundance, backed up by dark chocolate and the most savoury herbs – thyme and oregano. Whites, a blend of Marsanne and Roussanne, are rich and weighty, with flavours of roasted nuts and liquorice.

PRODUCERS: Chave, Guigal, Delas, M Sorrel, Faurie, Tardieu-Laurent, Chapoutier, Jaboulet's La Chapelle.

**Cornas** Enigmatic appellation for densely textured, tannic Syrah reds that never quite seem to open out into the fruit-filled glories of Hermitage. They can often resemble the burlier versions of Châteauneuf-du-Pape, with roasting meat aromas filling out Syrah's black-pepper character, but taking their time to do so.

PRODUCERS: Clape, Voge, Colombo, Allemand, Courbis, Tardieu-Laurent.

**St-Péray** Mainly noted for rather tough, unfriendly sparkling wine, made from the white Hermitage grapes (plus another fairly rare variety, Roussette), using the traditional method, but lacking elegance. Some strangely cream-cheesy, but often likable, still white is also made, worth trying if you see it.

PRODUCERS: Clape, Gripa, Thiers, Lemenicier.

*Vineyards of Côte-Rôtie, 'the roasted slope' (above), on the sunny left bank of the Rhône, overlooking the village of Ampuis.*

*Picking Viognier grapes at the four-hectare AC Château-Grillet (above), a single vineyard within Condrieu.*

*Vineyards of Châteauneuf-du-Pape (above), the most famous red wine of the southern Rhône.*

**SOUTHERN RHONE**

GRAPES: *Red – Grenache, Cinsault, Mourvèdre, Syrah, Carignan, Gamay; White – Clairette, Picpoul, Bourboulenc, Grenache Blanc, Roussanne, Marsanne, Muscat, Viognier*

## SOUTHERN RHÔNE

**Châteauneuf-du Pape** The most famous red wine of the southern Rhône, named after a palace built for one of the Avignon popes in the 14th century and flattened by Nazi bombers during the war, Châteauneuf always has a symbol of crossed keys embossed on its bottles. It embraces a wide stylistic range, from almost Beaujolais-light to fairly weighty, ink-dark wine with whopping tannic extraction. It always has very high alcohol (14 per cent is quite usual). Principally Grenache, it can draw on 13 varieties, though most producers make do with three or four. The lighter ones can be drinkable at three years old, but most need at least twice that to begin to lose their tannin. If there is a problem, it's often that the wines are not really about fruit, other than a sort of chewy fruitgum quality.

The white wines come from a cocktail of varieties les by such unlikely stars as Picpoul, Bourboulenc, Clairette and the white version of Grenache. They tend to be fairly neutral in aroma, but fat, structured and alcoholic in the mouth. Ch. de Beaucastel's white has much more character, and is worth keeping for three or four years.

PRODUCERS: Beaucastel, Mont-Redon, Clos du Mont-Olivet, Rayas, Vieux Télégraphe, Bonneau, la Janasse, la Charbonnière, Font de Michelle, Chapoutier, Fortia.

**Gigondas** A fierce, black-hearted red, often rigidly tannic and head-bangingly alcoholic. It needs plenty of time to soften up, but many of the wines are too austere to make the wait worthwhile. When good, it has a violent liquoricey majesty.

PRODUCERS: St-Gayan, Clos des Cazaux, Raspail-Ay, Santa Duc, Brusset, Moulin de la Gardette, Amadieu, Cassan.

**Lirac** On the opposite bank of the Rhône to Châteauneuf, this much underrated AOP makes wines in all three colours, all highly reliable. The reds have good fruit and considerable substance, the rosés are agreeably ripe and graceful, and the whites are strong and flavourful.

PRODUCERS: Maby, St-Roch, Lafond Roc-Epine, la Mordorée, Sabon.

**Tavel** An AOP, unusually, for rosés only. They tend to look more beige than pink, and are not exactly overflowing with fruit. Good with richly sauced crustacean dishes.

PRODUCERS: Genestière, Aquéria, Montézargues, la Mordorée.

**Vacqueyras** May be red, pink or (very rarely) white. The reds are good, spicy, gingery wines worth keeping for five years.

PRODUCERS: Ch. des Tours, Clos des Cazaux, Monardière, Montirius, Couroulu.

**Ventoux** Dusty, spicy reds from just south of Vacqueyras, with small amounts of the other two colours.

PRODUCERS: Martinelle, Anges, Cascavel.

**Coteaux du Tricastin** Mainly reds and rosés with plenty of earthy fruit. One of those appellations that has slowly but surely improved of late.

PRODUCERS: Grangeneuve, St-Luc.

**Côtes du Rhône-Villages** A whole swathe of villages, from the central Rhône districts of the Ardèche and the Drôme down through the southern section, are entitled to this AOP. Of those, 16 are allowed to append their names to the basic designation, among them Cairanne, Séguret, Sablet, Chusclun and Vinsobres. Quality across the board is quite dependable, and the price is mostly right.

**Côtes du Rhône** The basic AOP that covers all other villages, including those in the northern Rhône. Styles vary from light and fruity to tannin-driven red, via some delightful rosé, to a scant quantity of vaguely milky white. Quality is all over the place, but the wines are hardly ever pricy. Names to seek are Dom. de la Fonsalette and Guigal.

Other large areas around the southern Rhône make up a fair amount of the annual production. Most is uncomplicated everyday stuff, but there are occasional stars. The **Côtes du Lubéron** is good at hearty reds, as is the **Côtes du Vivarais**. **Costières de Nîmes** is technically in the Languedoc further south, but considers itself part of the Rhône, and its wines can be superbly complex (especially from Mourgues du Grès).

In the central sector are two wine regions, the **Coteaux de l'Ardèche** and the Drôme. The former can be a good source of varietal wines (Duboeuf makes a good Gamay there).

The Drôme encompasses the small but good AOP of **Châtillon-en-Diois**, which makes Gamay reds and Chardonnay and Aligoté whites, as well as an interesting sparkling wine, **Clairette de Die**. Made from a minimum of 75 per cent grapey Muscat blended with the neutral Clairette, it's a refreshing, frothy dead ringer for Italian Asti to the uninitiated.

## VINS DOUX NATURELS

These are sweet wine specialities of southern France. They are made naturally sweet by interrupting the fermentation of super-ripe grapes with the addition of spirit to produce a light fortified wine – basically the same method as is used for port.

**Muscat de Beaumes-de-Venise** The most celebrated of the fortified Muscats is a rich, golden dessert wine, tasting of sweet green grapes and mandarins, with a tongue-coating barley-sugar quality too. They should be drunk young and fresh, and served very well chilled. PRODUCERS: Dom. de Durban, Vidal-Fleury, Jaboulet, Delas, Bernardins.

**Rasteau** This comes as either red or white, from the respectively coloured versions of Grenache. The red can be good in a rough, young port-like style; the local co-op makes a passable example.

## VINTAGE GUIDE

For northern Rhône reds, the best recent vintages are *2023, 2022, 2020, 2019, 2017, 2016* and the truly outstanding *2015*.

In the south, the chance for blending means that more vintages are likely to produce something acceptable than if you have to pin all your hopes on the ripening of one grape variety. Good recent vintages are *2022, 2020, 2019, 2017, 2016, 2015, 2010* and *2009*.

*Harvested Muscat grapes being taken to the local cooperative in Beaumes-de-Venise (below), to make the luscious, rich, golden sweet wine of the same name.*

# PROVENCE AND CORSICA

*Traditionally known for its pale rosés, the Mediterranean region of Provence now grows a wider and better choice of grape varieties that are bringing some fine reds and whites to market.*

**PROVENCE**

*GRAPES: Red – Grenache, Mourvèdre, Cinsault, Syrah, Carignan, Cabernet Sauvignon, Tibouren, Braquet; White – Clairette, Ugni Blanc, Grenache Blanc, Rolle, Sauvignon Blanc, Marsanne, Terret*

IT IS HIGHLY PROBABLE that the much-loved region of Provence in southeast France was the cradle of French viticulture. Its ancient seaport of Marseilles was founded around 600 BC by Greek settlers, who brought their own wines with them, probably sourced from their colonies in what was eventually to become Rome. Later, when France – as Gaul – had become a major component of the Roman Empire, cultivation of the vine spread slowly westwards and northwards throughout the country from this sun-soaked corner.

Despite the fondness of European tourists, the British foremost among them, for Provence, its wines are still very little known outside the region. That remains a mystery, especially given the unusually high production of rosé wines, a style that has become extravagantly fashionable in the early years of the 21st century. Nearly all the wine is blended from a handful of grape varieties, some of them quite obscure, which means that Provence doesn't have varietalism on its side. But there is much healthy experimentation in the region, and its wines are worth trying.

**Côtes de Provence** By far the biggest AOP, covering the whole region, Côtes de Provence embraces a number of totally diverse areas in a broad sweep that runs from near Aix-en-Provence down via the coast at St-Tropez and back up to a mountainous enclave north of Nice. The greater part of the production (fully 80 per cent) is pink wines – known locally as 'little summer rosés' – targeted specifically at the tourist hordes, and sold in peculiar skittle-shaped bottles. The wines are largely based on the Midi varieties Grenache and Cinsault, but there is a good-quality local grape, Tibouren, that is used on its own by some producers, and makes characterful rosés that are a cut above the norm.

Reds have traditionally been based on the rather dull ubiquitous southern grape, Carignan, although since the 1980s, it may constitute no more than 40 per cent of the blend. Cabernet Sauvignon and Syrah are beginning to play significant roles in the vineyards instead. Only a small amount of white wine is made, but it can be unexpectedly fragrant and good. PRODUCERS: la Courtade, Ott, Richeaume, Rimauresq, Cressonnière.

**Coteaux d'Aix-en-Provence** The area around the old university town of Aix-en-Provence produces wines in all three colours, which are quite as varied as those from the main regional AOP, but at a higher overall standard of quality. Its performance has been on a steady upward trajectory since it was demarcated in the 1980s. Again, Cabernet and Syrah are beginning to make their presences felt, and some of the reds from this westernmost part of Provence have a tantalizingly claret-like profile. Rosés account for about a third of the output, while whites are very few and far between. PRODUCERS: Vignelaure, du Seuil, les Bastides, les Béates.

**Les Baux de Provence** Demarcated from the above AOP in 1995, Les Baux is a mountainous outpost of highly individual red and rosé wines, some of them from relatively recently planted vineyards. Cabernet and Syrah combine to do their stuff once more among the more traditional Provençal varieties, and encouragingly around 85 per cent of the appellation is run along organic or biodynamic lines. Indeed, so

*The broad sweep of the Provençal wine region, running from the cooler inland hills along the sun-soaked but Mistral-blown Mediterranean coast (below).*

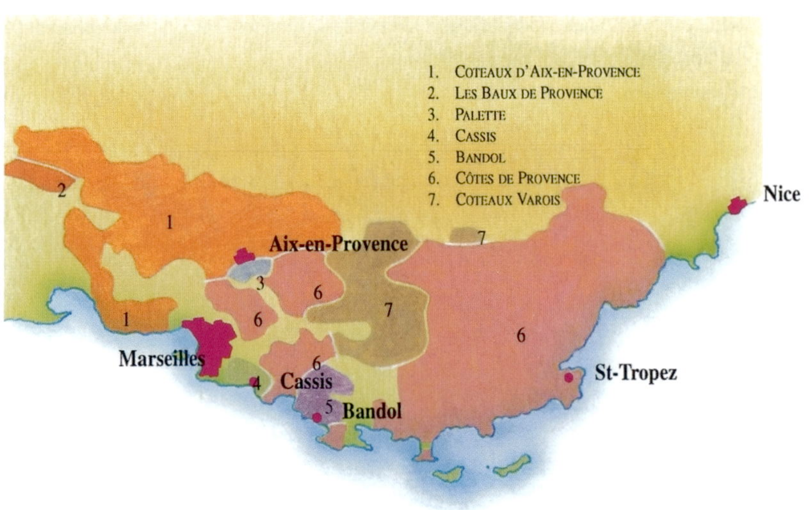

great is the local commitment to these methods that growers are lobbying for them to be made a stipulation of the AOP regulations.

PRODUCERS: Mas de Gourgonnier, Romanin, Terres Blanches, Hauvette.

**Bandol** Potentially the weightiest and most ageworthy reds in Provence come from this coastal appellation that also makes some good savoury rosé and a little crisp, appley white (some containing a dollop of Sauvignon Blanc). The reds have to be cask-aged for a minimum of 18 months, and they must include at least 50 per cent of the distinguished Mourvèdre grape, to achieve a dense-textured wine full of black plum fruit and herbs. They are slowly but surely acquiring a reputation outside the region – largely thanks to the first-named producer below – and represent a serious alternative to mid-range Bordeaux.

PRODUCERS: Tempier, Pibarnon, Pradeaux, Gaussen, Vannières.

**Cassis** Nothing to do with the blackcurrant liqueur of the same name, this tiny AOP a little further westwards along the coast from Bandol makes mainly white wines from a fascinating grab-bag of southern Rhône varieties – Marsanne among them – and Sauvignon Blanc. Mainly sold locally, they can be quite sturdy, but often possessed of an uncommonly beautiful aromatic allure. Reds and pinks use proportionately about as much Mourvèdre as those of Bandol.

PRODUCERS: Best is Clos Ste-Magdeleine.

**Bellet** Perched high up in the hills to the north of Nice, near the border with Italy, Bellet is seldom seen outside Provence. Because of its altitude, this is a cooler area, and the small production of reds, whites and rosés reflects that in noticeably higher acid levels. The grape varieties are shared with parts of western Italy, so that the Rolle of Bellet's whites is Vermentino to the Italians, while the Braquet used in its pinks is called Brachetto over the border. Outposts of Grenache and Cinsault make their appearance in the reds.

PRODUCERS: Ch. de Bellet, Ch. de Crémat.

**Palette** An historic enclave near Aix-en-Provence, about 75 per cent of which is owned by one property, Ch. Simone. In addition to the usual southern grape varieties, there are some microscopic plantings of all but forgotten local grapes on very aged vinestock, producing reds, whites and rosés. Reds and rosés can both make quite an impact in the best years.

**Coteaux Varois** Named after the *département* of the Var in which it is located, this AOP was carved out of the Côtes de Provence in 1993. The usual mixture of southern grape varieties is employed to mostly good effect, although the whites can be a shade dull.

PRODUCERS: Triennes, Miraval, Alysses.

## CORSICA

The Mediterranean island of Corsica may be French-controlled, but its vine culture owes much to neighbouring Italy. Once the source of basic slosh that went into the European wine lake, it set about radically improving its ways in the 1980s, with cautiously encouraging results to date, and an interesting spread of styles.

Corsica has a wide range of grapes, including the reds of the southern Rhône and Languedoc, as well as more fashionable international varieties. In the white Vermentino (known as Rolle in Provence) and two characterful reds (Nielluccio and Sciacarello), it has a handful of good indigenous grapes.

Only a small percentage of the island's production goes under one of the nine AOPs available. They are **Patrimonio**, **Ajaccio**, the island-wide **Vin de Corse** (all making emphatic use of the local grapes), five subdivisions of Vin de Corse – **Coteaux du Cap Corse**, **Calvi**, **Figari**, **Porto Vecchio** and **Sartène** – and a separate AOP for a *vin doux naturel*, **Muscat du Cap Corse**.

About 60 per cent of Corsican wine is made by powerful cooperatives as Vin de Pays de L'Ile de Beauté.

*Carefully tended vines at Dom. Clos Ste-Magdelaine (left), in the hot coastal hills of Cassis.*

*Houses tumble down the hillside (above) in the Corsican town of Sartène that gives its name to the local AOP, Vin de Corse Sartène.*

# LANGUEDOC-ROUSSILLON

*Better grape varieties and modern technology are assisting producers across Languedoc-Roussillon in their efforts to move away from everyday plonk to greater quality, with clean, stylish varietal wines.*

*Traditional bush-trained vines in the Languedoc-Roussillon region (above).*

*France's largest wine region (below), taking in Languedoc and the Côtes du Roussillon – once known as the Midi – which touches the Spanish border.*

THE CENTRAL-SOUTHERN swathe of France that is comprised of the twin regions of Languedoc and the Côtes du Roussillon – often referred to as the Midi – is where the most dynamic developments in the recent history of French wine have been taking place. This is the traditional grape-basket of France, and too often in the past simply a backwash area of over-production. Now it is the scene of frantic innovation, inspired to a significant degree from the 1990s on by the technical input of wine consultants from other countries.

A debate of gathering ferocity has been going on as to whether roving winemakers, with their technocratic ways, jetting in from Australia and elsewhere, and stopping just long enough to oversee the harvest, the grape-crushing and the vinification, are not guilty of homogenizing the taste of these wines. There has been some militant resistance on the part of local growers to superstar investors from the English-speaking world hoping to buy up land, and grow something akin to California Merlot in the rolling hills of southern France.

The potential of the Languedoc has nonetheless begun to emerge. Some of its key appellations were only upgraded to AOP status in the past 20 years, while a lot of the running has been made by growers working outside those regulations. These latter have been planting varieties that were not previously the norm in the region – Cabernet Sauvignon, Chardonnay, Sauvignon Blanc, even the odd outbreak of Pinot Noir. In consequence, the Languedoc is – with the exception of Alsace and its handful of traditional white grapes – the best bet for the varietally minded wine-lover starting out in France.

**Vin de Pays d'Oc** The Languedoc has done a smart job since the 1980s of turning wine tradition on its head by bottling much of its best wine under the catchall generic designation of *vin de pays*. Theoretically inferior to wines of AOP status, these would-be 'country wines', in many cases, put the produce of the appellations to shame in terms of quality. Prices for the most ambitious rose rapidly, as growers realized that an oak-aged Cabernet Sauvignon could fetch more in the market than Fitou.

The climate down here is more reliable than in most of the classic French regions, with relatively low rainfall and less severe spring frosts. Deep, blackcurranty Cabernets are nearly always better than cheap Bordeaux, Chardonnays range from the lightly oaked and lemony to strapping young things full of butterscotch and cream, while Sauvignons can be improbably crisp and fresh for such a warm climate. Soft juicy Merlots, peppery-plummy Syrahs, ripely apricotty Viogniers and the odd, rather lost Pinot Noir fill out the picture. PRODUCERS: Skalli-Fortant, Clovallon, Val d'Orbieu, Denois, Lurton.

**Vin de Pays de l'Hérault** If there were to be a *grand cru* of the *vins de pays* in the south, it would surely go to an estate called Mas de Daumas Gassac in the eastern Languedoc district of the Hérault. Here, powerfully aromatic whites, thick, strong, mountainous Cabernet-based reds of uncompromising intensity, and a delightful, madeira-like sweet wine, Vin de Laurence, have ripped up the formbook. Quality is on a definite upswing across the Hérault, though, and there are increasing numbers of stars. PRODUCERS: Mas de Daumas Gassac, Limbardié, Grange des Pères, Ch. Capion.

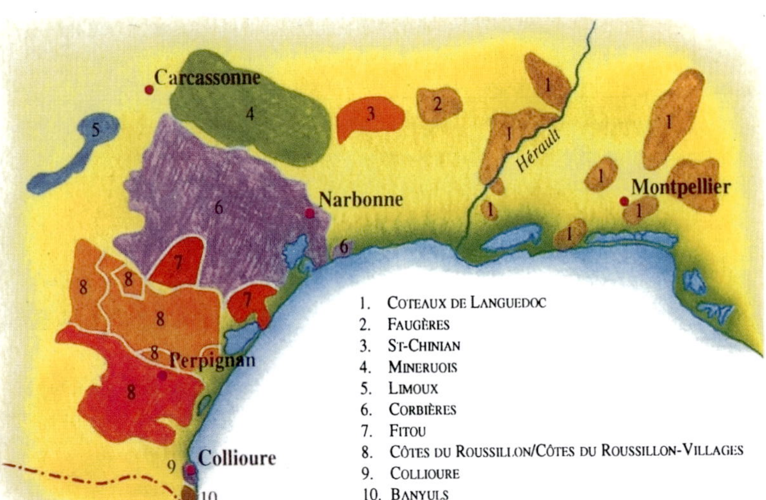

**Coteaux du Languedoc** A rather sprawling AOP for some of the best village wines of the Hérault, flanked by the eastern edge of the Aude and the western fringe of the Gard *départements*. The painstaking process of subdividing the Coteaux into recognizably distinct districts has been under way for some years, and includes the areas of Grès de Montpellier, La Clape, Pézenas, Pic-St-Loup, Picpoul de Pinet, Terrasses de Béziers, Terrasses du Larzac and Terres de Sommières. Within these, individual *crus* to look out for are Quatourze (La Clape), Cabrières (Pézenas) and Montpeyroux and St-Saturnin (Terrasses du Larzac).

The overall picture here is improving all the time, with Grenache, Syrah and Mourvèdre staking a claim to a larger share of the red blends, at the expense of the humdrum Carignan, and making some fragrant, pale pink rosé. Whites from Picpoul de Pinet have been impressive in a muscular, solidly textured way, while Clairette du Languedoc is a white of uncommon versatility, ranging in style from light, dry and neutral to heavily sweet and oxidized. Take your pick.

PRODUCERS: Mas Jullien, Prieuré St-Jean-de-Bébian, Clos Marie, Peyre Rose, Lacroix-Vanel.

Working our way around in a southwesterly arc from just north of Cabrières, the other appellations for unfortified wines in Languedoc-Roussillon are as follows:

**Faugères** Demarcated in 1982 out of the Coteaux du Languedoc, Faugères makes soft, berryish reds from Syrah, Grenache, Mourvèdre and a maximum proportion of 40 per cent Carignan. Small amount of fairly ordinary rosé. Excellent value.

PRODUCERS: Alquier, Barral, Estanilles, Lorgeril.

**St-Chinian** A little further west in the foothills of the Cévennes, St-Chinian shares the same history and grape varieties as Faugères, with light rosés and perhaps a little more heft to the reds, which can be impressively long-lived.

PRODUCERS: Cazal-Viel, Rimbert, Mas Champart, Berlou co-op.

**Minervois** As for Faugères and St-Chinian, with the addition of a little white. Quality here has steadily improved since it gained its AOP in 1985. Reds in particular can now be richly aromatic and ageworthy. Best wines come from a *cru* called La Livinière, which may be stated on the label, and represent excellent value.

PRODUCERS: Ste-Eulalie, Villerambert-Julien, Oupia, Senat, Clos Centeilles.

The old farmhouse at Mas de Daumas Gassac (above), star of the Vins de Pays de l'Hérault.

**Cabardès** North of Carcassonne on the cusp of Languedoc and the southwest, this AOP (since 1999) is allowed to use both Midi and Bordeaux grapes for hearty, meaty reds and rosés.

PRODUCERS: Jouclary, Cabrol.

**Côtes de la Malepère** West of Carcassonne, and very similar in style to Cabardès, this became an AOP in 2005.

PRODUCERS: Cave du Razès, Matibat.

**Limoux** Created in 1993 for white wines, Limoux represents a determined attempt to give the oaked-Chardonnay brigade a run for their money, so much so that oak-barrel treatment is compulsory. There are also plantings of Chenin Blanc and a crisply appley local variety, Mauzac. Since 2005, reds are permitted too from Merlot, Malbec and the Midi grapes.

PRODUCERS: Sieur d'Arques, d'Antugnac.

*Bush vines growing high in the hills of the Côtes du Roussillon (above), with the snow-capped Pyrenees and the Spanish border in the near distance.*

**Blanquette de Limoux/Crémant de Limoux** The former is the traditional sparkling wine of the region, made by the traditional method, but claiming an older lineage than champagne. Blanquette is a synonym for the local Mauzac grape, although there can be 10 per cent of Chardonnay or Chenin. Since 1990, any wine that contains up to 30 per cent of those, plus Pinot Noir, is Crémant.
PRODUCERS: Collin, Martinolles, l'Aigle.
**Corbières** One of the larger and more famous Languedoc AOPs covers a range of good, sturdy, often spicy reds, as well as small amounts of white and rosé from southern varieties. Includes a *cru* village, Boutenac. These are now some of the more fascinating, and fairly priced, examples of modern French winemaking. Buy with confidence.
PRODUCERS: les Ollieux, Voulte-Gasparets, Caraguilhes, Lastours, l'Anhel.
**Fitou** The oldest AOP in the Languedoc lies on the border of Languedoc and Roussillon, in two separate zones that are divided by part

of Corbières. There is still a fair amount of roughly undistinguished Fitou around, but the best is as good as Corbières now, a herb-tinged, sinewy red.
PRODUCERS: Mont-Tauch, Bertrand-Bergé, Roudène, Nouvelles, Lerys.
**Roussillon/Côtes du Roussillon/Côtes du Roussillon-Villages** The area south of Perpignan, bordering on Catalan country, is home to some rather more run-of-the-mill offerings. By far the best of these three designations is the last, which is for red wines only, and comprises the northern section of Roussillon, nearest to Fitou. Individual village names to look out for are Caramany, Latour-de-France, Lesquerde and Tautavel.
PRODUCERS: de Jau, Gauby, Mas Amiel, Cazes.
**Collioure** A coastal AOP of vertiginously steep vineyards, making some remarkable, thoroughly original reds in an ultra-ripe, expansive style, mainly from Grenache and Mourvèdre. Some rosé and white.
PRODUCERS: Mas Blanc, la Rectorie, Clos de Paulilles.

## OTHER WINES

There are a number of *vins doux naturels* produced in this region, both white and red. Winemaking techniques are the same as those for Muscat de Beaumes-de-Venise (see entry, Rhône), and the whites here all use either of two strains of Muscat. Frontignan, together with three other Muscats suffixed respectively by de Mireval, de Lunel and de St-Jean-de-Minervois, all use the Muscat Blanc à Petits Grains grape, and produce lightly fragrant, barley-sugar sweet wines of varying degrees of intensity. The chunkier, less attractive Muscat d'Alexandrie is permitted as well in Muscat de Rivesaltes, made north of Perpignan.
PRODUCERS: la Peyrade (Frontignan); Mas de Bellevue (Lunel); Clos Bagatelle (St-Jean-de-Minervois); Cazes (Rivesaltes).

Sweet red wines, usually made entirely or predominantly from Grenache, are made in **Rivesaltes, Maury** to the west of Fitou, and **Banyuls**, down on the Roussillon coast and overlapping with Collioure. Of those, Banyuls is about the best, with sweet strawberry fruit and a heady perfume sometimes reminiscent of good ruby port, but much less aggressive on the palate. Maury is characterful too, though.
PRODUCERS: Mas Blanc, la Rectorie (Banyuls); Mas Amiel (Maury).

# GASCONY AND THE SOUTHWEST

*These small wine areas, scattered from Bordeaux down to the Spanish border, offer a diverse and exciting range of wines that have been little influenced by passing fashions. These winemakers are proud of their traditions.*

WHEREAS MOST OF the appellations of the sprawling Languedoc region make use of the same basic collections of red and white grapes for their wines, a much more diverse picture prevails in the southwest. There is an umbrella trade organization for the wines of the southwest, but each AOP retains its own fiercely guarded identity, and many have one or two local grape varieties they are proud to call their own.

They also have a culinary tradition to be proud of. After Burgundy, this is probably the most celebrated gastronomic corner of France, home of magnificent pork and poultry, Toulouse sausages, duck confit, foie gras, sheep's-milk cheeses, prunes and armagnac.

The producers have been considerably less susceptible to the influence of foreign technologists around these parts than further east, and are consequently more fearful that their often little-known wines will continue to be swept aside in the varietal mania that has overcome the world markets. However, there remains at least a sporting chance that the next generation will discover Petit Manseng and

Négrette grapes, and then the southwest will have its day at last.

Wending our way circuitously down from just south of Bordeaux to the far southwest corner, the main appellations are as follows:

**Bergerac/Côtes de Bergerac** The first few AOPs in the immediate vicinity of Bordeaux were once considered part of its overall catchment area. They use the same grape varieties (chiefly Cabernet Sauvignon, Merlot and Cabernet Franc for reds and rosés, Sauvignon Blanc and Sémillon for whites). Bergerac and the theoretically slightly superior Côtes de Bergerac are to the east of the Côtes de Castillon sector of Bordeaux, on the river Dordogne. There are a few stars here, though a lot of the wine is pretty basic stuff from the local cooperative.

PRODUCERS: la Jaubertie, Bélingard, Tour des Gendres, l'Ancienne Cure.

**Montravel/Côtes de Montravel/Haut-Montravel** Traditionally a white-wine AOP at the western end of Bergerac, mainly planted with Sémillon. The three designations refer to dry, semi-sweet and very sweet wines respectively.

*Château de Crouseilles peering majestically over its vineyard in the Gascon red-wine enclave of Madiran (above).*

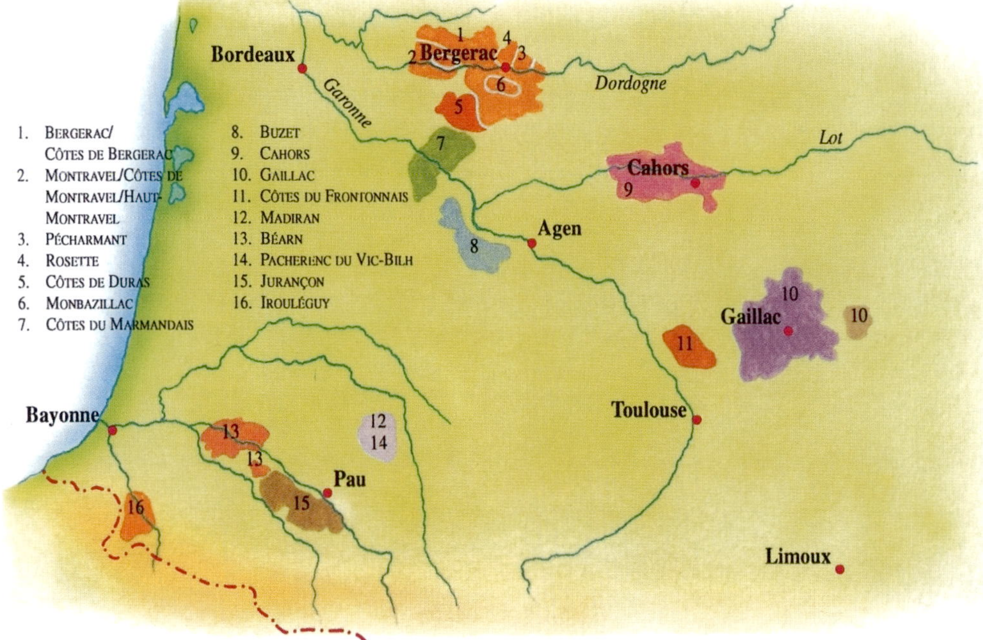


*The scattered appellations of Gascony and the southwest (left), from Bergerac, close to Bordeaux, down to Irouléguy on the border with Spain.*

**GASCONY & SOUTHWEST**

*GRAPES: the Bordeaux grape varieties and a wide collection of local varieties further south.*

*The old face of Cahors, in the Lot valley (below), an area once renowned for its 'black wine'.*

The dry Montravel wines are best, and much improved of late. Montravel may also now be red, from at least 50 per cent Merlot.
PRODUCERS: Jonc Blanc, du Bloy, Puy-Servain.
**Pécharmant** Red wines from Bergerac itself, using Bordeaux grapes with a preponderance of Merlot. Overall quality is high, classy and claret-like.
PRODUCERS: Tiregand, Chemins d'Orient.
**Rosette** Sweet-wines AOP overlapping into Pécharmant and using Sémillon, but now sadly dwindling towards extinction.
**Côtes de Duras** South of the Dordogne, the Duras makes some passable wines in the style of simple Bordeaux. The best shots are the Sauvignon whites, which can be agreeably crisp and clean.
PRODUCERS: Chater, Petit Malromé.
**Monbazillac** One of the southwest's unsung stars is the potentially glorious botrytized wine of Monbazillac. While Sauternes prices soar, this AOP further east along the Dordogne looks a ringer for great dessert wines at affordable prices. Sensational vintages in the late 1980s brought its name to a wider audience. Made from noble-rotted Sémillon, with Sauvignon and flowery Muscadelle, the best are full of golden, honeyed richness.

PRODUCERS: Tirecul-la-Gravière, Grande Maison, Haut-Bernasse, Theulet.
**Saussignac** Tiny AOP for sweet Sémillon-based whites, just west of Monbazillac. Of no great pedigree, though Ch. Court-les-Mûts produces a reasonably good one.
**Côtes du Marmandais** An AOP since 1990, the Marmandais straddles the river Garonne, south of Bordeaux. It makes principally reds (with a smidgen of rosé and white) in a no-nonsense, easy-drinking style. The Bordeaux varieties are allowed to constitute up to 75 per cent of the red blends, the remainder made up of Syrah, Gamay, the rough-natured southwestern grape Fer Servadou, and a Marmandais speciality, Abouriou. A couple of co-ops account for the bulk of production.
**Buzet** Although south of Marmandais, Buzet returns to the Bordeaux varieties for all colours of wine. Once again, the cooperative predominates, but its versatile range (look for its Baron d'Ardeuil) is good. The austerely concentrated reds are often as structured as *cru bourgeois* claret.
**Cahors** Situated northeast of Agen, Cahors spans the river Lot. Historically one of the more famous southwest names, it was once known as the 'black wine' because the grape juice was boiled to concentrate its colour. Now more sensitively vinified, it is made from a minimum 70 per cent of the Bordeaux variety Malbec (known locally as Auxerrois), backed up by Merlot and a fierce local grape Tannat, used only in judicious dashes. Light red fruits and modest tannins are the hallmarks of the wines now, but many have an intriguing violetty note too, and a lingering spicy sizzle.
PRODUCERS: Triguedina, Clos de Gamot, Haute-Serre, Lamartine, les Rigalets.
**Gaillac** A large AOP northeast of Toulouse, Gaillac makes a wide range of styles, from bone-dry as well as slightly sweet whites, via some sparkling wine using an old, single-ferment rural method, to firm full reds. Its proximity to Limoux means that Mauzac is an important variety, and the dry whites and fizzes have the same sort of tart, green-apple bite to them. It's supplemented by local grapes Len de l'El and Ondenc, as well as a soupçon of Sauvignon. The fizzes may be either just pétillant (Gaillac Perlé), or fully re-fermented and released with the yeast sediment still sloshing around in them. Reds include the local Duras and Fer Servadou, together with Syrah and Gamay, as

well as the big three Bordeaux varieties. There is a tendency to produce sturdy, oaky reds now, which require keeping.
PRODUCERS: Plageoles, Labarthe, la Ramaye.
**Fronton** Distinctive reds made from the local grape Négrette, which has a deliciously savoury pepperiness to it, fleshed out with the two Cabernets and Fer Servadou. Better than most country reds for sheer concentration and personality. Also makes a small amount of rosé.
PRODUCERS: Baudare, Bellevue-la-Forêt, Cahuzac.
**Tursan** Roughish, everyday reds from the muscular Tannat grape and the Cabernet duo, rosés from the Cabernets, and oak-matured white based on local variety Baroque.
**St-Mont** All shades of wine, dominated by the reliable Caves de Plaimont cooperative. Reds and pinks use Fer Servadou and Tannat, as well as the main Bordeaux trio; indigenous white grapes include such delights as Ruffiac and Courbu, among others. Some highly interesting flavours and oak experimentation are to be found, but quality remains uneven.
**Madiran** The unforgivingly brutal Tannat grape comes into its own in these fiery reds that always need a few years to soften, but never quite lose the power to intimidate. When fully ripe, they are spicily elegant. The two Cabernets are used to provide some fruit relief.
PRODUCERS: Montus, Aydie, Capmartin, Berthoumieu, Ch. de Crouseilles.
**Béarn** To the west of Madiran, and using the same grapes for reds and rosés. These are softer than Madiran, but not particularly characterful. Lapeyre makes a good one.
**Pacherenc du Vic-Bilh** A separate AOP within Madiran for generally sweet white wines made from the local grapes Ruffiac, Courbu and Gros and Petit Manseng, together with Sauvignon and Sémillon. Depending on the vintage conditions, Pacherenc may be made dry, but its sweeter wines made from grapes left to shrivel on the vine can be occasionally as distinguished as the sweet wines of Jurançon.
PRODUCERS: Aydie, Labranche-Laffont.
**Jurançon** Much underrated AOP south of Pau, making white wines principally from a blend of the twin varieties Gros Manseng and Petit Manseng (the latter the better for its piercing pineapple and apricot aromas), together with some Courbu. The wines may be refreshingly dry and full of tropical-fruit ripeness, or lusciously sweet from raisined grapes, as in Pacherenc. Excellent value.
PRODUCERS: Uroulat, Cauhapé, Lapeyre, Souch.
**Irouléguy** Practically on the Spanish border in the Pays Basque, this far-flung AOP takes in a number of young vineyards carved out of the Pyrenean rock by growers motivated by great regional pride. Tannat raises its wild head in the reds and rosés, but is tempered by the Cabernets, while the whites use the Jurançon varieties. As elsewhere, the regional co-op makes a fair amount of the wine, but Arretxea and Brana are also good.
**Vin de Pays des Côtes de Gascogne** Surplus grapes not used in the production of armagnac, the brandy of the southwest, go into white wines under this regional designation. Much comes from Ugni Blanc and is yawningly dull, although there is also some Sauvignon and both Mansengs to add aromatic appeal, and even a little Chardonnay and Sémillon. They should all be drunk young and fresh. There are smaller quantities of red and rosé too, with an equally broad palette of grapes to choose from – the three main Bordeaux varieties, plus Malbec, Tannat, Négrette, Duras and Fer Servadou. Styles tend to be on the lighter side, crisp but not especially memorable.
PRODUCERS: Tariquet, Brumont, St-Lannes, Caves Plaimont.

*The stunning Château de Monbazillac (above). The finest sweet wines of Monbazillac can rival those of Sauternes.*

*Cabernet Sauvignon grapes arriving at the Buzet cooperative (above). The Bordeaux varieties are used to make concentrated claret-style reds.*

# JURA, SAVOIE AND BUGEY

*To the east of Burgundy lie the three little-known regions of Jura, Savoie and the Bugey. Tucked up against the French Alps, the areas are dominated by white wines, and the unique styles of* vin jaune *and* vin de paille.

THESE THREE EASTERLY regions are among the most obscure and insular of all France's wine-growing areas. Not much of their wine is exported, and what is makes few compromises to modern tastes.

## JURA

The remote high-altitude vineyards of the Jura, not far from the Swiss border, harbour some of France's most individual wines. They do crop up in minute quantities on the export markets, but tend to be highly priced, and the house style of the region is not an especially fashionable one. That said – *vive la différence.*

There are two regional specialities – *vin jaune* and *vin de paille*. The former, 'yellow wine', is made in a similar way to dry sherry, in that it matures in cask for six years under a *voile*, or film, of yeast culture. As the wine oxidates, it turns yellow. About one-third also evaporates. The resulting wine is heavy-textured, dry as chalk-dust and alcoholic – rather like fino sherry, in fact. *Vin de paille*, 'straw wine', is equally rare and made from raisined grapes dried on straw mats. These are rich, powerful wines, capable of some bottle-age. Both these wines are only made in certain years and in small quantities, and are therefore pricy. Much of the *vin de paille* is found in Arbois, while *vin jaune* reigns supreme in L'Etoile and Château-Chalon.

**Arbois** The greatest volume of Jura wine is produced under this AOP in the northern part of the region, centred on the town of the same name. They may be red, white or rosé, and there are three important local grapes: two red varieties – Trousseau, which gives a deeply rich if unsubtle wine, and thin-skinned Poulsard, quite the opposite and good for rosés – as well as a white, the gloriously musky Savignin, a relative of Gewürztraminer.

Pinot Noir and Chardonnay are also grown, the latter more extensively in recent years. Some of the wine is made sparkling by the traditional method, and labelled Crémant du Jura, while wines from the best village, Pupillin, are allowed to add its name as a suffix.
PRODUCERS: Puffeney, Tissot, Maire.

**Côtes du Jura** The central and southern parts of the region take this AOP, but make the same broad range of styles from the same grapes as Arbois. Ch. d'Arlay is a good producer of *vin jaune*.

**L'Etoile** Tiny AOP largely represented by the local co-op, specializing in hazelnutty *vins jaunes* from Savagnin. Also straight white, and sparkling wine.

**Château-Chalon** The only AOP entirely for Savignin *vins jaunes*, Château-Chalon sits on a little hilltop, remaining completely aloof from the modern world. Wine is only made in years when the producers deem the harvest good enough to bother.
PRODUCERS: Bourdy, Berthet-Bondet, Macle.

*The vineyards of Jura and Savoie (below) lie on the lower slopes of the French Alps, close to the Swiss border.*

*The vineyards of Château-Chalon (left), the tiny AOP in the heart of Jura that makes only* vin jaune.

**Macvin du Jura** A fortified style in any colour, Macvin gained its AOP in 1991. It is unfermented sweet grape juice to which a slug of marc du Jura (grapeskin spirit) is added.

## SAVOIE

Lying due south of Geneva, Savoie is home to some indigenous grape varieties. Many of its wines have character, but are not much exported.

**Savoie** The overall AOP for any wine produced within the *départements* of Savoie and Haute-Savoie. Most are whites and are made from the local Jacquère grape in a crunchy-fresh style, supported by Chardonnay, some of the northern Rhône's Roussanne, and the neutral-tasting Chasselas much favoured in Switzerland. Reds use Pinot Noir and Gamay, as well as a local variety called Mondeuse, which makes something a little fleshier than the light-bodied norm. Seventeen privileged villages may add their names to the basic designation; they include Apremont, Abymes, Montmélian and Chautagne.

**Roussette de Savoie** The Savoyards consider the Roussette (aka Altesse) to be their best white grape. It has its own AOP throughout the region. The wines have a diverting floral perfume, and should be drunk young to catch their tingling acidity at its freshest. In four villages – Frangy, Marestel, Monterminod and Monthoux – the wines must be 100 per cent Roussette; elsewhere, they can be up to 50 per cent Chardonnay.

**Seyssel** Small AOP taking in dry white wines from Roussette and the local Molette. There is also a sparkling version, Seyssel Mousseux, based on Molette, but which has to contain at least 10 per cent of Roussette.

**Crépy** Chasselas makes the wines of this dry-whites appellation, and jolly dull they are too.

## BUGEY

Just west of Savoie, in the Ain *département*, is the Bugey. Historically part of Burgundy, it now constitutes a mini-region of its own, its grape varieties marking its identity as a sort of cross between Savoie and the Jura. Finding any outside the region is something of a teaser, though some make it as far as Lyon.

**Bugey** The main designation covers the whole region. An entire range of styles is made, from aromatic, crisply textured dry whites, through delicate rosés, to lightish reds using Gamay, Pinot Noir and also some Mondeuse. There are additionally two styles of fizz – lightly prickly (Pétillant) and fully sparkling (Mousseux). Much praise has been heaped on the region's Chardonnay varietals. Cerdon is perhaps the best of the handful of village names that may appear on the labels. A separate AOP, **Roussette du Bugey**, is for whites made entirely from Roussette (Altesse).

***JURA***

GRAPES: *White – Savagnin, Chardonnay;*
*Red – Trousseau, Poulsard, Pinot Noir*

***SAVOIE***

GRAPES: *White – Jacquère, Roussette, Molette, Roussanne, Chasselas, Chardonnay;*
*Red – Mondeuse, Gamay, Pinot Noir*

*The alpine town of Seyssel, in Savoie, on the river Rhône (left), that has given its name to the local white wine AOP.*

# IGP AND OTHER FRENCH WINES

*The IGP designation was created to encourage production of higher quality, easy-drinking red, white, and rosé wines, country wines that display the character of their region.*

MANY FRENCH WINES – about a quarter of the annual production – fall below the top category for quality wine, AOP (*appellation d'origine protégée*). The designation IGP (*indication géographique protégée*) came into effect in 2009 to accord with the EU-wide system of labelling products that come from a particular designated area but are not necessarily subject to the same stringent regulations as those in the top drawer. These are wines that don't qualify for AOP status, perhaps because the grower is using grape varieties not officially sanctioned within the locality, or perhaps because the vines were too young under the appellation regulations but are nonetheless better than the most basic products.

The entry-level quality category is straightforward French wine (*vin de France*), the labels of which will have scarcely any more detail than a brand name and the information that it's from France. Not all of these are crude slosh. The Rhône family Perrin makes a perfectly decent range under the VdF label, La Vieille Ferme, a constructive way of utilizing this basement category to turn out wines made to a consistent, dependable style.

Above the *vins de France*, the IGP wines broadly correspond to the old *vin de pays* designation, wines that are intended to be as representative in their way of regional characteristics as the AOP wines. There are three levels of IGP, depending on how specific the individual producer wants, or is able, to be. At the broadest, most inclusive level, the designation may cover one of five sprawling regions: Pays d'Oc (Languedoc-Roussillon, now the most geographically extensive single wine designation in the world); Val de Loire; Comtés Rhodaniens (the northern Rhône, Jura and Savoie); Méditerranée (the southeast); and Comté Tolosan (the southwest).

Then there are IGPs that use the name of the *département*, such as Alpes-Maritimes in Provence, Gers in Gascony or l'Hérault in the Languedoc. To use these, the wines must have been sourced from grapes grown entirely within that *département*. Within the confines of those, there are over 90 zones, or local areas, based on named patches of vineyard land, particular hillsides, geographical features, and so forth (such as the Coteaux de l'Ardèche in the Rhône Valley, a subdivision of the larger departmental Ardèche IGP. These last are the districts that are best qualified to be elevated to AOP status in due course, as indeed many have been in the most recent generation.

To qualify as an IGP, the wines must be made from certain grape varieties, and are not to be blended with wines from other areas. Many of them are single-varietal bottlings and, as such, are virtually the only French wines so labelled outside the Alsace region. At the outset of the *vin de pays* revolution, this amenity enabled the producers to compete with wines labelled Chardonnay, Merlot, and so on, from the rest of the world. Gradually, however, it has promoted recognition of some of the lesser-known varieties, such as the Viognier and Marsanne of the northern Rhône, giving consumers a hint of the kinds of flavours previously only familiar to drinkers of Condrieu or white Hermitage.

*IGPs that use the name of* département, *such as Ardèche (below), must contain grapes sourced only from within that district.*

Because the bulk of it is produced in the south of France, about three-quarters of all IGP wine is red, although the second most important area is the Loire, where much of the white IGP is produced.

## REGIONAL IGP WINES

**Vin de Pays d'Oc** Stretching across the Languedoc-Roussillon region of southern France, this is by far the most commonly seen IGP. A whole panoply of what are now international grape varieties is grown here, and styles range from crisp, nettly Sauvignon to big, burly Cabernet. Wines can be blends of more than one variety, the components stated on the label in descending order of their proportions in the bottle. Some of these combinations are innovative mixtures that are not permitted within any of the regional AOPs, hence their apparently lowlier designation, but the quality of the best can be little short of stunning.

**IGP Vin de Pays Val de Loire** Originally known as the Jardin de la France, this is the regional label for the whole of the Loire Valley. Varietally labelled white wines from Chardonnay or Sauvignon Blanc are common and can be engaging enough in a fairly simple style.

**Vin de Pays du Comté Tolosan** This covers much of the southwest, with wines that are generally blends of two or more of the regional grapes. Whites are distinctly underwhelming,

but there are some reasonable reds that tend to be on the lighter side.

**Vin de Pays de Méditerranée** Wines from Provence and the southeast corner, with breezy, fresh rosés a speciality.

**Vin de Pays des Comtés Rhodaniens** The designation for a sector of the northern Rhône Valley, together with the eastern regions of Jura and Savoie.

## DEPARTMENTAL IGP WINES

Among the more important of the 52 departmental classifications are the IGPs of **Vin de Pays du Gers** (in Gascony), **Vin de Pays de l'Hérault**, **Vin de Pays de l'Aude** and **Vin de Pays du Gard** (within the IGP Pays d'Oc region), **Vin de Pays du Var** and **Vin de Pays de Vaucluse** (in Provence) and **Vin de Pays de Charente-Maritime** (which is part of the Cognac region of western France).

## SOME LOCAL IGP WINES

**IGP Vin de Pays des Coteaux de l'Ardèche** The region in between the northern and southern sectors of the Rhône has proved to be a highly reliable source of varietal reds and whites, and might expect to be promoted to AOP before long, although its present spread of grape varieties – Syrah, Gamay, Merlot, Cabernet Sauvignon, Viognier, Chardonnay and Sauvignon Blanc – will be hard to reconcile into one overarching set of regulations.

**IGP Vin de Pays des Côtes de Thongue** A good source of spicy reds from within the Hérault, northeast of Béziers.

**IGP Vin de Pays des Côtes Catalanes** Sturdy whites and herb-tinged, concentrated reds from Roussillon in the deep south.

**IGP Vin de Pays des Côtes de Gascogne** Mostly crisp, clean, herbaceous whites from the Armagnac production area in the southwest.

*These vineyards of Château Capion, in Hérault (above), grow Cabernet Sauvignon, Chardonnay and Merlot for Vin de Pays d'Oc.*

*Hand-picking of grapes near Reuilly in the upper Loire (above), destined for one of the region's comparatively rare red IPGs.*

*Grapes growing in the spectacular Ardèche gorge for use in the region's highly regarded Vin de Pays des Coteaux de l'Ardèche (left).*

# EUROPE, AFRICA AND THE EAST

*The 11th-century Castillo de Milmanda (above), owned by the famous winemaking family, Torres, in Catalonia.*

*Picking grapes for Vinho Verde (above), on Portugal's 'Green Coast'.*

When the first edition of this book was published, back in 1996, I reported that the world of wine was convulsed by a struggle for supremacy, billed as France versus the New World. Varietalism (naming wine after the grape variety or varieties it contained) was king. Serious consumers had grown tired of the often badly made and boring wines of the rest of Europe and, other than the abiding French classics, had largely bailed out of Europe, and were chasing the easy-drinking wines of the sunnier (and largely English-speaking) parts of the viticultural world.

In the years since that diagnosis, things have changed considerably. The picture has become productively more complicated, and there are signs of hope springing up all over, not just in the old European heartlands, but in some surprising new quarters too.

The single biggest factor influencing the way wine is made, sold and indeed talked about is the development of the theory of *terroir. Terroir* is a famously untranslatable French word for the entire mass of geographical, climatic and cultural circumstances in which a wine (or speciality food) is produced. It is the main reason that an unoaked Chardonnay grown in the *département* of the Yonne in northern France tastes like Chablis, while one grown in the Santa Ynez Valley, California (or, for that matter, a little way south of the Yonne in the Mâconnais) doesn't.

At one time, producers outside Europe congratulated themselves on the fact that they were not in hock to the pettifogging regulations of the continental wine bureaucracies, but by the mid-1990s, that attitude was discernibly shifting. Now producers all over the Americas, Australasia, South America and South Africa were beginning to demarcate the specific locations of which their wine industry was comprised. Now there were AVAs, GIs and WOs to match the European AOPs, DOCs and so forth. Which meant, did it not, a wholesale victory for the *terroir*-based appellation systems of Europe?

Well, yes and no. If we struggle to define *terroir* precisely, that is at least partly because it isn't in itself a wholly stable concept. This is a point that receives too little acknowledgement among its defenders (of whom I am unequivocally one). Tradition is important in wine, but dynamism, innovation, a wholesale commitment to learning from mistakes and moving on, are even more so.

One of the principal drivers for reform, and one that is bound to become more important, is climate change. If the appellations of southern Europe are going to become hotter and drier over the next generation, that will have profound implications for what happens in their vineyards. Certain grape varieties will become unfeasible. At worst, whole vineyard regions may have to be abandoned, to be replaced by new ones in northern Europe.

Even more than global warming, though, for the time being, is the Herculean effort being made by the ever-expanding European Union to harmonize the respective quality systems in place among all its wine-producing member countries. What that enterprise often foundered on was the attempt to reconcile the irreconcilable, to cater for all the niceties of individual national systems within a roughly recognizable overarching structure.

If there is one complaint consumers have about the various appellation systems, it is that they are too complicated. The everyday drinker accepts that he or she doesn't need to memorize the names of every last one of the hundreds of denominated wines in each country, but it is often the structure itself that baffles. As I write, they are just in the process of abandoning a little-used intermediate classification in French wines (VDQS, *vin délimité de qualité supérieur*) that sat awkwardly in between AOP and *vin de pays*. It only accounted for about one per cent of total production, but justifying its existence was always a headache. Now they need to do something about the subdivisions and sub-subdivisions within the *vin de pays* framework.

Similarly, by the end of the first decade of the 21st century, Italy had saddled itself with a system that began with *vino da tavola* (the entry-level table wine designation that nonetheless included some of the greatest wines of Italy, produced outside the DOC regulations), went on up through the *vin de pays* equivalent, IGT, and on to the top wines awarded DOC, the analogue for the French AOP. Except that DOC itself was further subdivided into around three dozen DOCGs, theoretically super-dooper wines, the absolute *crema* – except that they happened to include Albana di Romagna, a snoozingly dull white made near Bologna.

From 2009 onwards, Italy creditably began the long, potentially fraught process of streamlining all that into two broad categories, a regional country-wine designation to be known as IGP, with a rationalized DOP category for the upper echelon. Noses were put out of joint right and left as many wines were reclassified, but the end-result will be a more readily accessible set-up – and one that, with any luck, will obviate the need for further tinkering in the forseeable future.

Italy remains the great *terra incognita* of European wine, a country festooned top to toe with interesting indigenous grape varieties (and a few depressing dullards too, to be sure), and yet one that barely registers in the high-street retail trade beyond the over-familiar names of bulk producers of Chianti, Valpolicella, Soave and deracinated Pinot Grigio. But grapes like Sangiovese, Nebbiolo, Barbera, Dolcetto, Negroamaro, Aglianico and Primitivo (that last the European precursor of California's Zinfandel) should be on the radar of any self-respecting wine-lover.

As should Spain's Tempranillo, Verdejo, and a handful of others. Spanish wine is struggling to emerge from its traditional bad habits, which included over-ageing many red wines in cask until they tasted well and truly past it. I worry that too much regional identity is being sacrificed here to international winemaking theory, but we'll see. In the meantime, sparkling cava has suddenly got good.

Portugal has more indigenous grapes than Spain, despite its much more limited production. Some talented small producers have emerged all the over the country, with regions like the Alentejo, Ribatejo and the Douro pointing the way. For me, the best thing about the Portuguese wine industry is that it remains, among the advanced winemaking countries, by far the least wedded to varietal thinking. Why churn out more tankerloads of Chardonnay and

Cabernet when you have such sumptuous and inimitable native styles to call on? It's a self-defeating strategy they've resisted.

Poor old Germany is in real trouble. It has to find a way of convincing the world to try its premium Rieslings, list them in restaurants and bars, and drink them at the table in other words, rebuild the world from the ground up. They remain its strongest suit, but who will buy? Meanwhile, neighbouring Austria capitalizes on its greater diversity, and the novelty value of its wines, to win new converts.

The countries of the former Soviet bloc have had mixed fortunes since its breakup in the early 1990s. For a while, Hungary forged ahead, while Bulgaria fell spectacularly back. Moldova began to emerge, while Romania may have been sitting on some of the best-kept secrets of the lot. In time, Russia and Georgia will become important players. Once again, there are plenty of fascinating grape varieties, and some (though by no means enough) outside investment.

Greece, after years of lagging inexplicably behind, is now entering the big time, with scores of innovative, quality-conscious producers working magic from a menu of fascinating native grapes. I expect the handful of quality producers on Malta to elevate its small but exciting wine industry to international acclaim one fine day.

Outside Europe, there are exciting things afoot in east Asia, where Japan, Thailand and (most promisingly of all) China are working out how to apply international know-how to the biggest untapped domestic audiences for grape wine left on the planet. Watch this space.

*Autumn arrives in the vineyards of Germany's Mosel region (above), above the town of Piesport.*

*The dramatic modernist bodega (below) was built in 1918 for the Spanish producer Raimat.*

# ITALY

*The invading Greeks called it Oenotria, the land of wine. Italy has remained steeped in viticulture, has an extravagantly diverse range of styles, and today usually produces more wine than any other country in the world.*

VITIS VINIFERA, the wine-grape species, has been growing on the Italian mainland since several centuries before the birth of Christ. For a long time, the archaeological orthodoxy was that invading Greeks brought the vine to Italy in the era before the rise of the Roman Empire. It is now known that some tribal cultures, notably the Etruscans whose domain extended along the western coast of the peninsula, already possessed viticultural knowledge, and that the Greeks did little more than introduce new vine varieties to southern Italy when they arrived.

The clue to the central importance of viticulture in the ancient world is in the name that the Greeks gave to their new territory, Oenotria (land of wine). Over the centuries that followed, Roman ingenuity extended the possibilities of winemaking considerably, until it had far surpassed the Greek model. Wines of particular vintages came to be valued, as did the wines of specific regions, such as Lazio, Campania and Toscana (Tuscany).

Wherever the conquering Roman armies went, they took their vine-growing expertise with them, to keep their troops supplied with better wines than were locally available in such benighted outposts as Spain, France and even Britain. As Greek civilization entered its long decline, Italy became the heartland of European wine culture in the ancient world.

Nowadays, in terms of volume, Italy remains in most years the most significant wine producer in the world, knocking France into second place. Wine is still central to Italian family life, in a way that has all but vanished among modern urban families in France. No part of Italy is a no-go area for the vine, from the Tyrolean north to the Calabrian south, not forgetting the islands of Sicily and Sardinia. There are now over one million vineyard holdings throughout the country, an astonishing figure for its size. To a great and overarching extent, Italian agriculture just is wine.

Ongoing efforts simultaneously to refine and simplify the Italian wine classification system are a sign of progress. When the DOC system was drawn up in the 1960s, it did little more than acknowledge which wines were most commercially important, regardless of quality. That began to change in the early 1990s, when a genuine attempt to ensure quality within the regulations was initiated, with maximum yields and minimum ripeness levels specified, and wines that fell within the top DOCG category expected to pass muster among professional tasting panels.

The customary styles of many Italian wines have played an unfortunate part in holding the country back in the international markets. Most of the traditional dry white wines, to be frank, are pointless, boring, vapid creations that might taste agreeable enough if knocked back well-chilled at lunchtime while you're on holiday

*Italy's foremost agricultural industry is grape-growing. Vines are planted across the country, from the northern borders to its heel in the south (below).*

there, but have no obvious role in world viticulture now. The breakout success in recent years, Pinot Grigio, made across a whole swathe of northern Italy, has mostly only succeeded in replacing the watery white wines of the north with a watery white wine with a varietal name on it.

Reds were always better, but too often marked by what is technically known as volatile acidity, and which, bluntly simplified, meant there was more than a faint air of vinegariness to them. Many of the reds were anaemically pale and thin – not just the Merlots of the northeast either, but much of what flowed out of the Chianti region too.

Much of this is now receding into a past worth forgetting, while the true treasure-trove of Italian viticulture, its cornucopia of fine indigenous grape varieties, comes to the fore. Wines made in central Italy outside the DOC regulations, those that came to be known as the super-Tuscans, pointed the way out of the quality impasse, encouraging the production of better wines at the more affordable end of the scale. And just as Italian domestic cooking has been the single most important influence on global food fashion since the demise of French haute cuisine, so the world wants something to drink with it. And there remains no better accompaniment to tomato-based pasta dishes, Italian cured meats, risottos, gnocchi, pesto, Italian cheeses, even pizza, than Italian wine.

The pages that follow reflect the classification system as it existed up to 2025. It can be assumed that DOC (*denominazione di origine controllata*) and DOCG (*denominazione di origine controllata e garantita*) wines will eventually fall within the DOP (*denominazione di origine protetta*) category, with IGT (*indicazione geografica tipica*) regional wines becoming IGP (*indicazione geografica protetta*). It'll all be much simpler – honestly.

## PIEMONTE

The northwestern region of Piemonte (Piedmont in English), in the foothills of the Alps, is one of Italy's premium wine-growing districts. Styles range from the lightest of whites through delicate sweet sparklers to thundering, fabulously complex reds of great longevity. They are listed here alphabetically.

**Arneis** A DOC since 1989 for white wines made from the grape of the same name. They are made of sterner stuff than many Italian dry

*The Barbaresco DOCG (above) in Piedmont, the foothills of the Alps.*

whites, with a fruit like fresh pears, often mixed with a discernible hint of almond. Grown in the Langhe hills around Alba, and also in Roero to the northwest of the town, where it becomes DOCG. One of Italy's better whites.
PRODUCERS: Giacosa, Vietti, Prunotto, Deltetto.

**Asti** Formerly known as Asti Spumante, the famous frothy sweet fizz produced around the town of Asti is one of Italy's classic styles, a DOCG no less. Made from Moscato, low in alcohol (usually about 7 per cent) from a procedure that involves chilling it to halt the fermentation, and full of the flavours of ripe green grapes and sugared almonds, it is one of the most approachable sparkling wines in the world. Quality is extremely reliable.
PRODUCERS: Fontanafredda, Contero, Bera, Martini & Rossi.

**Barbaresco** This and Barolo (see below) are the two most important reds produced from the excellent Nebbiolo grape. Centred on the eponymous village, the Barbaresco DOCG is often held to produce slightly more elegant Nebbiolos than Barolo, but the difference is pretty subtle. These are huge, tannic, exotically scented wines, monstrously tough in youth, but ageing well to a savoury, chocolatey maturity. Single-vineyard wines can be monumental.
PRODUCERS: Giacosa, Gaja, Pio Cesare, Sottimano, Rocca, La Spinetta, Ceretto.

**Barbera d'Alba/d'Asti/del Monferrato** The Barbera grape, suffixed by any of these regional names, produces a sharply acidic but agreeably cherry-fruited red that is usually fairly light in both body and alcohol, though barrel-aged wines are becoming more common. Otherwise best drunk young and fresh, its undeniable potential as a variety has carried it to the vineyards of California.
PRODUCERS: Voerzio, Aldo Conterno, Giacomo Conterno, Bertelli, Prunotto, Correggia.

*Scything poppies in springtime (above) in Barolo.*

*PIEDMONT:*
*ARNEIS*
GRAPE: *Arneis*
*ASTI*
GRAPE: *Moscato*
*BARBARESCO*
GRAPE: *Nebbiolo*
*BARBERA D'ALBA/*
*D'ASTI/DEL*
*MONFERRATO*
GRAPE: *Barbera*
*BAROLO*
GRAPE: *Nebbiolo*

***BRACHETTO D'ACQUI***
Grape: *Brachetto*
***DOLCETTO***
Grape: *Dolcetto*
***FAVORITA***
Grape: *Favorita*
***FREISA D'ASTI/***
***DI CHIERI***
Grape: *Freisa*
***GATTINARA***
Grapes: *Nebbiolo, Bonarda*
***GAVI/CORTESE DI GAVI***
Grape: *Cortese*
***MOSCATO D'ASTI***
Grape: *Moscato*
***SPANNA***
Grape: *Nebbiolo*

***LOMBARDY:***
***OLTREPO PAVESE***
Grapes: *Red – Barbera,*
*Bonarda, Croatina, Uva*
*Rara, Pinot Nero; White –*
*Riesling Italico, Pinot Bianco,*
*Pinot Grigio*
***VALTELLINA***
Grape: *Nebbiolo*
***FRANCIACORTA***
Grapes: *Red – Cabernet*
*Sauvignon, Merlot, Pinot*
*Nero; White – Chardonnay*
***LUGANA WHITE***
Grape: *Trebbiano di Lugana*

*High on the alpine slopes of*
*Valle d'Aosta, vines are often*
*still trained up traditional*
*low pergolas (above).*

**Barolo** King of the Piedmontese reds, Barolo is one of Italy's most travelled DOCG wines, even though it's often very difficult to know when to drink Barolo to catch it at its best. In its youth, it is absolutely rigid with tannin, although its colour starts to fade surprisingly quickly. It then acquires an extraordinary range of flavours that includes violets, black plums, bitter chocolate and wild herbs, but even at 20 years old (when it may be quite brown), it obstinately refuses to let go of that heavyweight tannin. In the main, its growers have refused to compromise with modern tastes, so that Barolo remains one of the world's most gloriously unreconstructed red wines. Best vineyard sites (e.g. Ginestra, Monfalletto, Arione) may be specified on the label.
PRODUCERS: Giacomo Conterno, Bartolo Mascarello, Giuseppe Mascarello, Sandrone, Roberto Voerzio, Einaudi, Altare, Ceretto.

**Brachetto d'Acqui** Light red or rosé wine from the aromatic Brachetto grape, often slightly spritzy to add a dash of character.

**Carema** Tiny DOC for lighter Nebbiolo reds, in the far north.

**Dolcetto** Eleven DOCs in Piedmont make red wines from this grape. They include Dolcetto d'Alba (the best), Diano d'Alba, Dolcetto d'Acqui, Dolcetto d'Asti, Ovada, Monferrato and Langhe Monregalesi. There is also a DOCG for it in Dogliani. The wine is a bright purple, light-bodied, exuberantly fresh product, crammed with blueberry fruit, for drinking young. A more gently priced alternative to Beaujolais.
PRODUCERS: Giuseppe Mascarello, Vajra, Ratti, Bongiovanni, Chionetti, Pecchenino.

**Erbaluce di Caluso** Light, fairly soft dry whites, some fizz, and a famed but rare golden dessert wines (Caluso Passito), made from the not especially distinguished Erbaluce grape.
PRODUCERS: Ferrando, Orsolani.

**Favorita** White variety making pleasantly lemony wine on both banks of the Tanaro.

**Freisa d'Asti/di Chieri** A pair of DOCs, the latter very near Turin, for an intensely scented, light, floral red. Can be sparkling.

**Gattinara** Most important of the lesser-known DOC reds based on Nebbiolo. Intense, potentially long-lived wines.
PRODUCERS: Travaglini, Antoniolo.

**Gavi/Cortese di Gavi** Ambitiously priced dry whites from the herbaceous Cortese grape. Held in preposterously high esteem locally, hence its outlandish price. Gavi di Gavi is the top wine, with some creamy, nutty substance to it.

PRODUCERS: Chiarlo, La Scolca, Giustiniana.
**Grignolino** Light quaffable varietal red made near Asti, almost as fruity as Dolcetto.
**Moscato d'Asti** Made in the same region and from the same grape as Asti, but less fizzy and even less alcoholic (5 per cent is typical). An appetizing mouthful of citric freshness.
PRODUCERS: Ascheri, La Caudrina, La Spinetta, Bava, Giacosa, Saracco.
**Ruchè** Small DOC making full-bodied, herbal-scented reds in the Monferrato region.
**Spanna** Widely used synonym for Nebbiolo, often seen on richly textured reds from a number of localities.

## VALLE D'AOSTA
The far northwestern corner of Italy is occupied by a small river valley bordering on both France and Switzerland. Wines produced here are made from a number of native grapes, backed up by a smattering of Nebbiolo and Moscato, and plantings of Burgundy and Alsace varieties. They are almost all consumed locally.

## LIGURIA
An arc-shaped mountainous region that runs along the Mediterranean coast of northwest Italy, Liguria's main commercial centre is Genoa. It isn't particularly significant in terms of exports, and some of its traditional wines, such as syrupy dessert wines made from raisined grapes, are dying out. **Cinque Terre** is a dry white based on the local Bosco grape, usually blended with Vermentino. Rossese is an important native red variety, and has its own DOC, **Dolceacqua**, in the west of Liguria. Some Dolcetto is produced in the DOC of **Ormeasco**, and is known by that name there.

## LOMBARDIA
Centred on Milan, Lombardia runs from the Alpine border with Switzerland down to the river Po, which forms its southern extremity. It is geographically the largest of Italy's wine regions, and has been in recent years one of the quality leaders.
**Oltrepò Pavese** In classic Italian fashion, this name covers almost any style of wine, only some of which qualifies for the DOC. The best is a good sturdy red based on Barbera, while the dry whites from Riesling Italico (not the noble Riesling) are largely forgettable. Traditional-method fizzes use the Pinot family.
PRODUCERS: Frecciarossa, Verdi, Montelio.

*The castle of Soave (left), in the Veneto, that gives its name to one of Italy's most famous dry white wines.*

*Drying grapes for Amarone and Recioto (above) at the Masi winery, in Veneto's Valpolicella DOC.*

**Valtellina** The largest volume of Nebbiolo in Italy is produced in this DOC near the Swiss border. As well as basic DOC Valtellina and the slightly better DOCG Superiore version, there are four recognized sub-regions for the better wines: Inferno, Grumello, Sassella and Valgella. These are much lighter than Piedmont Nebbiolo, but the best do attain a purity of fruit and staying-power on the palate. Some powerful wine is made from shrivelled grapes fermented until fully dry, labelled Sforzato.

**Franciacorta** Created a DOCG in 1995 for potentially excellent traditional-method sparklers. Still wines are labelled DOC Terre di Franciacorta, and tend to use classic French varieties and techniques.
PRODUCERS: Ca' del Bosco, Bellavista, Cavalleri, Berlucchi.

**Lugana** White DOC for dry wines based on a local variant of the dreaded Trebbiano grape. The odd one has a little herbaceous snap to it. Zenato is a good producer. (Lugana overlaps into the Veneto region.)

## TRENTINO-ALTO ADIGE

Hard by the Austrian border is Italy's northernmost wine region. The Alto Adige is known to the Austrians, as well as the many German-speaking Italians in these parts, as the Südtirol. The lower half of the region takes its name from the city of Trento. It's a portmanteau region, like Languedoc-Roussillon.

In the last 30 years, producers here have made a name for the region by making some light but impressive wines from international varieties, most notably the two Cabernets, Merlot and Pinot Noir, as well as Chardonnay, Pinot Gris and Pinot Blanc.

Some of the Chardonnay is barrel-aged and has carved itself a niche in the international market for oaky white wines, but prices have sometimes been too stiff for their own good. Local red varietals of particular note are the sour-cherryish **Marzemino**, the richly chocolatey Lagrein (which can make sinewy reds such as **Lagrein Dunkel**, as well as graceful rosés known as **Lagrein Kretzer**), and the blackcurranty Teroldego, which has its own DOC in **Teroldego Rotaliano**.
PRODUCERS: Ferrari, San Leonardo, Haas, Lageder, Tiefenbrunner, Walch.

## VENETO

The Veneto is the major wine-producing region of northeast Italy, extending from east of Lake Garda across to Venice and up to the Austrian border. There are some important DOCs and commonly recognized names like Soave and Valpolicella, but overall quality is dogged by excessive production and some ill-considered matching of grape varieties to vineyard sites. However, the Veneto is putting its house in order, and some enterprising growers are beginning to realize the region's potential.

*Cases of Soave leaving
the packing shed (right).*

**VENETO:**
**BARDOLINO**
GRAPES: *Red – Corvina,
Molinara, Rondinella*
**BIANCO DI CUSTOZA**
GRAPES: *White – Trebbiano
Toscano, Garganega,
Tocai Friulano*
**BREGANZE**
GRAPES: *Red – Cabernet
Sauvignon, Cabernet Franc,
Merlot; White – Tocai
Friulano, Pinot Bianco,
Sauvignon Blanc,
Chardonnay*
**PIAVE**
GRAPES: *Red – Merlot,
Cabernet Sauvignon; White
– Tocai Friulano, Verduzzo*
**SOAVE**
GRAPES: *White – Garganega,
Trebbiano di Soave,
Chardonnay, Pinot Bianco*
**VALPOLICELLA**
GRAPES: *Red – Corvina,
Molinara, Rondinella*

**Bardolino** Featherlight reds from a trio of local grapes, for drinking young and fresh but not lingering over. Wines labelled Superiore should have a bit more oomph. The rosé version is called Chiaretto.
PRODUCERS: Masi, Le Vigne di San Pietro.
**Bianco di Custoza** Mostly neutral dry whites from a cocktail of grapes, none of them of much character. Some have a little tutti-frutti personality, if you try hard enough.
PRODUCERS: Le Vigne di San Petro, Gorgo.
**Breganze** One of those DOCs making waves by trying out international varietals, though there is plenty of ordinary stuff too. The reds made from the Bordeaux blend can be extraordinarily good. Maculan is the best producer by some distance.
**Gambellara** Dry whites that bear a marked resemblance to Soave, from the same grapes. Blandly inoffensive.
**Piave** The area immediately behind Venice produces large quantities of indifferent varietal wine, the lion's share of it thin, grassy Merlot.
**Prosecco di Conegliano/di Valdobbiadene** Named after its principal grape, Prosecco can be a still dry white, but its more celebrated manifestation is as a sparkler, using the Charmat method in which the second fermentation is induced in a large tank before bottling. Once useful mainly for mixing with peach juice to make the famous Bellini cocktail, Prosecco has now come up in the world, with more complex, elegant wines, in many cases rivalling Spanish cava.
PRODUCERS: Carpenè Mavolti, Bisol, Adami.
**Soave** One of Italy's most famous dry whites, synonymous for too long with the bone-dry, totally neutral, flavour-free image of Italian

white wine. Very gradually, Soave is getting better. Some of it now has a little Chardonnay in it, and some is cautiously oak-aged. At its best, and with plenty of the traditional Garganega grape in the blend, it can be a deeply appealing, gently silky white with a touch of almond paste and a faintly toasty note, perfect with lunchtime salads. **Recioto di Soave** is a sweet but austere version made from raisined grapes.
PRODUCERS: Pieropan, Anselmi, Prà, Ca' Rugate, Coffele, Suavia.
**Valpolicella** A red wine DOC that covers a multitude of styles, from very dilute pinkish wines of no great character to deliciously concentrated, berryish, chocolatey reds of considerable ageing potential. As well as the basic style (and the slightly stronger Superiore version), there are some high-octane traditional Valpolicellas produced from grapes that have been dried on straw mats. **Recioto** is a silky-sweet version that can resemble port, while **Amarone** (DOCG since 2009) is fermented out to full dryness, is hugely alcoholic (often 15–16 per cent, without fortification) and almost painfully bitter – its name coming from the Italian for bitter, *amaro*. **Ripasso** is a sort of compromise, an ordinary Valpolicella that has been allowed to run over the skins of grapes used to make Amarone or Recioto. These can be good too, though.
PRODUCERS: Allegrini, Quintarelli, Masi, Tedeschi, Le Ragose, Dal Forno, Bussola.

## FRIULI

The easternmost wine region of Italy borders Austria to the north and Slovenia to the east, forming part of the Adriatic coastline that extends down to Trieste. It is sometimes known as Friuli-Venezia Giulia. This is another region that has achieved some notable successes with international varieties, and the main production within DOC regions such as **Collio** or the **Colli Orientali** is of varietally named wines.

Best reds so far have been Cabernet Sauvignon and Merlot, particularly from the commercially important DOC of **Grave del Friuli**, Cabernet Franc from Collio, and local grapes Refosco, which makes a sharp-textured but appetizing red, and spicy Schioppettino. Successful dry whites have been Pinot Grigio, the tantalizingly flowery Tocai Friulano, crisp Sauvignon, and even some subtly perfumed Gewürztraminer. The improving DOC of

**Isonzo** has scored with most of these varieties too. There are also a pair of very rare, austerely almondy, golden DOCG dessert wines made by the raisining method, one from a grape called **Picolit**, the other – a stern tannic white called **Ramandalo** – from Verduzzo Friulano. Snap them up if you see them, but expect to pay.
REGIONAL PRODUCERS: Borgo Magredo, Pecorari, Puiatti, Edi Kante, Colmello di Grotta.

## EMILIA-ROMAGNA

A sprawling region south of the river Po, comprised of Emilia in the west and Romagna on the Adriatic coast, with the ancient city of Bologna at its heart, Emilia-Romagna is one of the bulk-producing wine regions of Italy. Very little of the wine is of DOC standard, and much of it is drunk in a slightly fizzy state, whatever the provenance. The epitome of this tendency is **Lambrusco**, which comes in all colours but is usually sparkling, high in acidity and of often dreadful quality.

A hillside district bordering on Lombardia, in the northwest of the region, the Colli Piacentini, is one of the better zones for quality wines. **Gutturnio** (made from Barbera and Croatina grapes) is a good hearty red, and there are some refreshing white varietals, including Sauvignon Blanc. Down in the southern part of Romagna, **Albana di Romagna** is noteworthy only for being the first white wine to receive the DOCG, a questionable choice for an unexceptional wine made from the workaday Albana grape. Some steadily improving red wine is made from Sangiovese, the great red grape of Tuscany. Labelled **Sangiovese di Romagna**, it is best drunk young while there is still a bracing acid edge to it. Try Cesari's.

## TOSCANA

Along with Piedmont, Tuscany is the most significant part of Italy in quality wine terms, and occupies a special place at the cultural heart of the country. In addition to the beautiful old cities of Florence and Siena, the rolling landscape of olive trees and vines is one of the best-loved on the European tourist trail.

For many newcomers to wine in the 1960s, Chianti – usually sold in straw-covered bottles – came to be synonymous with Italian red wine. More than in any other region, however, it was here that the *vino da tavola* revolution really took off, with the launch of a generation of wines made without reference to the DOC

stipulations. These proved once and for all that Italian growers are capable of producing world-class wines. Many are superb.

**Bolgheri** The Tuscan wine scene was transformed in the 1970s with the release of the first vintages of Sassicaia, brainchild of the Incisa della Rochetta family. Blended from the two Cabernets, it was an explicit attempt to produce a premium wine in the image of a classed-growth Bordeaux. For all there are no Italian varieties in it, it does still taste quintessentially Tuscan, the rich cassis-and-plum fruit always having a savoury edge like bitter herbs. It was a mere *vino da tavola* until 1994, when the Bolgheri DOC was drawn up to include it. The rest is history.
PRODUCERS: Ornellaia, Le Macchiole, Grattamacco, Satta, Poggio al Tesoro.

**Brunello di Montalcino** Created single-handedly by the Biondi-Santi family in the late 19th century, Brunello is made from a particularly fine clone of Sangiovese. It is only since the second world war that any other producer has made Brunello. One of Tuscany's greatest reds, it's deeper and richer than Chianti, full of sour black cherries and pungent herbs, and capable of long evolution. It has to be aged for three years in cask under the regulations (which many feel is too long). Prices are stratospherically high. A separate DOC, **Rosso di Montalcino**, has been created for wines released at one year old; these represent excellent value.
PRODUCERS: Biondi-Santi, Talenti, il Poggione, Castelgiocondo, La Gerla, Case Basse.

*Merlot vineyard in the Bolgheri DOC (above), destined for the 'super-Tuscan' Tenuta Ornellaia.*

*TUSCANY:*
***BOLGHERI***
GRAPES: Red – *Cabernet Sauvignon, Cabernet Franc*
***BRUNELLO DI MONTALCINO***
GRAPE: Red – *Sangiovese*

*CARMIGNANO*

GRAPES: *Red – Sangiovese,*
*Cabernet Sauvignon*

*CHIANTI*

GRAPES: *Red – Sangiovese,*
*Cabernet Sauvignon,*
*Canaiolo; White –*
*Trebbiano, Malvasia*

*VERNACCIA DI SAN*
*GIMIGNANO*

GRAPES: *White – Vernaccia,*
*Chardonnay*

*VINO NOBILE*
*DI MONTEPULCIANO*

GRAPES: *Red – Sangiovese,*
*Canaiolo; White –*
*Trebbiano, Malvasia*

*VIN SANTO*

GRAPES: *White – Trebbiano,*
*Malvasia, Pinot Grigio,*
*Pinot Bianco, Sauvignon*
*Blanc, Chardonnay*

*Grapes hanging from the*
*rafters (above) to dry out*
*for the sweet Tuscan wine,*
*Vin Santo.*

**Carmignano** Cabernet Sauvignon was allowed into Carmignano before it gained admittance to any other Tuscan red. The proportion isn't huge, but the Sangiovese is generally ripe enough not to need the extra dimension of intensity conferred by Cabernet. Impressive quality has been rewarded by elevation to DOCG. Capezzana is a highly reliable producer.

**Chianti** Inevitably for such a high-volume wine region, Chianti spans the quality range from heavenly wines of tremendous, often oak-powered concentration down to vapid, thin apologies for red wine that have only undermined it over the years. Part of the problem is that the boundaries for the region are much too inclusive. It consists of seven sub-zones: Chianti Classico (the heart of the region between Florence and Siena), Chianti Rufina in the northeast, Chianti Montalbano, and four hillside areas named after the cities they adjoin – Colli Fiorentini (Florence), Colli Senesi (Siena), Colli Aretini (Arezzo) and Colli Pisane (Pisa). Of these, only the first two are generally dependable for quality, and will always carry their regional names.

Wines given longer in cask from any of the sub-zones are labelled Riserva, not necessarily an infallible indicator of a fine wine, since much Chianti is too frail to withstand long periods in wood. The traditional Sangiovese and Canaiolo blend has been joined by Cabernet, but the allowance of the white grapes Trebbiano and Malvasia has only hindered the production of quality wine, and many of the better producers don't bother with them.

Typically, Chianti was always an orangey-red wine with an aroma of dried berry fruits, perhaps some plum tomato, and savoury herbs, feeling quite sharp on the palate from high acidity and a faint peppery edge. Modern production methods are now seeing wines with much richer colour and riper fruit, some with obvious Cabernet presence.
PRODUCERS: Volpaia, Fonterutoli, Villa di Vetrice, Isole e Olena, San Polo in Rosso, Fontodi, Selvapiana, Frescobaldi, Querciabella.

**Galestro** Water-white, low-alcohol, flavourless dry white used for mopping up the surplus Trebbiano no longer used in Chianti. Malvasia can add some interest.

**Vernaccia di San Gimignano** The local Vernaccia grape forms the basis for this highly prized, but low-volume white wine made within sight of the famous towers of San Gimignano.

Elevated to DOCG in 1993, it may now contain up to 10 per cent Chardonnay. At its best, it has an intriguingly waxy feel and attractive almond-paste character. Too much falls blandly short.
PRODUCERS: Teruzzi & Puthod, Casale-Falchini, Vagnoni, Cesani.

**Vino Nobile di Montepulciano** There is a grape called Montepulciano, but it doesn't feature in this DOCG made in the hills southeast of Florence from the classic Chianti grape mix (minus Cabernet). The wines can be powerfully intense, with strong purple fruit and a dash of liquorice, but they tend to stop just short of the pedigree of top Chianti. Two years' cask-ageing is mandatory. Again, the better producers ignore the white grapes. Younger wine may be released as **Rosso di Montepulciano** under its own DOC.
PRODUCERS: Avignonesi, Trerose, Boscarelli, Dei, Poliziano, Salcheto.

**Vin Santo** Undoubtedly the best manifestation of the undistinguished white grapes of Tuscany is as Vin Santo, a tawny, often lusciously sweet raisined wine. The grapes are hung up or laid out in the warmest part of the winery to lose their moisture. A small amount is fermented out to a nutty dryness like the driest sherry. There are DOCs for Vin Santo throughout Tuscany (one of the best being **Colli dell'Etruria Centrale**), some permitting the use of non-Italian varieties. Long cask-ageing of the wines is the norm, and many are made in a deliberately oxidized style, but retain an attractive orange-peel-and-walnuts allure.
PRODUCERS: Isole e Olena, Avignonesi, Selvapiana, Fontodi, Bindella.

## LE MARCHE

An eastern region on the Adriatic coast, with the city of Ancona its main commercial centre. Its best wines are a pair of red DOCs, **Rosso Conero** and **Rosso Piceno**, made from blends of the eastern Italian grape Montepulciano with Tuscany's Sangiovese. (In the case of Rosso Conero, the former predominates, while Rosso Piceno must be not less than 60 per cent Sangiovese.) Both are full-bodied, spicy reds with notable ageing potential. Verdicchio is the regional white grape, most often seen in **Verdicchio dei Castelli di Jesi**, one of those uninspiringly neutral-tasting whites that Italy seems to specialize in (although the best producers coax some peanutty aromatic quality out of it). **Verdicchio di Matelica** is a superior, rarer version. Garofoli makes an oak-aged Verdicchio of impressive concentration. The house of Umani Ronchi is a reliable regional producer.

## UMBRIA

Wedged between Tuscany and the Marches, the small landlocked region of Umbria is centred on the city of Perugia. Its most famous wine is **Orvieto**, which lays claim to a distinctive local grape variety in Grechetto, swamped in too many wines with admixtures of Trebbiano and Malvasia. It comes in three basic styles, a simple dry wine (*secco*), which often has the tartness of Conference pears, a medium-sweet, in-between version (*abboccato*), and a fully sweet, often rotted dessert wine (*amabile*). Overall quality isn't great, but Decugnano dei Barbi shines out.

**Torgiano** is the best red wine, now classified a DOCG. It is made from Sangiovese in a dense, concentrated style (look for Lungarotti's wines). **Montefalco** is a DOC near Assisi for Grechetto-Chardonnay whites, as well as Sangiovese reds blended with a little of the local variety, Sagrantino. Vinified alone in this region, this latter grape also has its own DOCG, **Sagrantino di Montefalco**.

## LAZIO

Lazio is the region surrounding Rome, chiefly responsible for large quantities of indifferent white wine, the most famous of which, **Frascati**, is one of Italy's best-known names. Trebbiano and Malvasia hold sway here too, so most Frascati is fairly dull stuff. Decent producers include Colli di Catone and Fontana Candida. Drink young to catch their tangy, crème fraîche character. The most overbearingly named wine in Italy, **Est! Est!! Est!!! di Montefiascone**, is also Trebbiano-based, and rarely tastes as if it justifies one exclamation mark, let alone six. Some Cabernet and Merlot is grown in this region, but otherwise there are no particularly remarkable reds.

## ABRUZZI

The reputation of this mountainous region on the Adriatic coast, south of the Marches, rests on a trio of DOC wines, one of each colour. The red, **Montepulciano d'Abruzzo**, is by far the more famous of the three. Made from the grape of the same name, it is always a softly plummy, low-tannin, easy-going wine with a strange but unmistakable waft of sea air about it. Despite its strong reliability, it has never become expensive on the export markets, and is often a surefire bet for a modestly priced Italian red with more depth than most of its equals. Umani Ronchi and Masciarelli make fine ones. **Cerasuolo** is the deeply coloured rosé version.

The white, **Trebbiano d'Abruzzo**, is hampered by its name alone. It is mostly actually made from a southern variety with the rather splendid name of Bombino, but the less reputable Tuscan Trebbiano may also be used. Valentini has single-handedly made a name for this DOC with a hazelnutty dry wine of quite uncommon intensity.

## MOLISE

Small and quantitatively unimportant region south of the Abruzzi, specializing in *vini da tavola* from international varieties such as Chardonnay and Riesling. **Biferno** is a regional DOC for wines in all three colours, the reds and rosés based on the Montepulciano grape, the whites on Bombino, Trebbiano and Malvasia.

*Bottles of Montepulciano d'Abruzzo being packed at the Illuminati winery in eastern-central Italy (below). The wine is regularly one of the country's most reliable and reasonably priced reds.*

*Vines compete for space with houses on the coastal cliffs at Amalfi (above), in Campania.*

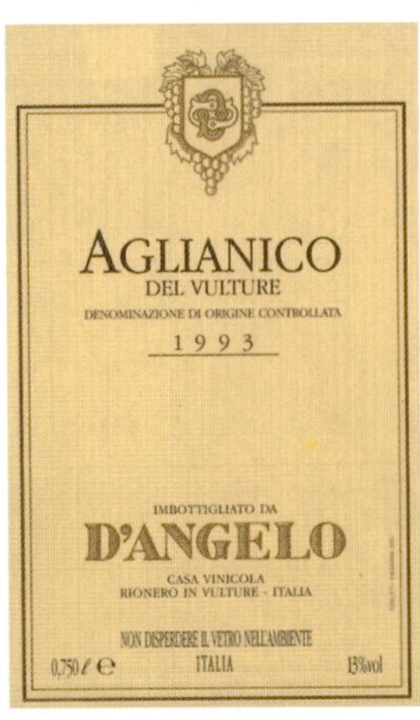

## PUGLIA

The heel of Italy, Puglia incorporates the Adriatic port of Bari, and is responsible for one of the largest annual productions of any of the country's wine regions. Only a small proportion of this is of DOC standard, however. The extreme southeastern province of Salento is where the finest reds come from. Here, the spicily exciting Negroamaro grape is the claim to fame. Its best DOC is **Salice Salentino**, a richly plummy, often interestingly honeyed red wine of enormous appeal. (Candido's Riserva is especially good.) There are now also two white wines here, the straight **Bianco** containing a minimum 70 per cent Chardonnay, and one made from **Pinot Bianco**. Negroamaro also crops up in the wines of **Copertino**, **Squinzano** and **Brindisi** among others, sometimes given extra bite with another local grape, Malvasia Nera. These are good meaty reds.

**Primitivo di Manduria** makes colossally alcoholic reds from the Primitivo grape (aka Zinfandel in California). **Castel del Monte** is another DOC with its own local red grape, the intriguing Uva di Troia. Otherwise, the grapes of Abruzzi are relatively important for reds and whites, and there is the usual smattering of international varieties.

## CAMPANIA

The Neapolitan southwest has the most venerable winemaking tradition of any part of Italy, but the lowest percentage of wine qualifying as DOC. And yet the DOC areas have undoubted potential. **Taurasi** DOCG is a fierce and exciting, if tannic, red made from a fine local variety, Aglianico. **Falerno del Massico** is a newish DOC seeking to recreate the lost glory of Falernian, the much-revered wine of classical antiquity; the red is a blend of Aglianico and the local Piedirosso with Primitivo and Barbera. Early indications are that it is promising enough to investigate.

The main white DOCGs are **Greco di Tufo**, a mildly lemony wine of some charm, and **Fiano d'Avellino**, which can have a haunting taste of ripe pears. Both are named after their grapes. **Lacryma Christi del Vesuvio** is one of the region's more famous wines, appearing in both red and white versions, both fairly underwhelming. Another interesting local white grape is Falanghina, often vinified as a varietal. Mastroberardino is the reference name among Campania producers.

## BASILICATA

This very poor southern region makes only minuscule quantities of wine. Far and away its best shot is the DOC **Aglianico del Vulture**, from the red grape of that name. Here it is grown in vineyards around the extinct Vulture volcano, and produces an astonishingly lush-textured wine with a lovely coffeeish aroma, worth seeking out.

## CALABRIA

**Cirò** is the only DOC wine you might see outside the region that forms the toe of Italy's boot. Based on the local Gaglioppo grape, the full-bodied reds and rosés may, as with many other Italian reds, be blended with some white grapes, inevitably including Trebbiano. On the south coast, a rather sophisticated DOC dessert wine, **Greco di Bianco**, is produced from semi-dried Greco grapes.

## SICILIA AND PANTELLERIA

The island of Sicily is one of the most copiously productive regions of Italy. Much of its produce is of no more than table wine standard, but there are isolated pockets of improving quality which suggest that Sicilian wines may well one day be among Italy's finest.

Its most celebrated product is the fortified wine **Marsala**, produced in the west of the island. In common with southern Europe's other classic fortified wines, it remains one of the great original wine styles, quite unlike any other. Various methods of fortification are used, including a rather clumsy one that uses cooked concentrated grape juice, *mosto cotto*. The best grades of Marsala, however, **Superiore** and **Vergine**, are not permitted to use this method.

Styles range from the austerely dry (*secco*) to the liquorously sweet (*dolce*), but common to all of them is a smoky, almost acrid, burnt-toffee tang that is Marsala's unique selling-point. These days, much of it is consumed in tiramisu and zabaglione, but the best Marsalas, such as those from de Bortoli, deserve to be appreciated on their own as stimulating alternatives to the more familiar after-dinner tipples.

Two of the white grapes used in Marsala make good dry unfortified IGT wines elsewhere on the island. They are **Inzolia** and **Catarratto**, both capable of producing lightly aromatic wines of some character. **Nero d'Avola** is the best of the native red grapes, and blends containing a healthy percentage of it are often among the best. The wines are robust and savoury in style, with blackberry fruit and a suggestion of spice.

Regaleali is one of the leading producers of quality Sicilian wines. Its reds can be monumentally complex and ageworthy, as can Corvo Rosso, a long-lived, excitingly spicy IGT red made by Duca di Salaparuta. Settesoli, the main co-op, makes some decent simple reds.

The tiny island of Pantelleria, halfway between Sicily and Tunisia, has revived one of the legendary dessert wines of history in **Moscato di Pantelleria**, made from dried Moscato grapes given delicious richness with oak-ageing. Try it if you're on vacation.

## SARDEGNA

Sardinia's wine production continues to be hampered by its very insular approach to marketing, and the ridiculously high yields permitted under the DOC regulations for what could otherwise be interesting wines. **Cannonau** is one of the most important red varieties (claimed by some to be related to Grenache), and can make an inky, full-bodied red where yields are restricted. **Monica** produces a much lighter, sharper, Beaujolais-like red for early drinking.

**Nuragus** is one of the more significant white grapes, but its wines tend to the classic Italian neutrality, partly again because of over-cropping. **Vernaccia di Oristano** can be a diverting curiosity for those on holiday – a bone-dry, nutty, often oxidized white that may remind you of a basic fino sherry.

## OTHER CLASSIC WINES OF ITALY

As the redesigning of Italy's wine classification system continues apace, one of its central concerns has been to draw into its embrace all those quality wines that were being produced outside the regulations as *vini da tavola*, but actually comparable to the most illustrious wines of France. The ground-breaking Sassicaia is now DOC Bolgheri, as is Ornellaia. The other wines listed here have all been designated IGT Toscana. A lot depends on whether the individual producers care to play a part in the official system. Many don't as yet.

**Balifico** (Castello Volpaia): Sangiovese-Cabernet Sauvignon blend aged in French oak.
**Cepparello** (Isole e Olena): Attractively ripe varietal Sangiovese fleshed out with new oak.

**Flaccianello della Pieve** (Fontodi): 100 per cent Sangiovese similar in style to Cepparello, but with more obvious Tuscan bitterness to it.
**Grifi** (Avignonesi): Sangiovese-Cabernet Franc from a fine Vino Nobile producer.
**Ornellaia** (Lodovico Antinori): Massively concentrated blend of Bordeaux grapes, built for long life.
**Sammarco** (Castello dei Rampolla): Predominantly brambly Cabernet with a dash of Sangiovese.
**Solaia** (Piero Antinori): Cabernet-Sangiovese of great distinction, full of classical intensity.
**Tignanello** (Piero Antinori): A Sangiovese-Cabernet blend, Tignanello is a hugely exciting, long-lived red that combines gorgeously ripe purple fruits with chocolatey richness.

RECENT VINTAGES FOR REDS
It remains tricky to generalize about Italian vintages, as there is such microclimatic variation from one site to the next. But here goes.
*Piedmont: 2021 ****   2020 *****   2019 *****
*2016 *****   2015 ****   2010 ******
*2009 ****   2004 *****   2001 ******
*Tuscany: 2023 ****   2022 ****   2020 *****
*2019 ****   2018 ****   2015 ****   2012 *****
*2010 *****   2006 *****   2004 ******

*Ancient farmhouse in the hills of Basilicata (above), surrounded by ploughed land ready for planting with new vines.*

*Sicilian vineyard (below) planted on black volcanic soils in the shadow of Mount Etna.*

# SPAIN

*A proud winemaking tradition, and the producers' commitment to quality, are placing Spain at the forefront of Europe's great wine nations. Freshness and fruit are now the bywords for the best wines, rather than old-fashioned wood flavour.*

*The castle of Peñafiel (above) perches above the vineyards of the dynamic Ribera del Duero region.*

*Renowned for its sherries and oaked wines, the arrival on Spain's map of new wine regions is bringing impressive still and sparkling wines to the market (right).*

MODERN SPAIN has more land devoted to vine cultivation than any country in the world, although its average annual production is normally behind those of both Italy and France. Part of the explanation for that paradox lay traditionally in the abnormally low yields that its vines produced, a situation that has been rectified to some degree in the modern era.

Its viticultural industry has slowly but surely come to terms over the past 30 years with what the modern world expects of wine. The old habit of according extended cask-ageing to both red and white wines tended to see off any fruit, with the result that wines labelled Gran Reserva often tasted like museum-pieces. Today, there are vibrant, fresh wines bursting out all over, based on indigenous grape varieties. Tempranillo and Garnacha still lead the pack, but Bobal, Albariño and Loureiro are coming up on the inside track.

The classification system in operation has been taken more seriously in Spain than it often has in parts of Italy. It has equivalents of *vin de table* and *vin de pays* in *vino de mesa* and *vino de la tierra*, respectively, while the appellation wines are DO (*denominación de origen*). An upper level, the rough equivalent of Italy's DOCG, has been created in DOCa (*denominación de origen calificada*), but has been used sparingly so far, with only Rioja and Priorat (where it takes the Catalan DOQ) being elevated. An innovative category, *vino de pago*, has been established for the best single-estate wines, currently covering Castilla-La Mancha, Navarra, Castilla y León, Aragon and Valencia.

In sherry, Spain has one of the great, and now jealously protected, fortified wines of Europe, easily a match for port and madeira in its versatility and complexity. There is even decent wine being made these days in the Balearics.

1. RIOJA
2. NAVARRA
3. RIAS BAIXAS
4. RIBEIRO
5. VALDEORRAS
6. EL BIERZO
7. TORO
8. RUEDA
9. CIGALES
10. RIBERA DEL DUERO
11. CHACOLI DE GUETARIA
12. CALATAYUD
13. CAMPO DE BORJA
14. SOMONTANO
15. TERRA ALTA
16. COSTERS DEL SEGRE
17. PRIORATO
18. TARRAGONA
19. CARIÑENA
20. CONCA DE BARBERÁ
21. PENEDÉS
22. ALELLA
23. AMPURDÁN-COSTA BRAVA
24. MÉNTRIDA
25. LA MANCHA
26. VALDEPEÑAS
27. UTIEL-REQUENA
28. VALENCIA
29. ALMANSA
30. JUMILLA
31. YECLA
32. ALICANTE
33. MONTILLA-MORILES
34. MÁLAGA
35. CONDADO DE HUELVA
36. JEREZ

All that can go wrong now is climate change reducing much of the interior of Spain to unproductive desert. Perish the thought.

# RIOJA

Spain's most visible export wines for years have come from the Rioja region surrounding the river Ebro in the north of the country. The red wine in particular, with its strawberry-flavoured fruit and smooth, creamy texture derived from ageing in oak, became a much-loved style in the 1970s, and it remains the pre-eminent Spanish red for many drinkers. When the new super-category of DOCa wines was created, Rioja was its first recipient, reflecting its importance in Spanish wine history.

The region is subdivided into three districts: the Rioja Alta, west of Logroño (generally held to produce the wines of highest pedigree); the Rioja Baja, southeast of the same town; and the Rioja Alavesa, which forms part of the province of Alava, in the southern Basque country. All three regions make reds, whites and rosés, the last known as rosados in Spanish.

The hierarchy of classification for the wines depends on the length of maturation in barrel and bottle they receive before being released on to the market. At the bottom of the pile, young new wine may be released as **Joven** (meaning 'young'). It can have a delicious, sweet-cherry appeal, and responds well to chilling.

**Crianza** wines must be aged for one year in barrel and a further year in bottle before release. Many commentators feel that this is probably the optimum period for most wines, producing an oaky red that still retains some decent fruit. **Reserva** spends a year in barrel, but a further two in the bottle, while **Gran Reserva** is aged for at least two years in wood before being held in the bottle for a further three.

Traditionally, the type of wood favoured for the production of both red and white Rioja was American oak, which gives a much more pronounced sweet vanilla flavour than the softer French oak. More producers are now turning to French coopers, however, in order to achieve a subtler wood influence in their wines, and the innovation seems to be paying off in the form of more balanced wines.

Tempranillo is the principal grape of the reds, contributing flavours of summery red fruits to young wines, but often turning fascinatingly gamey (almost like Pinot Noir) as it ages. It is supported mainly by Garnacha (Grenache),

which usually lends a spicy edge and some structure to the softer Tempranillo, as well as Graciano and Mazuelo, with a little Cabernet Sauvignon in the wines of producers who always had historic plantings of it.

As to white Rioja, or **Blanco**, there are two distinct schools of thought. The traditional preference is for heavily oaked and deliberately oxidized wines of golden-yellow hue. They often smell tantalizingly like dry sherry, yet possess a bitter tang like dried citrus peel. Sipped in small quantities, they can be impressive wines to mull over, but you'd be mulling over them a long time before the word 'refreshing' suggested itself.

The newer style is all about squeaky-clean fermentation in stainless steel, at low temperatures, to maximize fruitiness and freshness. Often made entiely without the use of oak, these light, lemony wines may not be as imposing as their barrel-fermented cousins, but they do cater more obviously to modern tastes. Rioja's white grapes are the relatively neutral Viura (often seen unblended in the modern styles) and the muskier, more headily perfumed Malvasia.

The **Rosado** can be utterly charming, a little too alcoholic for its own good perhaps, but crammed full of just-picked summer berry fruit. Served properly chilled, it can be a great accompaniment to meaty tapas.

PRODUCERS: La Rioja Alta, Artadi, Montecillo, Marqués de Murrieta, López de Heredía, Remírez de Ganuza, Marqués de Cáceres, Marqués de Riscal, Faustino, Remelluri, Baron de Ley, Marqués de Vargas.

*Oak barrels piled up outside the winery at Rioja producer Bodegas López de Heredía (above).*

### RIOJA

GRAPES: *Red – Tempranillo, Garnacha, Mazuelo, Graciano; White – Viura, Malvasia*

*Splashes of red mark the autumnal vineyards of Valdeorras (above), where increasingly characterful wines are being created.*

**NAVARRA**
GRAPES: *Red – Garnacha, Tempranillo, Cabernet Sauvignon, Merlot; White – Viura, Chardonnay*

**RIAS BAIXAS**
GRAPES: *Albariño, Treixadura, Loureiro, Caiña Blanca*

**RIBEIRO**
GRAPES: *White – Treixadura, Torrontés, etc; Red – Garnacha, etc.*

**VALDEORRAS**
GRAPES: *White – Palomino, Godello, etc; Red – Garnacha, Mencía, etc.*

**EL BIERZO**
GRAPES: *Red – Mencía*

**TORO**
GRAPES: *Red – Tinto de Toro*

## NAVARRA

Just to the east of Rioja, but also on the river Ebro, is the increasingly fashionable DO region of Navarra. While Navarra grows essentially the same grapes as neighbouring Rioja, its wines are quite different. There has been increasing interest in incorporating some of the classic French varieties into the more ambitious oak-aged wines, so that it is not uncommon to see a white wine labelled Viura-Chardonnay. Unlike the traditional oaky wines of white Rioja, these are much fresher, with a gently buttery quality reminiscent of the lighter whites of Burgundy.

Navarra makes a much higher proportion of rosado than Rioja, and most of it benefits from attractively juicy strawberry fruit and exemplary freshness. Red wines range from the relatively light in style, a little like midweight Côtes du Rhône, to seriously weighty, world-class wines from the aspirational producers. There is also some sweet Moscatel.

PRODUCERS: Chivite, Inurrieta, Ochoa, Magaña, Nekeas, Príncipe de Viana, Camino del Villar.

## RIAS BAIXAS

Rias Baixas has lately been one of the more talked-about regions of northern Spain. Situated in Galicia in the northwest, its reputation has been founded on some unexpectedly fragrant, concentrated dry white wines, mainly based on a fine local grape variety called Albariño. The DO is subdivided into three areas: Val de Salnes on the western coast; O Rosal and Condado de Tea on the Portuguese border; and Soutomaior and Ribera de Ulla near the city of Pontevedra. As in much of the rest of Spain, the typical yields are low, and although other varieties are permitted in the wines, including the scented Loureiro, they don't generally account for much of the blend. Quite expensive, but highly attractive.

PRODUCERS: Lagar de Fornelos, Codax, Lagar de Cervera, Condes de Albarei, Terras Gauda, Lusco do Miño, Besada, La Val.

## RIBEIRO

The region's name means 'riverside', and the vineyards occupy the land around the river Miño, which extends up from northern Portugal. There is some fairly inconsequential red, but – as in Rias Baixas – the main business is white wine, and here quality is much improved of late. Some recently established plantings of Torrontés are adding character to the whites. This is a florally aromatic grape with strong notes of orange blossom and roses (now starring in many Argentinian wines). Often blended with Treixadura.

## VALDEORRAS

Small region in the east of Galicia that is progressing slowly but surely from making dull, bland plonk to wines of burgeoning character. Palomino, the sherry grape, has long been the curse of northwestern whites, but is now being replaced by more promising varieties such as the local Godello, which gives good, modestly aromatic, dry whites. The ubiquitous Garnacha goes into many of the reds, but some attractively grassy, fresh-tasting reds are being made from the native Mencía grape, in a style not dissimilar to the lighter reds of the Loire valley, but with gentler acidity.

## BIERZO

Just to the northeast of Valdeorras, the Bierzo DO is also beginning to explore its potential. The main focus of interest so far is good ripe Loire-like reds made from the local Mencía grape. More richly structured wines come from the Palacios family vineyards.

## TORO

The wines of Toro are produced in some of the most inhospitable conditions of any of Spain's vineyard regions. Planted at high altitude along the river Duero, the grape responsible for the thunderously powerful Toro reds, Tinta de Toro, is a local mutation of Spain's premier red variety, Tempranillo. Alcohol levels are typically at least 13.5 per cent, but the wines mostly wear it well, the thick, liquoricey flavours of the grape more than adequately rounding out the spirity finish. Insignificant quantities of weighty rosado and white are also produced.

PRODUCERS: Numanthia-Termes, Fariña, Telmo Rodriguez.

## RUEDA

A DO region since 1980, Rueda makes white wines only, and has now carved out a reputation for some of the freshest and tangiest dry whites in all of Spain. The native variety here is Verdejo, which gives snappy, herbaceous whites with good texture. It is sometimes given a little citrus tang with a dash of Viura, but more often brought into focus with a sharp dose of nettly Sauvignon Blanc. Straight Rueda must be at least 50 per cent Verdejo, while wines labelled Rueda Superior have to contain a minimum of 85 per cent of the grape. Oak-aged wines can be surprisingly good.

PRODUCERS: Marqués de Riscal, Belondrade y Lurton, Sila, La Vieja, de Medina.

## CIGALES

North of the river Duero, Cigales is not much known to the outside world. It principally makes dry rosados and a little red from the two main red grapes of Rioja.

## RIBERA DEL DUERO

For many, this dynamic, forward-looking region is now at the head of the Spanish pack. Across the board, its carefully crafted wines are highly dependable, and its producers have absorbed the lessons to be learned from global trends in premium red wine production. Its principal variety is another local variation of Tempranillo, Tinto Fino, often appearing unblended. Controlled plantings of some of the Bordeaux varieties are permitted in specific sectors of the region, and a little plummy rosado is produced too. A proportion of juice from the local white grape, Albillo Mayor, may be used to soften the intensity of the red wine, but since the 2020 vintage, the DO regulations now extend to the production of varietal Albillo white. One superstar producer has provided much of the impetus, but there are now dozens of quality names here.

The best wines of Ribera del Duero have concentrated blackberry or plum fruit, and usually a fair amount of oak influence. This can be either the exotic vanilla of American oak or the more muted, subtler tones of French. The system of ageing in cask and bottle is analogous to that of Rioja: Joven, Crianza, Reserva and Gran Reserva.

In the west of the region is a property called Vega Sicilia, which makes an enormously opulent, totally individual range of red wines, using Tinto Fino with the French varieties and a modicum of Albillo. Valbuena is a five-year-old oak-aged red with an astonishing and unforgettable mixture of perfumes – orange essence, loganberries and milk chocolate. Unico is its top wine, made only in the most promising vintages. The wine is released at about ten years old, after undergoing an elaborate ageing procedure in various types of wood (including large old casks that allow a fair amount of oxygen to seep into the wine) and in bottle. It has been fairly compared to the top classed growths of Bordeaux, in majesty if not in flavour.

OTHER PRODUCERS: Pesquera, Aalto, Carraovejas, los Capellanes, Aster, Moro.

## CHACOLI DE GUETARIA

A tiny DO region (Spain's smallest) in the Basque country to the west of San Sebastian. Its mainly white wine is light and spritzy, and made in such modest quantities that it isn't really viable as an export product. The equally light red is even rarer.

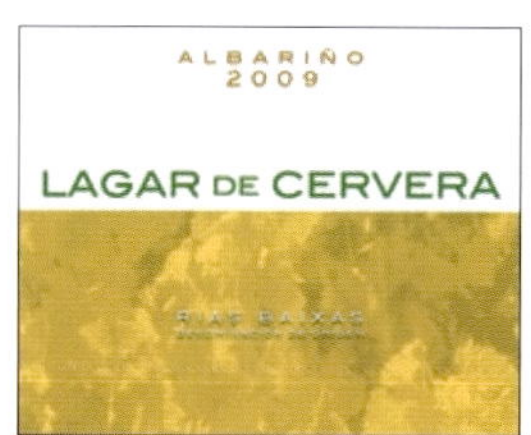

*The church of Santa Maria la Mayor in Toro (left). On Spain's high central plain, the wine region of Toro makes big, powerful reds.*

*The 17th-century castle of Raimat, in Catalonia (right), where the Raventos family has extensive high-altitude vineyards.*

**CHACOLI DE GUETARIA**
*Grapes: White – Hondarrabi Zuri; Red – Hondarrabi Beltz*
**CALATAYUD**
*Grapes: Red – Garnacha, Tempranillo, Mazuelo, Graciano; White – Viura, Malvasia*
**CAMPO DE BORJA**
*Grapes: Red – Garnacha, Cariñena, Tempranillo; White – Viura*
**CARINENA**
*Grapes: Red – Garnacha, Tempranillo, Cariñena; White – Viura, Garnacha Blanca, Parellada*
**SOMONTANO**
*Grapes: Red – Moristel, Garnacha, Tempranillo, Cabernet Sauvignon, Merlot; White – Viura, Alcañón, Chardonnay, Chenin Blanc, Gewürztraminer*
**TERRA ALTA**
*Grapes: White – Garnacha Blanca, Macabeo; Red – Garnacha*
**COSTERS DEL SEGRE**
*Grapes: Red – Tempranillo, Garnacha, Cabernet Sauvignon, Merlot, Pinot Noir; White – Chardonnay, Parellada, Macabeo*

## CALATAYUD

In the Aragón region on the river Jalón, Calatayud is dominated by cooperative producers, but not much geared for export. The varieties are essentially the same as for Rioja, and the wines come in all three colours, the unsubtle, alcoholic reds being the surest indicator of local taste.

## CAMPO DE BORJA

Stunningly alcoholic reds are the speciality of this DO near the town of Borja in the province of Aragón. Made mainly from Garnacha, they also incorporate the other Rioja varieties, along with the big two Bordeaux grapes and a little Syrah. Again, cooperatives rule the roost, and again, most of the wine is drunk in the vicinity.

## CARINENA

Much the most promising so far of the DO regions of Aragón, Cariñena – southwest of Zaragoza – is named after the grape variety that originated and once flourished here. (It's the same grape as Rioja's Mazuelo and France's

Carignan.) Garnacha is these days the star of the show for the big opulent reds in which the region specializes and, as in other parts of Aragón, they can attain spine-tingling levels of alcohol. Some Tempranillo is often blended in to soften the impact. Whites are largely fresh and clean, and some use a little of the Chardonnay-like Parellada grape more typically associated with the white wines of Penedés further east. A small quantity of Spain's traditional-method sparkler, cava, is made in Cariñena and isn't bad either, although it too is more at home in Penedés.
PRODUCERS: San Valero, Añadas, Victoria.

## SOMONTANO

A healthily outward-looking DO region in the Pyrenean foothills to the east of Navarra, Somontano makes reds, whites and rosados from a tempting mixture of local grapes (including the indigenous red Moristel and Parraleta, and white Alcañón), and a catholic range of French varieties, including some convincingly perfumed Gewürztraminer and full-bodied Chardonnay. As in Cariñena, a small amount of cava is produced.
PRODUCERS: Blecua, Enate, Laus, Irius.

## TERRA ALTA

As its name suggests, Terra Alta is a high-altitude vineyard region in the west of Catalonia, currently making the familiarly northern Spanish shift from heavy fortified wines to light dry whites in the modern idiom. Reds are galumphing Garnachas in the old unsubtle jammy style.

## COSTERS DEL SEGRE

Split rather messily into six separate sub-regions, Costers del Segre has made waves outside Spain, despite its starting life as inauspicious desert land. The six zones are: Artesa, Valls de Riucorb, Garrigues, Raimat and (since 1998) Pallars Jussà and Segrià, the last entirely encircled by Raimat. The principal exporter has been the Raimat winery in Lleida (Lérida), which makes a range of fine varietals, from softly velvety Tempranillo to densely meaty Merlot, as well as some Chardonnay fizz of impressive richness, and Franco-Spanish blends with Cabernet Sauvignon. Prices have stayed sane, with the result that this is definitely a region worth watching.
OTHER PRODUCERS: Castell del Remei, Cusiné.

## PRIORAT

Practically a legend in its own right, Priorat makes one of the most uncompromising styles of red wine anywhere in Europe. Yields from the older vines in the region are minuscule, and the rules specify a minimum alcoholic strength of 13.5 per cent for the wine to qualify as DOQ (the Catalan for DOCa). The result is not hard to imagine – fiercely concentrated, heady stuff, with a pugnacious peppery edge to it, capable of ageing for many years in the bottle. It's predominantly Garnacha and Cariñena, although French varieties are being planted here too, with stunning results. Worth a flutter for one of the unique tastes of Spain.
PRODUCERS: Mas Doix, Scala Dei, Finca Dofi, Clos Mogador, Clos Erasmus, Cims de Porrera.

## TARRAGONA

After once enjoying a reputation for sweet red port-style wines, Tarragona now contents itself largely with producing unambitious blending material for bulk producers elsewhere. Its limited local wine production, in all three colours but mostly white, is quite forgettable.

## CONCA DE BARBERA

Considered virtually a western extension of Penedés, Conca de Barberà produces some pleasantly fresh dry whites from the Catalan varieties (see Penedés below), as well as some hearty blended reds, rosados from the local Trepat grape, and a great deal of sparkling cava. The region became a DO in 1985, and has since benefited from substantial investment from the Penedés giant, Torres.

## PENEDÉS

The largest of the DO regions of Catalonia, Penedés has two main claims to fame. It is the centre of the cava industry, and it is the base of one of the most successful wine dynasties of Europe – the house of Torres.

Cava is a peculiarity in terms of its regulations, in that it can technically be made elsewhere in Spain; the DO is not specific to Penedés. In practice, most of it is made in this northeastern region near Barcelona. The method used is the same as that for champagne, but the grapes are nearly all native varieties: Parellada, Macabeo and Xarel-lo. In addition to those, Chardonnay is being grown to a much greater extent than hitherto, although it is by no means taking over. The rosados use Garnacha and the local Monastrell, and may also now use Pinot Noir. Cava has to be aged on its yeast lees for a minimum of nine months (or two years for vintage cava), but in practice, many houses age it for significantly longer.

Once upon a time, much of it was bedevilled by disturbing, rubbery off flavours, but that syndrome is now receding rapidly into the past. In fact, cava is on one of the most exciting quality upswings of all Spanish wine, with many producers both big and small producing deeply elegant, complex, toasty sparklers, as well as some lemony-light wines that make perfect aperitifs. The rosados have improved hugely too, the best having sensational raspberry fruit and graceful texture. Some are now boldly aiming, in both style and price, to give champagne a run for its money, and are frankly often capable of outshining some of France's famous names.
PRODUCERS: Raventos i Blanc, Codorníu, Gramona, Rovellats, Torello, Jané Ventura.

The pioneering work of the late Miguel Torres established Penedés as the most outward-looking wine region in the country. He planted international grape varieties alongside the indigenous ones, in many cases blending them together, creating a formidable and enduring reputation in the process for both his company and the region.

Among the more successful Torres whites are the basic Viña Sol (a reliably straightforward, clean house white), Fransola (mouth-wateringly crisp Sauvignon and Parellada), Viña Esmeralda (a honey-and-lemon, off-dry blend of Muscat and Gewürztraminer), and Milmanda (a buttery oaked Chardonnay in the Burgundian style).

The notable reds include Gran Sangre de Toro (earthy Garnacha, Cariñena and Syrah), Atrium (a soft varietal Merlot), Mas Borràs (a classically cherry-scented, gamey Pinot Noir), and Mas La Plana (a premium bottling of intensely dark, austerely tannic Cabernet Sauvignon). At the top of the tree is Reserva Real, a Bordeaux blend for long ageing. (Torres also produces a rather good Gran Reserva brandy.)

Jean León is another grower of note to have followed the international varietal trail here. His Chardonnay, Merlot, Cabernet Sauvignon and Syrah are made in the thoroughly modern style, with lashings of ripe, vibrant fruit and unabashed levels of oaky richness.
OTHER STILL WINE PRODUCERS: Can Rafols dels Caus, Albet i Noya, Puig i Roca.

*Old Garnacha and Cariñena vines yield powerful, heady reds that have drawn attention to the small Priorato region in Catalonia (above).*

## ALELLA

Alella is a tiny DO north of Barcelona, in which the Marqués de Alella cooperative is the predominant producer. The output is attractive dry whites, in which the assertive character of Xarel-lo (here known as Pansa Blanca) is frequently softened with a modicum of Chardonnay, as well as sparkling cava labelled Parxet, which may also contain a freshening dash of Chenin Blanc. A varietal Chardonnay and Viognier are also made.

## AMPURDAN-COSTA BRAVA

This is a small DO situated on the opposite side of the border to the French Côtes du Roussillon. Nearly all the wine made here is drunk *in situ* – mostly simple rosados for the tourist market. There are also some rustic reds and, this being Catalonia, some cava from the traditional grapes. A recent innovation is rush-released Vin Novell, an Iberian answer to Beaujolais Nouveau. Er, no thanks.

## MENTRIDA

A DO region immediately to the south and west of Madrid in central Spain, Méntrida's principal business is rough-and-ready Garnacha reds of no obvious pedigree. However, the excellent winery of Marqués de Griñón is also situated near here. Since 2003, it has had its own *vino de pago* DO near Toledo, **Dominio de Valdepusa**, and the wines, including stunning varietal Cabernet Sauvignon, Petit Verdot and Syrah, as well as a premium bottling, Eméritus, a blend of all three, are among the most fabulously rich and opulent Spanish reds of all.

## LA MANCHA

The largest DO region in Spain is also the largest individual appellation in Europe. La Mancha occupies the broiling, arid dustlands of the centre of Spain from Madrid down to Valdepeñas, about 125 miles from top to bottom. The pre-eminent grape variety grown here, the white Airén, is actually the most extensively planted wine grape in the world. Given that it's grown virtually nowhere outside Spain, that gives some idea of the sprawling vastness of La Mancha's vineyards.

Once seen as a workhorse area, dedicated as much to producing alcohol for industry as everyday table wines, La Mancha is now set on an upward course to quality. The Airén, previously dismissed as boringly neutral, turns out to make quite refreshing, simple, lemony whites in the right hands, and since the predominant red grape is Tempranillo (here adopting another of its many pseudonyms, Cencibel), the prospects for classy reds too are good. They are generally somewhat lighter than those of Rioja, but have the pronounced strawberry fruit of the grape, together with appealingly smooth contours. The cosmopolitan duo of Cabernet and Chardonnay are beginning to make their presences felt, reflecting the scale of ambition among many of the small proprietors.

In short, La Mancha is set fair to prove that, even in the world of wine, big can be beautiful. It is expected, however, that sooner or later the region will have to be broken up into more manageable chunks.

## VALDEPENAS

Valdepeñas is the southernmost outpost of the huge central plateau of La Mancha. Its wines are thought sufficiently distinctive to merit a separate DO, and the growers have been quicker off the draw in penetrating the export markets than their neighbours to the north. Red wines from Cencibel (Tempranillo) are the main business. Often given long cask-ageing, and labelled as Reserva or Gran Reserva, they can suffer from an excess of petrolly oak flavours on a basically rather light fruit base, but the better producers are managing to achieve better balance. Some straightforward, thin dry white is also made from Airén, but a fair amount of it, depressingly enough, goes into the red wines below Reserva level, reducing them to insipid irrelevance.
PRODUCERS: Los Llanos, Solis, Megía.

## UTIEL-REQUENA

In the province of Levante, to the west of Valencia, Utiel-Requena's speciality is the Bobal grape – a good red variety that yields fairly beefy wine with a distinctive raisiny flavour. The reds can be a little clumsy, but the rosados are improving, and can be agreeably refreshing on a hot day. Mustiguillo is the outstanding producer and has, since 2003, had its own country wine designation in **Vino de la Tierra El Terrerazo**.

## VALENCIA

The eastern port of Valencia lends its name to a DO region inland from the city. White wines run the gamut from dullish dry wines, made from the less than inspiring local Merseguera grape, to the well-known sweet wine, Moscatel de Valencia. The Moscatel doesn't undergo normal fermentation, but is made by adding grape spirit to freshly pressed Muscat juice (a style known as *mistela* in Spanish). Red wines can be surprisingly thin and acidic when made from the Garnacha variant grown in these parts (rosados are better), but the Monastrell grape produces a firmer, beefier style of red. PRODUCERS: Cambra, Gandia.

## ALMANSA

A relatively unimportant Levantine DO that has concentrated much of its effort hitherto on making blending wine for other regions. When it does bottle its own red wines, they tend to the heavyweight end of the spectrum. Varietal Tempranillos are the best bets, but the conscientiously made blends of Piqueras are pretty good.

## JUMILLA

Much the same applies in Jumilla as for neighbouring Almansa. A lot of blending wine is produced, alongside some strong-limbed Monastrell reds and Merseguera whites that lack excitement. Improvements are afoot, though, particularly among the red wines. El Nido is the go-to producer, but there are also impressive wines from Castillo.

## YECLA

Another DO making large quantities of blending wine, with a vast cooperative at the centre of operations. Big beefy reds are the name of the game once more, supplemented by weedy Merseguera whites.

## ALICANTE

The typical Levantine pattern of giant cooperatives producing mainly blending wine is repeated in the Alicante DO, which extends inland from the coastal city of that name. A sweet fortified wine, **Fondillón**, using the same ageing method as in sherry, brightens the picture a little, and Tempranillo is beginning to lend some sophistication to the generally rustic reds.

## THE ISLANDS

The holidaymakers of the Balearic islands are kept well supplied with wine by the **Binissalem** and **Plà i Llevant** DOs on the island of Mallorca. Two indigenous grape varieties, plus Catalonia's white grapes, make some simple whites, gluggable rosados and increasingly good reds.

Among the Canaries, there are a total of 11 DOs (including **Lanzarote**, where the sweet Malvasia can prove a hit in small doses), with fresh dry whites and juicy reds aplenty.

*ALMANSA*
*GRAPES: Red – Monastrell, Garnacha, Tempranillo*
*JUMILLA*
*GRAPES: Red – Monastrell; White – Merseguera*
*YECLA*
*GRAPES: Red – Monastrell, Garnacha; White – Merseguera*
*ALICANTE*
*GRAPES: Red – Monastrell, Garnacha, Bobal, Tempranillo; White – Merseguera*
*BINISSALEM*
*GRAPES: Red – Manto Negro; White – Moll, Xarel-lo, Parellada*

*La Mancha, in the hot, arid centre of Spain (below left). This vast vineyard area is Europe's largest single appellation.*

**SHERRY**

*GRAPES: Palomino,
Pedro Ximénez, Moscatel*

*The finest vineyards of the
sherry region, as here at
Osborne's Viña el Caballo
west of Jerez (below), are
planted on chalk-white
albariza soil.*

## SHERRY AND OTHER FORTIFIED WINES

The province of Andalucía, in the south of
Spain, is home to a range of traditional fortified
wines, the most celebrated of which is sherry.
At one time, fortified wines were produced all
over Spain, but as the fashion gradually shifted
towards lighter table wines, so the other regions
abandoned their frequently poor efforts, and
Jerez and its satellites cornered the market.

It is, alas, a dwindling market. Tastes have
changed, and the image of sherry has suffered
both from its preferment by drinkers of a certain
age, and its exasperating association with
inferior products from elsewhere that had no
moral (or now legal) right to the name. Neither
has the preponderance of simple sweet styles
of the real thing much helped. People have a
tendency to grow out of cream sherry. Since
1996, the word 'sherry' has at least been
reserved rightfully for the first of the fortified
wines discussed below.

**Sherry** The wine takes its name from the city
of Jerez de la Frontera in Andalucía, but the
region also encompasses the major towns
of Puerto de Santa María and Sanlúcar de
Barrameda. These are the three principal
locations for the maturation of the region's
wines. Their quality rests fundamentally on the
geology of the Jerez DO. The soil at the heart
of the region is a mixture of limestone, sand
and clay that looks deceptively like chalk,
so blindingly white does it glare at you in
the brilliance of a summer day. The local

name for it is *albariza*, and most of the best
vineyard holdings are planted on this type of
soil. Because of its proximity to the ocean,
moreover, Jerez does not suffer quite the
summer heat-stress that, say, La Mancha does.
Although the summer months are relentlessly
dry, cooling Atlantic breezes waft across the
vines and the falling night-time temperatures
mitigate the roaring heat of day.

Palomino is the main grape variety in sherry
production. Nearly all the wines, from the palest
and driest up to the most liquorously treacly, are
based on that grape. The variable element lies in
how the producers decide which lots of the base
wine will end up as which style.

After the light Palomino base wine has
completed its fermentation, it is fortified with
grape spirit up to anything from 15 to 20 per
cent alcohol. Generally, the lighter fortification
will be used for wines that are destined to be
sold as **fino**, the palest, most elegant version
of dry sherry. This is because fino sherries are
matured in casks underneath a film of naturally
forming yeast called *flor*, derived from wild
yeasts that are present in the atmosphere of the
cellars. The *flor* protects the developing wine
from the influence of too much oxygen, and
also imparts a characteristic nutty taste (like
fresh peanuts) to classic fino. Fortification
above 15 per cent will inhibit the growth of *flor*,
which is why fino sherries are lower in alcohol
than darker and sweeter styles.

Sometimes the *flor* doesn't quite form a solid
enough layer to produce fino. It breaks up and
sinks to the bottom of the cask, and the more
direct exposure to oxygen causes the wine's
colour to darken. This becomes the style known
as **amontillado**. (The best amontillados are
still bone-dry, the popular conception of it
as a medium-sweet style being derived from
commercial brands that have been sugared up.)

The heaviest, darkest version of sherry
is **oloroso**, which is fortified to the highest
alcoholic degree of all, and is aged with
maximum oxygen contact so that the colour is a
deep burnished brown. Most olorosos are given
a sweetening dose of juice pressed from raisined
grapes, Pedro Ximénez (or PX) giving the best
quality, although Palomino may be treated in
this way too. As with amontillado, however, there
is a certain amount of totally dry oloroso made,
labelled oloroso seco. Austere and intense,
with a flavour of bitter walnuts, it is one of
the greatest taste experiences wine can offer.

Other sherry styles commonly encountered are **palo cortado** (which is a kind of naturally evolved median stage between amontillado and oloroso, generally given some sweetening), **cream** (sweetened, blended brown sherries, eternally typified by Harvey's Bristol Cream) and **pale cream** (a sweetened fino epitomized by Croft Original). **Manzanilla** is the official name of fino sherries matured in the town of Sanlúcar de Barrameda. They are popularly supposed to have a distinct salty whiff of the local sea air in them, and on a good day, with a spanking-fresh bottle, they really seem to.

Some houses make a speciality of bottling their raisined **PX** wine unblended. The result is an oleaginous, nearly-black essence of mind-blowing sweetness, so glutinously thick that it can scarcely be swirled in the glass. Everybody should try at least a mouthful, but it is admittedly hard to know what to do with a whole bottle. Its more or less dignified fate is to be used as a very grown-up kind of ice-cream topping.

The traditional method of sherry maturation, now extensively abandoned by many houses, was the so-called *solera* system (or fractional blending). This consisted of massed ranks of barrels containing wines that dated back a century or more. With each bottling, a third of the wine would be drawn off the oldest barrels, which would then be topped up with wine from the next oldest, and so on up to the youngest at the top of the pile, which would be topped up with newly made wine.

Given the painstaking labour involved in operating and maintaining such a system, it isn't entirely surprising that modern economics have decreed the abandonment of it in many cases. Wine that has been aged in a *solera*, however, will be labelled with the date of the oldest wine in it; there will thus be some 1895 wine in a bottle so labelled, but only a microscopic amount.

A note about serving the different types of sherry: Fino and manzanilla sherries *must* be served well-chilled, or they will taste lifeless, but no other sherries should be. Equally as important with the paler sherries is to drink them promptly after opening, as soon as you would drink leftover white wine. They aren't that much stronger, after all.

BEST SHERRIES: FINO: Tio Pepe, Don Zoilo, Hidalgo, Lustau, Williams and Humbert, Valdespino Inocente.

MANZANILLA: Barbadillo Príncipe, Hidalgo La Guita, Don Zoilo, Valdespino, Lustau Manzanilla Pasada (an older, darker version than the norm).

AMONTILLADO: Gonzalez Byass Amontillado del Duque, Valdespino Tio Diego and Coliseo, Hidalgo Napoleon, Lustau Almacenista.

OLOROSO: Gonzalez Byass Matúsalem and Apostoles, Valdespino Don Gonzalo, Williams and Humbert Dos Cortados, Lustau Muy Viejo Almacenista.

PX: Valdespino, Hidalgo, Garvey.

**Montilla-Moriles** A region to the northeast of Jerez that makes entirely analogous styles of fortified wine to sherry. However, it is generally somewhat behind the best sherries in terms of quality because of its inland location and less promising soils, and also the fact that the main sherry grape Palomino has not been able to make itself at home here. The wines can be good though, and are always cheaper than the corresponding sherry.

PRODUCERS: Alvear, Pérez Barquero, Toro Albalá, Garcia Hermanos, Aragón.

**Málaga** Made in the hinterland behind the Mediterranean port of the same name, the fate of Málaga stands as a salutary warning to what can happen to an original and inimitable style of wine when nobody wants to drink it any more. In the 19th century, it was highly revered, particularly in Britain where it was known as Mountain, owing to the steep hillside locations of its vineyards. By the end of the 20th century, hardly anybody had heard of it, and the last major producers in the region were close to shutting up shop. At the death, it was reprieved, as news of its possible demise caused a modest resurgence of interest. Made from PX and Moscatel, it is usually mahogany-coloured, and has a gentle raisins-in-caramel sweetness that is somehow never cloying. López Hermanos is a great producer.

**Condado de Huelva** To the west of Jerez towards the border with southern Portugal, Condado de Huelva is now sunk in obscurity as far as the outside world is concerned. Some fortified wine is still made, based on a grape called Zalema. There's a kind of fino that develops under *flor* called Condado Palido, and a darker, oloroso-type wine, Condado Viejo, aged in a *solera* system. The emphasis is slowly shifting, though, towards the production of an unfortified table wine, Vino Joven, and white-wine vinegars.

*Fino sherry is matured in oak butts (above) under a film of* flor, *a natural yeast that imparts a characteristic nutty taste to classic fino.*

# PORTUGAL

*Shaking off its old-fashioned attitudes, Portugal has rediscovered its greatest treasure – a range of exciting grape varieties – to prove that it can produce more than the world's top fortified wines.*

At their best, traditional aged Portuguese reds (above) are liquoricey and spicy in character.

1. VINHO VERDE
2. PORTO/DOURO
3. DÃO
4. BAIRRADA
5. OESTE
6. RIBATEJO
7. BUCELAS
8. COLARES
9. PALMELA
10. ARRÁBIDA
11. ALENTEJO
12. ALGARVE
13. SETÚBAL.MOSCATEL
14. CARCAVELOS
15. MADEIRA

Portugal offers a striking range of wine styles (right), the two most renowned – port and Vinho Verde – coming from the north.

### VINHO VERDE

GRAPES: White – Loureiro, Trajadura, Arinto, Avesso, Alvarinho; Red – Vinhão, Azal, Espadeiro, etc.

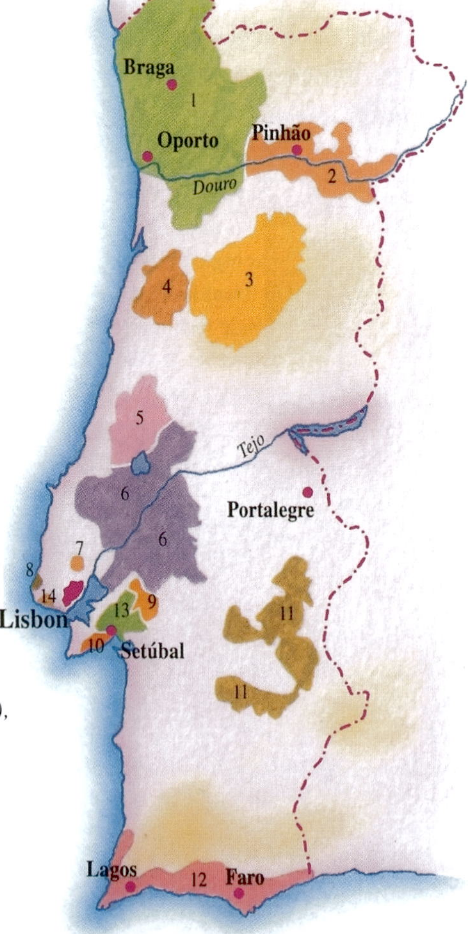


THE EMERGENCE OF PORTUGAL into the international limelight in the past 30 years has been one of the more heartening stories in European wine. For centuries, it occupied a place at the top table on the strength of its two famous fortified wine styles, port and madeira. The latter, particularly, was responsible for opening up Atlantic trade in the period prior to the war of independence in what was to become the United States. And as for the British, they had always drunk port (having more or less invented it), firstly as a matter of patriotic observance during the regular bouts of hostilities with the French, but also as a matter of national taste.

Nobody really paid much attention to the unfortified table wines of Portugal, though. And, to be brutally honest, they weren't much worth paying attention to. You might drink them on holiday in the Algarve, but they weren't a taste you acquired. The whites were flat and often musty. The reds might be palatable, but there was better in Spain, Italy and France.

That state of affairs has been swept away completely. Investment funds began to flow when Portugal joined the European Union in 1986. The flying winemakers flew in, like they do, and were sensible enough to work with the grain of what they found. And what they found was a benign climate, much influenced by coastal breezes, great soils, and – best of all – a cornucopia of fascinating indigenous grape varieties. These last make it possible to say that, apart from the still emergent Greek wine industry, Portugal is, among the Old World wine countries, the least in hock to international varietalism. If you don't know Portuguese wines, now's the time to come on in.

The classification of the wines follows the three-tier system that EU regulators devised on the basis of the original French model. At the top, the equivalent of *appellation contrôlée* is DOC (*denominação de origem controlada*). Then comes IPG (*indicação geográfica protegida*), a sort of waiting-room category for promotion to DOC; which incorporates the old regional classification of *vinho regional*, and finally simple table wine, *vinho*.

## VINHO VERDE

This is Portugal's largest DOC region by far, up in the northwest corner of the country around Porto. The sheer volumes produced and exported have made Vinho Verde one of Portugal's better-known wines internationally. At least, it's the white version that is popular; many consumers are unaware that just over half of all Vinho Verde is red, probably because the

Portuguese keep nearly all of it to themselves. The name means 'green wine', not, as is often thought, in reference to the greenish tinge in many of the whites, but to the fact that the wine, both red and white, is released young for quick consumption. Its youth means there is usually a slight pétillance, even a positive sparkle, in many bottles (indeed, some wines are deliberately carbonated before bottling), as well as generous dollops of raw, palate-scouring acidity. Fruit? Don't ask.

Most wines are blends of various local grapes, and each sub-region has its own particular specialities, Loureiro and Trajadura for example being especially favoured in the central part of the DOC. The whites are a simple, bracing, lemony slap to the tonsils that can be appealing enough at the height of summer. Sensitive souls may gag on the reds, however, which are astringently dry as well as slightly fizzy, not a combination familiar from any other European wine.

PRODUCERS: Tamariz, Aveleda, Azevedo, Soalheiro, Baguinha.

## DOURO

Named after the river Douro, which has its origin in Spain (as the Duero), the Douro valley's most celebrated product is port (see pages 176–177), but the DOC for the region as a whole also encompasses some exciting unfortified wines. Growers here are not exactly short of choice when it comes to the right grape to grow on each patch – they have nearly 100 at their disposal, including all the varieties used in port for a start.

Just as Spain has its premium red wine in Vega Sicilia, Portugal has Barca Velha, launched in the 1950s by the port house of Ferreira. It is a complex, subtly spicy red made only in the best vintages and given long cask-ageing – a profound and inspired wine.

Notable successes have been achieved with blends of international varieties such as Cabernet Sauvignon, but the non-traditional grapes are not allowed DOC status, the wines taking the regional designation, Terras Durienses. There has been a slight tendency to the over-enthusiastic use of oak from some producers, but better balance is now emerging across the board. Reds can be sumptuously deep, herb- and spice-scented beauties, while whites from vineyards planted higher up can be florally perfumed and fresh.

If there has been a problem during this initial period of heady experimentation in Douro, it has tended to lie in over-eager extraction of tannin in the red wines. We take the point that they are intended for ageing (and can easily take a decade in their stride at best), but they are after all meant to be table wines, not vintage port.

PRODUCERS: Ferreira Barca Velha, Crasto, Vale Meao, Côtto, Galvosa, Chryseia, Vale Dona Maria, Casal de Loivos.

## DÃO

Dão, a large mountainous DOC just to the north of central Portugal, makes one of the higher-profile red wines, as well as a small quantity of fairly undistinguished white. The reds were bedevilled in the past by sloppy winemaking, and even now can be dried out and robbed of their fruit by extended cask-ageing. When good, though, they can show that spicy, liquoricey appeal that characterizes the country's best reds. The whites were also traditionally over-aged, but there are now real aromatic trail-blazers from companies like Sogrape and Quinta das Maias.

PRODUCERS: Pellada, São João, Roques, Vegia, Aliança, Sogrape Quinta dos Carvalhais.

*The port house of Ferreira has gained a reputation for a fine red wine, from grapes grown on the steep hillsides (above) of the Douro valley.*

### DOURO

*GRAPES: Red – Touriga Nacional, Tinta Roriz, Tinta Cão; White – Gouveio, Malvasia, Viosinho*

### DÃO

*GRAPES: Red – Touriga Nacional, Bastardo, Tinta Pinheira, Tinta Roriz, Alfrocheiro Preto, etc; White – Encruzado, Bical*

*A timeless scene outside the 19th-century adega (above) at Bairrada's most innovative producer, Luis Pato.*

## BAIRRADA

To the west of Dão, the Bairrada DOC shares some of the same problems as its neighbour, in that its production has been dominated by poorly equipped cooperatives using rather backward vinification methods. The picture is slowly brightening, however, as more of the small growers decide to cut out the co-ops and bottle their own wine.

Three-quarters of Bairrada is red, and the main grape, Baga, is one of Portugal's more assertive red varieties, although since 2003, a clutch of other Portuguese and international grapes may now be blended in. Clumsily vinified, it can be depressingly tannic and rough, but the smarter operators are coaxing some ripe plummy fruit out of it and showing its potential. White Bairrada, given a gentle touch of oak by one or two producers, can be splendidly smoky and appley, but the majority is still fairly bland. That remains hard to account for as its main grape varieties, Maria Gomes and Bical, are good ones.

This is also the region in which the Sogrape company makes its famed Mateus Rosé. Originally a sweetish pink fizz, it has now gone fashionably drier, with clean, peachy fruit that makes it a respectable proposition on a hot day. PRODUCERS: São João, Aliança, Sogrape, de Sousa, Baixo, Campolargo.

## ESTREMADURA

Quantitatively the most important region of Portugal, this western coastal region north of Lisbon encompasses nine DOCs and a number of IPG regions. **Alenquer** is a quality DOC with mature plantings of the local red Castelão, Trincadeira, Touriga Nacional and Aragonez (Spain's Tempranillo) grapes, with some French interlopers, such as Cabernet and Syrah, mingled in. Other constantly improving DOCs include **Arruda**, **Obidos**, **Torres Vedras**, **Lourinhã** and **Encostas d'Aire** (and its sub-region **Alcobaça**), but much of the wine is still given the regional designation **Lisboa**, after the capital city. Monte d'Oiro is one of the producers setting the pace.

**Bucelas** is a tiny DOC to the south of Arruda. It came perilously close to extinction in the 1980s, when there was just one producer, Caves Velhas, remaining. There are now a handful of new estates determined to restore its historically lofty reputation. It makes white wines only in a light, crisply acidic style from the Arinto grape, which also crops up in white port, together with Esgana, which (as Sercial) is one of the four noble grapes of madeira. Traditionally, the wines were kept for many years in bottle, for all that their grape varieties seem to be telling us to drink them young.

**Colares** is another of the DOC minnows, perched high on the wind-battered clifftops above the Atlantic Ocean, northwest of Lisbon. Its claim to fame, the noble Ramisco grape, makes some fine, concentrated, ageworthy reds, both on the coast as well as further inland. Whites, based on Madeira's Malvasia, are fairly heavy and less interesting.

## RIBATEJO

Inland from Estremadura, also north of Lisbon, Ribatejo also contains a patchwork of districts, which all fall under the regional DOC. From north to south, these are **Tomar**, **Santarém**, **Chamusca**, **Almeirim**, **Cartaxo** and **Coruche**. The potential for outstanding quality here is manifest. The main red grape, Periquita (locally called Castelão Frances) is a good one, giving deeply coloured, spicy wine, while the whites are based on Fernão Pires (aka Maria Gomes in Bairrada). They can be enticingly fresh and floral, and even lightly oaked from those with the resources.

PRODUCERS: Casal Branco, Lagoalva de Cima, Cadaval, Fiuza & Bright.

## SETUBAL

**Palmela**, in the northern part of the Setúbal peninsula, was made a DOC in 2003, incorporating the former IPG of Arrábida, and has gradually made a name for itself as a quality region. The fine red Periquita grape makes intriguingly spicy, peppery wines with good plum and raisin fruit, as well as a small amount of fresh rosé.

The IGP here is labelled **Peninsula de Setúbal** (formerly Terras do Sado), and includes a slew of excellent savoury reds and scented whites. Some of Portugal's best large companies are based here, including DFJ Vinhos, José Maria da Fonseca and the Pegôes co-op. Sparklers are also becoming a speciality. This is a region to watch.

The **Setúbal** DOC is for fortified sweet Muscats (see page 183).

## ALENTEJO

In the southeast of the country, not far from the Spanish border, the Alentejo region has become one of the hottest names on the Portuguese wine scene. Indeed, this was where the quality revolution really began. Much experimentation has taken place, and the evident standard of the predominantly red wines speaks for itself.

The Alentejo is divided into eight sub-regions, all formerly either DOCs or IPGs in their own right, but which were amalgamated into the overall Alentejo DOC in 2003. From north to south, these are: Portalegre, Borba, Redondo, Evora, Reguengos, Granja-Amareleja, Vidigueira and Moura. The IGP wines are labelled **Alentejano**.

Grapes are all first-class, with reds led by Aragonez, Trincadeira, Moreto and Periquita, the whites by the gently spicy Roupeiro, and there is the usual crowd of well-controlled French interlopers among them. Careful site selection and judicious oak-ageing are the hallmarks of the best efforts in what is for me Portugal's most dynamic region.

PRODUCERS: João Portugal Ramos, Esporão, JM de Fonseca, Bacalhôa, Malhadinha Nova, Mouchão, Cortes de Cima, Mouro.

## ALGARVE

The southern coastal strip of Portugal may be much-loved as a holiday destination, but it hasn't tended to produce much in the way of quality wine. It consists of four DOCs – from west to east, **Lagos**, **Portimão**, **Lagoa** and **Tavira** – mostly making burly reds of no particular charm. Wines from the Cantor estate, bottled as Vida Nova and Onda Nova, might just change that. A long-forgotten pale dry fortified wine is still made by the local cooperative.

*Ripe bunches of Periquita grapes (below) destined for Tinto da Anfora, a blended red from the Alentejo region.*

*Taylor's Quinta de Vargellas, source of one of the most successful single-estate ports (above).*

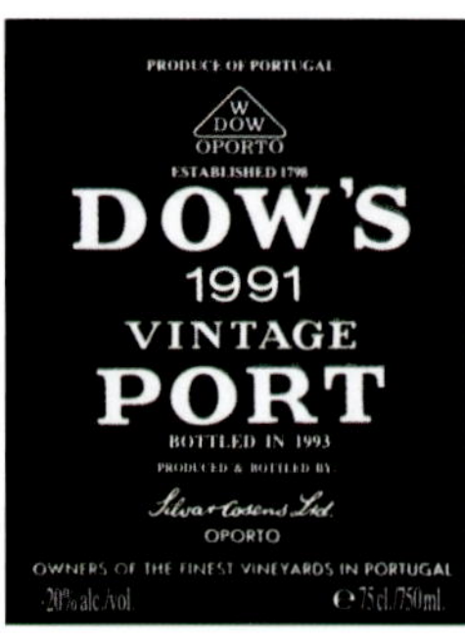

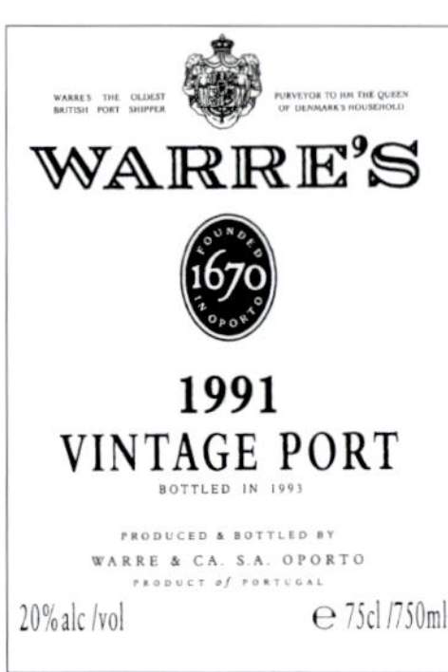

## PORT

The origins of port, as of all fortified wines, lie in the need to stabilize light table wines and protect them from spoilage during long sea voyages. When the English merchants found themselves having to pay punitive tariffs to import French wines, as a result of the 17th-century wars with France, they turned to Portugal as their next best source. The thin white wines of northern Portugal (the modern Vinho Verde DOC) were not much to anyone's taste but, venturing into the Douro valley, the importers chanced upon the fiery red brews of what was to become port country.

Imported in barrel, the wines had inevitably spoiled by the time they reached England, and so the shippers learned to add a little brandy to them in order to preserve them. At this point, therefore, port would have been a potent but dry wine. It wasn't until some while later that the English began systematically adding the brandy before the red wine had finished fermenting. That stopped the yeasts dead in their tracks before all of the grape sugar had been consumed, and so port became naturally sweet as well as strong. A legendary fortified wine was born.

Today, the fortifying agent is a more neutral, colourless grape spirit rather than actual brandy, but the production process is otherwise not much changed from the 1600s. In the mid-18th century, in a drive to protect port from poor imitations from other regions, the Douro valley was demarcated as the only area that could produce genuine port. It was thus the first ever denominated appellation, predating the French system by about 180 years.

Of all the European fortified wines, port is the most confusing to the unsuspecting. The following is a summary of the range of port styles now offered.

**Ruby** The most basic style of all, blended from the produce of several harvests and aged for no more than a couple of years. Many shippers produce a house brand that may or may not call itself Ruby (the term is somewhat debased now), but if it has no other description, this is what it will essentially be.

**Vintage Character** If ever a wine term were ripe for abolition, it is Vintage Character port. These are basic rubies, aged for longer (about five years on average) that theoretically have something of the depth of flavour of true vintage port. In practice, they simply never do, and if you're going to trade up from basic ruby, it is far more advisable to move on to the next category, Late Bottled Vintage.

**Late Bottled Vintage (LBV)** Unlike Vintage Character, these really are the produce of a single vintage, which will be specified on the label. They are basically the years that are not quite deemed good enough to make true vintage port, but the quality is nonetheless generally good. They are aged for between four and six years, and the best ones will have been bottled without being filtered, so that the wine throws a sediment and requires decanting. Some companies filter their LBVs in order to avoid the need for that, largely because many consumers wrongly imagine that decanting is more technical than it is (see page 15). Buy an unfiltered LBV in preference to a filtered one; the flavours are far more resonant and complex.

**Vintage port** At the top of the pyramid, vintage port is the product of a single year, stated on the label as with ordinary table wine, that is bottled after two or three years' cask-ageing. Each shipper must decide within two years of the harvest whether the wine of a particular year is going to be fine enough to be released, unblended, as a vintage port. This is known as 'declaring' the vintage. Good years such as 2003 may result in a universal declaration among the major shippers. Vintage port requires ageing in the bottle by the customer, and will always throw a sediment. Some, such as the relatively light 1980, will only need a few years; other vintages, like the legendary 1977, may take a quarter of a century and more before they are ready for drinking.

**Single quinta** Vintage wines made from the grapes of single estates or quintas. Since these grapes normally play a part in a shipper's best vintage port, the single-estate wines tend to be produced in the marginally less good years, but quality is still fine (above LBV in most cases). Names to look for are Quinta do Bomfim from the house of Dow, Quinta de Vargellas from Taylor, and Quinta da Cavadinha from Warre.

**Crusted port** So called because it forms a crust of sediment in the bottle, crusted or crusting port is a kind of cross between vintage port and LBV. It is not the produce of a single year, but is treated like a vintage port and bottled unfiltered. The style is a speciality of the British-owned port houses, and is intended as an economically kinder alternative to true vintage port.

**Tawny port** Traditionally a basic blended port that is aged for several years longer than ruby, so that its colour drops out and the flavour goes almost drily nutty with oxidation. Some tawny is now made by simply adding a little white port to the base of paler red wines to lighten the colour.

**Aged tawny** These are invariably true tawny ports, aged for many years in cask. The difference from basic tawny is that the label will state the average age of the wines that have gone into the blend, calculated in multiples

of ten. A 10-year-old tawny, such as the perennially superb example from Dow, may well be the optimum age. Twenty-, 30- and 40-year-old wines will increase correspondingly in price, but may yield diminishing returns as to appreciable complexity.

**Colheitas** A *colheita* port is essentially a vintage tawny. The wines from a single year receive a minimum of seven years in cask, so that their colour fades. Many are only released at grand old ages, and the prices – compared to early-bottled vintage port – can look immensely attractive.

**White and rosé port** Among the cocktail of 80-plus grape varieties that are permitted in port are a few white ones. Some houses produce a port solely from white grapes (largely Arinto, Gouveio, Malvasia and Viosinho), which is fortified by the same method as the red. They may be dry or sweet and are not particularly great wines. The dry white has nothing like the pedigree of good fino sherry, for instance, but can be appealing served well-chilled in small quantities. Rosé port is the latest innovation, but not one that was crying out to be introduced.

BEST NAMES IN PORT: Dow, Taylor, Graham, Cálem, Fonseca, Warre, Ferreira, Niepoort, Burmester. Quinta do Noval makes a famously brilliant vintage wine called Nacional from ancient vines, selling at a once-in-a-lifetime price.
PORT VINTAGES: 2020 **** 2019 **** 2018 **** 2017 ***** 2016 ***** 2011 ***** 2008 ***** 2007 ***** 2005 **** 2003 ***** 2000 ***** 1977 *****

*Back-breaking manual harvesting in the terraced vineyards of Quinta do Bomfim in the Douro (above).*

*A traditional barco rabelo sails through Oporto (below), on the Portuguese coast. These boats were used to carry the pipes of port down the Douro to the port houses.*

## MADEIRA

The history of madeira is perhaps the single most remarkable example of human dedication to the cause of fine wine. The island of Madeira is a volcanic tropical outcrop in the Atlantic Ocean, nearer to the coast of north Africa than to the Portugal of which it forms an autonomously governed province. Its soil contains a great quantity of ash from a conflagration that raged across the island many centuries ago, and its mountainous terrain means that its vineyards are among the most inaccessible in the world.

Like port, Madeira's wines were once light table wines that came to be fortified so that they might better survive long sea transportation. In the case of madeira, though, the shippers stumbled on an extraordinary discovery. Carried aboard the great trading vessels of the Dutch East India Company, the wine's voyage east was a more arduous matter than simply ferrying port from northern Portugal to the south of England. It was noticed that, when the wine arrived in India, it was unspoiled; in fact it was positively improved. So, just for good measure, the shippers left some to complete a round trip back to Europe, and that turned out even better.

No other wine has ever, before or since, proved so improbably masochistic. It sailed the heaving oceans in raging heat for weeks at a time, the barrels clattering around in the hold, and nothing could destroy it. For many decades, every bottle of madeira sold had been on this round-the-world cruise, until a way was found to simulate those conditions in its place of origin.

In the 19th century, a maturation system known as the *estufa*, or stove, was introduced. The *lagares* – the storage houses in which the wine is aged – were equipped with central-heating systems, hot-water pipes that ran around the walls (or occasionally through the vats of wine themselves) in order to cook it, as it had been in its maritime days. Some wines known as *canteiros*, reputedly the best, were cooked by simple exposure to the tropical summer sun.

Simple blended madeira is often based on a red grape variety called Tinta Negra Mole that used also to find its way into any of the four varietal styles of madeira. These must now, as a result of intervention by the European Union, be made up of no less than 85 per cent of the named varietal, although Tinta Negra Mole itself has now been accepted as Madeira's fifth varietal, which seems fair enough.

*All of Madeira's agriculture, including its vineyards, is planted in terraces on sheer hillside land such as this (right). The fearsome gradients mean that any form of mechanized harvesting is out of the question.*

The white varietal wines are, from lightest and driest to richest and sweetest, **Sercial**, **Verdelho**, **Bual** and **Malmsey** (the last name being an anglicized corruption of Malvasia). Even at its very sweetest, madeira always has a streak of balancing acid running through it to complement the amazing flavours of molasses, toffee, Christmas cake, sweet spices, dates and walnuts. There is also often a telltale whiff of mature cheese about it, rather like old dry Cheshire, and just to complete its range of peculiar attributes, it generally has a distinct green hue at the rim.

Labels may state the age of the blend (ten-year-old is significantly more rewarding than five), or may use such vague-sounding, but in practice fairly precise, terminologies as Finest (about three years old), Reserve (five), Special Reserve (ten) or Extra Reserve (15).

A small quantity of vintage-dated madeira is made, which sells for a fraction of the price of vintage port. As the history of this fabulous, unique wine suggests, it is virtually indestructible. Definitely worth trying.

BEST NAMES IN MADEIRA: Blandy, Henriques & Henriques, Barbeito, Cossart Gordon, Rutherford & Miles, Leacock.

## SETUBAL

Three variants of the Muscat grape, the main one Muscat of Alexandria, make a port-method sweet fortified wine on the Setúbal peninsula, **Moscatel de Setúbal**. After the fortification, the skins of the grapes are left to infuse in the new wines for several months, so that a particularly pronounced aroma and flavour of fresh Moscatel grapes is imparted to it. It is usually aged in cask for five years before bottling, though some premium wines are given up to 25 years' maturation, resulting in a nuttily oxidized, deep brown wine. Most examples taste fairly heavy on the palate, but some attain the graceful balance of the best southern French fortified Muscats. JM da Fonseca makes excellent ones. Wines with less than 85 per cent Moscatel in them are labelled as simple **Setúbal**.

## CARCAVELOS

Decreasingly important coastal DOC just west of Lisbon that once tried to rival port as a producer of quality fortified wine. The wines are made in much the same way, from both red and white grapes, and generally resemble basic tawny. Quinta dos Pesos is a recently established estate determined to keep the flame alive.

*Traditional thatched A-frame houses, like this one at Palheiros (below), are a characteristic feature of Madeira's vineyards.*

# GERMANY

*Germany's wines have struggled to earn respect abroad in the modern era,
yet the country's conscientious producers can offer the very best of fine,
light wines in a whole range of styles.*

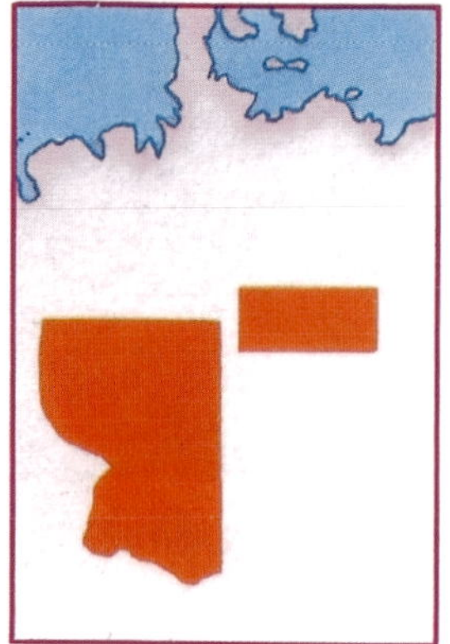

*Germany's famous wine
regions hug the river Rhine
and its tributaries, along the
southwestern borders (below).
Saale-Unstrut and Sachsen
are two additions since the
fall of the Berlin Wall.*

IMAGE PROBLEM? What image problem?
Everybody knows that Germany produces
some of the finest light fermented drinks in the
world. Indeed, it set the European standard, and
remains an enviable beacon of integrity when
set against the mass-produced stuff churned out
to satisfy everyday tastes elsewhere in Europe.
That's right. German beers are second to none.

Wine? That – sadly, agonizingly, notoriously
– is another story. It hardly seems necessary
to rehearse again the long decline of German
wine over the 20th century. War reparations
following the Treaty of Versailles in 1919
devastating a wine industry that had enjoyed a
continent-wide reputation for quality since the
Middle Ages. The invention of a new product
(sweetened-up slop, to be sure, but a unique
style anyway) in order to move in on the

undemanding end of the market. The graduation
of international taste to dry, full-bodied, barrel-
fermented white wines and sturdy, ultra-ripe
reds when all you've got is delicately lacy
white wines that nearly all have some degree
of sweetness to them. What's a wine producer
to do? People always enjoy a glass of fizz,
perhaps, but then even your sparkling wines
are mostly rubbish.

All in all, the modern wine world has been
more of a challenge for Germany than it has
been for any other established wine-producing
country. The first signs of a way out of the
impasse began to emerge in the early 1990s.
If the world wanted dry wines, German
winemakers would produce them. Early
attempts at fermenting out the Rieslings to full
dryness were often grotesque, unbalanced and
painfully bitter, but with the right varieties in
the right sites, decent dry whites are now being
produced. They're not world-shattering, but
they don't taste unripe any longer.

What's more encouraging is that the best
growers – and Germany has some of the most
talented winemakers on the face of the earth –
have excelled in the past couple of decades at
extending their range, and modernizing their
approach. There are wines being made along the
Mosel, in the Rheingau, the Pfalz and the Nahe,
by no means exclusively from Riesling, for
which only the word 'beautiful' will do. 'But
what do we drink them with?' is the parrot-cry
of the food-and-wine chatterati. Don't drink
them with anything if nothing seems to work.
Drink them on their own, if you prefer, but
drink them. They're too good to miss.

The only problem you'll encounter is finding
any, since most high-street retailers, restaurants
and wine-bars bailed out of quality German
wine a long time ago. And that, which returns
us to the whole question of image, really is
what you call a problem.

A wine classification system comparable to
the French standard was established in 1971.
At its lowest level, is the basic table wine,
*Deutscher Wein*, to be avoided here as
elsewhere. A step up is the *vin de pays* category,

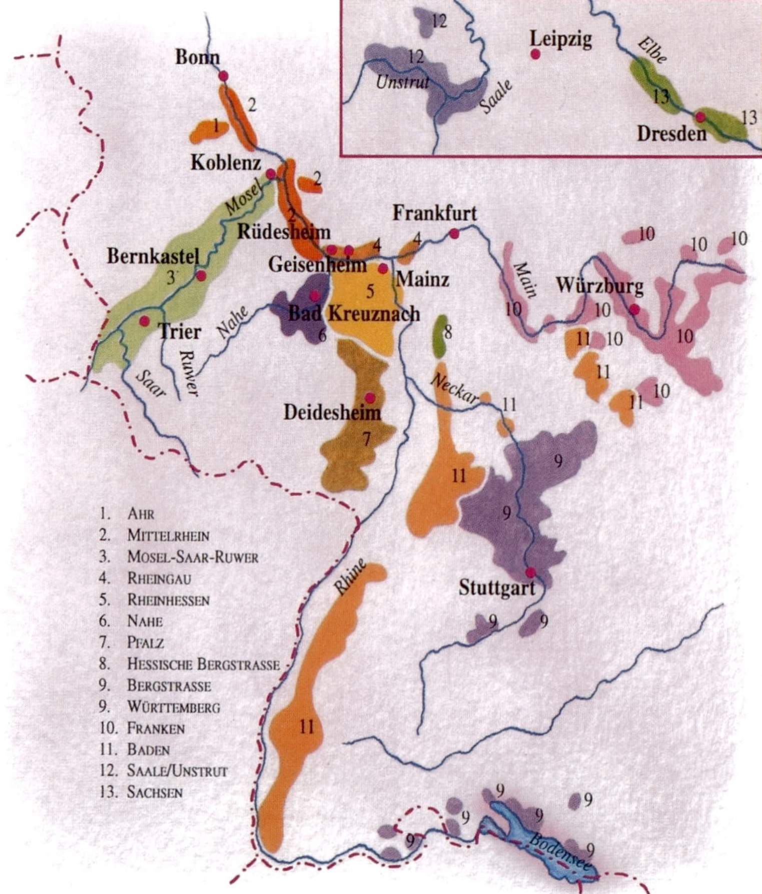

*Landwein*, which may come from any of 19 large demarcated regions. Above that is *Qualitätswein* ('quality wine'). This is the volume category, but represents a significant step up. It covers 13 strictly demarcated regions, in which the juice of underripe grapes may be sweetened to increase the final alcohol level.

At the top is *Prädikatswein*, formerly QmP (*Qualitätswein mit Prädikat*, 'quality wine with pedigree'). These wines are subdivided according to how much natural sugar the harvested grapes possess; they must not be artificially sweetened. In ascending order of sweetness, they are: Kabinett, Spätlese, Auslese, Beerenauslese and Trockenbeerenauslese. The separate category Eiswein ('ice wine' made from frozen ultra-ripe grapes picked in the dead of winter) also counts as *Prädikatswein*. It usually falls somewhere between the last two categories in terms of sweetness.

Dry wines are labelled Trocken, the semi-dry Feinherb (the latter term unofficially replacing the original Halbtrocken).

It remains true that its Rieslings are still Germany's best shot, but there are other varieties to contend with, many of them grown in different regions. In an effort to find grapes that will ripen more dependably than Riesling in the cold northern climate, viticultural researchers have produced crossed varieties, and even crossed the crossings. The results have been decidedly mixed, and remain mostly specific to Germany. Grapes familiar from elsewhere are a safer bet, but you'll need to know their German names – Weissburgunder (Pinot Blanc), Grauburgunder or Ruländer (Pinot Gris), Spätburgunder (Pinot Noir) and, more recognizably, Gewürztraminer.

## OTHER GRAPES

**Silvaner** Particularly valued in the Franken region around Würzburg, Silvaner is one of the best of the uncrossed grapes after Riesling. An earlier ripener, it gives wines with a whiff of cabbage leaves when young, but that can age to a silky, honey-laden maturity.

**Müller-Thurgau** A Riesling-based mix, this was the first of the crossings, developed in the 1880s. So grateful were the growers for its early-ripening properties that they fell upon it with unconfined zeal, to the extent that it became Germany's most widely planted grape, a position it no longer occupies. Indeed, it could have been the Holy Grail, were it not for the

fact that the wines it produces are unspeakably dull and watery. Unbelievably, though, new plantings of it are still being established.

**Kerner** One of the more successful new varieties, Kerner is a crossing of Riesling with the red Trollinger. It at least makes a crisp, lime-zesty wine with at least some of the elegance of the real thing, but plantings are declining.

**Scheurebe** A Riesling-Silvaner cross, Scheurebe has, when properly ripe, a distinct flavour of grapefruit, with the corollary that, if the summer hasn't been kind, its wines are agonizingly tart. In the right conditions, however, it gives excellent noble-rotted dessert wines of piercing intensity.

**Rieslaner** Probably the best of the Riesling-Silvaner crossings, the clumsily named Rieslaner can be stunning, full of almost tropical fruit from the best growers. Mostly only found in the Pfalz and Franken, it's a shame it hasn't become more widely favoured.

**Bacchus** Crossed from two other crossings, and with Riesling and Silvaner in its parentage, this can be an exhilarating aromatic variety, as some English growers have discovered. In Germany, it is of declining importance, planted mainly in Franken.

*The sundial (above) that gives the terraced Wehlener Sonnenuhr vineyard, one of the Mosel's premier sites, its name.*

*A misty winter morning dawns over the vineyard of Schwarzerde, near Kirchheim, Pfalz (above). German wines have to survive some of the severest cold-weather conditions in the world.*

*The village of Zeltingen (above), caught between the Mosel river and the steeply rising vineyards.*

**Dornfelder** A fine red variety produced from two other crossed grapes, Dornfelder has made inroads into various German regions, particularly along the Rhine. Its wines can be light and cherryish, a little like young Beaujolais occasionally, but with less alcohol. Some producers are attempting to coax a fuller, richer style from it suitable for oak-ageing.

**Blauer Portugieser** Not a Portuguese grape despite the name, it gives rather coarse reds with high acidity, and is now in decline.

**Lemberger** Known as Blaufränkisch in neighbouring Austria, this is a good, characterful red grape that produces light, but appetizingly spicy, even violetty wines with plenty of fresh acidity. Plantings of it are on the up.

**Trollinger** Planted mainly in the Württemberg region, Trollinger (known as Schiava in northern Italy) is a quality red grape that produces light, redcurranty wines, often with a gentle hint of nutmeg to them.

## THE REGIONS

**Ahr** This small northerly wine region, lying just south of the city of Bonn, specializes in red wines, mostly from Spätburgunder (Pinot Noir). They are inevitably light, in both texture and colour, as a result of being grown in such a marginal climate, but there are increasing numbers of good examples, notably from late-picked grapes that retain a gentle natural sweetness. The region's production is dominated by cooperatives, but Meyer-Näkel is a one of a handful of skilful smaller winemakers. There is also some Riesling, but it's losing ground as a percentage of total plantings.

**Mittelrhein** A small production area that extends from Bonn to south of Koblenz, the Mittelrhein is two-thirds Riesling – a high proportion for any German region. Vineyards are planted on both banks of the Rhine, often on steep hillsides. Pinot Noir is increasingly important here. Quality is good, but most of the wine is drunk *in situ* by the locals – or by tourists, as this is one of the most unspoiled parts of Germany. Toni Jost is a fine Mittelrhein winemaker who is exporting some of his sharply defined, exciting Rieslings.

**Mosel** The Mosel valley runs southwest of Koblenz, down past the city of Trier, and stops short at the intersection where Germany borders Luxembourg and France. The region also embraces two small tributaries of the river Mosel, the Saar and the Ruwer. It includes some of the most historically celebrated vineyards in German wine history, many of them located in the Bernkastel district in the centre of the valley. These are some of the world's most dramatically sited vineyards, clinging vertiginously to sheer hillsides on either bank of the river, completely inaccessible to any form of machine-harvesting. Here the Riesling achieves some of its great glories, wines that are almost miraculously subtle expressions of the variety, extremely low in alcohol and yet possessed of a fragile purity all their own.

The best vineyard sites (preceded by their village names) have been Erdener Treppchen, Wehlener Sonnenuhr, Graacher Himmelreich, Bernkasteler Doktor, Brauneberger Juffer and Piesporter Goldtröpfchen. Some of these, notably Piesport, have suffered by association with bland, mass-market products that are blended from the general district (or *Bereich*). Always choose a single-estate wine in preference to anything else.

Around the Saar, Wiltinger Scharzhofberg, Ockfener Bockstein and Ayler Kupp are the leading vineyards, while Maximin Grünhaus and Eitelsbacher Karthäuserhofberg are the jewels in Ruwer's crown.

PRODUCERS: Egon Müller (Scharzhofberger), Haag, Dr Loosen, von Schubert, JJ Prüm, Thanisch, Saarstein, Pauly-Bergweiler, Molitor.

**Rheingau** The Rheingau mostly occupies the right bank of the Rhine to the east of the Mittelrhein region. In some ways, it represents the nerve-centre of German winemaking. Rheingau boasts some of the most highly regarded wine estates in the country, growing a great preponderance of Riesling. At Geisenheim, the viticultural research institute has been responsible for so much of the work in creating new vine varieties.

A range of disparate vineyard conditions makes up the Rheingau. Around Rüdesheim, steeply shelving slaty soils produce some ethereally light Rieslings, while more robust wines, known and much favoured once as 'hock', come from the more gently contoured land around Hochheim.

At the heart of Rheingau production is a group of about four dozen winemakers calling itself the Charta Association. To qualify for the seal of approval (look for an emblem of twin arches embossed on the brown bottles), Charta wines must pass a rigorous taste test, which only Rieslings may enter. It is a quality initiative that other German regions would do well to emulate.

The two most famous properties are the ancient estates of Schloss Vollrads and Schloss Johannisberg. In a region dominated by small producers rather than cooperatives, the names of outstanding individual growers are a better guide to quality than the vineyard sites themselves. Look out for the following.

PRODUCERS: Breuer, Johannishof, Künstler, Domdechant Werner, Kloster Eberbach, Leitz, Kesseler, Schönborn, Reinhartshausen.

**Rheinhessen** South of the Rheingau, the Rheinhessen is where a lot of the mass-market wines of Germany originate. Half of all Liebfraumilch is made here, and there are other regional names that will be familiar to English-speaking consumers, such as Niersteiner Gutes Domtal. Much of Germany's acreage of crossed grape varieties is planted in the Rheinhessen too, with Müller-Thurgau leading the way. Production is much larger than in the Rheingau, and this is not by and large a quality region. There are, however, always exceptions, increasingly so in the production of surprisingly sturdy reds from Spätburgunder and Dornfelder. Silvaner also makes good wine, although less of it than it once did.

PRODUCERS: Villa Sachsen, Guntrum, Heyl zu Herrnsheim, Keller, Wittmann.

**Nahe** The Nahe region, named after its river, lies to the west of the Rheinhessen. It is a fine, and considerably under-recognized, player on the German wine scene, its best estates as good as those in the Rheingau or Mosel. Some astonishingly concentrated Rieslings are made within the vicinity of the town of Bad Kreuznach, with Müller-Thurgau and Dornfelder making up most of the rest of the plantings. A concerted campaign to raise the profiles of the best growers has helped; it's also driven prices up, but this is still one of the best-value regions in Germany.

PRODUCERS: Dönnhoff, Diel, Crusius, Plettenberg.

*A tiny patch of red earth at the foot of the towering Rotenfels cliff (above) at Bad Münster, in the Nahe, yields intensely flavoured wines.*

*Assmannshausen, at the western end of the Rheingau (below). This wine region, like Burgundy, can trace an unbroken history back to the early days of the Benedictine and Cistercian monks.*

*Decorative architecture typical of Germany's wine villages (above).*

*Looking down over the town of Würzburg on the river Main in Franken (right), from the Marienberg vineyard.*

**Pfalz** Once known in English as the Palatinate, the Pfalz is a fast-improving and dynamic region to the south of Rheinhessen. The range of grapes grown is very broad. Not only Riesling, but Dornfelder, Spätburgunder, Grauburgunder and Gewürztraminer are all producing good things. Among the best villages are Deidesheim, Ruppertsberg and Wachenheim, but impressive wine is proliferating all over the Pfalz now. Some of the new-style Pinot Noir reds could give some négociant burgundy a run for its money these days; not only do they have richness and body, but they can often match Burgundian Pinot for alcohol too. Decent sparkling wine, known in Germany as Sekt bA, is also becoming something of a speciality.

The very best Pfalz estate is Müller-Catoir, whose range of varietals is frankly world-class. Not only does it make breathtaking Rieslings and Rieslaners, as well as some convincingly spicy Gewürz, but the estate has even been known to cajole some display of personality from that old dullard, Müller-Thurgau. PRODUCERS: Müller-Catoir, Lingenfelder, Bürklin-Wolf, Bassermann-Jordan, von Buhl, Köhler-Ruprecht.

**Hessische Bergstrasse** Germany's smallest region, to the east of Rheinhessen, does not export much of its wine, but quality is impressively high. About half the vineyard is Riesling, and the better growers manage to achieve levels of concentration similar to those around Hochheim. This has been one of the sectors of Germany that has wholeheartedly embraced the latter-day trend for fermenting out wines of *Prädikat* standard to Trocken or Feinherb styles. Vineyards owned by the state of Hesse are producing some of the best wine, including sumptuous Eiswein; Simon-Bürkle is a commendable individual estate.

**Württemberg** A large region centred on Stuttgart, Württemberg is not greatly renowned beyond its own boundaries. Riesling and Kerner are the principal white varieties, Trollinger the main red. The region in fact specializes in red wines, with some also made from Spätburgunder, Lemberger and Schwarzriesling (the last better known as Champagne's Pinot Meunier). Trollingers are light in both colour and body, but have an attractive, summery, red-fruit nature.

**Franken** The region through which the river Main runs was traditionally famous as the mainstay of the Silvaner grape, although that now only accounts for about a fifth of the area under vine. The local taste is for austerely dry wines, the best of which come in a flat round bottle called a *Bocksbeutel*. Nowadays, Müller-Thurgau has, somewhat depressingly, made inroads into the vineyards, but there are also some delicately floral wines from that much-crossed variety Bacchus. The wines are exported to some degree, but prices tend to be off-putting. PRODUCERS: Wirsching, Ruck, Juliusspital.

**Baden** The principal region of southwest Germany , just over the border from Alsace, Baden has been on most people's lists as one of the more exciting European wine regions of recent years. It encompasses a long stretch between Franken and the border with Switzerland, with some vineyards situated in the vicinity of Lake Constance (or the Bodensee in German). Although there is a fairly high percentage of Müller-Thurgau in the vineyards, there is also fine, boldly delineated Riesling, musky dry Grauburgunder, spicy Gewürztraminer and – perhaps most promising of all in these warmer southern climes – plenty of intensely ripe, deeply raspberryish Spätburgunder, some of it benefiting from oak influence.
PRODUCERS: Königschaffhausen co-op.

**Saale-Unstrut** One of two small regions that fell within the boundaries of the former GDR (East Germany), Saale-Unstrut is named after the two rivers at whose confluence it lies. Müller-Thurgau, Weissburgunder, Silvaner and others are used to make dry, relatively full-bodied wines, but the region wasn't much blessed with investment by the old state authority, and it can still only be considered emergent as yet. Lützkendorf is a producer worth noting.

**Sachsen** The most northerly and easterly wine region in Germany, Sachsen (Saxony in English) is centred on the old city of Dresden, its vineyards planted along the banks of the river Elbe. Like Saale-Unstrut, it makes dry

white wines from good varieties, but the prospects for quality wine are noticeably higher. Müller-Thurgau rules the roost, but Riesling, Weissburgunder, Gewürztraminer and Grauburgunder all play their parts. The wine is mostly made by a single large cooperative of numerous small growers, but Zimmerling is a good solo performer.

## SPARKLING WINES

German sparkling wine covers a multitude of sins. It comes in four basic categories, the best of which is **Sekt bA** (*Sekt bestimmter Anbaugebiete*), which must come from one of the 13 *Qualitätswein* districts, indicated on the label (e.g. Pfalz Sekt bA). Most is made by the Charmat or tank method. Wonderfully fresh, lime-scented sparkling Rieslings at all levels of sweetness are getting better and better.

**Deutscher Sekt** is a step down, and may be blended from anywhere in the country. Basic **Sekt**, which accounts for about 90 per cent of German fizz, lacks the adjective Deutscher for the simple reason that it contains wines from other countries, mainly the unwanted slosh of Italy, Spain and France. Lowest of the low is carbonated **Schaumwein**, the most unbelievably atrocious fizzy wine made anywhere.

Recent german vintages: 2023 ****
2022 ****   2020 ****   2019 *****
2018 ****   2013 ****   2011 ****
2009 *****   2005 *****   2001 *****

*Netting keeps birds off the sweet shrivelled Riesling grapes left on the vine after harvest to botrytize (above), in the Ungeheuer vineyard at Forst, in the Pfalz.*

# UNITED KINGDOM

*In the relatively short period of the last 30 years, the UK's wine industry has developed dramatically. It may not ever become prolific but when the weather is kind, the quality is there.*

*A mechanical harvester at work at Denbies, in Surrey (above), the UK's largest producer at 250ha.*

*Most of the UK's vineyards (below) are clustered in the southeast, and are tiny, averaging less than one hectare.*

WINEMAKING in the British Isles was revived at a purely speculative level in the years following the second world war. For a long time, it was a rash hobbyist's pursuit, which involved rummaging through the back cupboard of Germany's experimental grape laboratories to find varieties that might care to ripen in the famously damp summers. The amount of investment needed to establish a vineyard meant that the resulting produce had to be sold at prices that made the wine look like a luxury item, compared to Muscadet or Bulgarian Merlot.

Quantities were tiny, so most of the wine was sold out of the vineyards themselves. Where anything was produced in sufficient quantity for one of the high-street multiples to take them, they belly-flopped commercially. The labels looked frumpy, the wines had names like Huxelrebe and Madeleine Angevine in a world of Chardonnay and Cabernet, and the tastes were something else. The French winemaker who commented with a sniff that English wine tasted of rain wasn't far wrong (although he perhaps hadn't tasted a great deal of Muscadet lately). Slow sales meant that a lot of wineries routinely offered light white and rosé wines for sale at six and seven years old, long past their notional sell-by dates.

If the British are noted for anything, though, it is the dogged refusal to know when they're beaten. Painstaking experimentation continued throughout the 1980s, and then in 1992, the national output of wine exceeded 25,000 hectolitres, triggering the institution of a European classification system, which has been retained in the post-EU era. There are two appellations – **England** and **Wales**. The top-drawer category is PDO (Protected Designation of Origin), for which the grapes must be sourced from a defined region. Below that is the looser PGI (Protected Geographical Indication), which allows for grapes from further afield.

That marked some sort of coming of age, but the single biggest story to happen to English wine since then has been fizz.

## SPARKLING WINES

The soils of whole swathes of southern England are part of the same geological chalk deposit as is found in Champagne. A cool climate is auspicious for yielding just the kind of low-alcohol, high-acid base wine that good fizzes need, and all three of the champagne grape varieties – Chardonnay, Pinot Noir and Pinot Meunier – have proved they will grow in England.

The result is a generation of sparkling wines that are every bit as good as decent champagne. They have the same toasty warmth, depth and concentration of their French cousins, whether vintage or non-vintage, and even though the prices are scarcely any different, the best wines are fully worth the outlay. The rosés, arguably, need a bit more work (many still taste rather heavy and solid), but the whites are little short of fabulous. When one of the champagne houses turns up, as it has, to buy four hectares of prime Hampshire real estate, England's sparkling wine producers can fairly claim to have arrived.

Look especially for the wines of Nyetimber and Ridgeview (both from West Sussex), Camel Valley (Cornwall) and Theale (Berkshire), but there will be many more stars in the years to come.

## OTHER WINES

Otherwise, Britain's cool, damp northerly climate means that the range of grape varieties that can be successfully grown, even given some climatic warming, is pretty narrow. There may be the odd heatwave, it's true, but vines need to keep producing year after year to earn their keep, and from where I'm sitting writing this on the south coast of England, I'm looking out of the window at the fourth wet August in a row. That's not good.

On the other hand, if there has been a reasonable summer, followed by a dampish, misty autumn, botrytis can set in, and there have in the opening years of the 21st century been some astonishing noble-rotted dessert wines. They could even cause the next wave of excitement, to follow up the success of the sparklers.

The single most important determining factor in the style of an English or Welsh wine is the grape or grapes it contains. Regional characteristics are not sufficiently sharply delineated as yet. The great tragedy, in a sense, of UK winemaking is that Riesling – hero of the German vineyards – just won't ripen here, which is where all those crossed grapes come into play. The following are some of the most commonly planted.

**Seyval Blanc** Seyval is something of an albatross to the English wine industry, in that it's a hybrid variety. This means that it has some non-*vinifera* parentage, thus outlawing it within EU rules from any appellation wine. As a varietal, it gives generally dull, thin, neutral-tasting wine, and is best blended with grapes that have a little more to say for themselves. The fact that it has gained in vineyard share to become the country's most planted grape can only hold English wine back.

**Reichensteiner** A three-way cross, Reichensteiner can occasionally make an exotically scented (and often slightly sweet) varietal. Some have achieved partial success with it by giving it a period in oak.

**Müller-Thurgau** The widely planted German workhorse grape was once England's most common variety, but it has lost ground since the 1990s. This is no bad thing, as its wines are no more thrilling than they are in the Rheinhessen.

*Breaky Bottom, in Sussex (above). Frost and birds are two menaces facing growers.*

Some producers add a little sweetening to it before bottling to create a more commercially appealing style. Enough said.

**Bacchus** A cross involving Silvaner, Riesling and Müller-Thurgau, Bacchus is quite a good grape. At its best, it has the flowery hedgerow scents that somehow suit English wine.

Other good white grapes include the perfumed Schönburger and Ortega, a little grapefruity Scheurebe, a pinch of Gewürztraminer, and growing quantities of good old Chardonnay – not all of which is going into the sparklers.

Red wines account for only about a quarter of the overall production. Germany's Dornfelder is doing well, the hybrids Rondo and Regent have produced some surprisingly robust, beefy reds, and we may one day see some exciting varietal results with Pinot Noir.

Only a tiny amount of wine is made in the south of Wales, most of it consumed locally. Monnow Valley in Monmouth has made some good, crisply refreshing whites.

# AUSTRIA

*After many years in Germany's shadow, Austria's wine industry has come out swinging, with a complex and evolving classification system, and some truly original wine flavours – led by indigenous grape Grüner Veltliner.*

*This highly ornamental gateway (above) leads to the wine cellars of Gustav Feiler at Rust, in the Burgenland region of eastern Austria.*

*Austria's vineyards lie in the eastern half of the country (right), producing mainly full-bodied dry white wines, now being joined by some rapidly improving reds. Around the Neusiedlersee lake in Burgenland, the regular occurrence of noble rot provides some of Europe's best-value dessert wines.*

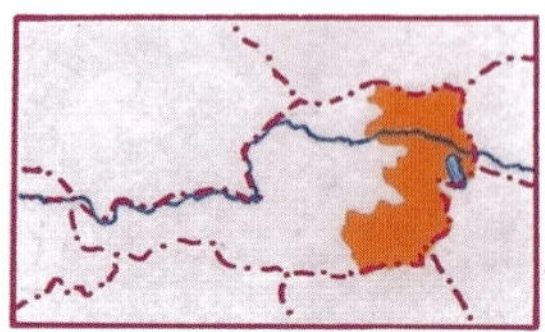

THE VINEYARD REGIONS of Austria are almost all located in the eastern half of the country, along its borders with the Czech Republic, Slovakia, Hungary and Slovenia. Germanic as well as French grape varieties are grown, but being that much more southerly than most of Germany's wine regions, Austria is able to produce a wider spectrum of wine styles in a more benign climate.

Its classification system has been a work in progress ever since Austria joined the EU. Originally modelled on the German system, it consists of *Wein* and *Landwein* at the lower end, above which is a *Qualitätswein* category for 16 demarcated regions (comparable to the German category), and then *Prädikatswein*, the major difference being that Kabinett wines (the sweetness category below Spätlese) are not included, but sit in their own category. In the **Wachau** district of Lower Austria, a three-tier classification for dry wines consists of (in ascending order of ripeness and potential alcohol) Steinfeder, Federspiel and Smaragd.

So far, so Germanic. Austria is also in the process of instituting a geographically based classification too, on the model of the French appellations. The category has been given a Latin title (there's posh!): *Districtus Austriae Controllatus* (DAC). There are 18 of these to date, including Weinviertel, Mittelburgenland, Traisental, Kremstal, Kamptal, Leithaberg and Eisenberg. Each may grown only certain designated grapes, mostly Grüner Veltliner and/or Riesling for whites, Blaufränkisch for reds.

## GRAPES AND WINE STYLES

The local grape made good in Austria is Grüner Veltliner; it occupies just over a third of all vineyard land. The wine it yields is quite unique, mediumweight to hefty on the palate, with an extraordinary dry spice like white pepper, and often quite biting acidity. It's fair to say the less carefully balanced ones can be more of a mouthful than you're expecting from a dry white wine, but they lack nothing in personality.

Otherwise, among whites, there's Müller-Thurgau (slowly being abandoned), Weissburgunder (Pinot Blanc), Chardonnay, Gewürztraminer, Ruländer (Pinot Gris), a dash of Sauvignon Blanc, and growing amounts of Riesling. Another white grape widely grown in these parts, **Welschriesling** (which has nothing to do with the real Riesling), occupies nearly a tenth of the Austrian vineyard. Normally, a clumsy oaf of a grape, it has achieved some improbably tasty results here. Then there are **Rotgipfler** and **Zierfandler**, the Rosencrantz and Guildenstern of Austrian wine, which together go into a peculiarly heavy wine called **Gumpoldskirchner**, made just south of Vienna.

Red varieties are the indigenous **Zweigelt**, which gives an often purple-hued wine with a Dolcetto-like taste of blueberries. The German varieties Blaufränkisch and Blauer Portugieser also appear, as well as some impressive Cabernet Sauvignon and Pinot Noir (often termed Blauerburgunder). St Laurent is a central

European grape gaining a reputation, now making gently spicy, raspberryish reds in the style of classic meaty burgundy.

Before its emergence as a producer of fine dry wines, though, Austria was noted for its botrytized dessert wines. These are mostly produced around the Neusiedlersee, a large lake on the Hungarian border. Conditions for the development of noble rot are so obliging most years that Austria can sell its sweet wines for much less than the top German examples. The categories for dessert wines are essentially the same as Germany's, including Eiswein, though with one extra classification – Ausbruch – inserted between Beerenauslese and Trockenbeerenauslese. Another sweet speciality is Strohwein (straw wine), made from naturally overripe grapes that are dried on straw mats, as in the production of Spanish *mistela* or the French *vin de paille*.

## REGIONS

**Niederösterreich (Lower Austria)** The northernmost wine zone, north of the Danube. Its wines are mostly dry or medium-dry whites from Grüner Veltliner, Riesling and Welschriesling. Kamptal, on the western fringe, makes richly intense Grüners and racy Rieslings, while Wachau has sharply defined Rieslings (some botrytized) to rival those of the Rhine valley. PRODUCERS: Brundlmayer, Loimer, Nigl, Nikolaihof, Malat, Salomon, Winzerhaus.

**Wien** Vienna is a little wine region in itself, unique among European capitals. Grüner, Riesling and Weissburgunder are the best wines, nearly all drunk locally. Traditional taverns known as *Heurigen* are cheery hostelries in the city's outskirts, where growers sell the wines of the new vintage, half-fizzing and still cloudy from the tank. Look for Wieninger's.

**Burgenland** On the Hungarian border, this is the region that includes the Neusiedlersee. A versatile range of dry table wines is made here, as well as fabulously opulent dessert wines from grapes such as Welschriesling, Gewürztraminer, the local Bouvier, and others. Dry whites take in firmly textured Weissburgunder, as well as creamy oaked Chardonnay and gooseberryish Sauvignon, while Zweigelt and Blaufränkisch reds are often packed with savoury spice, increasingly barrel-matured. One or two growers have produced breathtakingly concentrated Cabernet Sauvignon.

*The imposing white church gives its name to the village of Weissenkirchen (above) in the Wachau region of Austria, source of some of the country's finest Riesling wines.*

PRODUCERS: Kracher, Opitz, Umathum, Velich, Feiler-Artinger.

**Steiermark (Styria)** The southernmost sector. It's predominantly white wine country and, while extensive, only accounts for a modest fraction of the national output. The style, whether for Sauvignon, Chardonnay (often known by the pseudonym Morillon), Gewürztraminer or dry Muscat (Gelber Muskateller) is extremely dry, often tart, with sharply emphasized acidity. In the west, around Graz, a red grape called Blauer Wildbacher makes Schilcher, a highly regarded rosé. PRODUCERS: Gross, Polz, Tement.

*The wine village of Rust (left) in the Neusiedlersee region, where many opulent dessert wines are made.*

# CENTRAL AND SOUTHERN EUROPE

*The wine regions of central and southern Europe – stretching from Switzerland
to Slovakia – are becoming increasingly important in the global arena.
Internationally familiar grape varieties will help them to compete.*

*Trimly tended vineyards
cluster around the
village church at Conthey
(above), in the Valais,
western Switzerland.*

THE CENTRAL EUROPEAN countries,
some of them former members of the old
Soviet bloc, were only of marginal importance
to the international wine scene at one time but,
with the exceptions of Switzerland and Serbia,
all the countries on these pages are now members
of the European Union. Things are changing
fast, as their wine industries are brought within
the purview of continental regulations, and
improvements in quality – dizzyingly rapid
in some instances – have followed. Foreign
consultants have played their parts, and as the
old wine countries of western Europe have in
many areas begun to seem arrogantly distant
from the ordinary consumer, these newer players
are poised to dazzle. They just need adventurous
consumers prepared to try the wines.

## SWITZERLAND

The stunningly beautiful wine-growing areas
of Switzerland are concentrated near the
country's borders – with France in the west,
Germany to the north, and Italy in the south.
Its wines are not exported in any great quantity
and tend to be horrifyingly expensive even in
situ. Unless a path to better value can be found,
they are only ever likely to have curiosity status
in external markets.

Around the continuation of the river Rhône
in the west, the **Valais** and **Vaud** regions
specialize in French varieties, although the
favoured white grape, Chasselas (sometimes
known as Fendant), is not much prized in its
mother country, traditionally yielding a thin,
unassuming, sometimes minerally, but not
conspicuously fruity white. These wines are
gradually becoming more attractive, though,
the delicate purity that was once a handicap
having been conjured into a selling point, many
of them enlivened by a gentle spritz. Sylvaner
does well here, and there are isolated outposts
of Chardonnay and Pinot Gris.

Pinot Noir, the most planted grape with 30
per cent of the land, makes reasonably ripe
light reds, sometimes in a blend with smaller
proportions of Gamay. These are labelled **Dôle**
in the Valais, **Savagnin** in the Vaud. A white
version of the Valais blend, **Dôle Blanche**, is
made by avoiding maceration of the grapeskins.
East of France's Jura is Neuchâtel, where the
local claim to fame is a delicate Pinot Noir rosé,
**Oeil-de-Perdrix** ('partridge-eye').

Clustered around the southwestern end of the
lake of the same name is the **Geneva** region,
where Gamay has elbowed Chasselas aside to
claim more of the vineyard land. Some of the

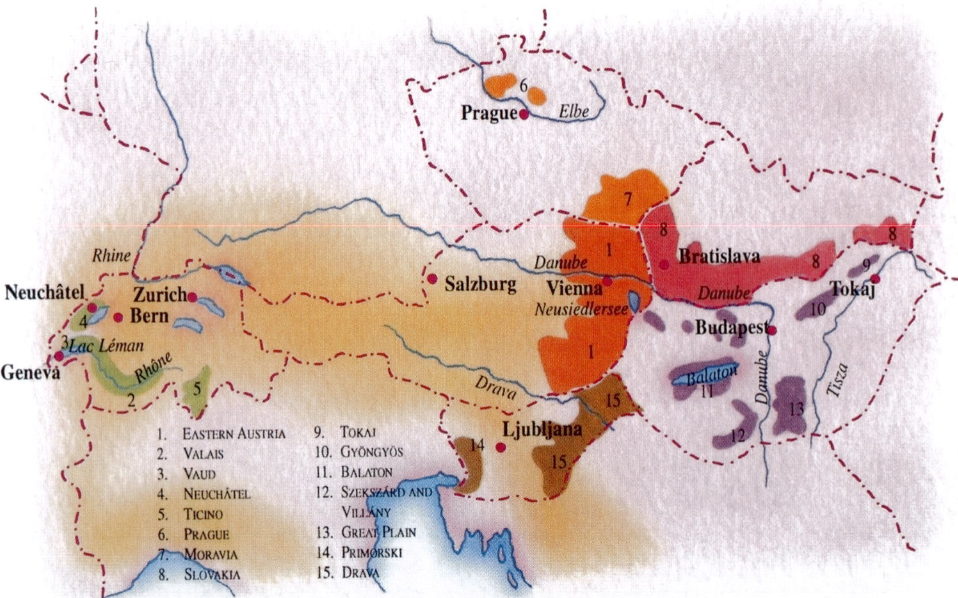


*Through the heart of
Europe stretches a band
of cool vineyards (right).
Once under the rule of
empires or else 20th-century
communist control, they
produce mainly white wines.*

minority German grapes Scheurebe and Kerner
have been planted here, as has a little speculative
Sauvignon Blanc. An ambitious cooperative, La
Cave de Genève, founded in 1994 at Satigny, is
leading the way in innovation.

**Ticino** in the south is the Italian-speaking
sector. Here production is overwhelmingly
dominated by Merlot reds, some light and
grassy, others with a bit of sinew to them,
helped along by judicious application of oak.

The most encouraging aspect of Switzerland's
wine industry is that the country also harbours
a wealth of fascinating indigenous grapes, such
as the red Cornalin (also known as Rouge du
Pays) and Humagne, and the white Arvine,
all specialities of the Valais. It also has small
but significant plantings of newer crossings of
more well-known varieties. Among the latter
are Gamaret (Gamay x Reichensteiner) and
Carminoir, an enterprising cross of Cabernet
Sauvignon and Pinot Noir.

## LUXEMBOURG

Müller-Thurgau (known here as Rivaner)
and a pallid-tasting variety called Elbling
are joined by most of the Alsace varieties in
Luxembourg's vineyards. Nearly all the wine is
white, with a little Pinot Noir for frail rosés, and
is labelled by variety. There is just one AOP,
**Moselle Luxembourgeoise**. Perhaps the most
interesting wine is **Crémant de Luxembourg**,
a denomination that came into effect in 1991 for
the country's traditional-method fizz, both white
and rosé. Quality is good, but you'll probably
have to go to the Grand Duchy to taste it.

## CZECHIA AND SLOVAKIA

Both halves of the former Czechoslovakia have
performed dynamically in the modern wine
world after decades of insularity under the state-
controlled Soviet bloc system.

**Czechia** is the greater of the two players
at the moment. Its vineyards are largely
concentrated in the southeastern region of
Moravia, on the Austrian and Slovak borders,
although an insignificant quantity of wine is
also made north of Prague in Bohemia. An
appellation system began to be formulated in
2009, under which wines are designated VOC
(*vína originální certifikace*, wines of original
certification), with new demarcated areas being
added periodically. The wines are labelled by grape
variety, and classified according to their ripeness
levels, on analogy with the German system.

*The mighty Mosel river
(above), at the point where
it separates Germany from
Luxembourg.*

International varietals to look for are Pinot
Noir for often surprisingly intense reds, along
with some Cabernet Sauvignon and Merlot, and
Pinot Gris, Pinot Blanc, Chardonnay, Riesling and
Traminer (as in Gewürz-) for whites. Plantings
of the Austrian Grüner Veltliner, together with
Müller-Thurgau, are responsible for increasing
quantities of fragrant dry white wine. St Laurent
makes appetisingly rustic red, and the violetty
Blaufränkisch crops up as Frankovka. There are
sweet wines from a local crossing, Moravian
Muscat, in the region of that name.

**Slovakia**'s vineyard regions extend in a
virtually unbroken line along the country's
southern borders, all the way from Austria to
Russia. Varieties are mostly the same as in
Czechia, with Grüner Veltliner the most widely
cultivated grape. The most important red variety
is Frankovka, which makes decent midweight
reds and fresh rosés. A curiosity is the **Irsai
Olivér** grape, a crossing originating in Hungary,
source of gracefully aromatic white wines, with
more than a waft of scented soap about them,
in the Nitra region – strange but appealing. The
labelling is by variety and grape sugars, as in
Czechia, but at the time of writing, Slovakia
lacks a formal VOC classification system.

A versatile range of sweet wine styles is
produced, made according to some of the
classic historic methods – ice wines from
grapes left to freeze on the vine, straw wines
from grapes that have been dried in the sun on
straw mats, and even **Slovak Tokaj**. The last,
often made from the syrupy exudation of fully
botrytized berries, is allowed to retain the Tokaj
name because its vineyards are effectively an
extension of the Tokaji region of northeast
Hungary, an area partitioned under the terms

*Vineyards below the
picturesque village of
Znojmo (above), southern
Moravia, Czechia.*

*Checking on the development of sweet Tokaji in the mould-coated cellars of the Tokaji Wine Trust, Hungary (above).*

*Vineyards at Nova Gora in Slovenia (below), one of central Europe's emergent wine nations.*

of the Treaty of Trianon in the aftermath of the First World War.

Orange wines from an indigenous crossed variety, **Pesecká Leánka**, tasting of dried citrus peel and orange blossom, are a clear indication that Slovak winemakers are joining the brave new world.

## HUNGARY

First things first. Hungary can lay claim to one of the greatest, most carefully curated, classic wines of Europe, namely **Tokaji**. Made in one form or another for the past four centuries, it is very possibly the origin story of quality European sweet winemaking – ahead of Rhine Valley Riesling and French Sauternes. Tokaji wasn't just incidentally sweet. Its producers perfected techniques for making it intentionally sweet in every vintage, and it retains a vinification regime, a whole series of them in fact, of awe-inspiring complexity.

There are dry and semi-sweet styles, but the excitement really begins with wines labelled Aszú. These are made from a mix of traditionally harvested grapes alongside ones that have been affected by botrytis. The rotted berries are pounded into a paste, added in varying quantities to the base wine, measured out in custom-made hods called *puttonyos*, the label stating the number added, from three up to a sticky-sweet six or seven. A burnished deep brown in colour, these wines have a flavour that can be superficially similar to sherry (although Tokaji isn't a fortified wine). Indeed, the drier styles result from maturation in large casks

under a film of naturally formed yeast, rather like the *flor* of the Jerez region.

**Tokaji Eszencia**, the sweetest style of all, appears only in occasional vintages, and is made from the free-run juice of mouldering grapes, cask-aged for at least five years. The sugar levels are so glutinously high that yeasts can barely function in it, meaning that Eszencia is a micro-alcoholic version, literally an 'essence', of all the sweetest wines in the world, often barely more than 2 per cent strength, but lacking nothing in complex, shrivelled, apricot-pulp and quince-paste perfection.

There was a doldrum period for Tokaji that roughly coincided with the Soviet bloc era, during which the wines were often stalely oxidized and tasted more of root veg than celestial marmalade. Inward investment in the region in the most recent era, including from French and German interests, has restored the wines to their rightfully exalted reputation.

But that's not all. Hungary has probably the most exciting wine scene of all the former Soviet satellite countries, with quality on the up and up as the total area of vineyard land has dwindled. There are 22 officially recognized wine regions, many of the best grouped around Balaton, Europe's largest lake. Most of the major varieties of Burgundy, Bordeaux and Alsace are now planted in Hungary, and are yielding encouraging results. Chardonnay (both oaked and unoaked) and Sauvignon Blanc have been particularly good, initially in a simple, easy-drinking style, now increasingly complex and characterful.

Native white grapes include the Furmint and Hárslevelű used in Tokaji, but also in many straight dry whites, and the crisp but unremarkable Olaszrizling (Austria's Welschriesling). Red varieties include the temperamentally late-ripening Kadarka, which makes beefy reds in the southern regions to the west of the Danube, such as Szekszárd and Villány. It was once the backbone of the famous **Egri Bikavér** (better known as Bull's Blood), for which my student classmates always seemed to have a higher tolerance than me, back in the day, and is now being cautiously reintroduced into the Egri vineyards. Kékfrankos (Blaufränkisch) reds are full of summer berry fruit, and are probably now Hungary's leading red varietal.

There are sweet Muscats for those who haven't quite got the Tokaji bank loan sorted yet, some

intriguing Pinot Gris, varietal Cabernet Franc in the southern regions, and a little of that perfumed Irsai Olivér that we met in Slovakia. Orange wine blends, often given several days' maceration on the skins, are gradually becoming more than just a novelty sideline.

## SLOVENIA

The northwestern republic of the former Yugoslavia became an independent country in 1991. It was from here that one of the biggest-selling wine brands of the 1970s hailed – the palatable, but desperately ordinary, Lutomer Laski Rizling, made from the Welschriesling grape. They still make it (as Ljutomer Rizling now), and it's considerably better than it was.

These days, Slovene wine production is mixing it in the international quality league with a range of classic varietals. Expertise and influence are being absorbed from neighbouring Italy and Austria, in the Primorska and Podravje regions respectively. Šipon (Hungary's Furmint), Sauvignon Blanc, Cabernet Sauvignon and Merlot are all performing well, while the best of the Muscat family – Muscat Blanc à Petits Grains – can make refreshing, simple sweet wines.

## CROATIA

Wine-growing in Croatia and its islands can be traced all the way to ancient times, when Greek settlers arrived. The country, independent again since 1991, is host to well over 100 native grape varieties, and some international ones too. What was long thought to be a regional speciality, Crljenak Kaštelanski, has recently been identified by DNA analysis to be none other than the Zinfandel grape widely grown in California.

There are two broad areas of vineyard in the inland Continental region: **Slavonia and the Danube** lies to the east of the coastal Dinaric Alps mountain range, where the most popular grape is Graševina, for crisply textured, aromatic whites (and also a little botrytized dessert wine), while the **Croatian Uplands** is a region of terraced hillsides to the north of Zagreb, where white grapes such as Pušipel (Hungary's Furmint) and Sauvignon Blanc have thrived.

**Coastal Croatia** is where the most exciting action is. In a strip that stretches from white wines of Istria in the north to the southerly Dalmatia, where reds predominate, this is one of central Europe's cutting-edge regions. Istria's Malvazija Istarska makes sturdily constituted, waxy whites, often aged in barrels of acacia wood, where skin contact during fermentation and ageing was traditional long before it became an international vogue. In **Dalmatia**'s vertiginous coastal and island vineyards, the red grape Plavac Mali (a crossed variety that can claim Zinfandel as one of its forebears) rules the roost for potent, tannic but fruit-driven wines.

## SERBIA

The landlocked Balkan republic of Serbia can also lay claim to a viticultural lineage going back to antiquity. A rudimentary classification system was established during the Yugoslav 1970s, but was refined in 2013, when 22 regions were demarcated. Although production is still dominated by large industrial operations, the smaller vineyards under family ownership, as in Burgundy, are gradually bringing Serbian wine to international notice. Biodynamic winemaking, as well as modish experiments with amphora fermentation, look very promising, and as in Croatia, there is a slew of indigenous grapes.

The **Fruška Gora** hills in the northerly province of Vojvodina are a particularly distinguished region, turning out sharply defined, appley whites from Morava, as well as Grašac (Welschriesling), and encouraging experiments with Pinot Noir. Elsewhere, the principal French varieties, as well as Riesling, are achieving impressive results. Prokupac is a native red grape for robust reds and dusky rosés, while a variant of Black Muscat, known locally as Tamjanika, has been cultivated in the northeasterly **Negotin Valley** for over 500 years. It is often said to have the aroma of frankincense as it ripens on the vine through the mellow early autumn.

## MALTA

Still in its infancy, winemaking on Malta looks to have a bright future. Since 2007, it has had a European classification system, and is producing carefully crafted, well-defined varietals and blends from Italian grapes such as Vermentino, Zibibbo and Sangiovese, as well as Merlot, Syrah and Chardonnay. There is also a handful of local specialities like the cherryish red Gellewza. Grapes are grown both on Malta itself, and on the second island, Gozo. There are even traditional-method Chardonnay sparklers. Tourists should look for the wines of Meridiana, Delicata and Marsovin.

*Purple Prokupac grapes ripening on the vine (above) in the Fruška Gora region of Vojvodina, Serbia.*

*Vineyards (above) at the Marsovin winery on Gozo, Malta's second island.*

# EASTERN EUROPE

*Through the great empires of the Greeks, Byzantines and Ottomans who crossed eastern Europe, the vine has flourished and faded. Centuries on, winemaking is again enjoying a new momentum.*

AS WE MOVE TOWARDS the eastern fringes of Europe, we are nearing the birthplace of wine itself, the first homeland of the winemaking grape, *Vitis vinifera*. If things had all turned out differently, then Greece would have been the pre-eminent wine country in Europe ever since Classical antiquity.

But it didn't happen that way. The Greeks took their expertise into Rome and other parts of southern Europe, and the Roman Empire carried it on northwards and westwards. In time, the native varieties of what was to be France became the most highly prized of all wine grapes, the vineyards in which they grew were carefully delineated, and French wine ascended to greatness.

In the Middle Ages, Greece became part of the Byzantine Empire. The fateful decision of the Byzantine emperor Alexius to grant favourable trading status to the Venetian Republic in 1082, exempting the goods of Venice from export duties, undermined Greek winemaking more or less at a stroke. When an

*The swathe of eastern Europe, crossing Bulgaria, Romania and Moldova, Turkey and Greece (below), offers a vast range of styles and native grape varieties.*

enterprise becomes obsolete because others are able to practise it more cheaply, the inevitable decline is accompanied by a critical loss of skills and knowledge. So it was with Greek wine.

As the collapsing Byzantine Empire was in due course overrun by Ottoman Turks, the fate of Hellenic wine was sealed. The nation that had, in large measure, taught Europe the art of vinification saw its viticulture regress to a state of helpless infancy that was to endure right up to the most recent generations. Only now are the first tentative steps towards a reconstitution of Greek viticulture being taken. The going is heavy, and the acute devastation caused by the credit crisis of recent years can hardly help matters, but somewhere at the end of the tunnel is the light of a competitive modern wine culture that, I believe, will one day be at least as successful and exciting as that of Portugal has been.

In the eastern countries formerly in the Soviet sphere of influence, a quality wine industry was viewed as something of a luxury when the agricultural sector as a whole was so chronically fragile. The one exception was to be Bulgaria, where an experiment in flooding western markets with heavily subsidized state-produced wines was to be one of the more conspicuous economic successes of the Soviet era.

Today, eastern Europe, most of it absorbed into the European Union, is struggling to keep pace with developments in the southern hemisphere. The auguries are ultimately favourable, though, not least because of the mass of potentially interesting indigenous grape varieties found all over the area.

What the future holds for the wines of Russia and Belarus is difficult to say. The Russian invasion of Ukraine in 2022 put paid to any hope of Russian wines building on their already very marginal presence in western markets, and the full-throated support of Belarus for the Kremlin's ill-fated military adventure has likewise ensured that their wines won't even make it to the starting blocks. That's the thing about war. It takes a historical age before those who start it will be forgiven.

# GREECE

*No other wine-producing country in Europe inspires greater excitement today than does Greece. At the beginning of the 21st century, one of the oldest viticultural heritages was in terminal decline. And now? Look out, the Greeks are coming through.*

When Greece joined the EU in 1981, it had already put in place an appellation system so devotedly modelled on the French that it had appropriated the French terms *appellation contrôlée* and *vin de pays*. As in other countries, the better wines that have been treated to cask-ageing are labelled either Reserve or Grande Reserve. There are now around 30 appellations throughout the country, from Macedonia in the north down to the island of Crete, with Greek terminology now proudly elbowing aside the aspirational French. A significant quantity of the annual production, it should be said, is table wines, including branded wines of dubious repute, but we can pass those by in silence on our way to the beautiful beaches.

The appearance of Greek varietal wines on restaurant wine lists is always a cause for celebration. They offer genuinely original, compelling, sometimes even challenging, flavours, and they are excellent wines to go with food – not just Greek meze and classic dishes like kleftiko and moussaka, but with all kinds of other Mediterranean cooking. There is an astringent freshness to the dry whites, and herbal savouriness to many of the reds (bay leaves, thyme, even mint), that equips them handsomely for the table. True, there are international grapes, often in productive blends with the native varieties, but they have not been allowed to rule the roost as they have in certain regions elsewhere. If you have a roster of interesting raw materials that mostly aren't available to winemakers elsewhere, at least until they come shopping for cuttings from you, why not make the most of them? Seasoned wine-drinkers are always on the lookout for new and undiscovered flavours, and the trends that they spark often turn into more widely appreciated styles. The future looks bright.

**Macedonia and Thrace** The northern regions are especially noted for red wines. Xinomavro is the main indigenous red grape, making intense, oak-aged, raisiny reds in **Naoussa** and **Goumenissa**. Naoussa reds are frequently compared to the stately wines of Nebbiolo (think Barolo without the tannic fury), while in

Goumenissa, Xinomavro is typically blended with the local Negoska grape, fermented by carbonic maceration à la Beaujolais.

One of the first reds to be taken seriously in the early stages of the Greek wine renaissance was Porto Carras (or Château Carras, as it was known in the Francophone days) on the slopes of Mount Meliton on the Thraki (Thracian) peninsula. Its vines having been first planted in the mid-1960s, it was conceived as an authoritative Greek version of classic claret, brought into being with French expertise, and based, to the tune of about 70 per cent, on a good indigenous grape Limnio, backed up by Cabernets Sauvignon and Franc. Although its quality has fluctuated in latter times, it spawned the **Slopes of Meliton** PDO in central Chalkidiki in 1982, and launched a period of feverish experimentation with blending local and French grapes.

In the little PGI of **Epanomi**, Gerovassiliou makes a varietal white from the indigenous

*Picking Cabernet Sauvignon on the slopes of Mount Meliton, in Thrace (below), for the Porto Carras red. Styled on claret, this wine marked the birth of Greece's modern wine industry.*

*Hot and dry, Cephalonia, in the Ionian Sea (right), makes both fortified and varietal white wines.*

Malagousia, a forthrightly scented grape that makes fat-textured, mouth-filling wines, and that is now being planted all over Greece.

**Epirus and Thessaly** Vineyards are rather thinly spread over the central regions of Greece. In the west, not far from the Albanian border, a local variety called Debina makes an often slightly pétillant white wine at **Zitsa**. On the Aegean coast, the Xinomavro grape crops up again, this time in a blended, barrel-aged red, **Rapsani**, made in the shadow of Mount Olympus, abode of the gods. Further south, **Anchialos** is a crisp dry white made from native grapes Roditis and Savatiano, a successful

*A vineyard landscape (below) at Nemea on the Peloponnese peninsula.*

combination also much favoured in traditional retsina.

**Peloponnese** The southern peninsula is home to more of Greece's appellations than any other zone. The extensive vineyards in its northern sector produce wines that span the stylistic spectrum, from **Patras** itself, a light dry Roditis white, through fortified **Muscat of Patrus** (made in the same way as French *vin doux naturel*), to the fairly widely known **Mavrodaphne**, Greece's answer to port. Mavrodaphne is the eponymous main grape in it, and the vinification method is the same as for port, the fermentation interrupted by the addition of grape spirit while the wine still retains natural sugars. Extended cask-ageing is the norm, although the wine tends to retain its deep red colour. The best (try Kourtakis) are a rich and robust match for good LBV.

At **Nemea** in the northeast, another distinguished red grape, Agiorgitiko (named after the Christian martyr, St George), comes into its own, making full-bodied, concentrated, oaky reds at high altitudes. Some of the less good wine from vineyards lower down the valley is made slightly sweet. This intensively productive region is crying out to be demarcated into recognized smaller appellations to replace the monolithic Nemea designation.

On the central plateau of **Mantineia**, some of Greece's more arrestingly original wine is made from Moschofilero, one of the rare varieties of grape that may accurately be classed as pink, rather than red or white. Most of the wine is a highly scented, viscous white full of musky orange aromas, like a heavier version of dry Alsace Muscat, while some of it can be weighty and waxy, full of electrical nerviness, with notes of beeswax and polish, perhaps a little preserved lemon. The pigmentation of the skin means that a period of maceration can yield a full-fruited rosé. There is also some experimentation with a couple of white grapes – the aforementioned Malagousia, and the island grape Assyrtiko.

**Greek islands** In the Ionian Sea off the west coast of Greece, the island of **Cephalonia** makes its own versions of the fortified wines of Patras, along with a strong-limbed, heavy-going varietal white from the northern Italian Ribolla Gialla (here called Robola). There is also some Robola on the neighbouring island of **Zante** (Zakynthos), where it is often produced in an ancestral style called Verdea, picked slightly underripe so that the wine is full of coruscating

*A vineyard (left) of aromatic Assyrtiko grapes on the island of Santorini.*

acidity, but also subjected to oak-ageing (a little like the recherché wood-matured version of Muscadet). There is a summer-fruited, herb-tinged red speciality too from the Avgoustiatis grape, and some Xinomavro.

The Aegean islands of **Paros** and **Santorini** each have their own respective appellations, the former for a lightish red wine blended from the red Mandilaria grape with some white Malvasia, the latter for a dry, refreshingly crisp, lemon-lime white made from the local Assyrtiko, now one of the reference varieties of modern Greek winemaking.

Greece's most celebrated fortified Muscats, from the top-flight Muscat Blanc à Petits Grains, come from two islands in the Aegean. **Muscat of Samos**, from the island just off the Turkish coast, is the better-known, and comes in a range of styles from gently sweet to an almost unbearably concentrated nectar, made from fully raisined grapes. The version most often seen abroad is somewhere in the middle, a *vin doux naturel* like Muscat de Beaumes-de-Venise. Further north, **Lemnos** makes a similar style of sweet wine, as well as a small quantity of dry wine for local consumption, and a resinated Muscat wine more like retsina.

Rhodes has a trio of appellations, representing different wine styles. The dry white is made from a grape called **Athiri**, the red is from the **Mandilaria** seen on Paros, and there is also the inevitable dessert Muscat. Athiri also makes some attractive dry and demi-sec fizz.

Crete, which has been making wine since early antiquity, and is by far the most prolific producer of any of the Greek islands, has a good showing of native grape varieties. **Peza**, in the centre of the island, is the principal appellation, making both red and white wines from grapes such as red Liatiko and white Vilana. Dafni is a very promising herb-scented white.

PRODUCERS: Costa Lazaridi, Antonopoulos, Gerovassiliou, Tselepos, Biblia Chora, Argyros, Kourtaki, Tsantali.

**Retsina** The wine that was entirely synonymous with Greece in the early days of mass tourism and, for many, the very definition of the phrase 'acquired taste'. The style is based on techniques that date back to Classical times, when stone wine jars were sealed with pine resin to preserve their contents. Today, retsina is a simple dry white wine that has had lumps of resin, from the Aleppo pine, infused in it during fermentation. It's made all over Greece, but mainly in the area around Athens, where much of it continues to supply the tourist industry.

Served extremely cold in sherry-like quantities, it can be an interesting aperitif, but despite the defensive insistence of many wine commentators that there is practically nothing nicer in the raging broil of the Greek afternoon, I find a little does go a very long way. There's a rosé version too now. (And resinated wine in the same style is being made in isolated pockets of South Australia.)

*Tapping a pine tree for the resin used in the production of Retsina.*

*Pruning vines (above). Old-fashioned methods still rule in many of Cyprus's remote hilltop vineyards.*

*A vineyard worker attends to vines in the Bornova region (below), near Izmir, Turkey.*

## CYPRUS

Winemaking on the island of Cyprus has not exactly covered itself in glory in the modern era. Production is largely cornered by large industrial concerns whose installations are located near Limassol for easy export, a worryingly long way from the hillside vineyards. But there are very tentative signs of improvement, encouraged by the country's accession to the EU in 2004.

Two indigenous grapes dominate the vineyards. Mavro makes good fresh reds for drinking young. Xynisteri is a bit of a rough diamond that is theoretically capable of dry whites with some aromatic personality. Plantings of southern French varieties, plus Chardonnay, may well point the way forward for now. SODAP is a good volume producer.

As in other Mediterranean regions, Cyprus has a once-legendary, but now little-known, dessert wine. **Commandaria**, a fortified sweet wine made from sun-dried Mavro and Xynisteri grapes, is made in the foothills of the Troodos mountains. It is aged for a minimum of two years in cask – often much longer – arranged in some cases in a *solera* system. It became a legally protected name only in 1993.

The fortified wines once sold as 'Cyprus sherry' were mostly best forgotten, but there is some fino-style matured under *flor* and aged in a *solera*, which is quite like the best examples of the real thing. These are worth seeking out if you're on vacation there.

## TURKEY

Turkey's viticultural history dates back at least to Biblical times, when – as the story in Genesis chapter 9 has it – Noah established the first vineyard on Mount Ararat after the Flood. Excavations in the area have lent strong support to the theory that some of the very earliest systematic wine-growing did arise here, at least 7000 years ago, among the civilizations of ancient Anatolia, including the pugnacious Hittites.

The first commercial vineyards of the modern era were only planted in the 1920s, and Turkish winemaking has had a lot of catching up to do. Today, there are plantings of some of the southern French grapes, and even Riesling and Pinot Noir, in the European west of the country, while the Anatolian peninsula that makes up the bulk of the Turkish landmass in western Asia produces wines from mainly indigenous varieties that are better able to withstand the climatic extremes. A lot of the annual production of grapes goes into the anise-flavoured spirit, raki, often still preferred to wine by those Turks who drink.

At the western end of the country, near Istanbul, **Thrace-Marmara** is home to a broad array of French varieties, with Gamay and Viognier lurking among the usual suspects, but there are interesting local grapes, including the red Adakarası and Papazkarası, that are no longer being invariably blended into the Cabernet and Merlot. In the Aegean region inland from the coastal city of Izmir, French, Italian and Spanish grapes, including Sangiovese and Tempranillo, are being tried, and there are plenty of local varieties. This region accounts for a little over half of all Turkish wine production. The remainder comes from vineyards scattered throughout Central Anatolia, with much smaller plantings in the Eastern and Southeastern sectors.

The Doluca company makes some reasonably good reds and whites, while the Pendore winery in the Aegean region has benefited from an input of expertise from a renowned Bordeaux consultant. The enemy of promise is the increasingly restrictive government policy on alcohol retailing, not helped by the regular deferral of its accession to the EU that Turkey has been negotiating for what feels like forever. With more inward investment and a return to more liberal social policies, Turkish wine could take off, and

then names like Oküzgõzü, the country's most widely planted red grape (with a name meaning 'bull's eye'), often blended with Boğazkere for a wine actually called Buzbağ, could be on all our lips.

## BULGARIA

Bulgaria's phenomenal export success in the 1970s and 80s was built on a winemaking tradition among the most venerable in the world, extending back 6000 years. The Ottoman interdiction on alcohol consumption during the period that Bulgaria came under its sway contributed to a certain decline, but it was undoubtedly the investment in state-owned vineyards that communist Bulgaria initiated in the years after the Second World War that set the ball rolling once again.

A combination of uprooting and neglect, coupled with the economic upheaval that followed the reforms of the post-Soviet era, led initially to troubled times, As the vineyards were sold back into private hands, the result was a considerable setback in terms of quality.

Gradually, things have rallied, though. Bulgaria's accession to the EU in 2007 has helped, and a system of GCAOs (Guaranteed and Controlled Appellations of Origin – the assonance with the Italian quality system is not accidental) has emerged from the country's five main wine zones – Eastern, Northern, Southern, Southwestern, and Sub-Balkan. There are currently 41 designated GCAOs, all in the Northern and Southern regions, which may only grow approved grape varieties.

The varieties with which Bulgaria shot to prominence, and which are still planted extensively, were classic French reds led by Cabernet Sauvignon and Merlot, together with a small amount of Pinot Noir. Whites included reasonable Chardonnay, Sauvignon Blanc (which tended to lack aromatic definition), and rather flabby Riesling.

These are supplemented by some fine native red grapes such as Mavrud and Melnik, which both give appetisingly meaty wines, and Gamza, which turns out to be the same as Hungary's Kadarka. Rubin is an ingenious Bulgarian crossing of Nebbiolo and Syrah. Native white grapes are less inspiring, and include a variety called Dimiat, of no noticeable character, which has been crossed with Riesling to produce Misket, but still continues to be pretty tasteless. Welschriesling is there too.

There are considerable climatic variations among the regions, Northern having the most temperate conditions, while Southwestern, bordering Greece, is fairly torrid. Some of what are now the GCAO districts established solid reputations with particular varieties over the years when the wineries were state-controlled, achievements that have formed the backbone of the new regulations. These include the often distinctly claretty Cabernets of **Rousse** and

*Melnik, in the torrid southwestern region of Harsovo, Bulgaria (above). The native Melnik grape makes characterful, dark reds for ageing.*

*A truckload of freshly picked Chardonnay at Blatetz (below), in the Sub-Balkan region of Bulgaria.*

*At Cernavoda, east of Constanta in Romania, the vineyards lie alongside the canal (above).*

**Svishtov**, the voluptuously plummy Merlots of **Stambolovo**, and the fiery Mavruds of **Asenovgrad**.
PRODUCERS: Bessa Valley, Borovitza, Suhindol, Boyar.

## ROMANIA

The vineyard regions of Romania are comprehensively scattered across the country, from Teremia in the west to Murfatlar on the Black Sea coast. There are eight broadly defined wine zones, subdivided into a dozen regional PGIs and an array of DOCs that are each held to exhibit identifiable quality. The vast majority of wine produced, even since Romania's entry to the EU in 2007, is still consumed within its borders, although there is a driving will to fashion a significant export industry.

Western investment (especially French and Italian) has begun to flow, and so have plantings of international varieties. In time, Romania could well become the most reliable producer of quality wine of all the old Soviet bloc countries. Its climate is far more dependable than that of Bulgaria, for example, and it does have some excellent indigenous styles of wine.

Cabernet Sauvignon has been established extensively throughout the country, far more so than in Bulgaria, while Pinot Noir was the first varietal to make western commentators sit up and pay attention to Romania's potential. The wines, initially comparable to good

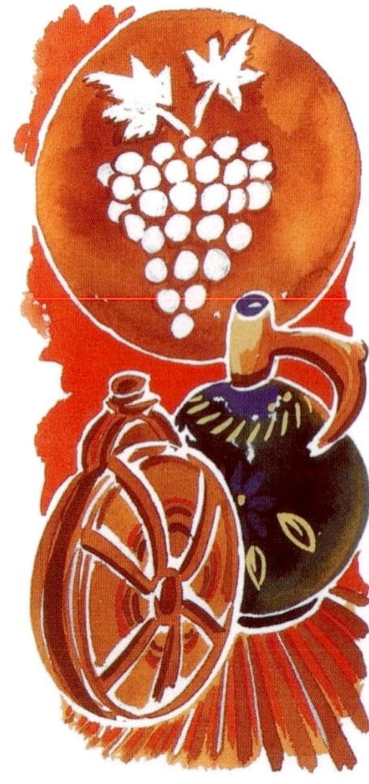

basic burgundies such as those of the Hautes-Côtes-de-Nuits, are now complex, savoury, raspberry-scented Pinots of indubitable Côte d'Or finesse. There are also plantings of Merlot, Chardonnay, Burgundy's Aligoté, Sauvignon Blanc and Pinot Gris. Two versions of a white grape called Fetească represent the most widely planted varieties of all, and are used in some of the sweet wines in which Romania has a long and distinguished tradition.

Tămâioasă Românească and Grasă are the two native ingredients of **Cotnari**, the country's greatest and most assertively concentrated botrytized dessert wine, with an aromatic profile of herb-tinged pears in syrup, which is made in the northeast of Romania, near the border with Moldova.

North of the capital Bucharest, the **Dealu Mare** region has made waves with its often sensational Pinot Noirs. At their most carefully vinified, they can be uncannily close to the style of good village burgundy. Continuing input from outside investors is now resulting in some world-class Romanian Pinot. Cabernet and Merlot make hearty reds in **Istria-Babadag** nearer the Black Sea. Lower down on the coast, **Murfatlar** also has a venerable dessert wine tradition, but its wines are less opulent than those of Cotnari, being much less prone to noble rot.
PRODUCERS: Cramele Recaş, Crama Oprişor, Halewood, Avincis.

## MOLDOVA

Moldova retains strong cultural ties to Romania, and speaks its language. Its vineyards are hugely extensive and, like its western neighbour, it looks set fair to ascend the quality scale in time. A very broad range of grape varieties is grown, including most of the major French names, some Russian varieties such as the white Rkatsiteli and the red Saperavi, plus a few of its own. Cabernet, Chardonnay and Sauvignon have inevitably been the first successful Moldovan wines seen in the west. Look out also for the near-legendary red wine of the Purcari estate in the southeast of the country. Its Negru de Purcari is a Cabernet-and-Saperavi blended red of ripe, figgy complexity and thumping potency, well worth the asking price.

As well as promising table wines, Moldova has a long-established tradition in sparkling wine, together with some high-potential fortified styles, some similar to sweet sherry, others to the Liqueur Muscats of Australia.

## GEORGIA

The oldest wine-producing region in the world, Georgia's South Caucasus is extensively planted with two eastern specialities, Rkatsiteli (which makes crisp, clean whites) and Saperavi (for fresh, black-cherry reds, which can also have guts and ageing potential when treated carefully), but there are no fewer than 500 indigenous grape varieties here. **Khvanchkara** from the **Racha-Lechkhumi** region, a semi- sweet red blend of two native grapes, Aleksandrouli and Mujuretuli, is one of the country's more diverting styles, reputedly a favourite of Stalin's, and there are some decent fortified wines.

The bulk of national wine production is in the **Kakheti** region in eastern Georgia, where 13 appellations have been ambitiously registered with the EU to increase the scope for exports. Here, and in **Kartii**, many wines are fermented and aged in bulbous clay amphorae known locally as *qvevri*. Once merely a quaint regional custom, amphora winemaking has now become an international vogue, but – just as with *Vitis vinifera* wine itself – Georgia can claim to have invented it. The clay pots are kept buried beneath the earth, and when the foot-trodden grape bunches, along with their stalks and pips, are stuffed into the *qvevri*, the wine is literally left to make itself, without the benefit of modern temperature control or of racking and fining

interventions. It could hardly be more low-tech. Even the white wines are made this way, originating the skin-contact style of what they call amber wine (known elsewhere as orange wine, and now all the rage). And guess what? The wines are fabulous. The whites are nothing like any white wine you have ever tasted before, and you might be glad to return afterwards to a glass of sleek, modern Chablis or Soave. But Georgia's *qvevri* tradition is a surviving organic cultural link, recognized by UNESCO in 2013 as an Intangible Heritage, to what wine must have tasted like in the ancient world.

## UKRAINE

Crimean reds were once celebrated far beyond the boundaries of the peninsula and may be once again if the country survives the Russian occupation of Crimea in 2014 and the wholesale invasion of Ukraine in 2022. When peace returns, as it must, investment will once more begin to flow in and help to rebuild a shattered economy. Widely planted international grapes include Cabernet Sauvignon, Riesling, Chardonnay, Merlot, Pinot Noir and Aligoté. As elsewhere in eastern Europe, there is an age-old tradition of sweet wines, many from Muscatel (in which style the Massandra winery near Yalta is considered a reliable name), and the taste for sweetness extends to the production of sparkling wines with plenty of sugar.

## RUSSIA AND BELARUS

These two countries are also significant wine producers but, for obvious geopolitical reasons, are hardly able to focus on finding western markets. The historic regional taste was for wines with palpable sweetness to them, even in the reds, but gradually a more global orientation has overtaken the industry. If dictatorship and political paranoia ever breathe their last, we may once again get to taste wines made from international grapes such as Cabernet Sauvignon, Merlot, Chardonnay, Sauvignon Blanc and Aligoté, along with Rkatsiteli whites and Saperavi reds.

Visitors to the old USSR may recall the great quantities of Soviet sparkling wine, fancifully termed Sovetskoye Shampanskoye, which, despite its name, was made by a variation on the tank method. It is still produced in gargantuan volumes, mainly from Chardonnay, Aligoté and Pinot Blanc, and is more often than not perfectly palatable.

*Wine cellar with* qvevri *wine pots (left) at the ancient Nekresi monastery winery in Kakheti, Georgia.*

*The winery of Château Purcari (above), in the region of the same name, in southeast Moldova.*

# MIDDLE EAST, NORTH AFRICA AND THE FAR EAST

*Israel and Lebanon are extending their reputation with classic grape varieties, while the wines of North Africa and the Far East remain little-known beyond their borders.*

*Historic barrels outside the Carmel winery (right), a huge cooperative that produces most of Israel's wine.*

B EYOND THE CONFINES of Europe, there are countries to the east and south of the Mediterranean that have been making wine for centuries, small amounts of which occasionally find their way into the export trade. These are areas that have been repeatedly beset by political turmoil and war, and it goes without saying that only when peace prevails will there be any positive chance for their wines to come to the international attention they deserve. In north Africa, the region's historical colonial links with France have benefited the wine styles and the emergence of reliable quality-control systems, while the ancient vinelands of Lebanon and Israel reach back to Biblical times, but are now brimming with innovative experimentation, allied to sound modern technique.

### LEBANON

The story of Lebanese wine in recent times has basically been the story of the Chateau Musar winery on the elevated slopes of the southern Beqaa Valley. Its presiding genius was the late Serge Hochar, who trained in Bordeaux, and established Musar's reputation for wines of stellar quality with massive ageing potential. They continue to be undoubtedly the region's most celebrated red wines, with virtually every bottle produced finding its way into the export trade. A blend of Cabernet Sauvignon, Cinsault and Carignan, the top cuvée is matured in both barrel and bottle for several years before release, and is a ferociously dark, intensely spicy and cedary wine with plenty of alcohol

and a haunting, savoury, balsamic character that lingers on the palate. Prices have gone through the roof, but when you consider the conditions under which the grapes are often harvested and vinified (sometimes not at all when the area comes under fire), that seems scarcely surprising. Small productions of white and rosé wine under the Jeune label are a distinct improvement on the original, rather heavy oaky white Musar once produced.

The volume producers in Lebanon are Ksara, where the first plantings were established by Jesuits in the mid-19th century, and Kefraya. French expertise from Bordeaux and the Rhône lies behind the success of Massaya, and there are other go-ahead producers who have planted Grenache, Viognier, Muscat and Semillon, particularly in the highly promising northerly region of Batroun. Rosé wines of convincing elegance and fragrant fruit prove that even in such sun-baked conditions as Lebanese vineyards contend with, winemaking ingenuity will find a way.

PRODUCERS: Musar, Massaya, Ch. St. Thomas, Dom. des Tourelles, Ksara, Kefraya.

*Lebanon's Beqaa Valley and Israel's Golan Heights (below), in the Middle East, offer especially favourable climes for grape-growing.*

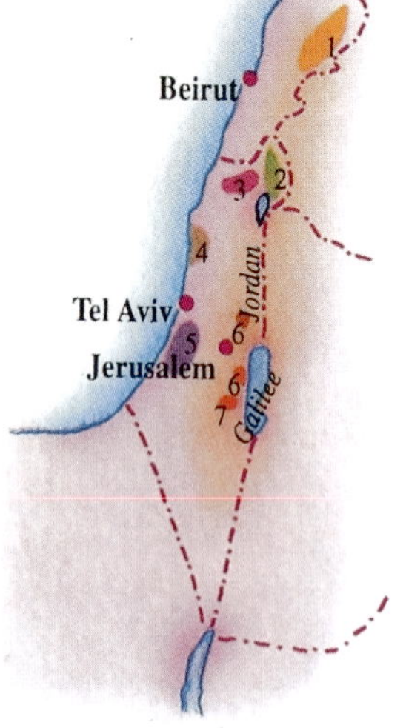

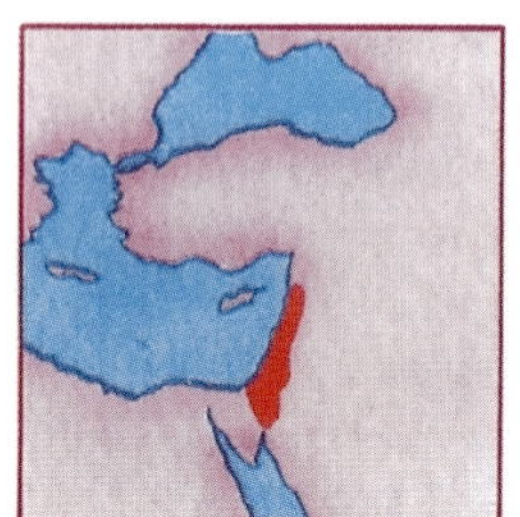

1. BEQAA VALLEY
2. GOLAN HEIGHTS
3. GALILEE
4. SHOMRAN
5. SAMSON
6. JUDEAN HILLS
7. NEGEV

*Ploughing a young vineyard at Enfidaville, Tunisia (left). Most of the country's vines are southern French varieties.*

## ISRAEL

The modern Israeli wine industry is a product of the early 1980s, when the country began to diversify from producing bulk kosher wine for export to worldwide Jewish communities into an expanding range of wines for general consumers. The climate is highly favourable, and viticulture is practised in five denominated regions: Galil, the Judean Hills, Shimshon, the Negev and Sharon.

French grape varieties predominate, with Cabernet Sauvignon, Merlot, Sauvignon Blanc and Chardonnay in the vanguard, but there are increasing plantings of Viognier, Marsanne and Roussanne. Shiraz is proving particularly successful. Red wines especially are beginning to demonstrate extraordinary complexity and ageing potential, and there is even some traditional-method sparkling wine. If the region ever reaches the political settlement with the Palestinian territories that has so far eluded it, the way could be clear for a major export drive. PRODUCERS: Dom. du Castel, Clos de Gat, Margalit, Yatir, Carmel's Upper Galilee range.

## NORTH AFRICA

**Morocco**'s wine industry benefits from intensive tourism, producing a fairly broad range of French varietals, including Cabernet Sauvignon, Syrah, Chenin Blanc and Chardonnay, for the holiday crowds. It has devoted the most ambitious efforts of all the north African countries to honing its appellation system into 14 designated AOGs (*appellations d'origine garantie*) within five broadly defined wine zones. The first AOC, intended as the top category, was created in 2001 for the Coteaux

de l'Atlas *premier cru*. Syrah reds and Cinsault rosés have been good, while the honeyed fortified wine, Muscat de Berkane, produced in the Eastern region, could well turn out to be a future eye-catcher. Substantial French investment in Moroccan wine will help the industry no end.

**Tunisia** also has tourists' thirsts to slake and does so with pretty rough-and-ready reds and a large volume of boldly assertive rosés, again largely from southern French grapes. Whites include rather leaden dry Muscat (made from the more ordinary Muscat of Alexandria variant). An appellation system has been constructed, consisting of seven AOCs, mostly concentrated in Res et-Teib, also known as the Cap Bon peninsula, in the northeast of the country.

**Algeria**'s vineyards are principally located in the Mediterranean northwest, where seven quality wine regions have been delineated, but are in a state of arrested development, owing to the country's indeterminate political identity. Should it become a full-fledged Islamic jurisdiction, wine production can be expected to recede. One of the better inland regions, for the time being, is the Coteaux de Mascara, which makes strapping meaty reds from a fistful of southern French varieties. James Bond fans may recall reference in some of the novels to a cheap Algerian red wine called Infuriator, a particular favourite of M. Incautious consumption of it was said to bring on a fit of aggression in the drinker. The legend was once powerful enough for a producer in the Coteaux de Tlemcen region to actually make a wine called Red Infuriator. They were different times.

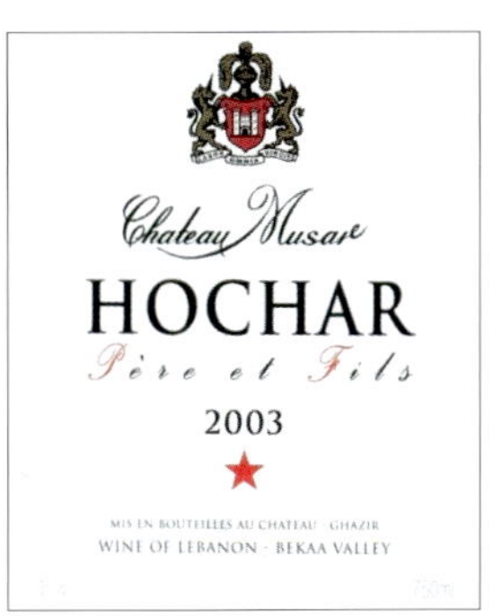

*A vineyard (above) in the foothills of the Batroun region of northern Lebanon.*

# INDIA AND EAST ASIA

*The countries here are among the newer names in world wine. They are cultures where grape wine in the European style had no tradition at all, and where tentative plantings in the 19th century were for the most part a matter of speculative curiosity.*

*A vineyard (above) planted outside Nashik in the state of Maharashtra, India.*

*Vines trained on bamboo frames (below) at a vineyard in Pengzhou, Sichuan province, China.*

INDIA'S WINE SCENE remains hampered by the fact that only a minuscule fraction of the world's most populous country drinks wine at all, and even they only drink a little. Contrast that with China, where elite and aspirant consumers are rushing to taste, to learn and to invest, and Japan, where growers are beginning to branch out from hybrid grapes into finely honed *vinifera* wines, and the difference is startling. With global wine consumers permanently on a quest for novelty, there could be some significant stirrings in the export markets before long for wines of the Far East. Even Thailand is getting in on the act.

## INDIA

Viticulture in India dates back to the time of the Bronze Age Indus Valley civilization, when the first grapevine cuttings were imported from Persia. In modern times, it was encouraged on a commercial scale by the colonial powers of Britain and Portugal, but following Indian independence in 1947, the industry dwindled to producing table grapes and raisins. A wave of innovation took hold, however, in the 1980s and 90s, spurred by economic gentrification, and the result is that India is now gradually on its way to becoming a regional wine producer to be reckoned with.

Vineyards are concentrated in a vast swathe of southern India, in the states of Maharashtra, Andhra Pradesh, Tamil Nadu, Karnataka and Goa. Winemaking in the disputed northerly zones of Kashmir and Punjab is bound to be a more perilous enterprise for the time being. That workhorse grape of the Turkish vineyards, Sultana, is currently the country's most widely planted grape, but Chenin Blanc, Sauvignon Blanc and Zinfandel have gained a foothold, and there are some potentially interesting indigenous varieties.

The Chateau Indage group, based in the Maharashtra hills east of Mumbai, is making much of the running so far, with a range of improving red and white varietals, as well as the trailblazing sparkler, Omar Khayyam, a full, dry, nutty Chardonnay fizz originally created with expertise from the Champagne house Piper-Heidsieck. What India really needs now is more domestic consumers of wine.
PRODUCERS: Chateau Indage, Sula, Grover.

## CHINA

As in much else, the People's Republic of China is set to be an extravagant success story as a wine producer in the 21st century. There is a burgeoning interest in wine among the aspirant business sector, and people are keen to take courses in the subject and learn the principles of tasting. A lot of this enthusiasm is driven by the urge to invest, and not only have private cellars become a feature of the country's upwardly mobile classes, but Chinese investment is in turn pouring into some of the old heartlands of European wines, notably in Bordeaux.

It was once the case that if you ordered a bottle of western grape wine in even a relatively upscale restaurant out in the suburbs, one of the waiters would be despatched to the corner shop to buy it. Now there are wine lists that wouldn't embarrass gastronomic hotspots in London and New York, and a growing clientele eager to demonstrate a knowledge of their wares. Apocryphal stories of businessmen ordering twenty-year-old bottles of Lafite, and then

adding Pepsi to the wine to make it palatable, need be accorded no further credence.

The country is awash with native grape varieties and has plenty of good vineyard land, especially in the northwestern province of Xinjiang, Shandong in the east, Gansu and Shanxi in the north, Yunnan in the southwest, and in the autonomous central region of Ningxia. Wild climatic extremes mean that careful vineyard siting is absolutely crucial, but the expertise is there, and close study of soil types and clonal selection are flourishing.

French and Australian investment has resulted in some astonishing early results from Chardonnay, Riesling and – best of all so far – red Bordeaux blends of deeply savoury complexity. Red wines are widely favoured, as much for connoisseurial reasons as for the fact that red is a propitious colour in Chinese folk culture, believed to ward off evil spirits and bring good fortune. There is Aglianico in Shanxi. What times are these.

Successful producers so far have been Changyu, the oldest winery in China, founded in 1892 with French vine cuttings; the Huadong winery at Qingdao (both in Shandong province); and Xintian, sold under the name Suntime, from Xinjiang. Grace Vineyard in Shanxi is producing world-class wine, including an impressive sparkler. Even the branded Great Wall wines, an offshoot of the state-owned

COFCO combine in Hebei province, are by no means as awful as that touristy name might suggest, as long as you're prepared for a lighter, grassier style of Cabernet Sauvignon, for example.

OTHER PRODUCERS: Silver Heights, Jia Bei Lan, Helan Mountain (all Ningxia).

## JAPAN

Grape wine is made on three of the four principal islands of Japan, the largest plantings being on Honshu and Hokkaido, although it has only recently become a viable industry. Giant industrial concerns such as Suntory kick-started the investment drive and have now been joined by the drinks companies Sapporo and Château Mercian. These large industrial players still dominate the wine scene, with smaller independent winemakers accounting for only a tiny, but growing, share.

Widely planted hybrid grape varieties don't help the cause, but the pink-skinned Koshu variety, which has a long historical lineage in Japan in the valley of the same name on Honshu, has proved itself the star indigenous grape for delicate unoaked, and richer wood-aged, whites. Styles range from dry to semi-sweet, and there is always a gracefully aromatic, floral-peachy character to the wines that, needless to say, makes them especially good for drinking with sushi and sashimi, assuming you can tear yourself away from the sake section of the drinks list.

Yamagata, Nagano and Yamanashi on Honshu have been among the premium regions to emerge. There are excellent Chardonnays and Merlots, a little Sauvignon Blanc, Cabernet Franc and Syrah, as well as those scented Koshu charmers. Pinot Noir grown on Hokkaido has been impressive enough to attract a little Burgundy investment, and there is decent Chardonnay on the southwestern island of Kyushu.

## THAILAND

Expect some interesting reds and whites from French varieties – Chenin Blanc whites and Syrah reds and rosés among them – to emerge from high-altitude vineyards in Thailand in years to come. Most of the plantings are in the Khao Yai region to the northeast of the capital, Bangkok. The Siam winery is one of the country's go-ahead producers, now exporting its wines to the Thai restaurant trade abroad.

*A vineyard worker (left) tending to trellised vines in Xinjiang province, China.*

*Vineyard worker thinning out grape bunches in early summer (above) in Suntory-owned vineyards, Japan.*

# REST OF THE WORLD

1993
FRANCISCAN
MONTEREY CHARDONNAY

*Vine leaves reddening
with the onset of autumn
in the Napa Valley,
California (above).*

*The dramatic landscape
of Marlborough,
New Zealand (below).*

No single factor did more to change the vinous world in the modern era than the advent of wines from North America and the southern hemisphere. These are the countries still amorphously lumped together in many European minds as the 'New World', basically the English-speaking nations, plus South America and South Africa.

The story has been well enough told of how, as their wine industries came of age, they kicked down the door of the old European wine temple, rewriting the rules with varietal labelling and wines that tasted of sun rather than northern chill. Everyday drinkers learned their wine vocabulary from these wines, gaining an appreciation of what kinds of flavours they could expect from bottles labelled Chardonnay, Cabernet Sauvignon, Pinot Noir, Sauvignon Blanc, and so on, and noticing that, when compared back against their Old World antecedents, they often tasted far more exuberant than the models on which they were originally based.

Although the term may have jangled on the sensibilities of American and Australian winemakers, the New World concept did in one sense do everybody a favour. It fixed in consumers' minds the idea that there was such a thing as a New World style, one that was in direct contrast to anything they might find in Europe. And the very shapelessness of this sprawling extra-European zone meant that wine-drinkers were prepared to explore the wines of far more countries than they might otherwise have done. The common identifying factor was that varietal labelling.

Following every major trend, however, is some kind of backlash. And what has happened in the years since the turn of the century is the beginnings of a disaffection with what has for so long been considered the primary New World style. A surging sense of liberation accompanied the first tastes of those big, belting, buttery Chardonnays and velvet-toned, crème de cassis Cabernets, precisely because they were nothing like the white wines of Burgundy or the red wines of Bordeaux. The problem (and only a surprising few of us, back in the early 1990s, saw this coming) was that these were *exhausting* flavours.

By that, I mean that the oak-powered richness, sweetish overripeness and head-clobbering alcohol levels of these wines eventually caused palate fatigue in those who drank them all the time. The venerable British wine authority who said that these wines were impressive enough in themselves, but you wouldn't want to drink them every day, was basically right. And, despite what the winemakers themselves continued to insist, they weren't great with food.

Some responsiveness to these criticisms was apparent even before the close of the 1990s. Much less oak was suddenly being used (especially in Australia, to its credit) for the simpler wines. Grapes, particularly white grapes, started to be shielded from the full blast of the sun on the vines, and were picked earlier than normal, in order to preserve some of their freshness and natural acidity. The alcohol levels were still through the roof, but you can't have everything.

To listen to the criticisms in some quarters is to realize that the pendulum is in danger of swinging too far back the other way. Nothing is to be gained from a revisionist wholesale return to Eurocentric thinking. There are profoundly exciting wines being made in the cooler-climate regions of the United States, Chile, South Africa and Australia, and much encouragement to be had from the planting of less familiar varieties, such as Barbera, Sangiovese, Marsanne and Petit Verdot, as well as Malbec, Torrontés and Tannat across South America.

Where there are problems, it is often with the varieties that initially led the charge. Boring Chardonnays that could have been made anywhere, overripe Cabernets and Merlots, baked, hyper-extracted Australian Shiraz and (here's something I never thought I'd hear myself say) too many cloying New Zealand Sauvignons with their sweet, juicy-fruit style, are all in need of new thinking.

There is much debate in wine these days about the homogenization of taste, of how the standard of wine may be streets ahead of what everybody except the super-rich were drinking a generation ago, but that it's all beginning to taste the same. Very often, that criticism is levelled at superstar wines made in the old European heartlands under the influence of a handful of grotesquely influential wine consultants, at least one of them French. But there is no escaping the fact that the standardized international idiom these wines are being made in is one that originated in the vineyards of North America and the southern hemisphere.

Increasingly, over the next few years, discerning customers will be seeking out those non-European wines that have better balance, are more food-friendly, and don't leave you feeling a hangover coming on after two glasses. Those wines will, I have no doubt, be the best wines produced within the emerging appellation systems that have been put in place all over the so-called New World. Painstaking selection of vineyard sites and grape varieties are what made the Old World classics so revered in the first place. And then, at last, the wines of Worlds Old and New will be fit to compete with each other on something like a level playing-field. I, for one, will drink to that.

*California poppies, the state flower, provide a splash of colour beneath the wire-trained vines of Kenwood Vineyards, Sonoma County (above).*

*An undulating vista of newly planted vineyards in South Australia's Clare Valley (left).*

# UNITED STATES

*Enthusiasm and the willingness to experiment has brought great success to the winemaking states of North America. Led by California and the Pacific Northwest, America's vineyards have made a great impact on wine-drinkers around the world.*

THE FIRST NORSE EXPLORERS to make landfall on the North American continent, finding the eastern seaboard carpeted with wild vines, called the place Vinland. These were not, as European settlers were later to discover, the same species as the common wine grape, *Vitis vinifera*, but a whole array of related species. Anybody who has ever tried a grape wine made from *Vitis labrusca*, to name just one, will know that it doesn't taste much – or indeed anything – like wine.

When the first *vinifera* vines were established from European cuttings at the dawn of American viticulture in the late 18th century, they quickly fell victim to the pests and diseases to which native vines were hardily resistant. Worst of all was the microscopic vine louse, phylloxera, which lives underground and feeds on sap in the vines' roots. You only know you have an infestation of that when your vines start looking brown and shrivelled.

Grafting *vinifera* vines on to the hardier rootstocks of native vine species turned out to be the answer to phylloxera (as was to be the universal recourse when American vine cuttings inadvertently introduced the menace into European vineyards, where it spread like wildfire, in the late 19th century). Even so, it was only really in the late 1800s that the fledgling American wine industry, based on good grape varieties, its winemakers learning on the job, finally took root.

The advent of Prohibition in 1919 put paid to that. For the 13 years that followed, it was officially illegal for citizens of the Land of the Free to drink alcohol. Although the ban was widely flouted, not least by ordinary Americans who bought the cakes of dried grape paste that were legally sold for reconstituting into juice, but which could be left to ferment into some sort of rudimentary 'wine', it had as devastating an impact on the wine industry as the closure of the playhouses in the Puritan 17th century had on the English theatre.

So it is that the contemporary American viticultural scene is pretty much a product of the latter half of the 20th century. In that respect, it is little short of astonishing that it has achieved such leaps and bounds in so short a span. It's almost as though America's winemakers were making up for lost time.

The first serious assault on external markets in the 1970s, as was very much the way at the time, was with cheap, simple 'jug' wines. A widely distributed California brand called Paul Masson really was sold in ugly, jug-shaped bottles, looking like something you might take on a picnic, but not want to put on the dinner-table. There was more commercial cunning in this than might at first have appeared, though. While other cheap mass-market wine products, such as Liebfraumilch, fizzy Lambrusco or the various branded French offerings like Hirondelle and Piat d'Or, seemed to be trying to make an ultimately self-defeating attempt to look like decent wine, Masson's jugs of light fruity red offered a new take on wine altogether. It was wine, but it wasn't asking to be taken too seriously, and nobody did.

The trick the California industry pulled off, and which was never repeated anywhere else, was not to allow its image as a whole to become inextricably associated with such mass products. In the same decade that those

*The US's top winemaking regions are centred on the west coast, in California, Washington and Oregon, but other areas are gaining reputations for fine wines.*

*The flat valley floor of Salinas in California's Monterey County (left). Monterey is cool, yet one of the state's most prolific grape-growing areas.*

cheapies first appeared, serious wines made from, and labelled with the names of, classic European grape varieties started to appear. They were ambitiously priced, but consumers tried them out of interest, in many cases learning the names of these grape varieties for the first time. They may have been drinking Chablis for years, but nobody knew it was made from Chardonnay. Now here were wines that were called Chardonnay.

What has happened in the years since then has been a cause for celebration – and a little frustration. The AVA (American Viticultural Area) appellation system, the beginnings of which were formulated back in 1983, now consists of close on 200 demarcated names. These are not restrictive as to grape varieties or vinification methods, but they do stipulate that, where a wine is labelled with an AVA, it must be made up at least 85 per cent from grapes grown in that area.

Of all the English-speaking wine countries, the USA is the most committed to the concept of *terroir*, and has engaged in what I believe to be the most productive exchange of all with French and other European growers. The political insularity for which Americans are, often unfairly, criticized in Europe doesn't at all extend to the country's winemakers, who retain a keen awareness of the cutting-edge of European achievement. They want to compete on the same field of play, and they have, in numerous instances, outpointed and excelled the European templates they began with.

The frustration I mentioned derives from two sources. One is that too many US wines, even at the top end, are being made in what has come to be demonized – from within the American wine commentariat as much as anywhere else – as the international style. Over-ripe grapes result in too much residual sugar in the wine, as well as too much alcohol. Many have too much charred new oak on them, leaving a mixture of smokiness and sweetness on the palate that ultimately only gets in the way. These tendencies, we can hopefully expect, will pass.

Pricing is the other bugbear. There does seem to be a preponderance of wineries wanting to produce and sell at the premium end of the market. I wouldn't for one minute want to see aspiration stifled. And anyway, the same could be said on the Côte d'Or. But what I think we are missing is enough wines in the mid-priced sector of the market that taste appealing and complex enough to make consumers want to choose those above, say, well-made everyday wines from the Languedoc or Castilla-La Mancha or, for that matter, from Chile.

Otherwise, it's all good. The range of grape varieties is vastly diversifying, the quality of sparkling wines has improved beyond recognition, and great wines are beginning to emerge from hitherto unfamiliar regions, such as the Pacific Northwest, New York State and Virginia. There appear to be no vinous challenges these days the Americans are unwilling to take on, and if that isn't the authentic pioneering spirit, I don't know what is.

*Modern technology in the vineyard and winery includes sterile winemaking equipment such as this crusher-destemmer (above).*

*California's own red grape variety, Zinfandel, arriving at the winery (above).*

*California's wine country (below) stretches the length of the state. Vineyards are planted on cool, hillside sites, in hot, inland valleys and close to the ocean.*

## CALIFORNIA

To say that the state of California is at the epicentre of the United States wine industry would be something of an understatement. Nine out of every ten bottles of American wine come from there. From Mendocino County, north of San Francisco, to the San Diego and Imperial Valley areas on the Mexican border, it's wine country practically all the way. Cross the Golden Gate Bridge heading north out of San Fran, and you soon enter the Napa Valley, California's grape-basket, where it's difficult to find anybody growing anything other than vines. From world-class traditional-method sparklers to idiosyncratic fortified Muscats and even brandy – if it's possible to make it, California does.

As in most of the wine regions outside Europe, the first of the running was made with largely French grape varieties. The most extensively planted is Cabernet Sauvignon, which still goes into many of the state's most aspirational red wines, either solo or blended with others of the Bordeaux varieties.

Chardonnay can be sweet and tropical, or else beguilingly Burgundian, but always with that sunny-natured core of ripe fruit running through it, as distinct from the often harder, chalky dryness of Burgundy's own offerings.

Next comes Merlot, which has suffered a little with its reputation, as much following a single line of vituperative dialogue in Alexander Payne's wine-based comic movie *Sideways* (2004) as anything else. It is now viewed by some as a kind of air-headed Cabernet substitute, but it generally lacks nothing in full-blooded, plummy ripeness. Pinot Noir has been the Holy Grail, here as elsewhere, best in the cooler-climate districts like Carneros. Sauvignon Blanc remains a problem, with too many winemakers interfering with its natural pungency and acidity, so that it too often comes across like a kid having to go to a party with a nerdy haircut. Syrah is showing its paces, with some exciting, spice-scented wines of inky concentration.

The state speciality, Zinfandel (southern Italy's Primitivo), makes a wide range of styles. There is a lot of deeply coloured purple-red wine of tremendous fruit concentration and rowdy alcohol, displaying ripe berry flavours like blueberries, together with something strangely herbal (fresh tea leaves are sometimes evoked). Some is much lighter, made in a quasi-Beaujolais idiom, and not generally as impressive. Then there is a usually slightly sweet pink style called Blush (or even, confusingly, White Zinfandel), which can be as refreshing as raspberry-ripple ice-cream, and just as sickly taken in quantity.

Beyond these international stars, enterprising growers are trying their hands at almost anything that takes their fancy, from native Italian and Spanish varieties (Barbera and Sangiovese have turned out some appetizing Italianate reds) to Rhône-style Viognier and the aromatic grapes of Alsace (cool, crisp dry Riesling, Muscat, Pinot Gris and Gewürztraminer).

The sparkling wine sector has benefited from substantial inward investment from an honour-guard of some of the most illustrious names in Champagne. In most cases, they have taken a hands-off approach, and left native California growers to get on with the elaboration of the wine itself. The result has been an array of traditional-method sparklers from Pinot Noir and Chardonnay that have depth, roundness and reliable levels of ripeness.

**Mendocino and Lake Counties** These two counties, through which runs the Russian River, lie at the northern end of California wine country. Mendocino, on the Pacific coast, encompasses a very broad range of microclimates as it extends inland, producing everything from delicately spiced Gewürztraminer and lightly leafy Sauvignon to big meaty Cabernets, Zinfandels and Zin-based blends labelled Coro. It forms part of the overall **North Coast** AVA, but smaller defined AVAs within Mendocino include the coastal **Anderson Valley** (a fine source of quality sparklers), and the warmer inland **McDowell** and **Potter** Valleys (which boast some richly textured reds).

In Lake County to the east, **Clear Lake** is the main AVA, while the smaller **Guenoc Valley** consists of only one winery of the same name, founded around the time of the first world war. Lake County is climatically less diverse than Mendocino, but has built a reputation for pleasantly green-fruited Sauvignons (some of California's more successful examples) and soft, approachable Cabernets.

MENDOCINO PRODUCERS: Navarro, Saracina, Lazy Creek, Fetzer, Handley, Roederer Estate, Scharffenberger (the last three producing fine Chardonnay-Pinot fizz).
LAKE PRODUCERS: Langtry Estate, Villa La Brenta, Brassfield.
**Sonoma** Sonoma is a coastal county north of San Francisco Bay, encompassing a valley of the same name, which forms its main sub-region. For a long time, the Sonoma region languished in the shadow of its eastern neighbour, Napa County, but its growers and wineries have worked assiduously to define its undeniable potential for quality, now reflected in 13 demarcated AVAs.

**Alexander Valley** has seen the most intensive programme of plantings in Sonoma in recent times. Grape varieties that grow nowhere near each other in France flourish here in happy juxtaposition. Cabernet Sauvignon produces some of its most compelling performances here, with strong support from muscular Zinfandel and seductively soft, curvaceous Merlot. Diverting, savoury Chardonnays can also be good.

*The herb garden at Fetzer winery (below), in Mendocino County, planted with hundreds of varieties of herbs.*

(Above) State-of-the-art
sparkling winemaking
at Domaine Chandon, in
Napa Valley, owned by
champagne house Moët &
Chandon (right). The fertile
valley floor of Napa Valley
is considered by many to be
the state's premier site for
Cabernet and Chardonnay.

The **Sonoma Valley** AVA itself includes some of California's oldest wineries, such as Buena Vista (established in the 19th century by a Hungarian migrant pioneer) and Sebastiani. Running north to south, the valley is blessed with subtle gradations of microclimate as it moves away from the cooling influence of the Bay. This means that a highly disparate range of grapes can be grown. At the southern end, it takes in a section of the celebrated **Carneros** region, which it shares with Napa County (see below).

One of the cooler Sonoma AVAs is the **Russian River Valley**. The impact of the morning fogs that roll in off the Bay is most keenly felt here, with the result that Pinot Noir is notably successful (especially from practitioners like Williams-Selyem, Dehlinger, Iron Horse, Marimar Torres and Rodney Strong). Chardonnay can be superbly balanced from the likes of De Loach, and there is fine sparkling wine too.

**Dry Creek Valley** AVA, formed around a little tributary of the Russian River, is making a name for itself with some sharply delineated Sauvignon from Preston and Dry Creek Vineyard, as well as one of the more memorable Zinfandels from Quivira.

The **Northern Sonoma** AVA is an important redoubt of E&J Gallo, planet Earth's largest wine producer. While the discriminating may be tempted to dismiss the produce of such a large powerful corporation, there are one or two decent wines among the premium bottlings of red varietals, especially Zinfandel and Cabernet. OTHER SONIMA PRODUCERS: Ravenswood, Laurel Glen, Kenwood, Matanzas Creek, Sonoma-Cutrer, Flowers, Simi, Jordan sparkling wines.

**Napa** If California is the premier state for American wine, the Napa Valley is its regional frontrunner. So much land has been planted with vines that the region is almost at capacity, forming a virtual grape monoculture. The Napa is the Côte d'Or of California, if such comparisons can be risked. Like Burgundy's prime patch, it is barely more than 20 miles from end to end, but embraces a dizzying degree of climatic variation. As with Sonoma, the southern end near the Bay is relatively cool and foggy, while the northern end at Calistoga is fiercely hot.

The overall **Napa Valley** AVA was organized into a plethora of smaller appellations from the 1990s onwards, based on the main towns along the valley highway. There are 15 at the time of writing. Cabernets and Merlots are made along this trail, varying in style as much because of their geographical location and altitude as because of the philosophies of individual winemakers.

The qualitatively important **Stag's Leap District** lies just to the north of town of Napa, and includes fine Cabernets and Merlots from

Stags' Leap Wine Cellars, Clos du Val and Shafer. **Howell Mountain** in the east of Napa is where La Jota makes some sensationally concentrated Cabernet. **Mount Veeder**, between Napa and Sonoma, has distinguished Chardonnays and Cabernets from the Hess Collection, and **Wild Horse Valley**, east of Napa itself, is turning out to be a good site for gracefully balanced Pinot Noir.

OTHER NAPA PRODUCERS: Newton, Silverado, Caymus, Phelps, ZD, Silver Oak, Diamond Creek, Heitz, Groth. Top premium wines come from Screaming Eagle, Dominus and Opus One. Good sparklers include Schramsberg and Cuvée Napa.

**Carneros** The Carneros district overlaps the southern ends of the Napa and Sonoma regions, and forms a distinctive AVA of its own. Being immediately to the north of the Bay, its climate is continually influenced by dawn fogs which often don't clear until around mid-morning. They mitigate the ferocious heat of summer to such a degree that Carneros qualifies as one of the coolest areas on average in all of California.

It shot to prominence in the 1980s for a handful of exquisitely crafted Pinot Noirs and Chardonnays from such wineries as Acacia, Saintsbury and Carneros Creek. The quality of the Pinots in particular – angular in youth, but packed with deep red fruit and roasted meat intensity – served notice that the citadel of Burgundian Pinot was about to be stormed.

Carneros has developed a reputation as a good producer of sparkling wines as well, with the champagne house Taittinger (Domaine Carneros) and cava producer Codorníu (Codorniu Napa) representing the European vote of confidence.

**Sierra Foothills** The foothills of the Sierra Nevada mountain range that forms the border with the state of Nevada encompass some of the oldest vineyard land in California, dating from the Gold Rush that began in 1849. Within the overall **Sierra Foothills** AVA are five sub-divisions. **El Dorado** County forms one, within which is the smaller, promisingly named **Fair Play** AVA, while Amador County to the south takes in **Shenandoah Valley** and **Fiddletown**. The usual diversity of grapes is grown, but the acreage of Zinfandel vines is among California's more venerable. The **North Yuba** AVA includes the Renaissance winery, famed for delicate Rieslings and Sauvignons and a totally contrasting Cabernet – a pitch-black study in rip-roaring tannins.

**Livermore Valley** East of the Bay in Alameda County, the **Livermore Valley** AVA was historically famed for its Bordeaux-style white blends, but has since followed the path of California diversity. One of the Livermore's oldest wineries is Wente Brothers, founded in 1883, and acclaimed now for its best *cuvées* of Chardonnay, as well as some tasty sparkling wines.

**Santa Clara Valley** South of Alameda, the **Santa Clara Valley** is now rather more about micro-electronics than wine, although it was one of the first AVAs.

**Santa Cruz** A coastal district south of San Francisco, the **Santa Cruz Mountains** AVA has been a whirlpool of innovative ferment on the California scene. This was one of the first regions to try producing great Pinot Noir, its proximity to the ocean making its climate cool enough not to overstress that notoriously fragile grape. Now all sorts of grapes have moved in, many of them under the creative aegis of Randall Grahm at the Bonny Doon winery. Plantings of Marsanne, Roussanne, Syrah, Grenache and Mourvèdre, just as everyone else was going hell-for-leather with Cabernet, earned Grahm the nickname of the Rhône Ranger, and helped to blaze a particularly fruitful trail. His entertainingly off-the-wall labels and wine names announce some genuinely original wines, marked by crystal-clear definition and great intensity.

*Clos Pegase, in the Napa Valley (above). This striking modern building contains not only the winery but an art gallery too.*

*New vines waiting to bud against a stark California landscape at Au Bon Climat, Santa Barbara (above).*

*Vineyards of Wente Brothers in Livermore Valley (above), east of San Francisco Bay in Alameda County.*

Paul Draper has been the other Santa Cruz colossus, producing monumental Cabernets and Zinfandels under single-estate names. More mainstream but still brilliant Cabernets and Chardonnays have come from Mount Eden, Ahlgren and Kathryn Kennedy, with gorgeously expressive Pinots from David Bruce.

**San Benito** San Benito is a smallish inland wine region west of Fresno, whose brightest star is Calera Vineyards, sole proprietor in the tiny **Mount Harlan** AVA. Calera's offerings include hauntingly scented Mills Pinot Noir, lovely, buttercream Chardonnay, and one of the most extraordinary Viogniers made anywhere outside Condrieu. It sells for about the same sort of giddy price as Condrieu, but the aromatic intensity and great length of the wine are powerfully persuasive.

**Monterey County** Monterey on the Central Coast is marked by both coolness and aridity, so that grape-growing has always been something of a challenge. Notwithstanding that, the county is one of the more densely planted California regions. Cool-climate grapes such as Pinot Noir, Riesling and even Chenin Blanc are now doing well here. Within the overall **Monterey** AVA, there are three flagship zones that represent Monterey's premier league: **Chalone** (overlapping into San Benito), **Arroyo Seco** and **Carmel Valley**. The first of those is home to Chalone Vineyards, maker of benchmark Chardonnay, surprisingly full Pinot Blanc and richly gamey Pinot Noir.

**San Luis Obispo** A little further south along the coast from Monterey, this county covers the climatic extremes, with the most highly

regarded wines tending to come from the cooler coastal areas, such as the **Edna Valley** AVA. The Edna Valley winery makes pace-setting Chardonnay here. North of Edna is the large elevated plain of **Paso Robles**, where the fiercer conditions are better for Cabernet and Zinfandel. South of Edna Valley, in the Arroyo Grande Valley AVA, the champagne house Deutz has established one of its overseas outposts, Maison Deutz.

**Santa Barbara** The southernmost of the Central Coast wine counties is fog-shrouded Santa Barbara, not far north of Los Angeles. Its best vineyards congregate in two AVAs – **Santa Maria** and **Santa Ynez Valley**. Both enjoy the cooling influence of the ocean and make good showings of Pinot Noir and Chardonnay, much as Carneros does, as well as some crisply textured Sauvignon and Riesling. Au Bon Climat and Sanford wineries set a tough standard with their effortlessly concentrated, raspberry-fruited Pinots, while Zaca Mesa has done improbably good things with Syrah, and Byron Vineyards scores highly for Chardonnay, Pinot Blanc and Pinot Gris.

In the south of California, three regions of no enormous viticultural significance are Riverside County (which includes the **Temecula Valley** AVA), San Diego County (including the tiny AVA of **San Pasqual Valley**) and the inland Imperial Valley.

## PACIFIC NORTHWEST

Three states in the far northwest of the USA have emerged in recent years from the long shadow cast by California's premier wine status. Of the three, it is Oregon, with its challenging climatic circumstances, that has generated the greatest excitement so far, but Washington State is making a strong showing as well, and inland Idaho will surely have a lot to offer future generations. Despite the favourable press they continue to receive, we still don't see enough of these wines in Europe.

**Oregon** Although *Vitis vinifera* vines were first planted in Oregon over a century ago, it is only comparatively recently that the state's potential as a quality wine producer has begun to bear fruit. There was some scepticism from the neighbours in California as to how likely it was that Oregon would turn out at all well, but early vintages of Eyrie Vineyards Pinot Noir, one of the great trailblazing American wines, were instrumental in proving them wrong.

Pinot Noir, the goal of aspirant winemakers everywhere at the time, became the Oregon buzz wine *par excellence*, so much so that for a while it looked as though there might be a surfeit of growers producing mediocre Pinot when they could be more profitably growing something easier. Where stunning Pinots have emerged, they have more often than not been made in the gently savoury, fruit-driven but attractively light style of the Côte de Beaune, rather than anything bigger and burlier. Alsace varieties have done remarkably well, providing dry, spicy, fragrant wines from Riesling, Gewürztraminer and – most successfully of all – Pinot Gris.

One long valley area dominates Oregon production – the **Willamette Valley** AVA. It occupies a northwestern corner of the state, near the Pacific coast, and enjoys the kinds of cool growing conditions that are to be found in parts of northern France. All of the finest Oregon producers are located here. The **Dundee Hills** is an especially propitious sub-regional AVA within the Willamette.

Adelsheim, Ponzi and Eyrie make full-blown, creamy Pinot Gris, and Eyrie is also tops for Chardonnay with its subtle, baked-appley Reserve bottling. As to the celebrated Pinot Noirs, Elk Cove, Bethel Heights, Ponzi, Argyle, Beaux Frères and Domaine Drouhin (owned by the Burgundy négociant house) all make state-of-the-art, sweetly cherryish, but ageworthy wines. **Washington State** In volume terms, Washington's production of *vinifera* wine is a very distant third in the American stakes, but some feel it's first runner-up for quality. The two halves of the state are, climatically, chalk and cheese. While the seaward side has temperate, dampish conditions, the eastern half has sweltering summers and unforgivingly cold winters.

Notwithstanding that, nearly all the vineyard land is in the east, where the overall **Columbia Valley** AVA accounts for most of the wine produced. An important sub-region of Columbia – the **Yakima Valley** AVA – is home to some of the state's oldest vineyards.

Cabernet, and particularly Merlot, have proved themselves adept at coping with the climatic torments of eastern Washington, and generally yield round, emphatically fruity wines that are drinkable quite early. Riesling, perhaps surprisingly, does well, and can produce outstandingly graceful dry and medium-dry styles; it seems a shame that the variety isn't especially popular among American consumers.

The inevitable Chardonnay, however, sells like hot cakes, and good, gently buttery stuff it is too. Semillon, not previously much lauded in the USA, has carved out a niche for itself; the style is a little like the minerally-dry unoaked examples of Australia's Hunter Valley.

Half of all Washington production is accounted for by one giant combine, Ste. Michelle Wine Estates, which puts out wines under a number of labels, such as Columbia Crest, Chateau Ste. Michelle, Snoqualmie and so forth. Quality is reasonable, if rarely idiosyncratic. Best of the smaller wineries include Delille, Quilceda Creek, Matthews, Hogue and Kiona (the last, in the Red Mountain AVA, is a specialist in late-harvest sweet wines from the Alsace varieties Gewürztraminer and Riesling, and also makes a Chenin Blanc ice wine).

**Idaho** Washington's eastern neighbour shares much the same climate as the Columbia Valley, except that Idaho's vineyards are planted at very high altitudes, making winter conditions here extremely severe. High-acid white varieties do better than Chardonnay, so Riesling and Chenin Blanc can be impressive. Against all the omens, Cabernet is now yielding some reassuringly ripe reds. A single high-volume producer, Ste. Michelle, rules the Idaho roost, and its wines are generally good. However, most of the state's production doesn't travel much further than Washington State.

*Oregon's cool Willamette Valley (above) dominates the state's wine industry, with the top producers clustered at the northern end of the valley.*

*While Oregon's vineyards lie close to the ocean, Washington's major wine regions are in the east, where the temperatures are more extreme, as in neighbouring Idaho (below).*

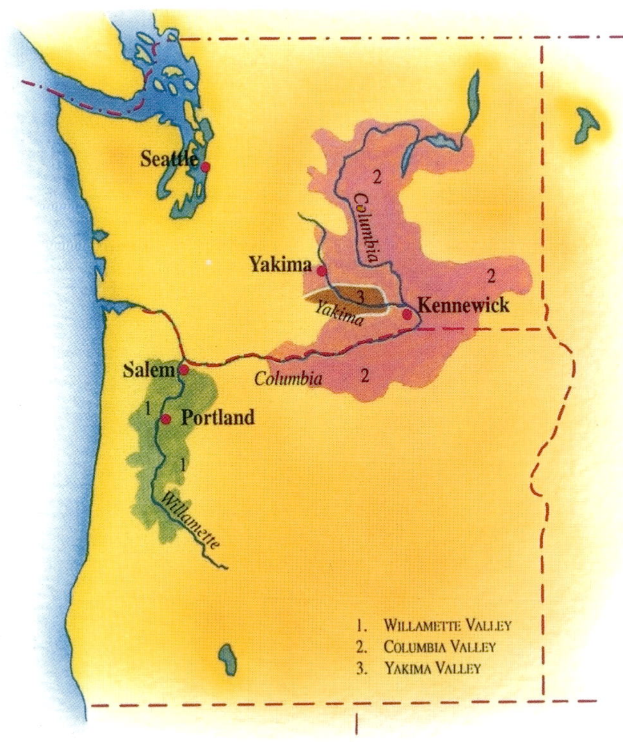

*Riesling vines of Idaho's main producer, Ste Chapelle (above).*

## OTHER STATES

**New York State** New York viticulture only really got under way in the early years of the 19th century, not much before California's, although the eastern state had of course been settled for much longer. Native American vine species dominated the wine industry into the most recent era, but that has now substantially changed, and New York is now the second most productive wine state in the USA (although, to put that into perspective, we're talking about four per cent of all American wine, as against California's 89 per cent).

The principal growing region is the **Finger Lakes** AVA, a group of long thin bodies of water in the centre of the state, south of Rochester. **Long Island** also has fairly extensive vineyards, and a pair of AVAs, **The Hamptons** and **North Fork**, within the overall regional designation. The cooler climates of these regions are beginning to produce some heartily encouraging, attractively balanced alternatives to the sun-soaked wines of Napa and Sonoma, their winemakers working with the grain of the climatic conditions.

*Vineyards spreading towards the water's edge in New York State's Finger Lakes AVA (right).*

Chardonnay has performed well, making appealing, lean, nutty whites that can stand a little oak. Classically steely Riesling is good enough to turn America's wine-drinkers on to that much underrated variety, and Cabernet-based blended reds have had something of the angular austerity of decent Bordeaux. Red grapes that do well in cooler conditions, though – including Pinot Noir and Cabernet Franc – will likely turn out to be the real stars.

Good producers include Fox Run, Anthony Road, Lamoreaux Landing and Wagner in Finger Lakes, and Bedell, Lenz and Pellegrini in Long Island.

**Texas** The Lone Star state develops apace, and now has eight AVAs, its most important one being the northerly **Texas High Plains**. Its wine industry is essentially a creation of the 1970s, when the Llano Estacado winery set the ball rolling, making Cabernet, Chardonnay and Sauvignon near Lubbock. In their wake have followed the likes of Fall Creek, McPherson, and the ambitious Ste Genevieve – a joint venture with a Bordeaux négociant. Good results are being posted with southern French

varieties such as Syrah and Viognier, as well as plantings of Spanish and Italian grapes like Tempranillo and Sangiovese.

**Virginia** Despite the fact that it has an uncompromisingly hot climate, some are tipping Virginia, with its six AVAs, as a forthcoming story in American wine. Unusually, given the pretty torrid conditions, it has proved itself most adept so far at white wine. The Chardonnays are luscious enough to give the best of California a run for their money, while Viognier, Semillon and Riesling also look promising. Reds are improving too, though, with Petit Verdot and Cabernet Franc among the likely stars of the future.

Other states poised to cause a stir in wine circles are **Missouri**, **Maryland**, **Pennsylvania** and **North Carolina**, but there is at least one winery in every single state of the Union now.

Going way out on a limb, you might enjoy some of the blueberry and rhubarb wines of **Alaska**, but they're probably beyond the scope of this book.

*A coming region is the state of Virginia (above), where new plantings of classic white varieties are proving successful.*

# CANADA

*Canada first attracted attention for its award-winning Icewines. Now, with plantings of popular international varieties, the country's producers are surging forward with an impressive range of styles.*

*Harvesting frozen Vidal grapes (above) in winter for Canada's speciality, icewine.*

*Canada's two important wine-growing regions are divided by the vast country itself, with Ontario on the east coast, bordering New York State, and British Columbia on the west.*

WHILE OTHER EMERGENT wine countries have targeted European markets with huge sales drives and promotional campaigning, Canada has quietly been developing its own industry at a rate that suits itself. Like New York State, it has made the necessary transition from reliance on ghastly hybrid grape varieties to *Vitis vinifera* types, although the harsh northern climate has made varietal and site selection much trickier than they have been in the States.

The Canadian summers are benign enough, but wintertime reliably brings several degrees of frost in most vineyard districts, which can be highly dangerous for the dormant vines. A clutch of French varieties has been established, though, mainly in Ontario and British Columbia, and even though many of the vines only came into full production towards the turn of the century, early showings have been highly encouraging.

Above and beyond the dry varietals, Canada's major speciality has been icewine, made in the same way as it is in Germany and Austria. After all, if you have sub-zero winters as a matter of course, you may as well put them to good use. The grapes are left to overripen on the vine, and then freeze as night-time temperatures start to plummet with the onset of winter. When the frozen berries are harvested, they are quickly pressed so that the ice-pellets of water remain behind in the presses, and the sweetly concentrated juice runs free.

Riesling has been, not unexpectedly, a favoured variety for icewine, but the other main grape is one of those hybrid varieties. Vidal isn't the most likely star turn for dry white wine, but has consistently yielded some of the most lusciously concentrated examples of Canada's icewine. It easily attains the kind of sugar levels found in all but the very sweetest German and Austrian versions of Eiswein. Good acidity balances the apricot-syrup sweetness of the wines, so that, although irresistibly easy to drink on release, they are also capable of ageing in the bottle.

So proficient a specialist at the icewine style has Canada become, indeed, that experiments with red icewine are now being tried. Cabernet Franc has been the leading grape so far, but the

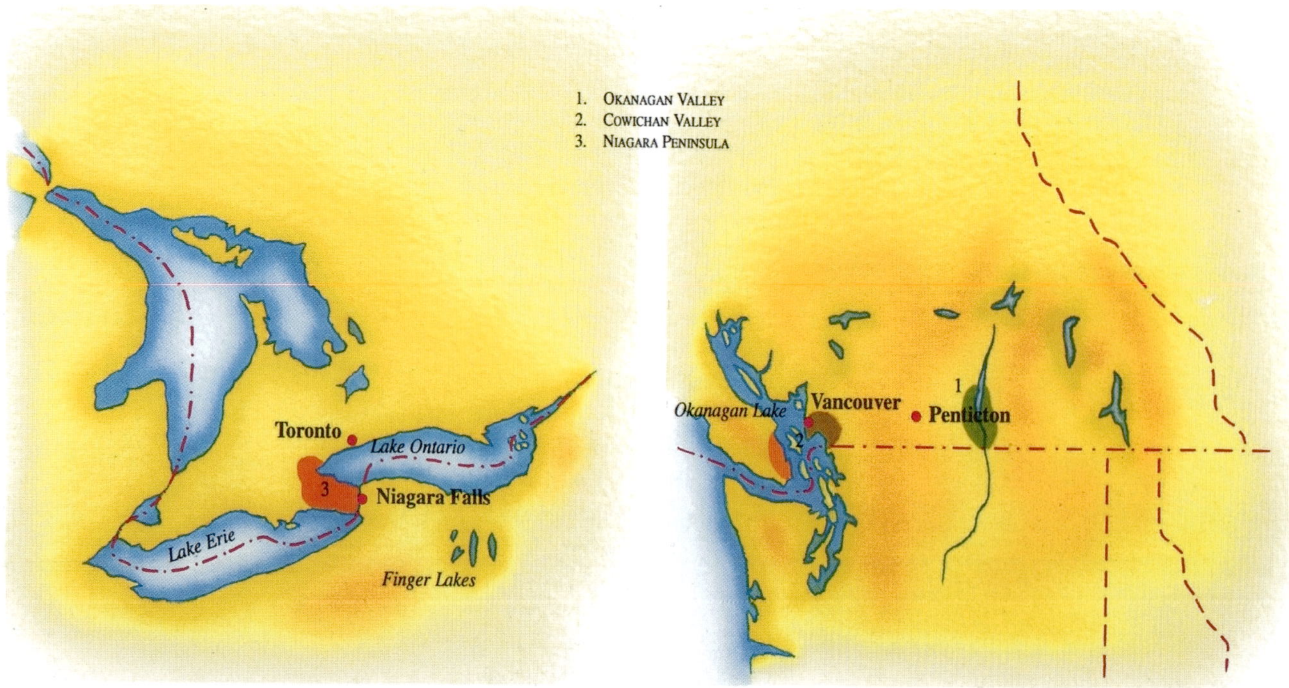

Pilliteri winery in Ontario has also branched out into Cabernet Sauvignon and even Shiraz icewines at the dawn of the new century. Red icewines tend to be quite delicately coloured and structured, but with lush aromas of red fruit purées and rose-petals. Try them with lighter chocolate-based desserts if you happen to come across them.

For dry wines, Chardonnay and Riesling are the best whites so far, but Gewürztraminer and Pinot Gris have also shown promise, while gently savoury Pinot Noir, cranberryish, Loire-style Cabernet Franc and lightly plummy Merlot have been the more successful reds. There is a certain amount of light-textured Cabernet Sauvignon from pioneering producers in British Columbia, but too much still tastes too thin to be convincing.

Canadian winemakers instituted an appellation system in 1988, the Vintners Quality Alliance. To make the VQA grade, wines must be sourced entirely from grapes grown in the defined regions, and to have achieved minimum levels of ripeness. Anything labelled 'Cellared in Canada' will have been made at least partly from the juice of imported grapes, a naïve and foolish practice that will surely undermine the efforts of winemakers working within the painstakingly elaborated VQA system.

Canada's vineyards are located in four of its provinces, of which the first two shown here are by far the most important for quantity.

**Ontario** The province that borders New York State has similarly cool, marginal growing conditions. A degree of natural protection is afforded by a high ridge overlooking the main vineyard area that mitigates the worst effects of the climate. Riesling is a star performer here, from crisp dry styles to the celebrated icewines, and Chardonnay too achieves good things in the style of steely Chablis, as well as softer, gently oaked examples. Pinot Noir grown in these cool climes may very well turn out to be among North America's finest.

It was in Ontario's **Niagara Peninsula** that the modern Canadian wine industry got going, with the innovative Inniskillin winery's first plantings in the 1970s. Its standard bottlings of Chardonnay and Riesling are still highly reliable, well-made wines.

PRODUCERS: Clos Jordanne, Hidden Bench, Tawse, Château des Charmes, Henry of Pelham.

**British Columbia** Whereas most of Canada's vineyards lie in the Atlantic east of the country, the western province of British Columbia, way out on its own Pacific limb, is also participating in the quality wine movement. The **Okanagan Valley** in the southwest of the province is where the best vineyards are found. Good varietals have been produced from Alsace grapes such as Pinot Blanc and Gewürztraminer, as well as Riesling of course. Delicate Chardonnays are good when not smothered with oak. Reds from the Bordeaux grapes are improving, but icewines are the cream of the crop.

PRODUCERS: Mission Hill, Black Hills, Sumac Ridge, Road 13.

**Quebec and Nova Scotia** The other two eastern provinces to make wine have only a sparse scattering of vineyards. So far, they are largely dedicated to the production of wines from hybrid grape varieties, although there are incipient plantings of Chardonnay.

*The beautiful Okanagan Valley in British Columbia (above) is carving a name for itself for Alsace grape varieties.*

# SOUTH AND CENTRAL AMERICA

*Led by the great successes of Chile and Argentina, South America has become an important player in the southern hemisphere. Mexico, from where vines initially headed south with the Spanish, is also enjoying a revival.*

*Climatically, Chile and Argentina offer the best wine-producing conditions in South America (below). There are also pockets of vineyards in Brazil and Uruguay.*

ALTHOUGH WILD VINES flourished in Central America just as they did in the north, there is no indication of any systematic wine production in pre-Columbian times. It took the arrival of Spanish and then Portuguese colonists to develop intensive viticulture in the central and southern sectors of the Americas, initially for the production of the Communion wine used in Christian worship. A rapid southward march from Mexico, down through what are now Peru, Chile and Argentina, carried the wine grape into those areas.

Peru was the original epicentre of wine cultivation on the South American continent, retaining its status throughout the 16th and 17th centuries, but its vineyards were gradually replaced by sugarcane and cotton through a combination of colonial diktat and natural disasters. In the present day, Peru is struggling to re-establish itself as a wine producer, but it will be a good while before we start seeing its wares in the global north.

In the meantime, Argentina produces the highest volume of all the Latin American countries, although it was Chile that made all the running in the export markets from the late 1980s onwards. What galvanized the progress of Chile to international renown was the arrival of some big European names in its vineyards. The early pace was set with sensationally rich, concentrated Cabernet Sauvignons and Merlots, as well as some fine opulent Chardonnays. There was also some often rather feeble Sauvignon Blanc, and that was basically it for quite a while. Greater diversification in the vineyard is now paying dividends, though, with Pinot Noir, Syrah and Viognier all turning out some stunners now.

The unique selling point of Chilean wine for some years was the fact that, alone among significant wine-producing countries, it was never invaded by the vine louse, phylloxera (see page 214). Chile's main protection lay in the circumstances of its geography. Since the country is, in essence, one long narrow Pacific coastal strip, nearly all of its soil is sand-based. And sand is the one type of soil in which phylloxera doesn't survive. Furthermore, the natural bulwark of the Andes mountains prevented what limited outbreaks of phylloxera arose in Argentina from spreading westwards. Thus it is that Chilean wines might fancifully be said to taste something like the wines of a century ago and more, although you might be rather dismayed if you found your bottle of Curico Valley Cabernet Sauvignon had been made with the vinification techniques of a hundred years ago.

While Chilean wines began to take the world by storm, Argentina's wine industry bided its time. Its growers were much less hidebound as to the varietals they produced. Malbec, one of the minor varieties in red Bordeaux, is accorded a status in Mendoza that it doesn't quite enjoy anywhere outside Cahors (see

1. BAJA CALIFORNIA
2. SONORA
3. HERMOSILLO
4. QUERETARO
5. ACONCAGUA
6. CENTRAL VALLEY
7. MENDOZA
8. RIO GRANDE DO SUL
9. CARPINTERIA
10. CERRO CHAPEU

*New vineyard plantings of Cabernet in Chile (left). Vines do not need grafting on to phylloxera-resistant roots as the pest cannot thrive in the sand-based soils.*

southwest France). The perfumed white variety Torrontes, nothing to do with the Spanish grape of the same name, is very widely planted, and can make intensely fragrant wines with clearly defined acidity.

These two countries between them are now making some of the most reliable – and also some of the most interesting – wine in the whole southern hemisphere. While there is the same impetus here as elsewhere (especially in Chile) to produce isolated superstar wines selling at crazy prices to satisfy the premium end of the market, the commitment to providing the export trade with good to great wines at prices all of us can afford has never wavered. The consequence is that the price-quality ratio of South American wines is unmatched anywhere on the planet. Chile's Cabernets and Merlots are considerably better than the same varietals from the Languedoc at the same prices. Argentina's best Torrontes can be had for a fraction of the cost of the equivalent spicy-flowery white varietals of Alsace. This is a cause for unalloyed celebration.

Brazil, despite its scale, has not so far been geared for a serious export push, other than to one or two of its neighbours. Hybrid grapes have been a big drawback, but so has finding the right sites for the good grapes. Even within the colossal Brazilian interior, site selection has not been a straightforward task, owing to the enervating heat and humidity most of the country endures. The southerly regions, which are decisively milder, will produce the best wines

in due course. Sparkling wines, to everyone's surprise, are showing exciting potential.

In spite of its diminutive size, Uruguay may turn out before too long to have as much untapped potential as Chile and Argentina once did. Established with Spanish and Italian expertise in the late 19th century, its vineyards are mostly clustered in the hills to the north of the beautiful capital city, Montevideo. Here they benefit from the temperate maritime climate and good soils. Determined not to be left behind in South America's international push, it has created its own niche for red wines from the widely planted Tannat grape of southwest France, as well as some impressive plantings of the Spanish Albariño, together with the expected crowd of Bordeaux reds, Chardonnay and Sauvignon Blanc. Rosé wines from Black Muscat are still a popular traditional local style.

Mexico, the only other wine producer of significant scale in Latin America, is where the whole American wine story started. Planted by Spanish conquistadors in the 1500s, the country's vineyards had gone into a seemingly terminal decline by the 20th century, as native wine was elbowed aside in the marketplace by tequila, mezcal and beer. The cautious beginnings of a reemergence, fuelled in part by Mexican migrant workers returning from stints in the California vineyards with a taste for wine, are now upon us. Southern French red varieties, as well as one or two minority stars such as Petite Sirah, have yielded some superlative results, and the only way is up.

# CHILE

*The meteoric rise of Chilean wine in both European and North American markets in the late 1980s was one of the more sensational (and also salutary) tales of latter times. Varietal diversification has been the most exciting recent development.*

*Cabernet grapes arriving at the Santa Rita bodega (right), in Chile's Maipo Valley.*

In the late 1980s, one of Chile's premium Cabernet Sauvignons, from the Los Vascos winery in Rapel, got sent to Bordeaux, where it muscled in among the top châteaux and set their annual wine-fair alight. Breathless notices in the French press called it 'Chile's *premier cru*'. And so Chile found itself hailed as the hot new property.

Certain members of the international wine aristocracy had, to be sure, been convinced of the potential of Chile's vineyards as far back as the 1970s, when the Torres family of Catalonia bought some land. Eventually, Bordeaux first-growth Château Lafite bought into Los Vascos, and soon there was California money coming in too. At the time, it felt like a case of too much, too soon, as the wines that emerged from this initial stampede turned out to be good enough, but ultimately rather limited in terms of their stylistic range.

Meanwhile, at the other end of the market, Chile looked like it was in danger of going too enthusiastically down the bargain-basement route, looking to mop up custom driven away from the other southern-hemisphere countries by rising prices. Fortunately, the story had a happy outcome, and Chile has since balanced the best of both worlds to emerge as, for my money, the most consistently rewarding winemaking country south of the Equator.

## THE GRAPES

What has been fascinating since the 1990s has been to see the meeting of northern- and southern-hemisphere thinking that Chile's staple varietals display. Many wines are made in a distinctly French style, the Cabernets with austere, backward tannins in their youth, the Chardonnays showing tantalizingly subtle oak seasoning and taut acidity. Others have nailed their colours to what we used to think of as the New World mast, with voluptuous, blackcurrant-essence Cabernets and muscular, wood-driven Chardonnays big on vanilla and alcohol.

Sauvignon used to be a perennial problem in that what a lot of growers had in their vineyards was not the true Sauvignon Blanc, but an inferior cousin of the grape called Sauvignonasse. That has been largely rectified now, and Chilean

Sauvignon usually offers a glass of crisply acidic, often distinctly Loire-like white tasting of gooseberries and asparagus, although where grown in the hotter regions, it can lack fruit and focus.

First-class Merlot is often Chile's trump card. The best wines have enveloping aromas of black fruits, evolving to well-hung game as they age, many of them withstanding comparison with good Pomerol. Even the Reserve wines have remained very competitively priced for their outstanding quality. One can only wish they wouldn't release them quite so young (they're frequently on the market even before their first birthdays), but then they are very supple and drinkable in their youth.

Chile has oodles of Semillon, but that has traditionally gone into roughly made plonk for domestic consumption. Small quantities of Riesling make fresh, simple, dry wine not too far from the New Zealand style, while Viognier is getting in on the fashion for big aromatic whites, with a little delicate Gewürztraminer tagging along behind.

Among the other reds, encouraging things are happening with Pinot Noir. Rather a lot is still made in a fiery, full-throttle style with surprising levels of tannin, but better-balanced wines may yet be good enough to compete with California's finest eventually. Syrah

*A long narrow strip of land caught between the Pacific and the Andes, Chile (below) is blessed with sandy soils. The vineyards lie mainly in the centre of the country, where the climate is benign.*

looks potentially very exciting, and is amply equipped in the warmer vineyard sites to produce richly concentrated wines. Also in the 'richly concentrated' bracket are reds from a grape called Carmenère (another wholesale misidentification once had this grape tagged as Merlot, partly because it turns out to be planted in Bordeaux too). Often blended with Merlot and/or Cabernet, Carmenère produces a thickly opulent, liquoricey wine with plenty of ageability.

Rosés in particular have been a notable success story in recent years. Made from the richer red varieties, such as Cabernet, Merlot and Syrah, they are full of juicy summer fruit, a little alcoholic perhaps, but far more satisfying than many of the pallid rosé styles of the northern hemisphere.

## THE REGIONS

Most of Chile's vineyards lie in the climatically benign central section of the country, immediately south of the capital, Santiago. The smouldering heat of summer is mitigated to a significant degree by the proximity of the vineyards to the cooling influence of the Pacific Ocean. Irrigation is as widely practised here as it is in Argentina, with mountain meltwater flowing through the soil. And no description of Chilean viticulture would be complete without mention of the celebrated fact that these mountain-protected, sandy vineyards are a no-go zone for the dreaded phylloxera.

**Aconcagua/Casablanca** The northernmost region for export wines is the Aconcagua, south of Santiago, incorporating the Aconcagua and Casablanca valley sub-regions. Cabernet Sauvignon is the grape best suited to the arid, broiling conditions in the former, where it achieves massive, pitch-black concentration in the premium wines.

To the southwest, nearer the coast and the city of Valparaiso, the Casablanca district has been the main talking-point of Chilean wine in recent years. Here, the climate is much cooler, so much so that frosts in the spring are not at all uncommon, and the summer swelter is constantly mitigated by ocean breezes. Here, a range of sharply defined varietals (notably from the eponymous Casablanca winery) has made the running, with some gorgeously aromatic, positively *Alsacien* Gewürztraminer and melon-scented Sauvignon in among the tropical-fruited Chardonnays, beautifully balanced Pinots and well-built Cabernets, the last stuffed

with brooding tannins and chewy damson fruit.
PRODUCERS: Casablanca, Ventisquero, Concha y Toro, Cono Sur, Casas del Bosque, Montes.
**Central Valley** South of Aconcagua, the vineyards of the Central Valley and its various sub-regions are concentrated midway between the Andes and the Pacific. At the northern end is **Maipo**, just south of the capital. Cabernet is king once again, but there are convincing Sauvignons too, and the Chablis grower William Fèvre has set up shop here.

The long-established Santa Rita winery produces an ultra-reliable range of basic varietals and Reservas, including top Cabernets. There's even a Zinfandel from the enterprising Canepa winery. One bastion of ancestral tradition is the Cousiño Macul estate, which makes Antiguas Reservas Cabernets that can age for 20 years to a gamey, claret-like venerability. Not to be missed.

Next south is **Rapel**, comprising the two valley districts of Cachapoal and Colchagua. The latter has been a conspicuous presence on the export markets, with brilliant Merlots, distinctive Cabernets and innovative Pinots. In Cachapoal, California's Clos du Val has invested in a winery called Viña Porta, which is making some first-division reds (including robust Pinot Noir) and Chardonnays.

The **Maule** area is cooler again than Rapel, and includes the important wine centres of **Curicó** and **Lontué**, both of which are good for white wines, crunchy Sauvignons as well as lightly creamy Chardonnays. In Maule itself to the south, Merlot has long shown real class as a varietal, as has Carmenère, along with some fresh, sappy Sauvignon.
PRODUCERS: Almaviva, Cousiño Macul, Carmen, De Martino, Quebrada de Macul, Canepa, Santa Rita (Maipo); Casa Lapostolle, Ventisquero, Anakena, Misiones de Rengo (Rapel); Gillmore, Caliboro, Valdivieso, Echeverria, Miguel Torres (Maule/Curico).
**Bio-Bio** The largest wine region, Bio-Bio, south of the Central Valley, is also the least interesting to date. It is considerably cooler and damper than Maule to the north, and is mostly carpeted with a dull pinkish-red variety called País (aka Criolla Chica in Argentina, where it produces much the same style of thin, tasteless semi-red). Undoubtedly, though, there is potential for the classic grapes, as soon as more of the big companies venture this far south. Concha y Toro has planted some Gewürztraminer here.

*All over central Chile new vineyard holdings are being established, making the country currently the most dynamic in South America (above).*

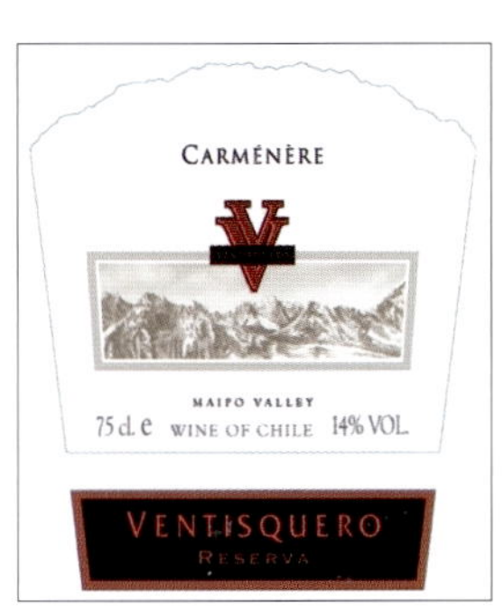

# ARGENTINA

*Following in the footsteps of its great rival to the west, Argentina made more cautious inroads into European markets, a strategy that paid handsome dividends. It is now the go-to country for rich Malbec reds, and much else besides.*



The vast majority of Argentina's vineyard land is in the western province of Mendoza, in the foothills of the Andes. This is a very arid region, and depends greatly on irrigation from melting mountain snow, which runs through the vineyards in intricately laid trenches to prevent them from becoming terminally parched.

As in other emerging wine countries, the quality revolution in Argentina has been led by investment in new technology, with wineries being built nearer to the vineyards themselves, and equipped with temperature-controlled fermentation facilities. Then too, the second-division grape varieties that once prevailed – among them Criolla, Cereza, Pedro Giménez (not the same as the PX grape of Spain's Jerez region) and the less exalted Alexandria member of the Muscat clan, used to make rather

clunking sweet wines – have gradually ceded vineyard land to the viticultural aristos.

Fine white wines are being made from the florally perfumed Torrontes Riojano variant, juicy Chardonnay and Semillon, and some powerful, apricot-and-citrus Viognier that works well when not overcropped.

For reds, Malbec leads the field. On its own, it can produce excellent midweight to full varietal reds, with sturdy meaty structure, unexpectedly supple tannins even in youth, and good ageing potential, the perfect accompaniment to the prodigious quantities of beefsteak consumed in Argentina. Some growers have been successfully blending it with Shiraz or Merlot. Shiraz on its own has been outstanding too. Italian grapes such as Nebbiolo, Barbera, Sangiovese and the relatively undistinguished Bonarda do well in this climate, as does Spain's Tempranillo. Cabernet Sauvignon adds to a rollcall that would make up most people's list of pedigree red varieties.

**Mendoza** This is where about two-thirds of all Argentine wine is made, and where most of the companies that have so far come to notice in the export markets are based. The **Luján de Cuyo** district south of the city of Mendoza, which became Argentina's first designated appellation in 1993, and the high-altitude vineyards of the **Uco Valley**, including the highly promising enclave of **Tupungato**, have been the most exciting regions to date.

The much-favoured Malbec heads the list of grapes planted, and is followed by Tempranillo,

Cabernet Sauvignon, Barbera and Sangiovese. By and large, Mendoza Malbecs are rich, opulently damsony reds, with controlled, streamlined tannins and fairly overt, but not unbalanced, oak influence. They can be surprisingly approachable in their youth, which makes them a very safe bet among mid-priced reds on retail shelves. Alcohol is usually high but is well integrated into the wines' overall structure. The Cabernets can be denser and darker still, often reminiscent of good *cru bourgeois* Médoc, while unblended Syrah can be monumentally, spicily intense.

White wines have featured fine, lightly buttery Chardonnay, some with beautifully weighted oak, solidly ripe, scented Viognier, and even a little sappy, citrussy Sauvignon Blanc. PRODUCERS: Catena, Norton, El Retiro, Terrazas de los Andes, Cobos, Clos de los Siete, Weinert, Trapiche, Trivento.

**San Juan** The area north of Mendoza is important in terms of volume, but not just yet of the quality to balance it. With a much less forgiving climate to contend with than the Mendozans, San Juan wineries have largely contented themselves with supplying the domestic market.

**La Rioja** The scattered vineyards of La Rioja lie to the northeast of San Juan. In the past, much of the production was given over to flabby Muscats, but there has been distinct improvement over the most recent generation. Torrontes from here is looking particularly impressive, and stirring red wines with plenty of muscle are being produced from both Syrah and Malbec. Much of the red wine from Italy's Bonarda grape is made here, in a midweight, redcurranty style that never quite thrills. The volume cooperative producer La Riojana is a reliable name.

**Salta** The northwestern province of Salta is currently producing the best Argentinian wine after Mendoza. Here, some gloriously ripe Cabernet Sauvignon and Malbec is made, and the speciality Torrontes Riojano, grown at the sort of altitudes to induce light-headedness, comes into its own. Within this region, the bulk of the wine is made in the exceptional appellation of **Cafayate** in the **Calchaqui Valley**. There is Malbec here (of course there is), some lightly currany Cabernet Franc, and – taking a leaf out of Uruguay's book – even a little Tannat. But for sheer, head-spinning, delirious beauty in a dry white wine, the

*Irrigation channels in a Mendoza vineyard (left). The water is sourced from the melting snowcaps of the Andes mountains.*

Torrontes is phenomenal. Etchart makes a fine example in Cafayate, all orange blossom and cinnamon on a crisp, appley base, and the winery's brambly Cabernet Sauvignon is also excellent. Colomé is another innovative producer, growing Pinot Noir and Sauvignon Blanc, as well as Malbec, at some of the highest vineyards in the world.

**Rio Negro** and **Neuquén** These two lower-altitude regions in the southern swathe of Argentina known as Patagonia look perhaps to have the best potential of all. The cooler climate and more propitious soil types (clay and sandy loam) are making them a happy hunting-ground for new investors. White varietals such as Torrontes, Sauvignon Blanc, Chenin Blanc and Chardonnay could well yet be among Argentina's finest. Pinot Noir is beginning to show its paces too, while sparkling wine production was given a substantial fillip in the 1990s by the arrival of a posse of Champagne VIPs with money to spend.

*Ploughing the old-fashioned way in Argentina.*

# BRAZIL

*The hulking behemoth of the South American continent presents problems with vineyard site selection, but where climatic conditions permit, astonishing wines are being produced. Look out particularly for stylish sparklers.*



BRAZIL'S VITICULTURAL history fits the general pattern of most of the Americas. Portuguese colonists and missionaries planted the vine, intially – and optimistically – in the environs of São Paulo. Slow vineyard expansion led to hybrid grapes churning out very basic wine by the 19th century. It wasn't until the 1970s, when foreign investors encouraged the planting of international varieties such as Chardonnay and Cabernet Sauvignon, that the seeds of a contemporary wine scene in Brazil were sown.

In the case of this South American giant, however, the progress has been more halting than it has elsewhere, despite the fact that it now has the third largest wine production on the continent, behind Argentina and Chile. Most of the expansive Brazilian landmass is simply too tropical for *Vitis vinifera* vines to cope with, with raging humidity and extremely high rainfall presenting an insuperable challenge even for the eminently adaptable Chardonnay. Only the more temperate areas are suitable for viticulture, which is where the state of Rio Grande do Sul, in the deep south of Brazil, comes into play. Ninety per cent of the country's wine is made here. In regions like **Serra Gaúcha** and **Campania Gaúcha**, the latter (formerly known as Fronteira) near the borders with Uruguay and Argentina, the best results so far are being achieved. As elsewhere in Latin America, high-altitude vineyard plantings look like producing the most distinguished wines of all.

For the time being, the problem remains that barely more than one-tenth of Brazil's vineyards are planted with *vinifera* grapes, the rest being a mixture of native species and hybrids. Pre-eminent among them is a grape called Isabella, which carpeted the vineyards of California in the dim distant past. None of these grapes will produce world-class wines – they hardly taste like wine at all when vinified – and one can only hope they start receding before too long.

Chardonnay, Syrah, and most of the Bordeaux varieties, red and white, represent the future. Plantings of Sauvignon Blanc, Pinot Blanc and Gewürztraminer are evidence of both enterprise and courage. Initially, the modern

wines tended to be made in a rather light and inconsequential style, with not-quite-ripe whites and featherlight reds predominating, as though in compensation for any potential overripeness the climate might deliver. That tendency has gradually been overcome, and better-balanced wines are emerging.

Perhaps surprisingly, there is a thriving and growing sparkling wine industry. Made mainly to cater for local tastes at first, it has now begun to attract attention with a range of styles from refreshingly dry to delicately sweet. The wines are made by the traditional method and subjected to careful ageing on their yeast lees to attain complexity, an indispensable element to success in quality fizz. Significantly, Champagne giant Moët & Chandon has a commercial interest here, just as it does in Argentina.

The coming decades will undoubtedly see a much bigger export push for Brazil's wines. Increasing quantities are presently being sold to the United States and China, as well as neighbouring South American countries, and western Europe is now firmly in Brazilian sights. Big players so far have been the Miolo, Salton and Aurora companies. The last of those is a gigantic, but quality-conscious, cooperative outfit consisting of more than 1100 growers. Visitors to Brazil should look out on restaurant wine lists for the wines of smaller family-run estates as well, such as Lidio Carraro, Casa Valduga, Cave Geisse's Chardonnay-Pinot Noir sparklers, and Pizzato's Fausto range.

# MEXICO

*There is more to Mexico's alcohol industry than agave spirits and beer, but its wines have a long way yet to go before they achieve visibility on the export markets. Nonetheless, the potential quality is undeniably there.*

WHEN THE CONQUISTADORS arrived from Spain in the wake of Columbus's voyages of discovery, Mexico was where they started their long exploratory sweep through Central and South America. Wherever anyone settled, vineyards were planted, so that something like the life back home could be replicated in the brave new Spanish world. The wine might not have tasted like the produce of the motherland, but at least it was wine.

Wine production has always taken a back seat to distillation in Mexico, and the fiery spirits tequila and mezcal have been supplemented by grape brandy. Mexico actually produces one of the world's biggest export brandies, Presidente, and much of the country's vineyard yield is destined for the stills. However, strengthening flickers of domestic interest, followed by the usual sporadic foreign investment and the emergence of a classification structure for quality wines, have created the bare bones of a modern wine industry.

Since the Spanish also occupied what is now California from their Central American base, it should come as no surprise to find most of the vineyard land concentrated in the north of the country near the United States border. The Mexican state of **Baja California** is its premium growing area, a long northwestern strip of breeze-cooled vineyard that receives the same morning fogs off the Pacific as does

the Napa Valley to the north. Along with the other main northern region, **Sonora**, this is where most of the wines with any chance of competing internationally will come from.

To the southeast of Sonora lies the La Laguna district, which straddles the two states of Coahuila and Durango, and further south again is the Central zone, which embraces Zacatecas, the relatively tiny enclave of Aguascalientes, and Querétaro. In 2025, this last became the first area to be awarded a protected quality designation (*Vinos de la Región Vitivinícola de Querétaro*) under Mexico's new wine denomination system, a bold entrée to the global stage.

Southern French red varieties constitute much of the area planted throughout the country, together with outposts of American continental grapes both old and new, including the historically significant Mission (Chile's País), a variety called Petite Sirah (not the same thing as Syrah, but actually another dark-skinned French grape, the brooding Durif, now seen virtually nowhere in France itself), and a spot of Zinfandel. There are small plantings too of Tempranillo and Italy's Dolcetto.

Petite Sirah has shown particular promise in producing thick savoury reds that have unwieldy tannins in their youth, but lots of exuberant blueberry fruit and chocolatey spice. Its flagship example has been the varietal wine made by the commercially important L. A. Cetto winery in the Guadelupe Valley, Baja California, which also makes excellent Cabernet Sauvignon.

When it comes to white wines, there is a fair bit of progress still to be made. The grapes grown were not always the more distinguished varieties, but the more recognisable names are now gaining a foothold, in the shapes of Chenin Blanc, Chardonnay, Sauvignon Blanc and Viognier. Sparklers may one day get a foot in the door too, if the presence of the Spanish Cava company Freixenet is anything to go by.

As well as L. A. Cetto, Santo Tomás, Casa de Piedra, Monte Xanic and Casa Madero have been among the producers to watch.

*An old timber-roofed wine bodega at Ensenada, Baja California, Mexico (above).*

*A vineyeard worker (left) trims vines during winter in the northerly Baja California region.*

## URUGUAY

If Brazil doesn't emerge to join Argentina and Chile as the next big South American wine country in the export markets, then Uruguay is where my money is going. There is so much potential here, and progress in recent years has been meteoric. The usual regional drawback of widespread hybrid vines is a factor, but a diminishing one, and a very broad-minded range of international *Vitis vinifera* varieties now offsets it. A simple quality classification system is in operation, with the serious wines being placed in the VCP (*vino de calidad preferente*) category. These must be made from *vinifera* grapes, and be sold in glass bottles, as distinct from the cartons that the basement-level wines are often packaged in.

Just as Argentina has its Malbec, so Uruguay has made an intriguing speciality of one of the lesser-known southern French grapes in Tannat, the often brutal red menace of Madiran (see southwest France). Uruguayan Tannat, however, seems better suited to its surroundings, with more supple texture and attractive ripe fruit than its French counterpart. Many of the wines spend several productive months in oak barrels, emerging full of intense purple berry flavours and dark chocolate richness, an absolute treat for lovers of full-bodied reds.

Vineyards are planted in nearly all of Uruguay's 19 administrative departments. Those to the north of the capital – **Canelones**, **Montevideo**, **Colonia** and **San José** – have the most extensive plantings, and are leading the country's quality wine revolution, but other regions such as **Maldonado** in the southeast, **Carpinteria** in the central Durazno department, and **Cerro Chapeu** in Rivera near the Brazilian border to the north are coming up fast on the inside track.

As well as Tannat, the Bordeaux varieties Merlot, Cabernet Sauvignon and Cabernet Franc are all producing outstanding wines now. Whites were at first a little overripe and inelegant, but better results are now being achieved with Chardonnay, Sauvignon Blanc and – perhaps most promisingly of all – Albariño. A lot of the traditional rosé is made from Black Muscat (aka Muscat Hamburg). You might be glad of a stone-cold glass of it at a waterfront bar in the sizzle of the late afternoon. (I know I was.) Quality sparkling wine will be increasingly important in years to come.

Bodegas Carrau's Castel Pujol bottlings of Tannat, either singly or blended with Merlot, are sumptuous. Among the Canelones wineries, Pisano makes a fine range of reds from French varieties, including premium Axis Mundi Tannat, and the family-run Carlos Pizzorno estate also has impressive Tannat Reserva. Best of all is the Bouza winery, which makes fabulously silky reds that wear their formidable alcohol levels lightly and are full of the kind of depth and spicy complexity that will help them to age excitingly. Among their whites are sharply defined lemony Albariño and astonishing dry Riesling with a fruit profile that's all nectarine and pear dancing around a classic core of petrol.

*Traditional low-trained vines in Uruguay (right). Viticulture is practised all over the country.*

## PERU

In centuries gone by, Peru was the dominant source of wine in South America and might well have been the scene of the very first exercise in vinification on the continent. Its vineyards cover an area of land nearly three times greater than those of Uruguay, but much of the wine that is sourced from them is destined for distillation into the regional grape spirit, pisco. Climatically, the country is comparable to Chile, so theoretically Peruvian wine could well play a significant part in South American wine output in the future.

Cabernet Sauvignon, Merlot, Malbec and Grenache have all taken root, but there are also plantings of Sauvignon Blanc, Torrontes (here known as Torontel) and a good northern Spanish variety, Albillo, with Italian Barbera to add variety to the palette of reds.

So far, the best of the wines, worth looking out for if you're on the Machu Picchu tourist trail, have come from the **Ica Valley** region, 250km to the south of the capital, Lima. This region is home to the Tacama winery, which boldly claims to be the oldest continuously active vineyard outside Europe, having been established during the Spanish conquest in the 1540s. They have an encouragingly complex Tannat, as well as some Malbec, Chardonnay and Sauvignon Blanc. Queirolo's Intipalka range includes savoury Cabernet Sauvignon and citrus-fresh Sauvignon Blanc, as well as a strawberryish Syrah rosé. Murga has a portfolio of modern styles bottled under eye-catching labels.

Vineyards (left) on the banks of the river Cañete, in the central coastal region of Peru, near the capital, Lima.

The Tarija valley (above), southern Bolivia, where these vineyards are planted lies between 1700 and 3000 metres.

## BOLIVIA

The lion's share of Bolivia's tiny production of wines comes from the southerly **Tarija** region, where vines were first established by Franciscan monks during the Spanish colonisation of South America in the 16th century. It was only in the 1960s and 70s that the rudiments of a modern wine industry began to emerge, and it has been very much a case of baby steps since then. As in Peru, much of the wine production (from Muscat of Alexandria) goes for distillation into a national grape spirit, in this case singani. The topography of Bolivia means that all its vineyards are of necessity planted at very high altitudes, which may be the mood of the moment in global wine right now but doesn't necessarily suit all grape varieties. Painstaking selection has been key.

A familiar range of classic grapes is grown, the reds including Cabernet Sauvignon, Merlot, Syrah, Malbec and Tannat, the whites encompassing Torrontes, Chenin Blanc, Chardonnay, Sauvignon Blanc and even a little speculative Riesling. The wines of the Solana winery are worth hunting down if you're passing through.

Other South American wine producers, of no real significance outside their own national boundaries, are Ecuador, Venezuela, Colombia and Paraguay.

# SOUTH AFRICA

*After a century of political strife, the South African wine industry is developing fast. The potential for quality wines is vast and expanding, and exciting times lie ahead for the country's most ambitious winemakers.*

*The Cape of Good Hope has always been the focus of wine-growing in South Africa (below). Even so, inland from the cooling Atlantic and Indian oceans, the climate here can still be hot and humid.*

1. OLIFANTS RIVER
2. SWARTLAND
3. PAARL
4. DURBANVILLE
5. CONSTATIA
6. STELLENBOSCH
7. ELGIN
8. WALKER BAY
9. WORCESTER/TULBAGH
10. ROBERTSON
11. KLEIN KAROO

VITICULTURE WAS among the very first enterprises of the Dutch settlers who arrived on the Cape of Good Hope in the mid-17th century. We don't know what grapes they brought with them, though it seems likely the cuttings would have come from Bordeaux. Early results were not exactly seized on with glee when they made their way back to the Netherlands, but a start had been made. What first put Cape winemaking on the map was one of those legendary dessert wines with which vinous history is strewn.

Constantia was the name of an estate near Cape Town planted by a colonial governor, Simon van der Stel, barely 40 years after the new territory had been claimed by the Dutch. It made sweet wines in both colours from grapes that were left to overripen and then dry out on the vine – a rudimentary version of the *passerillage* process still practised across much of southern Europe. There is some uncertainty as to whether they were fortified, although analysis of the contents of antique bottles opened in the 1990s suggests not, at least where they were intended for local consumption. (Some of the wines transported overseas may, however, have been fortified to preserve them, as was the developing practice at the time.) The wines took Europe by storm. In the 18th and

early 19th centuries, they enjoyed a reputation so exalted indeed that higher prices were paid for them than for any of the classic dessert or fortified wines of Europe.

If this was South African wine's early historic claim to glory, and a long enough moment in the spotlight at that, it was to be brutally extinguished from the latter half of the Victorian era onwards. The abolition in 1861 by the UK, then the colonial power on the Cape, of preferential treatment for goods coming in from outposts of the Empire forced South Africa's wines to compete, all but hopelessly, with wines being imported from much closer to home on the European continent. What need for wine merchants to pay for expensively imported Constantia when there were port, sherry and madeira readier to hand? The Cape export trade to its chief target market began to wither.

As the decline set in, it was aggravated by the depredations of the vine pest phylloxera, swinging through the Cape in the 1880s on its triumphal world tour. Many vineyards had to be uprooted, but even what was left was now producing at a rate that couldn't be absorbed either domestically or by export sales. A kind of forerunner of the European wine lake of the 1970s was the result, a surplus stagnant pool of unwanted wine that largely went to waste.

Something resembling a solution to that emerged in 1918 with the foundation of the Koöperatieve Wijnbouwers Vereniging (KWV).

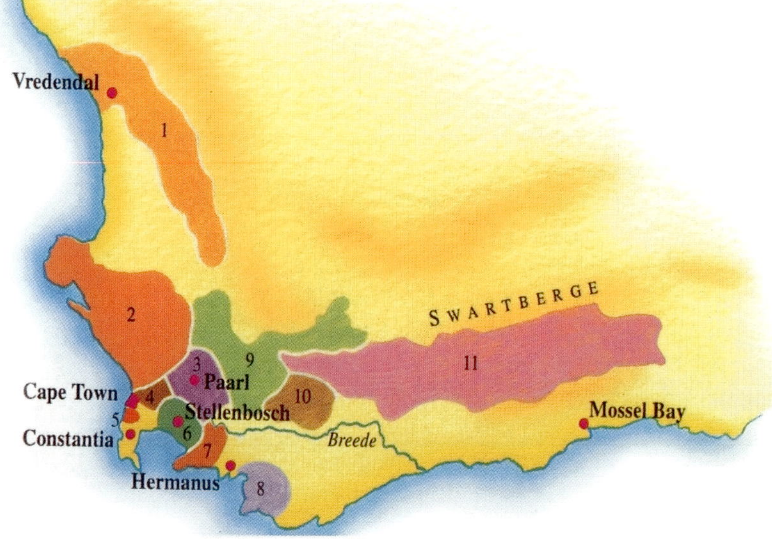


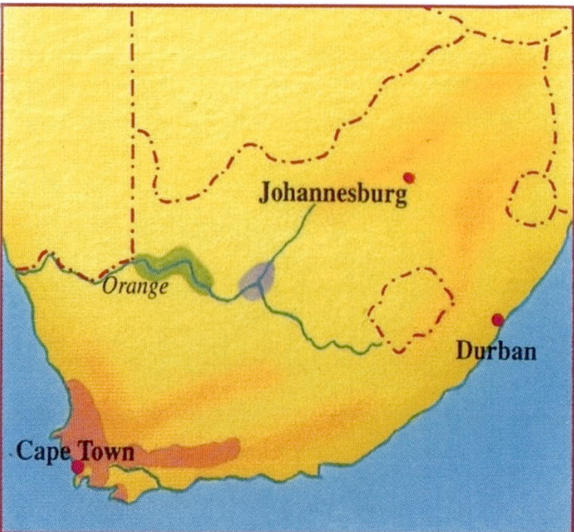

This huge organization was set up specifically to exercise a stranglehold over the South African wine industry, which it did with brutal efficiency until the 1990s. In many ways, it represented an outline of the European regulatory authorities, in that it declared what could be planted where, how much of it could be produced, and what the growers could sell it for. It worked, but at the cost of steamrollering diversity. For many years, the only wines seen in export markets were from the KWV.

Excess production, where it wasn't distilled into brandy, was often fortified to produce a range of wines – some resembling port, others madeira – that became minor Cape specialities. The table wines were generally thin and acidic, the whites based on the Cape's number one variety, Chenin Blanc, the reds on Cinsault.

The next calamity was entirely self-inflicted. Ruthless imposition of racial segregation during the apartheid era prompted a worldwide trade boycott of South African goods. Wines that had been only a minority percentage of the market anyway now basically failed to sell, their cause not at all helped by the fact that those consumers who were prepared to try them were regaled with an unrelieved diet of the KWV's insipid slosh.

With the political settlement of 1994 came the long-awaited denuding of the powers of the KWV. Small private growers began to plant the varieties they chose, inward investment started to flow, and in a few short years, South Africa has moved in among the other southern hemisphere giants and ruffled a few feathers. Complex varietal wines made from a broad canvas of grapes have achieved luminous intensity in a breathlessly short time, and there is a generation of sensational sparkling wines able to compete with the best from any continent.

The rather baggy appellation system that South Africa inaugurated in 1973 has gradually been honed into a fitter state of precision in recent years. The basic designation is Wine of Origin (WO), which is subdivided into progressively more defined areas. Geographical Units are the largest and least meaningful, but are divided further into Regions, then Districts, then Wards. Only the last really resemble the demarcations of the French AOP system, with appellations such as Elgin being identified for their specific *terroirs*. Wines labelled by grape variety must contain at least 85 per cent of that variety, and vintage-dated wines must be composed of at least 85 per cent of that year's wine. All this is encouraging.

*Harvesting Sauvignon grapes at Klein Constantia (above), in the Cape.*

*The manor house at Klein Constantia (below), the smallest of the three producers that make up the small, yet famous, Constantia wine region.*

*Looking out across the stunning Paarl region from Fairview Estate (above). Paarl produces the full range of South African wine styles.*

## THE GRAPES

In a country whose climate is so propitious for the production of concentrated, rich red wines, it may comes as a surprise to learn that no less than 82 per cent of the vineyard was planted with white varieties as recently as the late 1990s. That picture rapidly changed over the following decade, as the Cape began to win plaudits for its Bordeaux-style blends and Shiraz, and there is now virtual parity between reds and whites.

Chief among the whites is Steen (what most of the rest of the world, and now many of the winemakers themselves, know as Chenin Blanc). It is encouraged to perform to the full range of its versatility here, just as it does in France's Touraine. Its repertoire ranges from almost excruciatingly sharp, young dry wines, through fuller, richer, more substantial wines that have some of the palate profile of unoaked Chardonnay, to the ever-popular off-dry idiom (like demi-sec Vouvray) at which the grape excels, and all the way up to honeyed, liquorous dessert wines made from grapes picked after the main harvest.

Colombard, a French import from the Cognac region, was traditionally important in South Africa's brandy industry too, and is often used to make light dry whites. As a varietal, however, it has little character other than a waxy, sweetcorny coarseness not designed to endear it to the Chardonnay set.

Chardonnay itself is spreading like wildfire, as – just ahead of it – is Sauvignon Blanc, which, in some of the cooler areas, is turning out some superbly complex, smoky Loire-style wines. These are among the country's best white wines, increasingly showing better balance than the Loire's traditional main rivals in New Zealand. Riesling (once labelled as Weisser Riesling to distinguish it from a dreadful French variety, Crouchen, which had inappropriately become known as Cape Riesling) makes decent, lime-scented dry wines and some sweeties. Both of the two main Muscats are used for producing sweet and fortified wines and, promisingly, some growers are achieving highly impressive results with Gewürztraminer, especially in the Paarl region.

As to red grapes, Cabernet Sauvignon has come on in leaps and bounds. For a while, South Africa was burdened with rather inferior clones of Cabernet, meaning that its varietal wines from that grape often tasted oddly weedy, unclean and rubbery, but better clonal selection has now transformed it. It is often blended Bordeaux-style with Cabernet Franc and Merlot. Merlot itself is making some gorgeously intense, plummy reds on its own. Shiraz is coming up on the inside track, a real contender to match some of the pedigree Shiraz of Australia, and there are increasing quantities of quality Pinot Noir. Smatterings of Gamay and Zinfandel may produce interesting reds in time.

South Africa's equivalent of California's Zinfandel, a red grape it can call its own, is Pinotage, a crossing of the once ubiquitous Cinsault with Pinot Noir. If that sounds like a rather clumsily arranged marriage, many would agree. There are a number of Pinotage styles: simple rosés, light Beaujolais-like reds, and deeper, often barrel-aged versions. The uncomfortable truth is that the vast majority of it is unpleasantly coarse and ugly wine, with a

waft of burning rubber coming off it and a crude metallic aftertaste. At best, the lighter versions have a fruit flavour of little pippy berries like cranberries or redcurrants. Made in the more lavish idiom, from the better producers, it can be almost Rhône-like, with lush raspberry fruit and sinewy density of texture, reflecting one half at least of its parentage.

The Cape pantheon of red grapes also includes a French variety long since abandoned in its homeland. Pontac, named after one of the more illustrious families in Bordeaux history, is actually rather a rustic grape. Left to its own devices, it doesn't amount to much, but it was one of the minor components of Constantia, and is still grown on part of the old estate in readiness to play a role in the wine's resurgence.

*Vergelegen's highly functional* cuvier *(below) in Stellenbosch, where viticulture dates right back to the Dutch colonists' arrival in the 17th century.*

*Immaculate vineyard rows at Klein Genot wine estate in Franschhoek (below), a quality WO within the Paarl region.*

## THE REGIONS

Most of South Africa's wine regions are located in the southwest of the country, where the vineyards benefit to greater and lesser degrees from the cooling maritime influences of both the Atlantic and Indian Oceans. Most of the interior is too hot for successful viticulture, although there are some recently established vineyards around the Orange River in the centre of the country. Although winters are usually damp and windy, the growing season is characterized by prolonged hot and arid weather conditions. Irrigation is routinely practised in most Cape vineyards, albeit not quite to the extent that South American growers have to resort to.

The following guide to the regions moves anti-clockwise around the Cape.

**Olifants River** Primarily a source of bulk wine for distillation, the mountainous Olifants River area is home to several of the major Cape cooperative producers. The biggest of these, Vredendal, is actually one of the better practitioners, with some appetizing Chardonnays and Sauvignons. Its Goiya Kgeisje is an early-bottled, fruity-fresh Sauvignon-based white, its flavours presenting considerably less of a challenge to European tongues than its name. Sweet Muscat wines are locally popular. Red wine production is only a marginal activity, though Vredendal does a Cabernet Franc.

**Swartland** The blackish scrubland of this large, mostly very hot region gives the area its name ('black land'). Notwithstanding the heat, Sauvignon Blanc is curiously one of its best varietals, as in the smoky, nettly Reuilly or Quincy lookalike from the Swartland cooperative, for example. Pinotage does well, achieving some of its more concentrated wines here. A measure of how promising this sort of climatic context is for thick-skinned red varieties that can take more ripening than most is the success of Tinta Barocca. One of the mainstay grapes of port production, it makes an intriguing, plums-and-pepper varietal at the Allesverloren estate.

**Paarl** With Stellenbosch, this is one of the Cape regions that made early headlines in the export trade. It is where the once all-powerful KWV is based, and still represents the epicentre of the whole South African wine enterprise. One of the hotter regions as a result of lying completely inland, Paarl nonetheless produces the full range of South African wine styles, from crisp, light dry whites and sparklers to full, long-lived reds and excellent fortified wines, as well as some of the country's premium brandies.

All of the major varietals are made in Paarl. The Nederburg estate is one of the largest private producers, making some succulent Chardonnay and minty, chocolatey Cabernet Sauvignon. Fairview Estate is representative of the modern South African outlook, making an impressively diverse range of top varietals. These include enterprising reds such as peppery Mourvèdre and Petit Verdot, steely Chenin Blanc, peachy Viognier, and a particularly well-crafted Riesling, which often comes close to the fullness and weight of Alsace versions.

Villiera does good perfumed Gewürz, as well as sensationally intense Sauvignon (often with as much exuberant fruit as New Zealand growers typically obtain), while Backsberg makes creditable Chardonnay and Merlot. The Glen Carlou estate is notable for one of the Cape's best Pinot Noirs to date, with a headily perfumed Turkish Delight quality, as well as persuasively Burgundian Chardonnay.

In the southeast of the region is a valley enclave called **Franschhoek** (meaning 'French corner', after its original settlers). Many of Paarl's best wines come from here. High flyers so far have been Dieu Donné, whose superb Chardonnay is in the buttered-green-bean Côte de Beaune mode, La Motte with its brambly Shiraz, and the excellent Boekenhoutskloof, which has superlative premium bottlings of Cabernet, Syrah and Semillon, as well as an affordable mid-priced range called Porcupine Ridge. Clos Cabrière is a specialist in traditional-method fizz.

*Meerlust Estate in Stellenbosch (left), with the Helderberg mountain beyond.*

*Modern equipment and new oak barrels (above) at Klein Constantia.*

The KWV still makes its sherry-style fortifieds in Paarl, maturing the dry ones under a *flor*-style yeast layer and putting them through a *solera* system. Its portfolio doesn't stop at wine, however, but goes on to encompass several spirits, as well as the once popular Van der Hum, a kind of South African Grand Marnier whose name translates as something like 'Whatshisname'.

**Durbanville** Like many another small vineyard region that lies in the shadow of a major city, Durbanville's existence is being threatened by the urban expansion of Cape Town. It hasn't consequently played a significant role in South Africa's wine renaissance.

**Constantia** The old, sprawling estate where South Africa's historically greatest wines were made was initially broken up and divided among three proprietors, the largest of them – Groot Constantia – state-owned. Constantia went on to be considered a WO in its own right, though, and there are currently nine wineries based here. Of the privately owned estates, Steenberg has wonderfully edgy Sauvignon and luxurious, intense Merlot, while the smallest of them all, Klein Constantia, has so far proved itself the most visionary. As well as producing splendid modern varietals in the shape of Sauvignon and Chardonnay (together with an improving Bordeaux-blend red), it has been the first to make a serious attempt to revive the fortified Constantia of blessed memory, rechristened Vin de Constance. Recent efforts have been little short of sensational.

**Stellenbosch** Viticulture in the coastal Stellenbosch region, south of Paarl, dates back to the first generation of Dutch colonists. Today, it is home to more of South Africa's first-division wine estates than any other district. Benefiting from their proximity to the ocean, the vineyards of Stellenbosch regularly produce the best-balanced red wines of the Cape. At the heart of the region is the headquarters of the Republic's principal viticultural research institute.

Blended reds, often using all three main Bordeaux varieties are very often a better bet than varietal Cabernet. Warwick Farm's Trilogy is a fine blend, as are the sumptuous Rubicon from Meerlust, Paul Sauer from Kanonkop, and the sleek, sublime Faithful Hound from Mulderbosch.

Kanonkop also makes one of the more charming Pinotages. Neethlingshof is an enterprising producer, making an aromatic Alsace Gewürztraminer varietal, as well as an expressive late-picked Riesling, Maria.

Sauvignon Blanc from the Uitkyk estate is impressive, while Thelema has won plaudits for its rounded, golden Chardonnay and a seductively silky Merlot of great power and presence. Avontuur's Reserve is one of the more ripely concentrated Cabernets. Mulderbosch's Sauvignons are packed with varietal intensity – either oak-fermented or *au naturel* – and the Chenin Blanc has pleasing density of texture as well as aromatic lift. Stellenzicht makes a coffee-scented oaked Syrah, plus some luscious dessert wines, including a botrytized Riesling labelled Noble Late Harvest.

OTHER PRODUCERS: Beyerskloof, Grangehurst, Jordan, Rustenberg, Vergelegen, Simonsig, De Trafford.

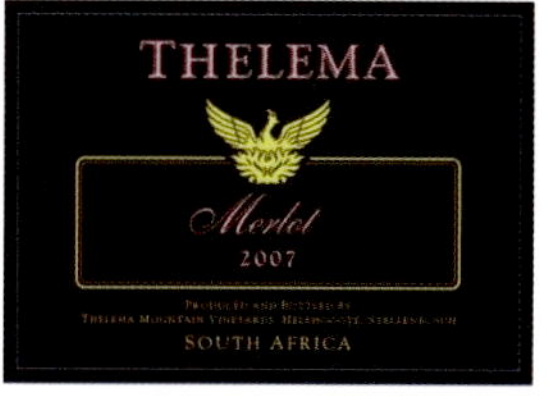

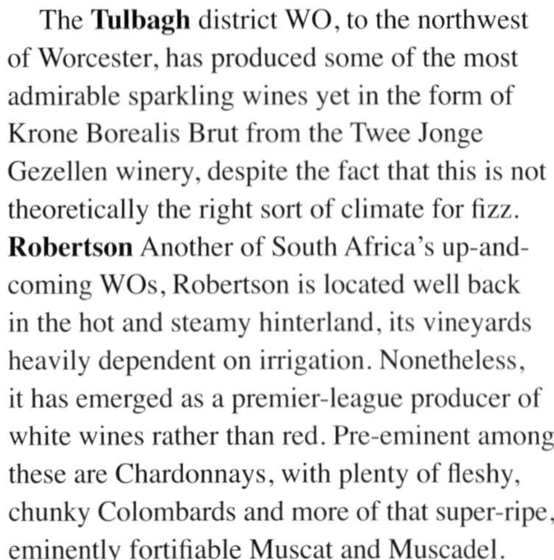

*Barrel cellar of Graham Beck Winery in the Robertson region (above), renowned for its Madeba Sauvignons.*

**Elgin** One of South Africa's newer regions, following the recent trend for planting vineyards at higher altitude in order to benefit from cooler growing conditions, the WO ward of Elgin is turning out to be a good source of varietals from northern French grapes such as Sauvignon, Chenin and especially Pinot Noir. Stellenbosch producer Neil Ellis has the best wines so far, including a thoroughly elegant Chardonnay.

**Walker Bay** Further east along the coast, near the town of Hermanus, Walker Bay stole a march on Elgin in the competition to produce cool-climate varietals, with many wines of great subtlety. Chardonnay and Pinot Noir are both looking good, and one of the larger Burgundy houses entered into a joint-venture here, Bouchard-Finlayson, to bring a little piece of the Côte d'Or to the Cape. Their wines, as well as those of Hamilton-Russell, show what can be done. Not all the vintages have been spot-on, but the potential is indisputable. Bouchard-Finlayson also makes a clean, snappy Sauvignon. The Wildekrans estate weighs in with some typically cranberryish Pinotage.

**Worcester** The Worcester and Tulbagh WOs lie well inland, northeast of Paarl, and are largely occupied by volume-producing cooperatives making old-fashioned fortifieds. The Muscat and Muscadel varieties (the latter may be red or white) are responsible for producing sweet wines in a number of styles. Jerepigo is made either from red or white Muscadel, the production similar to that used in Moscatel de Valencia. Intensely sweet, fresh grape juice is fortified with the addition of grape spirit before it has had a chance to ferment, resulting in a not unexpectedly grapy sweet wine at around 17 per cent alcohol. The whites are lightly refreshing, the reds more seriously blood-warming.

The **Tulbagh** district WO, to the northwest of Worcester, has produced some of the most admirable sparkling wines yet in the form of Krone Borealis Brut from the Twee Jonge Gezellen winery, despite the fact that this is not theoretically the right sort of climate for fizz.

**Robertson** Another of South Africa's up-and-coming WOs, Robertson is located well back in the hot and steamy hinterland, its vineyards heavily dependent on irrigation. Nonetheless, it has emerged as a premier-league producer of white wines rather than red. Pre-eminent among these are Chardonnays, with plenty of fleshy, chunky Colombards and more of that super-ripe, eminently fortifiable Muscat and Muscadel.

De Wetshof is leader of the pack for Chardonnay, its Danie de Wet *cuvées* aged on their lees to produce an indulgently rich, buttercream style with powerful appeal. Van Loveren's are almost as good. Sauvignons from this region are now exhibiting plenty of lush tropical fruit, replete with convincing gooseberry character from the Springfield and Graham Beck estates. Beck also makes fine unoaked Chardonnay called Waterside, and one of the region's more conspicuously successful sparklers. Among reds to look out for are the full-blooded Shirazes of the Zandvliet estate, and Springfield's Bordeaux blends and varietal Cabernets. Bon Courage makes fine dessert wines.

**Klein Karoo** Sprawling landlocked region where fortified Muscadels are best suited to the indomitable heat, though a few producers are chancing their arms with dry varietal table wines. Sauvignon Blanc may be the best bet.

**Mossel Bay** Like Walker Bay and Elgin, this easterly coastal area is a relatively new wine region, located to benefit from the ameliorating sea breezes, in this case blowing in from the Indian Ocean. Cool-climate varieties are what the growers have put their faith in, with Pinot Noir at the pinnacle of ambition as usual, supplemented by Riesling and Sauvignon Blanc. Given time to find a foothold, the wines should be excellent.

**Orange River** To the west of the landlocked state of Lesotho, the Orange River region is South Africa's climatically fiercest wine area, its riverside vineyards further from maritime influence than any on the Cape itself. Volume production is the chief activity; since the vines have to be so intensively irrigated, the amount of fruit they bear is correspondingly far too high for true quality.

## SPARKLING WINES

So important had South Africa's current generation of sparkling wines become by the 1990s that a new country-wide term, Méthode Cap Classique (MCC), was instituted to classify the best. It denotes any sparkler produced using the traditional secondary bottle fermentation method of champagne.

Many of these quality sparklers are made from the classic blend of Chardonny and Pinot Noir, while others may have a dash of Loire-like Chenin and even Sauvignon Blanc in them, but the overall quality is frankly breathtaking. Indeed, these may well be, along with those of southern England, the best such wines made anywhere outside Champagne itself. Given that the traditional method only started being used to any significant degree in South Africa in the 1980s, the progress is all the more astonishing.

Although fizz is made in many different WOs, including some of the warmer districts of Stellenbosch, the wines retain good crisp acidity and freshness in their youth. What has been so striking about many of the releases, however, is the yeast autolysis characters they display. Autolysis is the name for the biochemical interchange that takes place within the wine as it undergoes its second fermentation in the bottle. As the active yeasts die off, the dead cells impart a distinctive aroma and flavour to

*Pressing Chardonnay grapes (above) destined for the Cap Classique sparkler, Madeba Brut, at Graham Beck Winery in Robertson.*

the wine, a kind of toasty, wheatgrain character reminiscent of freshly baked bread. The more pronounced it is, the longer the wine must have spent maturing on its lees before being disgorged, and there is no surer sign that a sparkling wine producer means business than prolonged maturation of its wines.

That said, some of the wineries are now finding themselves tempted to release their wines too young to cope with the growing demand. This is a shame, but not exactly unknown of course within the Champagne region itself. Rosés could generally do with a little more fruit, but some are beginning to appear in a reasonably attractive, elegant style. Vintage-dated wines will in time be the classiest of all.

PRODUCERS: Twee Jonge Gezellen (Krone Borealis Brut), Cabrière Estates (Pierre Jourdan Brut and Blanc de Blancs), Bergkelder (Pongracz), Graham Beck (Graham Beck Brut), Simonsig (Kaapse Vonkel), Bon Courage (Jacques Bruére Brut Reserve), Steenberg (MCC Brut 1682), Villiera (Tradition Brut), Boschendal (Grande Cuvée Brut).

*This gleaming white, intricately gabled façade (left) belongs to the manor house of the Boschendal estate in Franschhoek, Paarl.*

# AUSTRALIA

*Leaders in the triumphal march of the varietal movement, Australia's winemakers have taken Chardonnay and Cabernet Sauvignon, added Shiraz to the list, and recreated them in styles all of their own.*

*Australia's vineyards run in a swathe across the southeast of the continent, as well as popping up in enclaves in Western Australia and on the island of Tasmania.*

OF ALL THE NEWER, non-European winemaking countries, Australia is the least in thrall to European ways of doing things. Its wine industry is scarcely any older than that of the USA, and quite considerably younger than South Africa's. (Some of the earliest imported vine cuttings came from the Cape.) The country had no wild vines, and so its industry didn't – unlike California's – have to go through the painful process of ridding itself of hybrid varieties. The slate it started with was blank and clean.

Barring the odd sighting of rough-and-ready fortified wines (mostly imitations of port), Australian wines were virtually unheard-of in the northern hemisphere as recently as the early 1980s. The first experimental cuttings of Chardonnay and Cabernet were only just going into the Australian dirt in the 1970s, when California's best were already winning prizes in French tastings. How, then, did Australian wine go from a tentative trickle to an almighty Eureka-style gush within one decade?

It was all a question of style. Winemakers in the Barossa and Hunter Valleys, in the Adelaide Hills and Victoria, taught the non-specialist wine consumer varietal recognition by making the wines thus labelled so easy to love. They removed the red-hot, mouth-furring tannins from Cabernet, and the razor-like acidity from a lot of traditional Chardonnay, and marinated them both in the sweet vanillin of brand new oak, and the world came running.

What helped to fuel this recipe for success was the wine-show system in Australia. All the country's wine-producing states regularly hold their own regional competitions, the results of which – rather like the UK's International Wine and Spirit Competition – have a galvanizing effect on the sales of wines that win medals. Many producers were driven by the competition phenomenon to craft wines made in a big, brash, love-me-or-leave-me style that would enable them to stand out in a lineup of their stylistic rivals.

These wines not only impacted on the show judges; they also exercised a siren-like allure for British and American retail buyers. By the early 1990s, nearly every bottle of Australian wine you opened tasted sweetly overripe, the over-maturity of the grapes accentuated by a lathering of oaky richness, all building up on the palate to an alcohol blast at the end that was like being punched in the head.

Along with the eggyolk-yellow Chardonnays came a raft of Cabernets, Shirazes, and blends thereof. These were red wines that had none of the harsh tannin or volatile sourness of French or Italian reds and, as such, they won over many of those who didn't think they liked red wine at all. Some of these wines were stunning in their depth of fruit and genuine complexity, but an awful lot of the others (mainly unblended Shiraz) tasted like overboiled jam, with gummy, cloying texture and a synthetic, un-winey aftertaste.

There were sparkling wines that tasted of ripe summer fruits, mango-scented whites and strawberry-perfumed rosés, selling for as little as a third the price of non-vintage champagne, for all that they weren't necessarily made by the traditional method and might be more likely to contain Semillon and Shiraz than Chardonnay or Pinot Noir. In time, these would be followed by more genuinely sophisticated fizz.

Behind them came a phalanx of fortified wines, Liqueur Muscats unlike any other *vins de liqueur* on earth, headily redolent of crystallized tangerine and creamy milk chocolate. It all added up to a non-stop scattergun strategy, and it worked like a dream.

The result of Australia-mania has been that the country is unable by quite some distance to supply the worldwide demand for its wines. They may still turn up their noses at them in continental Europe, but American and (especially) British consumers can't get enough of them – literally.

At present, in my view, the Australian wine industry is a great unanswered question. It established a solid bridgehead for itself into the global wine village more quickly and decisively than was achieved by any other emergent nation in wine history. The question is: which way does it go now? There is a tidal wave of crude-tasting, cheap Australian varietal wine on the world markets. They may have taken the oak out of the Chardonnay, but it still tastes sweet. Most Pinot Noirs remain maladroit offerings with hardly an iota of the elegance cool-climate New Zealand has achieved. Cheap Shiraz can be one of the unwisest ways of spending your money when you're dropping into the wine-shop for a simple hearty red to go with tonight's dinner.

*Opening the vintage (above) at the annual Barossa Festival, in South Australia.*

*Morning sunlight over the northern slopes of the Great Dividing Range (below), in Victoria.*

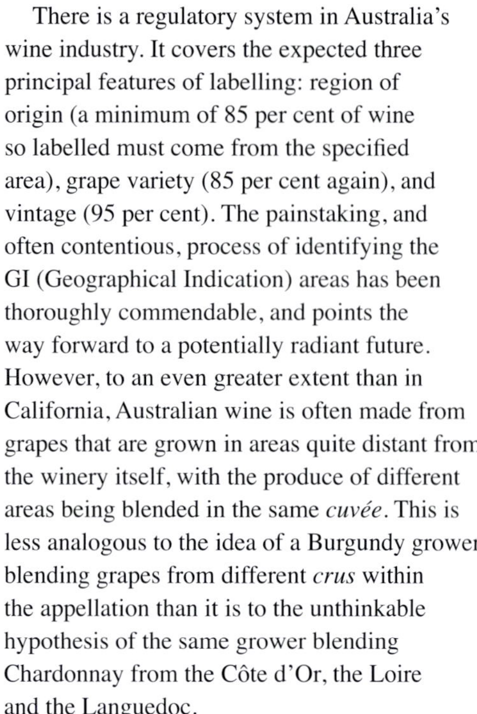

*Margaret River (above) is one of Australia's cooler wine-growing regions.*

Australia is hardly short of outstanding producers, from the pioneering Penfolds wines to the most talented growers in the Clare Valley and Margaret River GIs. These wines are worth the extra outlay, but they are being outshouted for the time being by the lowest-common-denominator stuff, all those boring branded wines with which your local supermarket shelves will reliably be groaning.

Most of Australia's regions experience reliably hot, dry growing conditions year on year. Within the overall pattern, however, there are cooler pockets where more temperate summers have a consequent effect on wine styles. They include the Margaret River GI of Western Australia, inland regions such as the Clare and Eden Valleys in South Australia, and much of Tasmania. By contrast, the vineyards of New South Wales and Queensland, being that much nearer the Equator, have a correspondingly fiercer climate to contend with, in which the spring can bring virtual drought while the harvest season suffers torrential rains.

The vineyards are strung throughout a swathe of southeast Australia, from north of Adelaide in the state of South Australia, through Victoria and up to the Hunter Valley, north of Sydney. There is a small outpost on a high plateau called the Granite Belt just into Queensland, as well as small but important plantings in the state of Western Australia. The cool-climate island of Tasmania, in the Tasman Sea south of Victoria, has isolated vineyards, mainly on its northern edge.

There is a regulatory system in Australia's wine industry. It covers the expected three principal features of labelling: region of origin (a minimum of 85 per cent of wine so labelled must come from the specified area), grape variety (85 per cent again), and vintage (95 per cent). The painstaking, and often contentious, process of identifying the GI (Geographical Indication) areas has been thoroughly commendable, and points the way forward to a potentially radiant future. However, to an even greater extent than in California, Australian wine is often made from grapes that are grown in areas quite distant from the winery itself, with the produce of different areas being blended in the same *cuvée*. This is less analogous to the idea of a Burgundy grower blending grapes from different *crus* within the appellation than it is to the unthinkable hypothesis of the same grower blending Chardonnay from the Côte d'Or, the Loire and the Languedoc.

## THE GRAPES

Australia's premium white grape varieties are led by Chardonnay, planted more or less wherever vines are grown. At its ripest, it produces the broad-beamed, sunny, golden wines the world has come to adore, but experiments with producing a leaner, more delicately complex style are likely to be the best. Subtle variations of style are as much to do with the vinification regimes of individual winemakers as they are of sites chosen. Some Chardonnay is kept back for blending as a crowd-pleasing component with other grapes such as Semillon and Colombard.

After Chardonnay comes Semillon, which gives a fatter, riper wine here than in Europe. In its dry, unoaked and unblended guise, this is very much an Australian original. Always popular at home, it has had to be patient in awaiting international consumer recognition, but these are definitely wines worth getting to know. Sauvignon Blanc is occasionally blended with Semillon, as in Bordeaux, but is more often seen on its own. It is a grape that many winemakers are only just learning how to handle, earlier examples often suffering from a lack of clarity or inappropriate excessive oaking.

Riesling is many ways the backbone of fine white wine production, and is particularly important in South Australia. Its fruit may be more plangently citric even than in dry Alsace

Riesling, and its acidity much less of a shock to the tastebuds, but the wines are quite as capable of developing interestingly in the bottle.

Other classic white grapes planted in small quantities include Gewürztraminer, the Rhône grapes Viognier and Marsanne (both of which have done well), and Chenin Blanc.

Less illustriously, there are widespread plantings in the irrigated Murray River region of South Australia of an indifferent white variety called Sultana. As its name implies, much of it ends up being processed as dried grapes, but a lot is still used for wine, often the bulk output of bag-in-box wines that accounts for an important proportion of the domestic market. Muscat of Alexandria, which goes under the local name of Muscat Gordo Blanco, also plays a role in volume production, and is not an ingredient of the premium Liqueur Muscats. Colombard is grown too, but on nothing like the scale that it appears in South Africa.

Chief among reds is Shiraz (the Syrah of the northern Rhône), another grape that Australia fashioned in its own image. The reds of the northern Rhône are varietal Syrahs too of course, but the southern-hemisphere style is hugely rich, creamy and blackberryish, with little or none of the black-pepper rasp or sharp tannins of young Rhône wines. At its least sensitively vinified, Shiraz turns out roaringly alcoholic wines (14.5 per cent is nothing) with a blurred, stewed flavour like cheap jam, the sweetness of which is then made the more repellent with oak (or oak-chip) treatment. At its best, it produces wines of monumental, unforgettable intensity, inky concentration, and a whole range of fruit and exotic spice notes.

Shiraz is frequently blended with Cabernet Sauvignon, generally forming the greater element in the mix. The effect can be to stiffen the sinew of the otherwise soft-centred ripe Shiraz, or to mitigate some of young Cabernet's severity where Shiraz is the junior partner. Cabernet is also valued as a varietal in its own right, though, and can offer incontrovertible evidence to those sceptical of the wine-taster's vocabulary that Cabernet Sauvignon really can taste intensely of blackcurrants.

Increasingly, where Cabernet is blended, it is with its traditional claret bedfellows, Merlot and Cabernet Franc (with dashes of Petit Verdot here and there). Merlot is now the third most widely planted red grape, one consequence of which in the future may well be more varietal

Merlot, not hitherto – and unusually in the southern hemisphere – one of the Australian industry's specialities.

Grenache looked until recently as if it might be doomed to die out as a humdrum variety used to bulk everyday reds. A wave of wines made according to the southern Rhône recipe, from Grenache, Shiraz and Mourvèdre (the last often known as Mataro), and styled as GSM blends, has pinpointed the potential of the perennially underrated Grenache.

Pinot Noir is gradually getting better. Much of what's grown goes into premium bottle-fermented sparkling wines conceived in the champagne image, but there are doughty souls, as there are wherever quality red wine is made, determined to make world-class red varietal Pinot. The first signs of modest success are with us, as suitable sites are identified for the famously unforgiving grape.

Minority red grapes include Tarrango, a crossing of white Sultana with the port grape Touriga Nacional (vinified by some in the style of a slightly more muscular north Italian red), and Italy's Nebbiolo and Sangiovese. A grape called Cienna, crossed from a minor Spanish variety with Cabernet Sauvignon, might one day set the world alight.

*The grounds of St Hallett's in the Barossa Valley (below), where 100-year-old Shiraz vines still yield fabulous wines.*

Red gum trees in Western
Australia (above) flower
at grape-harvest time,
distracting birds from
eating the grapes.

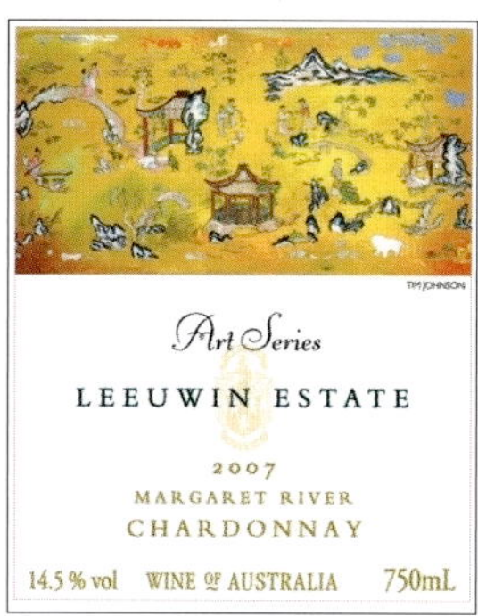

Western Australia's vineyards
lie at the southwestern tip of
the state (right), with the top
producers clustered in the
Margaret River region close
to the Indian Ocean.

## WESTERN AUSTRALIA

**Swan District** One of the very hottest regions
in a hot country, this GI in the Swan Valley
was once the main growing area of Western
Australia. For a while, it went into decline as a
result of the identification of cooler sites further
south, but is now re-emerging as a producer
of well-defined varietal wines. The Houghton
winery makes a range of good generic wines
here, together with improbable varietals bottled
under the Moondah Brook label, such as Chenin
Blanc and Verdelho (the latter one of the white
grapes of Madeira).
OTHER PRODUCERS: Sandalford, Lamont, Faber.

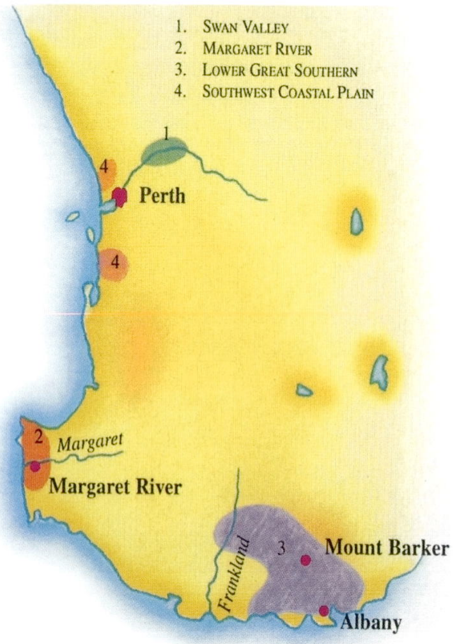


**Margaret River** One of the great talking-points
of Australian wine lately, the milder climate of
the Margaret River GI has led to the production
of some intriguing wines in a considerably less
upfront style than is traditionally associated
with Australia. Cooling breezes off the Indian
Ocean exert a moderating influence here, in a
country that doesn't generally receive the same
maritime amelioration that, say, South Africa
or the western US states do. Consequently, the
Margaret River's Chardonnays have an almost
Burgundian profile, and may require much
less acid adjustment than those from South
Australia, while the Cabernets are leaner
and more closed in their youth. Sauvignons
are briskly fresh and herbaceous, while the
Semillons are crisp but healthily rounded.

Cullens is one of Margaret River's best
estates, making nutty, savoury Chardonnay in
a restrained style. Moss Wood makes a slightly
richer version which, in some vintages, has the
unmistakable waft of buttered leeks familiar to
lovers of Puligny-Montrachet. Cullens also makes
a benchmark toasty Semillon without oak as
well as impressive Pinot Noir. Cape Mentelle,
the winery that founded the much-lauded
Cloudy Bay in New Zealand, has its Australian
base in this district, where it produces an apple-
and-melon blend of Semillon and Sauvignon,
and even has some plantings of Zinfandel.

Leeuwin Estate is one of the most ambitious
wineries in all of Australia. Its expensive but
indisputably brilliant Chardonnay is an object-
lesson to others. A varietally intense Cabernet
and pin-sharp, citrus-soaked Riesling show its
versatile abilities to the full. The long-established
Vasse Felix winery's Shiraz is plump and rich,
without slumping into jamminess.
OTHER PRODUCERS: Houghton, Pierro, Brookland
Valley, Voyager, Devil's Lair, Woodlands.

**Great Southern** Western Australia's largest
wine area is situated a little to the east of the
Margaret River. In the GIs of **Mount Barker**,
**Frankland River**, **Albany**, **Denmark** and
**Porongurup**, it is beginning to fulfil its early
promise quite emphatically. An entire range
of grapes succeeds here, including the finicky
Pinot and Sauvignon. The potential for
Rieslings in particular is extremely exciting.

A Mount Barker winery, Plantagenet, does all
sorts of things well, including a meaty Cabernet
to age, tropically juicy Riesling and lemon-
butter Chardonnay. Goundrey, also in Mount
Barker, has raised some eyebrows with its

good-value bottlings of creamy Chardonnay and cassis-scented Cabernet. Another sharply focused, lime-zesty Riesling is made by the Howard Park winery.

OTHER PRODUCERS: Harewood, Houghton, West Cape Howe, Castle Rock.

## SOUTH AUSTRALIA

The most copious wine-producing state of Australia is home to many internationally famous wineries. Its vineyard regions are fairly widely scattered throughout the southeast of the state, with the result that pronounced differences between them can actually be tasted in the glass. In the southern district of Coonawarra, South Australia boasts one of the most distinctive growing regions anywhere in the southern hemisphere. Almost every major variety performs well, and botrytized dessert wines – from Semillon and Riesling – have become a notable South Australia speciality.

**Clare Valley** One of the cooler growing regions, Clare consists of four interconnected valleys – the Clare, Skillogalee, Watervale and Polish River. The premium varietal here has to be Riesling, which achieves diamond-bright, intensely defined lime-juice and petrol characteristics from the best growers. Semillon is good too, in the austere, minerally, unwooded style, Viognier is elegantly aromatic, while Chardonnay can be a little on the shy and retiring side, unusual in Australia. Reds are lean as well, often with pronounced tannins and acidity, but for that reason do perform well if bottle-aged.

Tim Knappstein's Rieslings are indicative of the Clare style – smoky, full-bodied and zesty, and ageing to a delicious pungency. His Cabernet is good too. Skillogalee and Pikes are textbook Riesling specialists (the latter also makes a first-division Chardonnay). Another Tim, Tim Adams, makes spectacularly concentrated Semillon and deep, long-lived Shiraz. The Jim Barry winery attracts followers for its crisp Rieslings and Sauvignons, as well as a hauntingly aromatic Shiraz labelled Armagh. The Leasingham label, owned by the Constellation Wines conglomerate, is a good source of simple Clare varietals, including a ripely blackcurrant Shiraz.

OTHER PRODUCERS: Petaluma, Mount Horrocks, Wendouree, Grosset.

**Riverland** The backwash area of South Australia, making bulk wine for the bargain end of the market, is located on heavily irrigated vineyard land along the Murray River. Plantings of the more mundane varieties are concentrated here.

Among the better wines, Yalumba's Oxford Landing range is sourced from here, and includes a commendable GSM blend, a juicy Cabernet rosé, and an unexpectedly crisp Sauvignon. Angove is a decent volume producer, whose wines often appear under supermarket own-brands. Banrock Station is another widely seen Riverland wine brand. A substantial portion of Riverland production goes into wine-boxes, by no means of unacceptable quality, but best glugged back round the barbie.

*A springtime scene (above) in the Polish Hill area of South Australia's Clare Valley, home to fine whites.*

*Penfolds' space-age
Nuriootpa winery (right)
in the Barossa Valley,
South Australia.*

*The most prolific wine-
producer in Australia, South
Australia's vineyards extend
across the state (below),
offering distinctively
different styles of wine.*

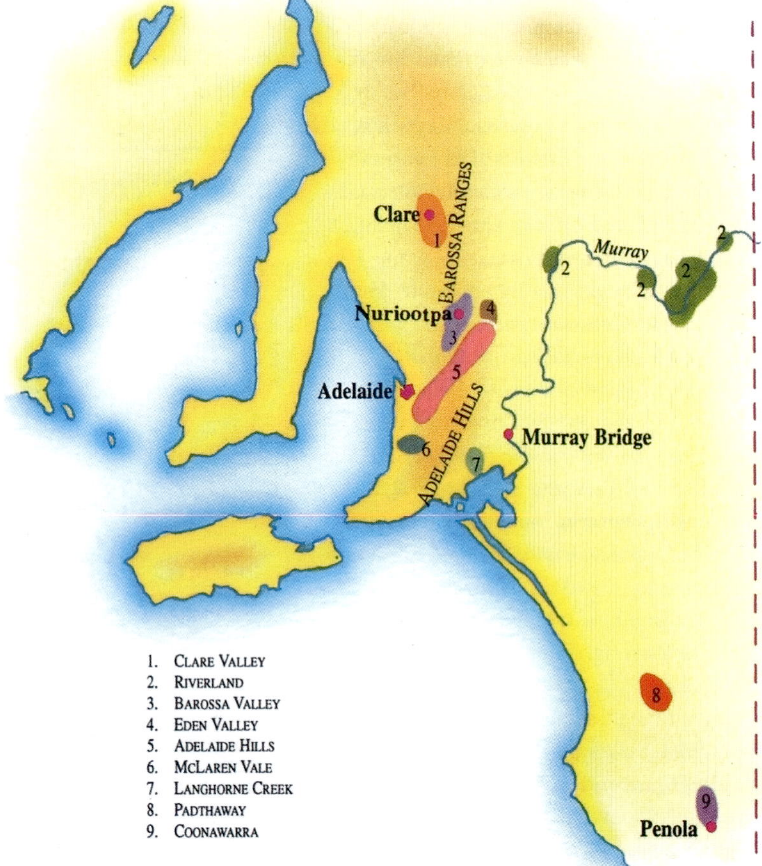


**Barossa Valley** One of the first regional names in Australian wine that overseas customers came to recognize, the hot Barossa Valley northeast of Adelaide is in many ways the epicentre of the whole industry. It was settled and planted by Germans and Poles in the 19th century, and today is where much of the harvest from neighbouring regions finds its way to be crushed. A high proportion of Barossa's wineries, therefore, are not necessarily making exclusively Barossa wine.

The bottom of the valley has the hottest microclimate, and is the source of some of Australia's most intensely coloured and alcoholic reds. Shiraz from this region attains incomparable levels of concentration, the epitome of which is Penfolds Grange, the Barossa's legendary *grand cru*. Growers in search of cooler conditions for the Rieslings and Chardonnays for which the area is equally famed have planted higher up on the valley hillsides.

Penfolds remains the pre-eminent Barossa name for a comprehensive range of varietals and blends to suit all pockets. From its simple, zesty Riesling and oak-driven, full-on Chardonnay, to its versatile and splendidly crafted reds, quality exudes from every bottle. Among the red highlights are the Bin 28 Kalimna Shiraz,

always a supple, brambly masterpiece, Bin 389 Cabernet-Shiraz, and the sensationally concentrated, ink-black Bin 707 Cabernet Sauvignon. The fabled Grange is nearly all Shiraz, a colossal yet immaculately graceful wine, full of the aromas of preserved purple fruits, soft leather and wild herbs, and capable of ageing in the bottle for decades. It isn't cheap, but it is still a fraction of the price of the Château Pétrus to which it has often been compared. Penfolds' bottlings of Coonawarra wines (see below), especially the Cabernet, are more purely indicative of the region than virtually any others.

Other large-scale operators include Orlando Wines, makers since 1976 of the best-selling Jacob's Creek range, and Seppelt, whose extraordinarily diverse portfolio takes in premium sparkling wines such as the bone-dry Salinger and trail-blazing sparkling Shiraz (think alcoholic fizzy blackcurrant cordial), together with authoritative fortifieds, among which the sherry styles stand out (see page 245).

A list of excellent smaller wineries would have to include Grant Burge (appetizingly nutty Zerk Vineyard Semillon-Viognier and a soft, plummy Hillcot Merlot), St Hallett (famous Old Block Shiraz from century-old vines), Peter Lehmann (minty, almost claret-like Stonewell Shiraz), Rockford (idiosyncratic, smooth-contoured Basket Press Shiraz) and Wolf Blass (a comprehensive range of generics, including good Gold Label Riesling).
OTHER PRODUCERS: Charles Melton, Turkey Flat, Duval, Barossa Valley Estate.

**Eden Valley** A group of high valleys in the Barossa Ranges, the Eden Valley GI is, properly speaking, a continuation of the Barossa region. It is considerably cooler than the Barossa Valley itself, though, and those gentler conditions show up in the wines, especially in the significant quantities of dry, citrically tangy Riesling the area produces.

One of the biggest names in Eden is Yalumba, which incorporates the Hill-Smith, Heggies and Pewsey Vale labels, as well as bottling under its own name. The Hill-Smith Sauvignon is an especially poignant wine, an eloquent riposte to those who claim that Australians don't understand the grape. Pewsey Vale and Heggies Rieslings both represent benchmark lemon-and-lime versions of that variety. Yalumba's own Octavius Shiraz is a triumph, a superbly complex red with a beguiling waft of coffee. The company's sparklers, such as the seriously complex Yalumba D Cuvée, and fortifieds like the chocolatey, caramelly Clocktower, are also to be reckoned with.

Henschke is another name to drop. It owns some of the oldest vineyard land for miles around, its shatteringly profound Hill of Grace Shiraz made from 100-year-old vines. Its Mount Edelstone is another top-drawer Shiraz, while Cyril Henschke is fine, concentrated Cabernet that demands ageing. The whites are good too, particularly the pungent, petrolly Julius Riesling, another one to age, and the nutty, lime-scented Louis Semillon.

*The hot, dry Barossa Valley (above) is South Australia's premier wine region.*

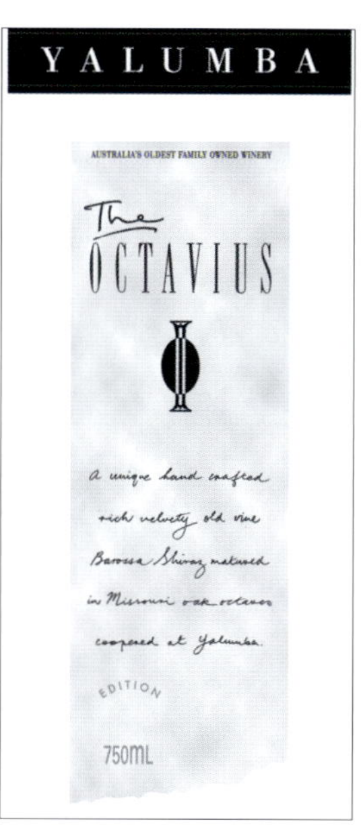

*A camel sanctuary amid the vines (below) in the flat expanse of South Australia's McLaren Vale.*

**Adelaide Hills** The hill ranges east of the city are fairly sparsely planted, but represent another favourable microclimate for growers looking for relief from South Australia's heat. Sparkling wines from here have been among the finest. Petaluma is the most widely-known name around here, although its more celebrated bottlings come from Coonawarra fruit (see below). Bridgewater Mill is its alternative label, and includes a good citrus-fresh Chardonnay. Pirramimma's Cabernet has an attractive eucalyptus note.

OTHER PRODUCERS: Nepenthe, Shaw & Smith, Geoff Weaver.

**McLaren Vale** South of Adelaide, this flat, expansive GI has carved out a regional identity for itself with wines that are increasingly being made in much subtler style than was once the case. Exquisite, richly constituted reds, including ground-breaking Shiraz-Viognier blends, are pouring forth. The climate remains a bit too baking for fully focused whites, though there are exceptions.

Chapel Hill has some superbly honed reds from Cabernet and Shiraz. Chateau Reynella makes powerhouse Basket Press Shiraz here too, under the auspices of the Constellation conglomerate. Among Cabernets, Wirra Wirra's Dead Ringer bottling exhibits all the cassis intensity looked for in South Australia, while Primo Estate's unctuous Joseph La Magia, a botrytized Riesling with a dollop of raisined Gewürztraminer, is a curvaceous charmer. Wandering winemaker Geoff Merrill is here too, making a range of good-value varietals, including a raspberryish rosé from Grenache, and some peachy Reserve Chardonnay.

OTHER PRODUCERS: Tatachilla, Clarendon Hills, SC Pannell, Fox Creek, Hardys.

**Langhorne Creek** The Langhorne Creek district is east of McLaren Vale, but shares much the same characteristics. Good reds from Cabernet and Shiraz, exotically perfumed Shiraz-Viognier blends after the northern Rhône idiom, and small but increasing quantities of dry Verdelho (one of the madeira grapes), are worth investigating.

**Padthaway** The Padthaway GI is a sort of northern outpost of the more famous Coonawarra region. Lying in the southeast corner of the state of South Australia, it is nearly as cool as its neighbour, and has a little of the prized *terra rossa* soil of Coonawarra. Whereas the latter has developed a reputation for red wines, Padthaway has become something of a white-wine enclave – specifically Chardonnay, Riesling and Sauvignon. Most of the vineyard land is owned by companies based in other areas, but who make special *cuvées* that carry the GI name on the label.

Orlando, Seppelt and Penfolds all have interests in Padthaway. Penfolds Chardonnay from the region is one of the most richly buttery, and the Lindemans Padthaway bottling is almost as powerful. Henry's Drive is an excellent producer with some sublimely aromatic Cabernet and Shiraz, and Constellation's Stonehaven is a reliable label.

**Coonawarra** Just south of Padthaway is the region that got everybody so excited about Australia in the first place. Declared a GI in 2001, Coonawarra's unique blend of cool climate and *terra rossa* soil – the paprika-coloured red loam that lends the vineyards such a striking appearance – is without doubt responsible for the obvious class of its wines.

Coonawarra's finest bottles provide the answer to that interminable rhetorical question that still fuels debates between the Old and New Worlds: does vineyard siting, or *terroir*, make a difference? Not all of Coonawarra's vines are planted on the red soil, and those that aren't do seem to lack that extra dimension of perfume and complexity boasted by those that are.

It is the reds, Shiraz and most notably Cabernet Sauvignon, that best demonstrate the regional identity, although there are some good Chardonnays and even Rieslings as well. The Cabernets are made in a positively French idiom, in that their youthful tannins can be decidedly severe, and the aromatic components stubbornly refuse at first to show themselves. When they do open out, however, there is nothing remotely French about them. They have a pronounced savoury quality, often resembling mocha coffee beans, sometimes a deliberate slight volatility like Worcestershire sauce, but underlying them is that dry, subtly spiced dark fruit, with the odd date or prune thrown in among the teeming blackcurrants.

There are more wineries actually based here than in Padthaway, but the headline-hitting wines have tended to be made by outsiders owning priceless Coonawarra land. Penfolds makes some of its most extravagantly beautiful Cabernet from grapes grown here; its range offers an obvious starting-point. Petaluma has long had a reputation for a hugely intense Cabernet-Merlot blend, simply called Petaluma Coonawarra. The high-volume Rosemount company from New South Wales has a well-made Coonawarra Show Reserve Cabernet too.

Among wineries located in the region, Hollick makes a glorious, challenging Ravenswood Cabernet, as well as a more immediately accessible Cabernet-Merlot blend and fresh, limey Riesling. Katnook Estate makes tobaccoey Cabernet and a big, fleshy Chardonnay, while Penley, a relative newcomer, produces densely textured Cabernet and a brambly, gamey Shiraz. Wynn's is a well-known name, and an ultra-reliable producer of ripe-fruited, unoaked Shiraz, smoky Chardonnay, a sweetly limey Riesling and a pitch-black, massively structured, top-of-the-range Cabernet called John Riddoch (it needs about ten years to come round). OTHER PRODUCERS: Majella, Balnaves, Brand's, Zema, Parker.

*The name that everyone recognizes as uniquely Australian (above), Coonawarra is the most southerly of South Australia's wine regions.*

*High-altitude cool vineyards of Victoria's Great Dividing Range (above), source of delicate Riesling and subtle Chardonnay.*

*From the cooler coastal areas to the hot inland regions, the smaller state of Victoria (right) produces a wide range of wine styles, including the famous liqueur Muscats made in the northeast.*

## VICTORIA

Victoria's vineyards suffered badly in the worldwide phylloxera plague (which South Australia managed to escape), but the cooler southern reaches of the state are now producing fine varietals and sparklers to compete with the best, and there are more than 500 wineries. In the northeast, Australia's celebrated fortified wines reach their apogee.

**Drumborg** Very cool western region, its main player being Seppelt, which uses grapes from here to make some attractive varietals, such as Pinot Gris and Riesling.

**Grampians/Pyrenees** These contiguous areas are further inland than Drumborg, and consequently somewhat warmer. They have a strong tradition in sparkling wines. Increasingly, though, it is becoming clear that the potential for Australia's two premier red grapes, Cabernet and Shiraz, is most exciting of all. Chardonnays tend to be fashioned in the rounded and richly oaked style.

Mount Langi Ghiran is one of the high fliers of this region, with a Shiraz in an intriguingly restrained style, and Cabernet with plenty of extract. Its Riesling has long been one of the best, and is structured for ageing. Cathcart Ridge makes a particularly lush, chocolatey Shiraz, while the Best's winery has a portfolio of cheap and cheerful varietals, including good, lemon-meringue Chardonnay.

OTHER PRODUCERS: Dalwhinnie, Summerfield, Redbank, The Story, Seppelt.

1. DRUMBORG
2. GREAT WESTERN
3. GEELONG
4. YARRA VALLEY
5. MORNINGTON PENINSULA
6. GOULBURN VALLEY
7. GLENROWAN-MILAWA
8. RUTHERGLEN
9. MURRAY RIVER
10. LAUNCESTON
11. BICHENO
12. HOBART

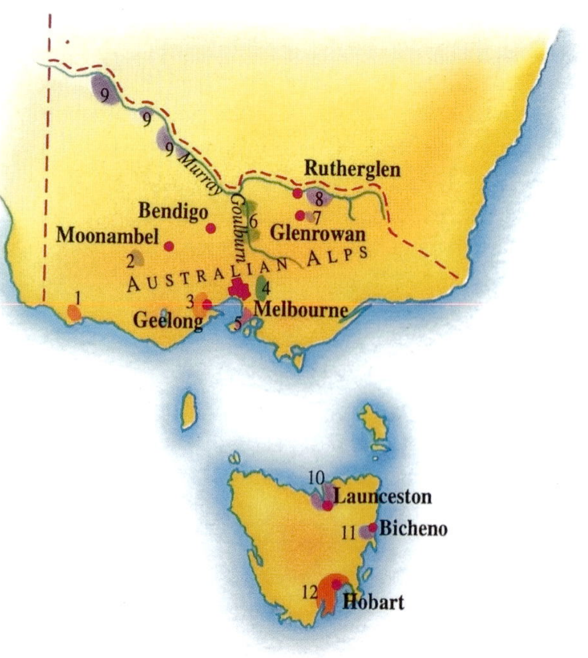

**Geelong** First of a ring of small regions surrounding Melbourne (Geelong is just west of the city), which are home to some of the more far-sighted and ambitious of Australia's current generation of winemakers. Bannockburn has a brilliant range of authentically Burgundian Chardonnays and Pinot Noirs, and nor does the Cabernet lack for anything in varietal richness. By Farr is a punning label for the Farr family's breathtaking Pinot Noirs and Shirazes.

**Yarra Valley** The temperate Yarra is Victoria's answer to South Australia's Coonawarra, a prime site for highly individual winemaking and superlative cool-climate varietals. This is one of the most promising areas in Australia for Pinot Noir, with fine examples from Green Point, Coldstream Hills, Tarrawarra and Mount Mary. There was a tendency in the past to overoak the wines, which is now thankfully being resisted. Green Point (the export name for Moët's Domaine Chandon) also makes a very classy, lightly buttery, nutmeggy Chardonnay – not a million miles from the style of California's Sonoma – as well as its much-praised fizz. The Cabernets and Shirazes of Yarra Yering are idiosyncratic creations fully worth the high asking price. St Huberts makes a deep, satisfying Cabernet to last.
OTHER PRODUCERS: Diamond Valley, Yering Station, Oakridge, Carlei.

**Mornington Peninsula** This little peninsula southeast of Melbourne has seen intensive new plantings in recent years, and is now crowded with boutique wineries. Like the Yarra, it is a region of stylistic pioneers making innovative waves. Kooyong has fabulous single-vineyard Pinot Noirs and Chardonnays, as does Moorooduc, fermented with wild yeasts. Stonier's Merricks has textbook Chardonnay in the full-blown opulent style, and some finely crafted sparklers.
OTHER PRODUCERS: Paringa, Hurley, Ten Minutes by Tractor.

**Goulburn Valley** North of the Yarra, Goulburn is an expansive valley region that contains some of the oldest wineries and vineyards in Australia, whose vines miraculously escaped the worst of the phylloxera wave. Tahbilk has some century-old vines; its Reserve bottlings of Shiraz and Cabernet are bursting with venerable class. This is one of the properties that pioneered varietal Marsanne in Australia. It certainly has a style all its own, but its clinging, top-heavy, buttery banana quality is too much

for some. The Mitchelton winery produces a Rhône-style blend of Marsanne, Roussanne and Viognier called Airstrip. Delatite offers a broadly based range from its high-altitude vineyards. Snappy Riesling, delicately scented Gewürztraminer, rose-petally Pinot Noir and an expressive, spicy Tempranillo called Donald supplement the excellent Shiraz and Cabernet.

**Glenrowan/Milawa** As you head into the northeastern sector of Victoria, you are heading towards fortified country (see page 245). At Milawa, though, table wines are made in quantity, the most important producer being Brown Brothers, one of the vanguard companies that blazed the trail for Australian wines in the UK and US. Its range is wide, and more stimulating than it used to be. Look out for finely etched Limited Release Chardonnay, the cherry-fruited Barbera lookalike Tarrango, earthy Patricia Cabernet Sauvignon, deliciously peachy late-picked Muscat, and some fine fizz from all three champagne grapes.

**Rutherglen** Pre-eminent for Liqueur Muscats (see page 257).

*New vineyards planted by Brown Brothers (below), one of hotter, inland Glenrowan-Milawa's top producers of table wines.*

*Vineyards of the Lower Hunter (above) suffer more from tropical rain storms than those in its more northerly partner, the Upper Hunter.*

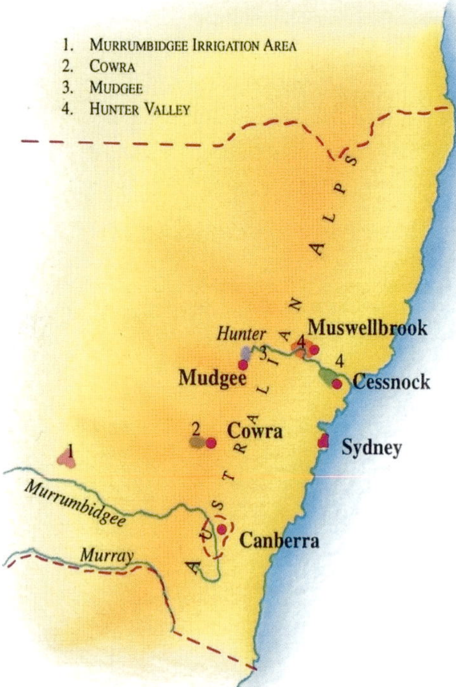



TYRRELL'S WINES
HUNTER VALLEY
Vat 47
Hunter Chardonnay

*The hot Hunter Valley, north of Sydney (right), is New South Wales' finest wine region.*

## NEW SOUTH WALES

Although it contains the Hunter Valley region of worldwide repute, New South Wales only accounts for a relatively tiny fraction of Australia's annual wine production. Its climate is as hot and hard for growers to contend with as parts of South Australia.

**Riverina** The lion's share of the output here is of wines destined for boxes and own-brand bottlings, grown on land irrigated by the Murrumbidgee River. Botrytized Semillon is an unlikely exception to the humdrum rule, and comes in especially distinguished form from the De Bortoli winery.

**Cowra** Small region supplying much of the Hunter Valley's raw material. Hunter winery Rothbury makes an impressive Cowra Chardonnay, though.

**Mudgee** The Mudgee district was sufficiently proud of its regional pedigree to have awarded itself an appellation even before the GI system was put into practice. A pity then that much of the produce of this hot dry region goes to beef up Hunter's wines when their harvests are hit by rain. Firm Cabernet and stout Shiraz are the baseline (Botobolar's opulent Shiraz is a stunner), but Chardonnays are improving too.

**Hunter Valley** Divided into Upper and Lower Hunter, this hot, extensive valley is the premium wine region of New South Wales. The Upper section is quite a way to the north of the Lower, and manages to escape the tropical rains that can disrupt the Lower Hunter vintage. Dry Semillon, practically an indigenous Hunter style of great lineage, is the proudest boast. It's often fairly low in alcohol, austerely hard and minerally, and famously takes on a burnt-toast quality as it matures in the bottle. This has fooled many a taster into thinking it has been aged in charred oak. Red wines can be a bit muddy – a lot of that sweet plum-jam style of Shiraz comes from the Hunter – but they are improving.

Good dry Semillons include McWilliams Elizabeth amd Lovedale wines, Tyrrell's Vat 1 and Brokenwood. Rothbury makes a slim but beguiling Shiraz, Rosemount a show-stopping, vegetally Burgundian Roxburgh Chardonnay, Tyrrell's an exciting, offbeat range sold under Vat numbers (such as the famed Vat 6 Pinot and the butterscotchy Vat 47 Chardonnay), and Brokenwood a reverberating Shiraz sombrely called Graveyard Vineyard.

OTHER PRODUCERS: Lake's Folly, Tower, Keith Tulloch, Thomas.

## QUEENSLAND

Right on the border with New South Wales is a GI area unromantically known as the **Granite Belt**. Its altitude always looked like making it a promising place to grow grapes, and there are now over 60 wineries established here. For the time being, not a lot of what they produce makes it much further than Sydney, but names to look out for in time will include Boireann, Robert Channon and Preston Peak.

## TASMANIA

Led by the visionary and multi-talented Andrew Pirie, a small band of Tasmania producers set out in the 1970s to show the world that the island can make sharply defined varietals, especially Pinot Noir and Chardonnay, in a distinctively European idiom. Although the whole island constitutes a single GI, it has two main centres of production at Launceston in the northeast and Hobart in the south.

Pipers Brook winery, in the northern region of the same name, makes exemplary Pinot Noir, hard in youth and needing time, a subtly steely Chardonnay and some crisp, zesty Riesling. Moorilla Estate produces good beefy Pinot, and improving Gewürztraminer. Heemskerk has some big Cabernets and has diversified into fizz, in association with the champagne house Louis Roederer, under the Jansz label. Tasmanian fizz has been superb across the board.
OTHER PRODUCERS: Bay of Fires, Freycinet, Frogmore Creek.

## FORTIFIED WINES

There are two basic categories of Australian fortified wine. One derives from the days when the hot southern-hemisphere countries all had a shot at imitating the traditional methods and flavours of port and sherry. Indeed, those terms were in widespread use in Australia itself, though they are now on the wane. Among the port-styles are extremely sweet, strawberry jam-like wines made from fortified Shiraz, of which some are vintage-dated. Extended wood-ageing washes out the colour of some, which are then referred to – as in the Douro – as Tawny. The sherry styles are even rarer, but can be much better. Seppelt makes a comprehensive range of tangy, salty fino (labelled DP117), hazelnutty amontillado (DP116) and toffeeish oloroso (DP38).

The second category is unique to Australia. Liqueur Muscat and Liqueur Tokay are breathtakingly rich fortified wines made from,

respectively, Muscat Blanc à Petits Grains (here known as Brown Muscat for the dun-skinned variant locally grown) or Muscadelle, the minority grape of Sauternes. The production area is mainly in northeast Victoria around the town of **Rutherglen**, although some are also made in **Glenrowan**, a little to the south.

Their production seems to combine a little of every traditional method for making liquorous dessert wines. Firstly, the grapes are left to shrivel on the vine. They are then pressed and the viscous juice partially fermented, but fortified with grape spirit long before the piercing sweetness has even begun to fade. After that, they are aged and blended from a barrel system something like the *soleras* of Jerez.

The Muscats, especially, are shockingly intense. Pure orange marmalade when you stick your nose in, they dissolve in the mouth into a glutinous amalgam of milk chocolate, sticky dates and candied orange rind, with a finish that persists on the back of the palate for minutes on end.
PRODUCERS: Stanton & Killeen, Chambers, Morris, Yalumba, Campbell's.

*Heemskerk Vineyards in the Pipers Brook region of Tasmania (above), makers of notably well-built Cabernet and elegant sparkling wines.*

# NEW ZEALAND

*In just 50 years, New Zealand's winemakers have taken the world by storm to become the fastest growing wine country in the world. Undaunted by geographical isolation, they have established a strong regional identity.*

THIS IS WHERE the global wine tour makes its final stop, at the world's most southerly vineyards on the North and South Islands of New Zealand. Any further, and we would be trying to make icewine in the Antarctic.

In terms of its age, the New Zealand wine industry really is the junior partner among the southern-hemisphere countries. Viticulture only really started being taken for a serious proposition here in the 1970s. Undoubtedly spurred by the prodigious worldwide success of Australia, New Zealand carved out its own niche. It could hardly have been otherwise. Not only are the volumes produced much smaller than Australia's, but the climate is entirely different.

The start was about as unpromising as it was almost everywhere else. Experimental plantings in the 19th century were quickly laid waste by phylloxera, and what they were replaced with was hybrid grapes of mixed *vinifera* and native American parentage. On top of that, national licensing laws were among the most restrictive in the English-speaking world, with supermarkets only being permitted to sell the country's own wines since the beginning of the 1990s.

What eventually put New Zealand on the map in the closing years of the 20th century was a single grape variety, and not exactly an unfamiliar one at that. If you had started planning a marketing push in the 1980s for a brand-new wine-producing country, and said that its vineyards looked like they were capable of excelling at one varietal wine in particular, you might have got people's attention. When you then, with the appropriate drum-roll and cymbal-clash, announced that that varietal was going to be Sauvignon Blanc, you might have been treated to a wall of uncomfortable silence.

It wasn't that Sauvignon wasn't a familiar and useful variety. Look at Sancerre, after all, and Pouilly-Fumé. It's just that it wasn't ever seen as being exactly on the A-list. Could a fledgling wine industry really establish itself on a grape that, at best, made simple, fruity quaffing wine, the sort of thing that was nice enough as a summer aperitif perhaps, but was hardly the stuff of legend?

The difference was that nobody had tasted Sauvignon Blanc that was anything like this before. If the grape had traditionally been viewed outside the Upper Loire as brash and unmalleable, or as just plain deadly dull when overcropped, Sauvignons from the Marlborough district of the South Island, New Zealand wine's Garden of Eden, rewrote the rulebook.

There is more uplifting, happy fruit flavour in Marlborough Sauvignon than there is in any other dry white wine on earth. It's a great wine to start off novice tasters with, because even when they struggle to sniff out the cherries in Pinot Noir or the honey in Semillon, the fruit

*The world's most southerly vineyards operate in a damp, cool climate. Except for South Island's Central Otago, New Zealand's wine regions (below) lie on or close to the coast.*

1. AUCKLAND
2. GISBORNE
3. HAWKE'S BAH
4. WAIRARAPA
5. NELSON
6. MARLBOROUGH
7. CANTERBURY
8. CENTRAL OTAGO

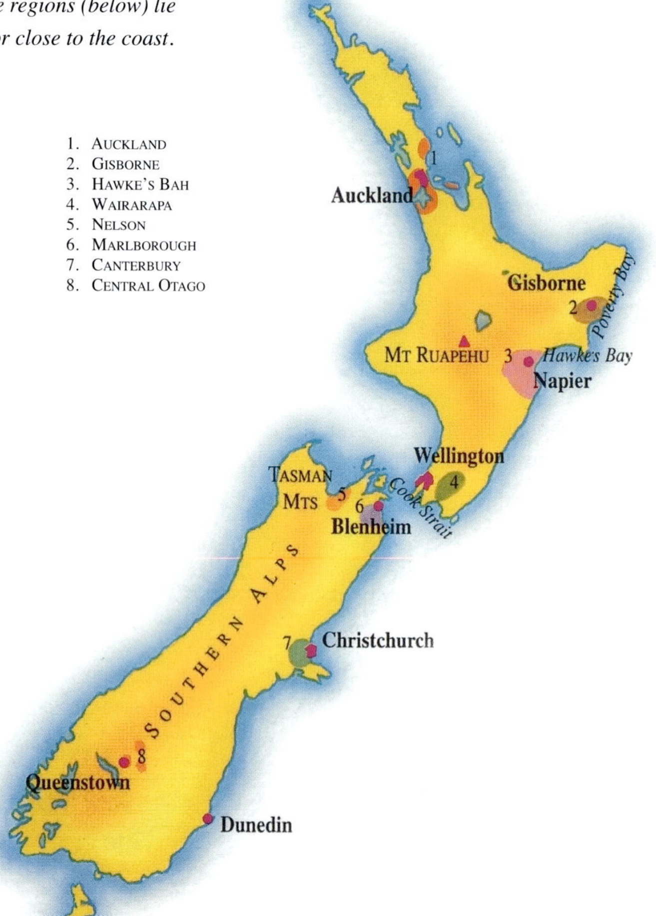

aromas that Marlborough Sauvignon throws out at you come almost too thick and fast to name. The Sauvignon was soon followed by almost equally fruit-fuelled Chardonnay and Riesling.

Reds lagged behind for a while, as one might have expected in a generally cool, damp climate. Much Cabernet Sauvignon was excessively light and herbaceous, its whiff of raw green pepper skin too often complaining of climatic indignities in the vineyard. With better selection of planting areas, and judicious blending with Merlot, that picture has now improved beyond recognition. Even better has been Pinot Noir, always a likelier bet in a cool climate, with wines that are now challenging the best of California for sheer opulence of fruit, and bright balancing acidity.

And what should the other cool-climate success be? Think northern France, think southern England. Sparkling wines made by the traditional method have also played a heroic part here, the results given the vote of confidence by the appearance of a Champagne delegation looking to invest. There is even a clutch of superb botrytized dessert wines.

It hasn't all been plain sailing commercially. The New Zealand wine industry has targeted the greater part of its export effort at the UK, which admittedly has paid off rather well. The path-breaking Cloudy Bay winery became the country's *grand cru* producer for Sauvignon and Chardonnay, some rich, concentrated red blends, and in time one of the more deeply flavoured fizzes. At the happy-go-lucky end of the market, Montana Sauvignon Blanc was one of the red-hot wines on the British market from the late 1980s on. But elsewhere?

While the British were knocking back New Zealand Sauvignon, the influential American wine constituency remained for a long time completely in the dark about the country's potential, while all the while Australia had stolen a march on it. That is slowly but surely changing, but when all is said and drunk, there basically just isn't that much New Zealand wine to go around each year, especially when growing and harvesting conditions can be so severe. In a good year, it produces about a tenth of what Australia does, and *they* haven't got enough to supply the demand.

Not only does New Zealand have a cool climate, it also has a damp one. Annual rainfall is plentifully distributed throughout the year, with the result that vines often yielded too

vigorously, giving low-quality fruit, or else the grapes were diluted by water penetration during the all-important ripening phase. New techniques in vineyard management, introduced towards the turn of the century, widely rectified those particular problems, but the fact remains that vintages are still subject to far wider variation than they are in sunny Australia, a thousand miles off in the distance. 2018 wasn't great for Sauvignon, for example, 2011 fairly awful for red varieties.

*The love-affair with Marlborough Sauvignon Blanc began with the wines of Montana. Machine-harvesters at work (above) picking Sauvignon grapes at Montana's Brancott Estate, Marlborough, South Island.*

*Stunning landscape of inland South Island (left), on the shore of Lake Wanaka in Central Otago.*

*Ngatarawa Winery and vineyards (above) in the well-established Hawke's Bay region of North Island.*

The growing regions are scattered throughout an extensive stretch of both islands, North and South, for all that the total acreage is still very modest. With the exception of southerly Otago, they are all situated on or near the coasts, mostly on the Pacific side.

The classification system, it's fair to say, is still in its infancy. The two principal designations, North and South Island, are subdivided into the ten regions listed below, but a lot of New Zealand wine is still blended from grapes grown by contract growers in different regions. In time, something like a true geographical appellation system will emerge. No other southern-hemisphere country is more obviously suited to one, after all.

## THE GRAPES

That old failsafe Müller-Thurgau once occupied pole position in the vineyards, but has now been put in its place rather decisively by Sauvignon and Chardonnay spreading like wildfire. Chardonnay achieves more overt fruit character in New Zealand than it does seemingly anywhere else. Aromas of peach, banana and pear are quite common, and not especially disguisable by oak treatments.

Some wineries have attempted to capture a more Burgundian ethos, with buttery richness as opposed to fruit-salad freshness, but they are by no means the norm. In the North Island's Gisborne especially, some of the country's finest pedigree Chardonnays are being produced, with stunning balance between richness of texture

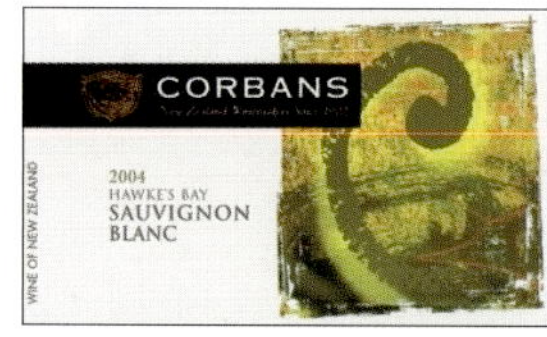

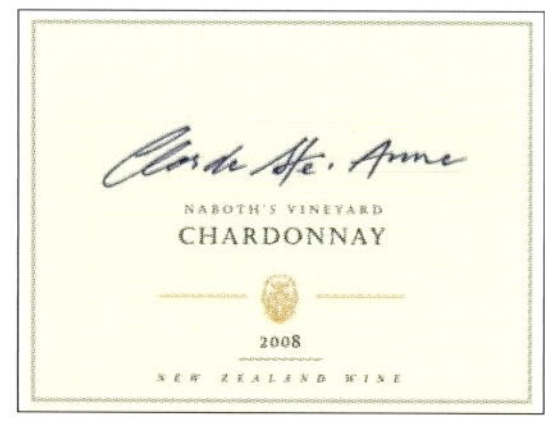

and freshening acidity, a palate profile more usually encountered among the white wines of the Côte d'Or.

Sauvignon Blanc has been the great white hope of New Zealand wine – better here than in the Loire, many think, for sheer fruit-powered dynamism. There are quite dramatic stylistic differences among the wineries, some emphasizing the green, herbaceous flavours of gooseberries, asparagus and freshly washed watercress, others plunging headlong into tropicality with mango, passion-fruit, pineapple and musky Charentais melon. I have tasted Marlborough Sauvignons with scents of red peppers, grated carrot, the purest blackcurrant juice, even candied cherries. It is one exciting wine when it wants to be.

On the other hand, the sheer success of Sauvignon has now resulted in some misconceived approaches to its production. There are quite a lot of wines that don't have the requisite acid balance, offering a mouthful of juicy fruit, but without the structure to pull it all into focus. At the opposite end, and even harder to like, are those wines, often from grapes picked earlier than the average, where acidity has been over-emphasized to the detriment of the fruit profile, so that the initial eye-watering attack is all bitter yellow grapefruit and hardly anything else. I hope we see the back of those before too long. Balanced blending, often of grapes sourced from sites with variant microclimatic conditions, is the key.

Riesling can achieve classical steeliness, without quite the petrolly pungency of Australian versions. The weakest examples used to taste rather limp and confected, with a touch of boiled sweet to them, but the overall quality is now much higher, and there are some wonderful noble-rotted sweet versions full of luscious marmalade intensity. Then there's a dash of Chenin Blanc, which should enjoy the climate, some delicate but recognizable Gewürztraminer, and limited plantings of so far rather unremarkable Semillon, better blended than made as a varietal.

Pinot Noir is now the most widely planted red grape, and is flexing its muscles on the world stage with wines of scintillating complexity, diamond-bright fruit and plenty of ageing potential, as thrilling and distinguished as the best of Carneros or Oregon. As well as being built on good, solid, raspberry fruit foundations, they also display a distinctly Burgundian reluctance to charm in their first flush, and nothing quite succeeds like a classy Pinot Noir that makes you do all the work. A fair amount of the Pinot goes into quality sparklers, white and rosé.

Merlot is striking out on its own in some parts, while playing its historically sanctioned role of chaperoning Cabernet Sauvignon in others. Cabernet itself has improved enormously. Those vegetal flavours that once dogged its image are occasionally still in evidence, but many are exhibiting much deeper, plummier concentration than before.

## NORTH ISLAND

**Northland** The whole New Zealand show began in the far north of the North Island, in what is just about the warmest part of the country. It's a narrow region, stretching from the Karikari Peninsula in the north to Mangawhai at the southern end. It nearly died out as a wine region, but its potential as a site for warm-climate varietals has been recognized, and there are now around 15 wineries here. Successful plantings of Merlot, Cabernet Sauvignon and Syrah have resulted in convincingly ripe wines, but white varietals from Chardonnay, Pinot Gris and Viognier are also looking good.

**Auckland** The area in the immediate vicinity of Auckland was also at one time in decline as a wine region, as attention was resolutely turned to more fashionable districts further south, but it's now gaining in status as an auspicious locale for well-built Bordeaux-blend reds. It is warm, but prone to harvest rains, which means fruit from elsewhere often has to be brought in to beef up the blends, but in the kinder years, it's looking good. The region includes a good sub-zone called **Matakana**, north of the city, as well as **Waiheke Island**, situated in the harbour. Kumeu River makes a profoundly Burgundian and quite atypical Chardonnay, while opulent reds from all five Bordeaux grapes come from Waiheke's Stonyridge.
OTHER PRODUCERS: Te Motu, Goldwater, Matua Valley, Coopers Creek, Te Whau.
**Waikato/Bay of Plenty** A small but expanding region just south of Auckland. It's fairly warm and is promising for Cabernet Sauvignon, but Chardonnay is the strongest suit so far.
**Gisborne** On the east coast of the North Island, Gisborne has now found its feet as a quality region. So good at premium white varietals has it become that it now styles itself Chardonnay Capital of New Zealand. As well as that hardy perennial, Gewürztraminer has performed creditably, as have Pinot Gris and Chenin Blanc, and there are some excellent traditional-method sparkling wines.

Millton Vineyards is an organic producer, making some of its wines according to biodynamic principles. Its Clos de Ste Anne

*The damp climate encourages vines to grow too vigorously. Pruning and leaf-trimming help control their growth here at Esk Valley vineyards in Hawke's Bay (above).*

*Vines were only planted in Marlborough (below) as recently as the 1970s, by big producer Brancott Estate. The region is now synonymous with fruit-rich Sauvignon.*

Chardonnay is a thunderously rich, complex wine. Matua Valley's Judd Estate version is equally impressive, while The Co-ordinates Ormond Chardonnay from Spade Oak emphasizes lush tropical fruit characters.
OTHER PRODUCERS: Vinoptima, Lake Road.
**Hawke's Bay** Further down the coast, in the environs of Napier, Hawke's Bay is one of New Zealand's longer-established wine regions. Its warm climate and poor gravelly soils, perfect for wine grapes, have conferred on it a reputation for outstanding reds, particularly from the richer, thicker-skinned varieties – Cabernet Sauvignon, Merlot and Syrah. These are among New Zealand's most opulent reds, and are worth the cellaring time that they demand. There are white wines too, but the Sauvignon is in the subtler, gentler style that suits it less well than cooler areas can produce. The Chardonnay, though, is pretty good, by and large. The best sub-regions are **Gimblett Gravels**, the **Bridge Pa Triangle** and the coastal **Te Awanga**.

Hawke's Bay winery Te Mata makes one of the most authoritative ranges of wines in the region, taking in soft, gooseberryish Sauvignon (Cape Crest), overtly buttery Chardonnay (Elston) and full-frontal, muscular Cabernet-Merlot (Coleraine), as well as some impressive, peppery Syrah (Bullnose). The Villa Maria conglomerate, which owns both the Vidal and Esk Valley labels, makes some outstanding Sauvignon, good, savoury Pinot Noir, and sensationally concentrated Bordeaux-blend reds. Ngatarawa makes ripely expressive Cabernet-Merlot, and fine noble-rotted Riesling.
OTHER PRODUCERS: Craggy Range, Trinity Hill, Unison, CJ Pask, Church Road, Sacred Hill.
**Wairarapa** At the very southern tip of the North Island, near the national capital, Wellington, Wairarapa is home to some of the country's best small growers. Reds are the declared speciality, whether from Pinot Noir or Cabernet, and many of the recent generation of wines are hugely impressive. A sub-region, **Martinborough**, has emerged as particularly superb for clean, raspberry-fruited, deeply complex Pinots with Burgundian levels of acidity and concentration. Brittle and nervy in their youth, they demand several years' bottle-age to show what they are capable of.

Other reds have included sturdy Cabernet Sauvignon and Syrah, and there are also impressively aromatic whites from the likes of Viognier, Pinot Gris and Riesling. Richly constituted Chardonnays and some particularly inspired, citrus-fresh Sauvignons are worth a look too. This is one of New Zealand's most versatile regions.

Martinborough Vineyards produces outstanding Pinot, and finely crafted Chardonnay and Riesling. Ata Rangi's Pinot is resonant, subtly spiced and meaty, its Célèbre Cabernet-Merlot blend rich, ripe and plumped up with a little Syrah, and its barrel-fermented Pinot Gris an exotically perfumed stunner. Paddy Borthwick has superbly defined, memorable Riesling and a vivid, appley Sauvignon Blanc. Dry River makes some of the most exceptionally concentrated Pinot Noirs in the world, as well as a range of gorgeous dry whites from Alsace varietals, including a violet-soaked Gewürztraminer and peachy Pinot Gris.
OTHER PRODUCERS: Craggy Range, Palliser Estate, Escarpment, Kusuda, Schubert.

*New Zealand's cool climate is showing itself adept as a source of* méthode traditionnelle *sparklers, especially in the Marlborough area (left).*

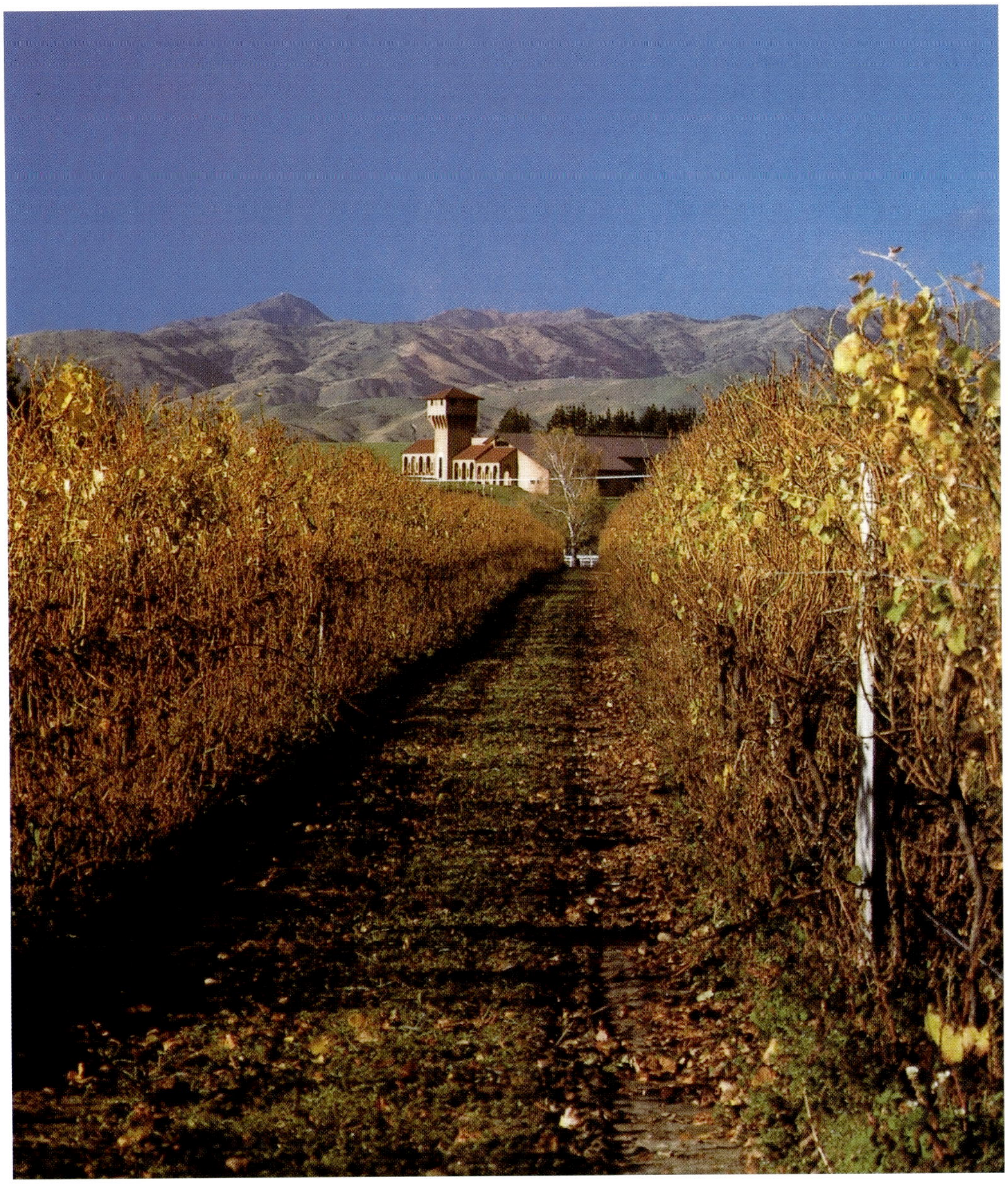

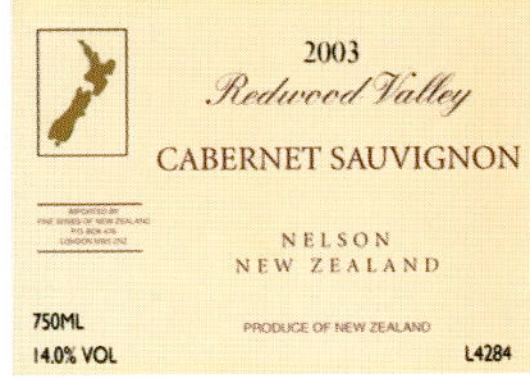

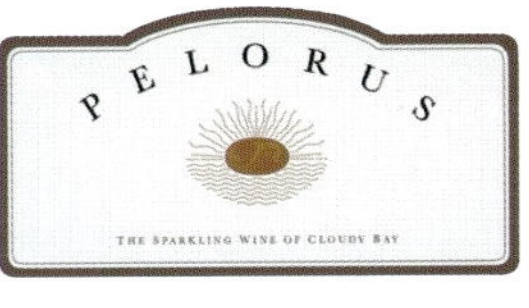

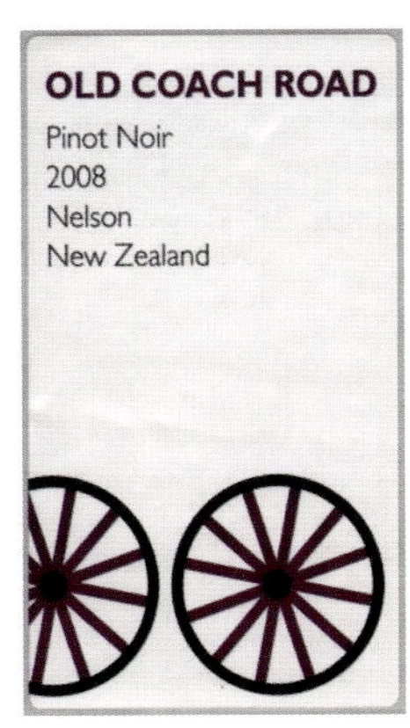

## SOUTH ISLAND

**Nelson** A hilly region on the fringes of the Tasman mountains, Nelson is Chardonnay country *par excellence*. Only a handful of wineries have made their home here, in a damp but otherwise promising cool-climate district, but the wine quality is very persuasive. Neudorf makes a finely honed Chardonnay, while Seifried has crisp Riesling in dry and lightly sweet versions, positively flavoured Pinot, rich Chardonnay and tangy Sauvignon.

**Marlborough** Centred on the town of Blenheim at the northern end of the South Island, Marlborough has been the greatest of all New Zealand wine regions. Little matter that it still doesn't have a particularly distinct reputation for red wines, it is the source of many of the country's most sharply definitive whites, with Sauvignon Blanc at the head of the pack. The region is cool but relatively dry, and its misty autumns mean that botrytized Rieslings are possible in most vintages. Chardonnay plays an important role too. The two most important districts are the **Wairau** and **Awatere Valleys**.

Brancott Estate (formerly Montana), the NZ wine colossus, basically invented Marlborough as a wine region in the 1970s when it planted the first vines here, and its top-value benchmark Sauvignon became a contemporary classic wine. It also makes some good dessert Riesling, and quietly impressive single-estate Pinot Noir.

Cloudy Bay was the second winery to startle the world with its much-sought limited

*An autumn vineyard scene (right) in the Bannockburn district of Central Otago, South Island.*

quantities of Marlborough Sauvignon, an expensive, but profoundly eloquent wine. It was joined by a deep, complex Chardonnay, a damson-rich Cabernet-Merlot blend, and a range of massively intense, richly toasty sparklers under the Pelorus label.

Hunter's Estate is another great name for opulent Sauvignon and Chardonnay, Jackson Estate makes soft biscuity Chardonnay and an emphatic, explosive Sauvignon, Framingham has a gloriously scented range of Alsace varietals, Seresin offers gooseberry-crammed Sauvignon, Wairau River has a taut, apple-fruited Sauvignon and melt-in-the-mouth Chardonnay, and Astrolabe makes brilliant Sauvignons teeming with orchard fruit.

Marlborough is also where most of New Zealand's traditional-method sparklers are made, often with expertise and investment from Champagne houses such as Veuve Clicquot and Deutz. Pinot Noir and Chardonnay are the grapes used, and many show just how distinguished sparkling wines can be from a cool climate. Acidity levels are sometimes a little eye-watering, but the overall balance and finesse of the best are beyond question.

Apart from Cloudy Bay's Pelorus, Deutz Marlborough Cuvée, released by Brancott, is crisp, dry and elegant. Nautilus Cuvée Brut is nutty, honeyed and complex, and Mumm

Marlborough Brut Prestige uses all three champagne grapes for a beautifully refined fizz. OTHER PRODUCERS: Fromm, Forrest, Dry Hills, Wither Hills, Dog Point, Morton Estate, Oyster Bay, Yealands, Saint Clair.

**Canterbury/Waipara Valley** Centred on the city of Christchurch, Canterbury's vineyards are cooler still than those of Marlborough, with the most elegant wines to date. Chardonnay and Pinot are the varietals of choice, but there is good Riesling too. Pegasus Bay offers ample-fleshed Chardonnays and Pinots, as does Giesen, which also makes noble-rotted Riesling when it can. Daniel Schuster has ostentatiously good Pinot, while St Helena has soft, creamy Pinot Gris and Pinot Blanc.

**Central Otago** East of the town of Queensland, Central Otago is the most dynamic region of all, and the world's most southerly. It's also the only inland region, with a rapidly growing number of innovative producers. Pinot Noirs (especially from Mt Difficulty and Peregrine) have been astonishing; there is scented Gewürztraminer, fine Riesling and some gently aromatic Pinot Gris.

In this lustrous region, where winemaking ambition runs sky-high, there are especially promising zones in **Bannockburn** and **Bendigo**, where the warmer conditions result in robust Pinot Noir, and could well see some exciting Syrah joining it before too long. On the western shore of Lake Dunstan, the **Lowburn** and **Pisa** districts have also provided auspicious growing conditions for Pinot. Lowburn's Burn Cottage Vineyard, in addition to its breathtaking Pinots, also makes an enterprising peach-and-pepper blend of Riesling and Grüner Veltliner. OTHER PRODUCERS: Felton Road, Quartz Reef, Carrick, Rippon, Mount Edward, Wild Earth.

*Rows of pruned winter vines (below) on trellises in the Canterbury region, South Island.*

# CONCLUSION

S O, HOW DO THINGS STAND with wine as we enter the middle years of the 21st century? In what settings do we expect to be drinking wine? And how do we want it to taste when we do?

Nothing dates any piece of commentary faster than expatiating on current trends. By the time somebody looks at this book five years or so after its publication, cartoon wine labels with jokes on them, to pluck a random example, might be long gone. Those flat bottles that are designed to fit through a standard letterbox, so that you don't have to worry about the online wine order arriving while you are at work and sitting invitingly on the doorstep all day, were, to some people at least, a stroke of genius marketing. If only they weren't always the same wine...

It's true that what kept a lot of consumers away from wine was the air of stuffy pomposity that surrounded it for so long. Novelty packaging is all part of the movement for destuffing and democratising wine as an everyday item of consumption. It can feel as though somebody else's sense of humour is being forced upon you, like the blathering of a drunken uncle at a wedding, but better that (perhaps) than the sanctimonious whispering of the pre-sale auction tastings I attended in my early years as a wine writer. 'Did you think the '86 Gevrey was showing a little reductiveness?' 'Indubitably, old boy.'

The chief problem with improving accessibility to any cultural product or activity is how to achieve it without the dreaded dumbing-down. As well as allegedly humorous labelling, another of the wine trade's strategies has been to bring back branded wines in a big way. There have always been wine brands. You might be surprised to find that some of them never went away. They still make Othello red in Cyprus. And then certain large-scale producers, particularly those owned by big multinational conglomerates, become brand-names after a fashion through sheer familiarity. Brancott Estate (formerly Montana Wines) in New Zealand springs to mind. Or what about the Perrin estate's basic *vins de France*, bottled under the name La Vieille Ferme? Nothing wrong with those.

If brands improve recognizability, though, they also create the ambience of an unvarying product, one that will taste the same from one year to the next. And that feels as though it is tugging in the wrong direction. True, the variability we so often celebrated in wines, especially European wines, of the past, was nothing more dignified than the fact that lovely vintages were interspersed with rotten ones. Now that the expertise exists to overcome all but the most inauspicious conditions during the growing season, that pattern is passing into sepia-tinted history, but that doesn't mean that the same producer's wine is not allowed to


*Immaculately trained vines (below) in the pioneering Marlborough region, South Island, New Zealand.*

*How many of us still have homes with well-stocked wine cellars full of maturing bottles (left)? Not me, for one.*

change. Different vintages highlight different characteristics in the wine – a year of mellow fruitfulness might follow one of robustly structured wines that will take longer to come round in the bottle but will still reward your patience. To me, that's more interesting than expecting the same wine brand to taste as doggedly consistent as your favourite brand of beer.

I talked in the Introduction about the problem of hotter growing conditions leading to sky-high levels of alcohol, and how that too often results in wines that lack balance. One answer to this has been the innovation of low-alcohol and no-alcohol wines. There have always been wines with very little alcohol – Mosel Rieslings, Asti – but even the 7 or 8 per cent of alcohol in those will make its presence felt eventually. The new generation of wines that have a mere 0.5 per cent ABV, or even absolute zero, are offering a genuine choice to those who want a period of abstinence.

The good news is that many of these products taste much more like wine than alcohol-free wine used to. A ghastly chemical taste from the dealcoholising process used to be the bane of this category, which is why most of us advised people to stick to fruit juice if they were having a dry spell. But if you are used to the flavour of wine, or you want something to drink with dinner that will give the atmosphere of wine without its intoxicating effect, a Chenin Blanc that actually tastes like Chenin Blanc could well be the lifeline. I wish they wouldn't promote these products as being the 'sober' alternative, as though regular wine-drinkers only drank to get drunk, but the health benefits

are fairly obvious, and the category now incorporates the full range of wine styles, from still to sparkling, bone-dry to lightly sweet.

Health figures large in all our considerations these days, and rightly so. In the 1990s, the news got about, based on a famous French research study led by a clinical cardiologist in Lyon, that wine – red wine pre-eminently – was supremely healthy. It broke down bad cholesterol in our arteries, and counteracted some of the danger of the excessive fat intake that characterizes so much of the Western diet. These findings were not necessarily exaggerated, but they were treated as a green light to carry on by people who really needed to cut their alcohol consumption. Red wine might be good for the heart to some extent, but too much of it still has the same negative impact

*Red wine fermenting in the vat under its cap of grapeskins (below. Its preventative effect on cholesterol build-up in the arteries was a health message of the 1990s.*

*These ripe Tempranillo grapes (above) awaiting harvest are destined to go into Spain's most celebrated red wine, Rioja.*

on the liver. 'Drink less, but better' was the cry in that era. And it isn't a bad watchword even now, if only better wine wasn't out of reach of ordinary pockets. Like much else in the food and drink sector, the price of wine has risen remorselessly throughout successive waves of global economic crisis, and many of the bottles that once looked like an inviting choice for a weekend dinner – Chablis, Rioja Reserva, Marlborough Sauvignon Blanc, Barossa Shiraz – have now ascended into the kind of price bracket that makes you at least hesitate, and probably come away with another bottle of Pinot Grigio delle Venezie.

That said, the positively outrageous success of Whispering Angel rosé from Provence confounds at a stroke any broad-brush theory about what people can and can't afford. Here is a branded wine to leave all the others on the starting-blocks, a delicate, gently cranberryish pallid pink from the Côtes de Provence AOP. Its producer, Château d'Esclans, reckons that it has such exemplary balance and concentration that it is probably the best rosé wine in the world. They're obviously ahead of me in having tasted all the others, but I honestly cannot see what justifies all the hype, let alone its seriously punchy price-tag. It has capitalized very successfully on the international thirst for pink wines, and instead of creating an entire category of luxury rosés, it still pretty much has the field to itself.

If I'm going to spend that sort of cash, I'd still rather have a bottle of decent own-brand supermarket champagne, or one of the outstanding new generation of English

sparkling wines, or a premier cru Chablis. If I want a dry, savoury pink with more body than most, a Merlot rosé from Chile delivers more convincing ripe fruit, to me, than most Provençal pink. But there we are. We are free to choose.

And that brings me to my last point. Choice. I said in the Introduction that our worries in the 1980s and 90s about the creeping homogenisation to which the wine world was succumbing had been decisively dispelled in the present era by the emergence of new wine-producing countries, and a growing familiarity among the wine-buying public with a broader range of grape varieties than was the case 30 years ago. That still stands, but you might be forgiven for not noticing it when you survey the shelves of your favourite retail outlet, including even those that once had higher reputations. What has happened to all the variety they once offered? Next time you are choosing a white wine, count up how many Sauvignons you can see. Outside the specialist wine merchants and bottle-shops, the retail trade has undergone a miserable retrenchment into what they consider their safest options.

Which is why it makes sense more than ever to buy from trusted independents. If you are lucky enough to have a wine shop nearby, pay them a regular visit. Get talking to the staff. Ask their advice. They know more about wine than anybody in the supermarket does. Many of them hold regular tastings for customers. Even if seems a bit of a splash financially, it's not as though you were shopping there every day, and the likelihood is that you will be drinking a much more satisfying, thought-provoking, even thrilling wine than you would if you were embarking on yet another bottle of multi-buy Silly Sausage Pinot Grigio with the cartoon label.

Whatever you are drinking, I hope you enjoy it. Wine is nothing other than a product of the agricultural cycle, a fermented liquid that is as old as the earth itself. We've come a long way from the bamboozlement of our archaic ancestors stumbling on alcohol by chance to the storied magnificence of the great wine estates of today. But the golden thread that links these two distant historical horizons is the happiness that spoiled fruit juice – call it single-vineyard Reserve Pinot Noir, if you wish – has brought to all epochs of humanity.

Your very good health!

*For wine drinkers everywhere*

This edition is published by Lorenz Books
an imprint of Anness Publishing Ltd
info@anness.com
www.lorenzbooks.com
www.annesspublishing.com

© Anness Publishing Ltd 2026

*Publisher*: Joanna Lorenz
*Editorial director*: Helen Sudell
*Senior editor*: Felicity Forster
*Designers*: Sheila Volpe and Ian Sandom
*Jacket design*: Nigel Partridge
*Picture researcher*: Lynda Marshall
*Special photography and styling*: Steve Baxter with Roisin Neild
*Illustrator*: Madeleine David
*Maps*: Steven Sweet
*Production Controller*: Ben Worley

*Photographs*: All photographic material supplied by Cephas Picture Library, with the following exceptions. Bridgeman Art Library: 8 (courtesy Pushkin Museum, Moscow), 9 (courtesy British Library, London). Eddie Parker: 228. German Wine Information Service: 188. Jane Hughes: 43 (right), 100, 105, 181 (bottom), 215 (bottom), 217, 219, 220 (bottom). Morris & Verdin/Robert Wheatcroft: 220 (top). Patrick Eager: 52–3, 243 (bottom). Shutterstock: 4, 10, 11, 38t, 46, 76t, 91, 96bl, br, 97tl, tr, 125t, 129, 138, 142t, 193br, 195 both, 197 both, 200bl, 201 both, 202 bl, 205 both, 207br, 208 both, 209tl, 230tr, 232bl, 233bl, 235 both, 264 both, 265, 266 both, 267. Sopexa (UK) Ltd: 134. South American Pictures: 234. SuperStock: 44, 45 (right), 63 (top) 240. Wines of Chile: 237.



A CIP catalogue record for this book is available from the British Library.

PUBLISHER'S NOTE
Although the advice and information in this book are believed to be accurate at the time of going to press, neither the author nor the publisher can accept any legal responsibility or liability for any errors or omissions that may have been made nor for any inaccuracies nor for any loss, harm or injury that comes about from following instructions or advice in this book.